Animals on the Agenda

Animals on the Agenda

Questions about Animals
for Theology and Ethics

Edited by
Andrew Linzey and Dorothy Yamamoto

University of Illinois Press

Urbana and Chicago

First Illinois paperback, 1998

© 1998 by Andrew Linzey and Dorothy Yamamoto
Introduction © 1998 by Andrew Linzey
Copyright to chapters 1–20 retained by
individual authors
Manufactured in the United States of America
P 6 5 4 3 2

First published in Great Britain in 1998
by SCM Press Ltd.
9-17 St Albans Place, London N1 0NX

Library of Congress Cataloging-in-Publication Data

Animals on the agenda : questions about animals for theology and
ethics / edited by Andrew Linzey and Dorothy Yamamoto. — Illini
books ed.
p. cm.
ISBN 10: 0-252-06761-4 (pbk. : alk. paper)/ISBN 13: 978-0-252-06761-7
1. Animals—Religious aspects—Christianity. I. Linzey, Andrew.
II. Yamamoto, Dorothy
BT746.A555 1998
241'.693—dc21   98-7118
CIP

Contents

Foreword

This volume has been many years in the making. It began its life as a research project of the Centre for the Study of Theology in the University of Essex. Members of the original Working Group included: The Very Reverend Dr Edward Carpenter (chair), former Dean of Westminster; Dr Stephen R. L. Clark, Professor of Philosophy at Liverpool University; Canon Paul Brett of Chelmsford Cathedral; Dr Una Kroll, medical doctor and Anglican priest; Cindy Milburn, then Director of Earthkind; Professor A. M. Allchin, then Director of the Saint Theosevia Centre, Oxford; and Dr Andrew Linzey (secretary), who was previously Director of Studies of the Centre for the Study of Theology in Essex University.

The aim of the Group was modest – 'to produce an agreed statement on the theological understanding of animals'. In the course of our long deliberations, it became clear that even this modest aim was over-ambitious. At the outset we had tried to isolate some of the major theological questions about animals that needed to be addressed. These included: What are animals for? Can animals have a relationship with God? Can animals praise God? Can animals sin? Are animals part of a fallen creation? Is nature God's will? Do animals have immortal souls? How does God value animals? Does Christ's reconciling work include animals? These apparently simple questions – and many others – occupied many hours of thoughtful and lively discussion, and it became clear that many of them raised in turn other fundamental questions about theology and how we do it. Struck by the sheer multifacetedness of the questions animals raise for theology, we began to select just some of them and wrestle with possible answers.

As the years passed, we drew into our conversations a variety of scholars, particularly from North America, who provided thoughtful answers to the list of questions we circulated. Among those who kindly assisted our efforts as corresponding members from time to time were Clive Hollands, Bishop John Austin Baker, Dr Michael W. Fox, Professor Jay McDaniel, Dr Petroc Willey, and Professor John B. Cobb, Jr. As a result, the initial aim of producing an agreed statement was superseded as papers came together to form a substantial collection, the first of its kind that tries to address fundamental theological questions about animals. When the time finally came for publication, we had exceeded our expectations and, sadly, not all papers – for reasons of space alone – could be included. Our special thanks to Professor Dan Cohn-Sherbok, Dr Katharine Dell, Bishop John Austin Baker, Cindy Milburn, Professor A. M. Allchin, Professor Bill French, and Dr Una Kroll for providing us with excellent drafts which helped stimulate discussion.

A number of funding bodies kindly assisted our work in its early stages or helped the completion of the project. We express our particular appreciation to the St Andrew Animal Fund, the Humane Research Trust, the David Shepherd Conservation Foundation, the Society of St John the Evangelist, and the International Fund for Animal Welfare. From its inception the Working Group received outstanding support from Theology Council Member, Dr David Capey, and the Centre's Administrative Director, Lynn Bowman-Burns. The project would have been impossible without the goodwill and encouragement of the Council of the Centre for the Study of Theology and we express our thanks to them for keeping faith with the project during times when completion seemed a distant goal.

Finally, a special word of thanks to our publishers, SCM Press, and in particular Margaret Lydamore, who provided expert guidance on the text. Collections are never easy for publishers, and it is to their credit that they were prepared to take on a substantial collection in a comparatively new field. If nothing else, this volume enhances the Press's wholly justified reputation for innovative theological publishing.

Andrew Linzey

Introduction

Is Christianity Irredeemably Speciesist?

Andrew Linzey

'Does God have a daughter?' The question was put to me some years ago by my eight-year-old daughter, Clair. I confess with pride that my daughter is perspicacious about issues in contemporary theology. Even so, her question and my awkward, fumbling, and, I fear, wholly unsatisfactory answers to it, have remained with me as a defining moment. For what *was* defined at that moment was a problem that even, and especially, professional theologians rarely see, namely a sense of alienation, of non-inclusion, brought about by the central Christian metaphor of Fatherhood and Sonship – a sense of exclusion so great that even an eight-year-old girl could feel it.

In her widely reviewed book *Theology and Feminism*, Daphne Hampson questions the confidence of many who maintain that Christianity and feminism are compatible. In her view, Christianity cannot help emancipate women, not only because of its historic rejection of equality between men and women, but principally because the foundational stories which give rise to Christian doctrine are inescapably patriarchal. The Christian faith is rooted in stories – indeed, in one particular story of Father and Son – which (so runs the argument) are exclusive of the female gender.[1] In fact, in her latest book, *After Christianity*, Hampson goes further, rejecting not only compatibility between Christianity and feminism but also coexistence. 'Within Christianity', she argues, 'there is no symbolic place for articulate, self-actualizing woman, the equal of man.'[2] In short: the Christian tradition is inimical to the true interests of women.

If such is true of women within Christianity, even more so of animals. It may have taken nineteen hundred years for women to arrive firmly on the theological agenda, but at least they *are* now unambiguously on the agenda. The same cannot be said of animals. Mainstream Christianity still propagates a range of ideas about animals which are hugely detrimental to their status and welfare. Animals are 'here for our use', indeed, 'made for us'. Animals have no immortal soul, no rationality, no intrinsic worth.

Animals are subordinate to humankind, who have been given 'dominion' (commonly understood as despotism) over them. How far these ideas are distinctly or authentically Christian is beside the point; the fact is that the Christian tradition has propagated them – and still defends them.

Indeed, those who wish to justify the exploitation of animals regard the Christian tradition as the last bastion of anti-progressive sentiment. The editorial of one daily newspaper, recording with distaste the growth of the modern animal rights movement, exclaimed: 'For centuries, it has been an inherent part of the Christian ethic that man is entitled to exploit lesser species for his own advantage, as do many fervently Catholic societies to this day.' Ethical sensitivity to animals, it was supposed, constitutes nothing less than a rejection of Christian values:

> It seems increasing part of a _post-Christian_ ethic, however, to nourish the belief that animals possess dignity, personality and spirit that entitle their interests to be considered in the same fashion as the rest of us.[3]

The question then must be faced: Is Christianity irredeemably speciesist? I do not mean by speciesism the recognition that there are boundaries between species and that each may have differing abilities or characteristics. Neither do I mean a recognition that particular species may have different needs, claims, or interests from others. Rather I define the word here as the '_arbitrary_ favouring of one species' interests over another'.[4]

Of course not all Christianity has been speciesist in this sense. There have been – for want of a better word – 'sub-traditions' of thought which have variously commended charity and generosity towards animals. A substantial, if non-canonical, strand from the second to the twelfth centuries associated Jesus and the apostles with peaceable co-operative relations with animals.[5] These 'apocryphal' stories were, it is true, officially disowned by the church and never included in any recognizable canon of scripture. But even after the twelfth century and the hardening of scholastic theology against animals, many canonized saints of East and West exemplified in their lives filial, respectful relations with animals. When in the eighteenth and nineteenth centuries movements sprang up for the protection of animals, they were able to draw inspiration, at least in part, from a tradition, albeit a derided one, that could justifiably claim some Christian antiquity. Elsewhere, I have tried to give some account of this 'alternative' tradition and its unexplored potential for contemporary theology.[6]

Nevertheless, it is true that systematic and moral theology has emerged in such a form that animals are substantially excluded. The thought of

Aristotle, Augustine, and Aquinas has been pivotal here. Although devotees of each dismiss the simple charge of 'speciesism' or moral callousness, it remains a fact that Aristotle *did* argue (typically or untypically) that since 'nature makes nothing to no purpose, it must be that nature has made them [animals and plants] for the sake of man'.[7] Augustine *did* maintain (however *ad hoc*) that 'Reason has not been given to them [animals] to have in common with us, and so, by the most just ordinances of the Creator, both their life and their death is subject to our use.'[8] And St Thomas (interpreting Aristotle rightly or wrongly) *did* write that 'It is not wrong for man to make use of them [animals] either by killing or in any other way whatever.'[9] Whatever higher thoughts they may have had – even probably did have – they cannot be entirely absolved of responsibility for the way their words have subsequently been interpreted, as stating that animals should be excluded from proper moral consideration. The lines of St Thomas (above, and others) have been used, it is true, by animal advocates eager to show the callousness of the tradition, but, before that, more often by Catholic authorities equally eager to absolve us of any direct moral obligation to the brutes.[10]

One discussion published as late as 1960 is revealing. While accepting that the Thomist conception of hierarchy means that 'animals were created to serve the use and benefit of human beings', it maintains that 'wanton' cruelty is sinful. But, most noteworthy, such cruelty is *not* classifiable as a 'sin of injustice' as such. Nor is it, we are assured, *per se* 'a mortal sin'. What kind of sin could it then be? Apparently wanton cruelty is only a 'violation of the virtue of temperance'. And in justification of this – surely the weakest of all delineations – St Thomas' view is offered that cruelty to animals may lead to similar cruelty to humans.[11]

Even now it is difficult to find one mainstream systematic theologian who has given animals space, except as a secondary or peripheral issue in ethics or theology. All the 'great' Christian thinkers (as distinct from doers) both Catholic and Protestant have kept clear of animals. There have of course been 'minor' theologians, writers, and poets who have championed the cause of animals, some impressively so. The eighteenth-century English poet William Cowper 'contented' himself with 'a humble theme', namely the 'worth of brutes', feeling 'recompensed if . . . verse of mine may stand between an animal and woe, and teach one tyrant pity for his drudge',[12] and such imaginative sympathy was characteristic of early humanitarian protest. But there is no evidence that the example of saints or the work of imaginative poets has had any lasting effect on systematic or moral theology, still less on the teachings of the church.

At the very least it must be conceded that contemporary theology remains firmly humanocentric – and that despite increasing ecological awareness. Even creation liturgies as now espoused in some quarters of the church make precious few references to animals, as though their status was little different morally from stones and trees.[13] It is not easy to find a locus, either in systematic theology, or liturgy, or church and synodical pronouncements, for the idea that individual sentient beings have worth before almighty God.

Without exaggeration we might say that contemporary speculative theology is more interested in aliens than animals. One such high-minded discussion recently concluded that

> If, in other worlds, there have evolved forms of intelligent life so different from our own as to entail an utterly different kind of experience, then there seems to be no theological reason why God should not also have assumed those forms of life in order to experience them for himself. And there seems no good reason to wish to deny such other species the opportunity to meet God as one of their own number, incarnate in their own flesh, just as we meet him in Jesus. Any lesser God would be far too small.[14]

Such theological open-mindedness, not to mention open-heartedness, to other non-human alien species is hardly ever directed to other non-human but non-alien animal species. Where has this theological commentator been? we may ask. Has he really not seen that God has already set the human species in the context of hundreds, even thousands, of 'other worlds' where life – some of which is undoubtedly intelligent – exists and abounds before our very eyes? If any 'lesser God' than the one who would meet and relate to them 'would be far too small', how is it that this non-lesser God is only apparently interested in alien non-human life forms, which may or may not actually exist, rather than the thousands of non-human, non-alien species that already do?

We may unravel this conundrum, and the similar ones that contemporary theology presents us with, if we begin to confront directly and honestly the theological investment in *not* addressing the animal issue. Christians are heirs to almost two thousand years of theologizing about the world. That we have been so neglectful of God's other creatures should give us some pause. As I have written elsewhere: Why is it that 'the community of faith which holds to the objective truth of the self-revelation of God in Christ should have advanced its world-affirming doctrine without much more than a passing thought for the millions of non-human inhabitants within creation itself?'[15] Two obvious answers present themselves: one reputable, the other less so.

The first is that throughout the centuries Christianity has demonstrated a penchant for articulating and defending its doctrines in a way that not only gives a high place to humanity but also defines that humanity *against* animals. It is difficult to find one historical or contemporary theological work on the status of humans that doesn't include the words 'unlike animals . . .' or others very similar to them. This – what I have called – 'difference-finding tendency'[16] has obscured humanity's relationship to creation and bolstered up a range of 'differences', many of which are now seen to be empirically questionable.

The theological rationale for this tendency is not difficult to discern. It is encapsulated in Karl Barth's view that 'God's eternal Son and Logos did not will to be an angel or animal but man' and that *'this and this alone* was the content of the eternal divine election of grace'.[17] Given this overarching divine election of humanity, it must follow that humankind *is* special, unique, distinct, superior, and so on. It is as if, given this guarantee of divine favour, no claim for specialness – humanly speaking – can be insufficient. The incarnation is used as the trump card to vanquish all other creaturely rights to specialness, intrinsic worth, and respectful treatment. And once perceived as central – as the doctrine of the incarnation surely is – all other doctrines are then reinforced from this centre. The result is a narrowing of theological focus. Contrary to the biblical evidence, the notion of covenant is applied solely to human subjects. Atonement doctrine specifically, if not exclusively, concerns humanity's redemption. The work of the creative Spirit is telescoped into the salvation of human souls. And creation is seen only as the background or theatre to the real work of God performed for, on behalf of, the divinely elected human species which is now viewed as God's exclusive concern.

This christological logic has become so pervasive within the tradition that it is now taken to be the essence of the tradition itself. To be for Christ is to be for humanity: for our true welfare, our final happiness, our salvation. Anything less produces among mainstream Catholics and Protestants a sense of dismay at not having understood the true Christian message. We have become, almost without knowing it, the exponents of humanism's most cherished hope: only human beings really matter in the world.

But what is taken to be the essence of incarnational doctrine is at best only an interpretation of it. Incarnation does not have to be viewed as only the vindication of humanity. The key to realizing this is provided by Barth in his use of the word 'man'. For if the particularity of the incarnation is allowed its full weight, incarnation concerns the election not of men and women but man alone (in fact a Jewish, circumcised male). And true to this particularity there have been Christians throughout the centuries who have seen the election of man in the incarnation as grounds for positing a divine ordering of creation in which women are clearly subordinate. Indeed, some of the most weighty theological objections to the ordination of women have focussed on precisely this: the appropriateness of specifically male persons for the eucharistic role of representing the male incarnate Christ.

Once we reject this implication (as we surely should) of the particularity of the incarnation, we are able to view the incarnation in broader terms which transcend even male and female humanity. Far from being God's Yes to male humanity alone, or male and female humanity, the incarnation can be viewed as God's Yes to creation: specifically to fleshly and sentient life. By becoming flesh, the Logos identifies, according to this paradigm, not only with humanity but with all creatures of flesh and blood.

I shall not deal here with the biblical and patristic evidence that justifies this wider view of the incarnation.[18] All that needs to be grasped is that the incarnation doesn't have to be seen as the objective privileging of the human species above all others – at least in a way that is derogatory to other species. It has undoubtedly been read that way. But it doesn't have to be. Indeed, nothing substantial is lost to Christian doctrine by this wider focus, and much, I shall argue, will be gained.

But is Christianity – in this one central doctrine alone – capable of reinterpretation, of embracing a wider paradigm? I think it's a real question. Real in the sense that we do not yet know the answer. If Hampson is right (as I fear she may well be) in rejecting a too-easily forged compatibility between Christianity and feminism, then even more should we be questioning whether historic Christianity is capable of becoming other-than-human species friendly.

Here we come to the second – and less reputable – answer to the question why mainstream Christianity has been neglectful of animals. It is simply this: humans are not animals. The point is not as trite as it sounds. There is an element of human self-interest in all theological endeavours – not surprisingly, perhaps, since, as traditionally conceived, the Christian Gospel means 'good news' for human beings. That allowed, and without supposing that all theology is simply the aggrandisement of the human species, there needs to be some frank acknowledgment that theology can be used for self-serving human ends. The point is easily grasped once it is also appreciated that theology has been used historically to serve specifically male interests – sometimes quite unconsciously so. Feminists have rightly alerted us to the way in which our interpretation of the Bible and the tradition reinforces a patriarchal, man-centred view of the world. And if it is true that some 'hermeneutics of suspicion' are appropriate when considering texts which may have been influenced by patriarchal prejudice, these are even more appropriate when it comes to more widely held speciesist prejudices against animals.

Rejecting humanocentric prejudices about animals may sound – probably *will* sound – like the most ludicrous latest expression of political correctness to those who hold fast to 'historical Christianity' and are fearful of what may be called 'postmodernist innovation'. But, in fact, the promise of real theology has always been that it will liberate us from humanocentrism, that is from a purely human view of the world to a truly God-centred one. Theology at its best has always claimed to be more than a purely human view of the world. Once grasped, the issue about animals is seen for what it is: a central test of the adequacy of Christian theology and its claim to offer an objective God-centred account of the world including some account of the purpose, meaning, and value of non-human creatures. To go on supposing that the meaning and value of other creatures can be determined solely by their relationship with human beings is untheological.[19] Confronting speciesism, then, is not about Christian theology's latest concession to secular fashion, it is an imperative derived from the heart of theology's mission: to render a truthful, non-partial account of the creation God has made.

What might a theology that took animals seriously look like? Recently I made a presentation, with Paul Waldau, at the American Academy of Religion on 'The Dog's Mess: Theology as if Animals Mattered'.[20] The dog's mess is defined by Albert Schweitzer. To describe the place of animals in European thought he used the image of a kitchen floor scrubbed clean by someone who is 'careful to see that the door is shut lest the dog should come in and ruin the finished job with its footprints'.[21] Certainly animals do make a mess of humanocentric theology, but in my view radical insights about the worth of animals can be incorporated into mainstream trinitarian theology and such doctrines as creation, incarnation, and redemption will themselves be enlarged and improved in the process.

Yes, odd as it may sound to liberals, a theology which took animals seriously would be a more fully trinitarian theology. A theology with real *theos*, *logos*, and *pneuma* in it. In brief, it would be a theology which celebrated God's universal creativity in relation not only to the human species but to all species of life;

recognized the God-givenness of all individual life, human or animal, as something to be honoured and respected;

was open to the work of the Spirit alive and abroad – not just within humankind but in all creation, especially sentient creatures;

affirmed human specialness as a commission to be not the master species but the servant species;

expounded the moral covenant between God and all creatures of all flesh;

celebrated the incarnation as God's love affair with the flesh – not only the flesh of humankind but all embodied, sentient creatures;

saw in the crucified Christ God's identification with all innocent suffering, both human and animal;

grasped that in their innocence and incomprehension sentient creatures represent the unacknowledged faces of Christ in our world;

felt God's own suffering in the pain and misery and futility of unredeemed creation, human and animal, and regarded it as grace that we are able to co-experience with God the passion of the world;

took to itself the Christlike paradigm of inclusive moral generosity to the weak, innocent, and vulnerable and applied that same paradigm to all sentient creatures;

articulated a vision of Christ's reconciling ministry to all suffering creatures and sought to place itself on God's side in the work of redemption and justice; and

looked to the completion and transformation of all things in Christ: the sabbath for all creatures, human and animal.

Doubtless this list is not exhaustive but it does illustrate the orientation required if theology were to move beyond humanocentric parochialism and begin to take God as Creator, Reconciler, and Redeemer seriously.

And is Christianity destined to remain irredeemably speciesist? Certainly non-speciesist theology is a promise in search of fulfilment. Much historical theology is not impartial in relation to animals, and neither is much in the foundational narratives of scripture. The struggle to secure correcting mechanisms in theology's own self-understanding is bound to be a long, slow process – paralleled (though only to a lesser degree) by the challenges presented by feminism itself. In my view, the question remains genuinely open.

But there are many sources of hope, two in particular. The first is expressed by those lines of Alasdair MacIntyre that 'an adequate sense of tradition manifests itself in a grasp of those future possibilities which the past has made available to us in the present', and, again, 'Traditions when vital embody continuities of conflict.'[22] Against the mainstream view that the purpose and value of animals can be wholly defined by reference to the species which controls them, there have been other voices within the tradition urging release from humanocentrism. These voices deserve a hearing, and at least some of them are represented in this collection. The biblical vision of a peaceable kingdom with animals has been largely relegated by Christian theology to the End Time but at least it has kept alive, however futuristically, the possibility of creatures living together in peace. The tradition which has distanced itself from its own vision is also the tradition capable of mediating a sense of its contemporary urgency.

The Christian tradition is not like a closed book with all the lines printed and the plot already worked out. There is an underlying trinitarian dynamic – of Father, Son, *and Holy Spirit* – to be grasped: not all truth is given in the past, the Spirit has something to give us in the present. It is untrinitarian to consistently oppose God's work in the past to what we may learn here and now. For myself, I cannot get away from the dominical promise that the Spirit 'will guide you into all the truth' (John 16.13, NEB). This must mean, *inter alia*, that there are new things to be learnt. The God revealed in Jesus Christ is the same God who reveals now through the Spirit. In the at least half-true words of David Jenkins, 'revelation is always now, or never'.[23] The Spirit which bears witness to the things of Christ is now able to help us learn what living the Christlike life means in relation to God's other sentient creatures.

The other source of hope is represented in a small but not insignificant way by this volume itself. For many centuries, questions about animals have effectively been answered by *not* addressing them. Indeed, the questions have not for the most part even been on the agenda. All disciplines of course are characterized by the asking of some questions to the exclusion of others. The question that most characterizes theology is this: 'What must be true about the nature of the world in the light of God's self-revelation in Jesus Christ?' It is striking that this question has been consistently asked in such a way that animals are rarely included even in the terms of reference. Historical Christianity has thus been marked by the questions it hasn't asked or allowed itself to answer. But the interrogative can be one means by which the Spirit penetrates and disturbs us. As I learnt from my daughter some years ago, the asking of questions can be undermining, even subversive, of standard answers. That theology has formulated its ideas without asking whether its doctrine of God was arbitrary or unjust to animals (and hence inadequate) ought to give us hope that in centuries to come a theology which did at least ask this question would be substantially different.

Theologians have a responsibility in this regard: to articulate a theological understanding in which 'the animal question' can be fairly put and answers assessed. What cannot be right is for practitioners – whether they be biblical scholars, historians, systematizers, or ethicists – to carry on their business as though the world of animals was invisible, and as if urgent and thoughtful questions cannot be raised about our theological understanding of the non-human world. A special word of thanks is therefore appropriate to our contributors, who have the accolade of being, if not the first, certainly among the first to ask questions and formulate answers.[24] The voices represented here have not been selected with any ulterior motive: on the contrary, we have searched out as many contrasting voices from as many traditions – Catholic, Protestant, Anglican, and Evangelical – as we can in order to allow the 'continuities of conflict' to show themselves and in turn stimulate new thought.

My particular hope is that in, say, ten, twenty, or thirty years, most authors will be pleased but also embarrassed by their contribution to this collection. Pleased because most are pioneering essays. Embarrassed because what true pioneers most love is for others to go even further than they have done and leave them behind. That we are still at the beginning of asking theological questions that matter about animals is painfully obvious.

For myself, I love collections. In their overly derided patchiness and disparateness they expose most constructively the strengths and weaknesses of current thinking on a given topic. Constructively because one person's omission or failure is another's creative opportunity. Animals are on the agenda, but the adequacy of theology is on the line.

PART ONE

Understanding Scriptural Perspectives

Introduction

Andrew Linzey

At first sight there is little in scripture to delight the modern-day animal advocate – indeed, there is much to provoke consternation, even dismay. On many pages in the Old Testament animals are slaughtered, sacrificed, treated as unclean, are even the victims of divine genocide. Disharmony rather than harmony, violence rather than peace pervade the biblical picture of human relations with animals. And when it comes to the New Testament there appear to be only incidental references to animals, and not many of these bear much stamp of humanity.

'It just goes to show', says the biblical critic of modernity or post-modernity, 'that we shouldn't judge scripture by modern-day standards.' Quite so in one sense. But only in *one* sense. For it can be argued that if we do feel consternation, even revulsion, at the violence humans do to animals, we are no less biblical than our forebears; indeed, arguably we are following direct biblical warrant. For the first chapter of Genesis describes a creation at peace with itself and its Maker. Humans, it is true, have 'dominion' over animals (v. 28) but the following verse makes clear that the diet enjoined by the Creator, on animals as well as humans, is strictly vegetarian: 'I give you all plants that bear seed everywhere on earth, and every tree bearing fruit which yields seed: they shall be yours for food' (v. 29, NEB). It is this creation that God describes as 'very good'.

The notion, then, that violence between creatures is not what God originally intended is not some latest animal-rights propaganda. On the contrary, it can lay claim to form part of one of the earliest strands of biblical reflection. Animal advocates have not invented a world in which God makes us and all creation vegetarian; neither have they invented a world in which the lion lies down with the lamb. Both insights are given in the Judaeo-Christian tradition and rekindled afresh in a new generation. Far from modern advocacy diminishing biblical insights, in crucial respects it *depends* upon them.

Yet we know that is not the whole picture. While Genesis 1.29 commands vegetarianism, Genesis 9 allows carnivorousness, and that with equal specificity. 'Every creature that lives and moves shall be food for you; I give you them all, as once I gave you all green plants' (v. 3, NEB). Of course, as many commentators have pointed out, between Genesis 1 and 9 lies the great gulf represented by the Fall and the Flood: the difference between the world God intended and the world as humans have made it. Scripture then appears to position us – and all creation – between two worlds: one in which violence and disorder are inevitable, even divinely sanctioned, and another represented by the continuing hope of Isaiah in which the lion does not eat the lamb but lies down next to it.

How then are we to live in this apparently interim state between present violence and realized peaceableness? In this context what did it mean, for example, to sacrifice animals? At the outset John Rogerson warns us against any 'one single understanding' that can account for a practice spread over a thousand years of biblical history. Ideas of bonding, expiation for sin, even scapegoating, may explain some forms of sacrifice but not others. In the end Rogerson comes down against the theory that sacrifice 'constituted the institutionalization of violence against animals'. For the Priestly writers it was less of an institution and more of an ideology symbolizing, at least for some, 'the failure of humanity as represented by Israel to live in the world as God intended'. So it may be that sacrifice – far from being the gratuitous destruction of God's creatures – became one means of both registering human failure and also, paradoxically, reinforcing the very hope of a restoration of a conflict-free creation.

And if sacrifice apparently kept alive the very hope which its practice appeared to deny, what are we to say of the widespread biblical view that some animals are classifiable as 'clean' or 'unclean'? Similarly, Walter Houston maintains that the rationale for such classification is best located in the Priestly narrative of an originally peaceful world fallen into unpeaceableness. The dietary laws help demarcate 'the opposition of wild and tame, of civilization and the desert . . . of the divine and the demonic', and thus 'mediate the contradiction between the ideal of a non-violent world and the fact of unrestrained violence against animals'. Such signposts, he argues, whilst inevitably superseded by the Christian tradition, represented layers of meaning which have sadly been lost in our current interaction with nature.

In addition to abandoning the dietary laws, did early Christian teaching offer an otherworldly gospel of escape from creation? Not so, argues John Muddiman. Although there were later Christian formulations associated with platonizing philosophy, when read in terms of the Jewish doctrine of creation, New Testament teaching about salvation 'begins to look rather different – not individualistic and escapist but historical, material, and corporate – and its understanding of human nature, focussed as it is on the person of Jesus Christ, not so much anthropocentric as theocentric and holistic'. If the demons come into the Gospel they are, maintains Muddiman, largely an alien import; and if they sometimes figure prominently it is only to illustrate how Jesus cast them out – reclaiming the monistic view 'against a prevailing first-century dualism'. John's Prologue, sometimes viewed as a triumph of Hellenistic spiritualizing, actually offers us an incarnation of flesh – a term which, according to Muddiman, 'defines the solidarity of humanity with the rest of creation in its bodiliness'.

Reading the New in terms of the presuppositions of the Old is also essential, argues Richard Bauckham, in order to understand Jesus' teaching about animals. To the objection that there isn't any, Bauckham insists that the various allusions to animals make good sense when the Jewish background is understood. Thus the verses in Matthew and Luke about rescuing an animal fallen into a pit on the sabbath entirely cohere with rabbinic teaching that care for life supersedes the requirement to observe the sabbath law. According to Bauckham, Jesus stands firmly within the Jewish tradition in its biblically derived principle of *tsaar baalei hayyim*, the obligation to avoid pain to living creatures. An apocryphal Coptic story of Jesus healing a mule is, whatever its historical provenance, indicative of what we may presume about Jesus' compassion for animals. Likewise Jesus' much-discussed concern for sparrows – sold as cheap meat in the market – is based on the view that God is not concerned only with species but with 'each individual of the species'. And, in a crucial piece of elaboration, Bauckham explains that even if a hierarchy of creation is presupposed by the notion that humans are worth more than sparrows, it is not a hierarchy in which, contrary to later theologians, humans therefore 'have no ethical responsibilities towards animals'.

So far, then, the picture of Jesus' dealings with animals appears wholly benign. But Bauckham does not avoid confronting the less than benign evidence – and uncompromisingly too. In his view, Jesus *did* send the demons into the Gadarene swine, which involved their destruction, thus 'permit[ting] a lesser evil'. Jesus *did* eat not only fish but also lamb at the Passover and elsewhere. Moreover, 'we can scarcely doubt that Jesus participated in the sacrificial system' and so *did* himself sacrifice animals in the Temple.

Bauckham's scholarship is impressive and clearly demonstrates the difficulty in reading present-day sensitivities into the life of the historical Jesus. Even so, his portrait inevitably raises questions of coherence and consistency. Are we to believe that the 'sinless' Jesus really allows the destruction of innocent non-human creatures on the grounds that otherwise non-human demons might also perish (since demons, according to contemporary thought, required a 'living being' to inhabit)? Are we really to believe that while Jesus can – in Bauckham's words – 'deliver people from the power of the demonic', he is oddly circumscribed in relation to the non-human creation? If Jesus is sinless, how can he tolerate, let alone 'permit', what Bauckham calls 'a lesser evil'. A meat-eating Jesus is not without problems either. Since there were vegetarian contemporaries of Jesus (including, we may reliably suppose, his brother James), did Jesus then endorse the killing of animals beyond strict necessity? Moreover, did the sinless Jesus really perpetuate sacrifices in the Temple even though the early church within a very short period of time effectively repudiated them? Did the rejection of animal sacrifices by the early church owe nothing to Jesus' example and teaching?

The puzzle is intensified by Bauckham's eloquent exposition of Mark 1.13. By his peaceable presence with the wild animals Jesus fulfils Jewish messianic hopes concerning 'the righting of all wrongs' between humans and animals, including an endorsement of the 'original vegetarianism of all living creatures'. Are we then to believe that the bearer of messianic peaceableness himself failed to live up to that vision in his own treatment of animals? Bauckham concludes that 'Like all aspects of Jesus' inauguration of the kingdom of God, its fullness will be realized only in the eschatological future, but it can be significantly anticipated in the present.' The question is inevitable: Did Jesus then fail to anticipate the kingdom – in this one regard – in his *own* presence?

Perhaps our review only demonstrates the impossibility of drawing ethical imperatives valid for our own time from scant details in the life of the historical Jesus. It is not for no reason that Christian ethics has never followed the route of imitation *simpliciter*. (I guess that a Christian church which nowadays initiated animal sacrifice on the grounds that it was imitating the practice of its Lord would get a rough ride from even theological critics.) Rather, perhaps, we have no choice in this matter, as in many others, but to follow the contours (since the details are missing). And the contours appear to be that Jesus' teaching involves compassionate ministry to the suffering, the outcast, and the vulnerable, and that, according to Bauckham's own research, implicitly or explicitly, includes animals as well.

The underlying question remains: How are we to live in the interim time between creation and consummation, seeking to anticipate the biblical vision of universal peaceableness, a vision which Jesus, however incompletely, witnesses to in his own life and whose Spirit now mediates a sense of its contemporary urgency?

I

What was the Meaning of Animal Sacrifice?

J. W. Rogerson

There is no simple or straightforward answer to the question posed by the title of this chapter, as is shown once we ask 'meaning for whom?' Do we have in mind, for example, 'ordinary Israelites' (whoever they might have been)? If the answer is yes, difficulties are immediately apparent. First, whenever it was finally edited into the form familiar to us, the Old Testament claims to witness to over a thousand years of religious and political life in ancient Israel, during which time there were vast social changes and political upheavals. It would be surprising if a single understanding of animal sacrifice had prevailed during such a period. Second, account must be taken of the different attitudes that probably existed among different classes of people, and even among individuals. Thus, priests would see things differently from village laypeople, and, if there is truth in the generalization that in any given society, 'primitive' or 'advanced', a mixture of sceptics, conformists, and 'believers' can be found,[1] some ancient Israelites would have believed in the efficacy of animal sacrifices, others would have performed them as a matter of course, while others would have conformed while remaining sceptical about their efficacy.

The Old Testament itself provides ample evidence for a diversity of viewpoints about animal sacrifices. The sons of Eli are represented, in their attitude to sacrifices, as 'worthless men' (Hebrew: 'sons of Belial') who used their position as priests to further their own gain (I Sam. 2.12–17). (It is not suggested, of course, that they were typical of priests.) An attitude to sacrifice that saw it as merely a conformist religious duty without any moral implications is often criticized in prophetic literature, as in Amos 4.4–5. On the other hand, Job is portrayed as an utterly sincere man who went beyond the call of duty in making burnt offerings on behalf of his sons in case they had sinned and cursed God in their hearts (Job 1.5). Another well-known viewpoint in the Old Testament 'spiritualizes' sacrifice in order to emphasize that it is less important than the attitude of the individual worshipper. Psalm 51.17 is an excellent example:

The sacrifice acceptable to God is a broken spirit; a broken and contrite heart, O God, thou wilt not despise.

Finally, there are passages that are outrightly hostile to sacrifice, such as the exclamation in Isaiah 66.3:

He who slaughters an ox is like him who kills a man; he who sacrifices a lamb, like him who breaks a dog's neck.

In giving these examples, I have made no assumptions about the historicity or otherwise of, for example, Job or the sons of Eli. My point is that the passages cited portray what for Israelite writers or readers must have been plausible differing attitudes to animal sacrifice.

As soon as one asks historical questions about animal sacrifice, one encounters some of the most difficult questions of Old Testament criticism.[2] Whereas the Old Testament states that Israel's priestly and sacrificial system was revealed by God to Moses at Mount Sinai, the broad consensus of nineteenth-century critical scholarship divided Israelite religion into three main periods. In the first, that of the early monarchy (*c*.10th–7th centuries BCE), Israelites worshipped at many local shrines, and not only local priests but heads of families or leaders such as Samuel (I Sam. 10.8) offered animal sacrifices, especially whole burnt offerings or sacrifices that were mainly eaten at a festive meal (cf. I Sam. 20.5–6). The second period saw the centralization of worship in Jerusalem during the reign of Josiah (639–609 BCE; cf. II Kings 23.1–25), with an early form of Deuteronomy providing the rationale for the reform (cf. Deut. 12). The local shrines were closed down and sacrifices could only be offered in Jerusalem. The third period, indicated by the Priestly material in Exodus, Leviticus, and Numbers, contained the developed sacrificial system of the Second Temple period, with an emphasis on guilt and reparation offerings as well as ceremonies such as the annual Day of Atonement (Lev. 16). A possible corollary of this view was that animal sacrifice in the first period had been joyful and spontaneous, and had bound the worshippers and God together in fellowship, especially when the sacrifice was consumed as a meal. In contrast, the third period was one which emphasized the holiness of God, who could be approached only by elaborate sacrificial rituals of atonement.[3] If this view is correct (a different interpretation of the Priestly material will be suggested later), then the 'meaning' of animal sacrifice varied at different historical periods. Although many criticisms of points of detail can be made of the nineteenth-century consensus just outlined, it has not so far been replaced by any more plausible theory, and it will be accepted here as a working hypothesis, without its corollary concerning attitudes to sacrifice.

While the Old Testament credits Moses with giving ancient Israel its system of priesthood and sacrifice, it accepts animal sacrifice itself as being older than Moses, and as practised by other nations than Israel. Thus Abel is said to have offered (sacrificed?) the firstlings of his flock and their fat portions (Gen. 4.4), while Noah, after the Flood, offers every clean animal and bird as a burnt offering to God (Gen. 8.20). An extreme instance of a foreigner offering a sacrifice is the king of Moab, who sacrifices his eldest son when surrounded by the Israelites (II Kings 3.26–7). The fact that animal sacrifice was not peculiar to ancient Israel brings us into the realm of social anthropology, where theories have been put forward about the general 'meaning' and function of animal sacrifice in religion, and then applied specifically to the Old Testament.

The best-known theories are those of W. Robertson Smith, who argued that animal and plant sacrifices established communion between a group and its totem deity, and of H. Hubert and M. Mauss, who saw sacrifices as essentially a gift to the deity.[4] Robertson Smith applied his own theory to the Old Testament, while the gift theory was worked out in regard to the Old Testament by G. B. Gray.[5] There is undoubtedly some truth in both views, once one has discarded Robertson Smith's theories about totemism.[6] Two more recent approaches will be mentioned, the one because it enables something positive to be said about *some* Old Testament sacrifices, the other because it raises what will become the main concern of this chapter.

By modifying the suggestions made by Edmund Leach in his *Culture and Communication*, Douglas Davies has argued that animal sacrifices enabled boundaries to be crossed, boundaries which separated the ordinary sphere of public life from, on the one hand, the holy place, and, on the other, from the world of disorder.[7] In ancient Israel, the wilderness was seen as a place of disorder because it was inhabited by wild beasts and, it was popularly believed, by demons. The ritual of the Day of Atonement illustrates this clearly (Lev. 16). Its principal scenes are the holy place (the tent of meeting, the mercy seat, and the altar), the camp, and the wilderness. A bull offering enables Aaron to approach the mercy seat, and a goat offering is then made in the holy place, for the sins of the people. A second goat is then used to 'bear' the sins, transgressions, and iniquities of Israel. Aaron lays his hands on the goat's head, confesses Israel's wrongdoings, and then causes it to be led from the holy place through the camp to the wilderness. The ceremony achieves two things. First, the holy place is cleansed from the defilement of Israel's wrongdoings,[8] and, second, these wrongdoings are symbolically removed from among the people as the goat proceeds from the holy place through the camp and out into the wilderness. Davies also points out how sacrifices enable barriers to be crossed when a priest is consecrated and thus passes to the sphere of the holy place from the camp, or when a 'leper' is rehabilitated and passes from outside the camp back into the ordered network of social relationships.[9] The rituals for the priest and 'leper' are similar, and involve a transition period of seven days when the person is in an intermediate state between the two spheres. Davies' approach differs from earlier theories in that it is not an individual psychological theory: that is to say, it does not ask how individual worshippers might have thought that the sacrifice 'worked'. It is, rather, a structural-functional theory which tries to relate the sacrifices to the communal need to remove wrongdoing from the society, or enable people such as priests to move into the sphere of the holy or 'lepers' to be readmitted to society.

Whether or not it is fair to call René Girard's theory a structural-functional one, it has some superficial resemblances to what has been said about the Day of Atonement as a means of removing wrongdoing from society.[10] Girard believes that societies purge themselves by identifying and punishing or killing persons who become scapegoats. Where, instead of humans, animals are killed in sacrifice, violence is institutionalized, but in such a way as to allow a society to relieve itself of potentially destructive forces. Girard's theory of animal sacrifice as institutionalized violence raises the question that will occupy the remainder of this chapter. How are we to reconcile the priestly system of animal sacrifice with the fact that the Priestly account of the origins of the world presents us with an original creation that was vegetarian?

In those parts of Genesis 1–11 that belong to the Priestly source, there is a contrast between the creation that existed before the Flood and that which exists after it.[11] That the pre-Flood creation was vegetarian is indicated by Genesis 1.30:

> to every beast of the earth, and to every bird of the air, and to everything that creeps on the earth, everything that has the breath of life, I have given every green plant for food.

The Flood that is brought by God to destroy the earth is an undoing of that creation, as the agents that restrain the waters that are above and beneath the earth are removed (Gen. 7.11). When everything has been destroyed except those in the ark, God causes a wind to blow over the earth (Gen. 8.1:

the link with the wind/spirit of God that moves over the watery chaos at the beginning of creation is unmistakable), the waters above and below the earth are restrained (Gen. 8.2), and the Flood subsides. The mandate to the human race to be fruitful and multiply is renewed (Gen. 9.1), but there are two differences from the mandate of Genesis 1.28. First, whereas the mandate in 1.28 implies a caring role in regard to animals, that in 9.2 introduces an element of hostility:

> The fear of you and the dread of you shall be upon every beast of the earth, and upon every bird of the air, upon everything that creeps on the ground and all the fish of the sea; into your hand they are delivered.

Second, the human race is given authority to eat meat, provided that the blood is drained from it:

> Every moving thing that lives shall be food for you; and as I gave you the green plants, I give you everything. Only you shall not eat flesh with its life, that is, its blood (Gen. 9.3–4).

Taken together, the pre- and post-Flood mandates imply that the world of our experience is not the world as God intended or intends it to be. That original world was one in which, since the animals were vegetarians, there was no predatory violence within nature. Neither was there violence in the relationships between humans and animals. It is only after the Flood that the world of our experience comes into being, with violence in both these realms. In visions of a re-created world, the vegetarian world reappears. Thus, in Isaiah 65.17–25, where new heavens and a new earth are promised, they include the situation in which

> The wolf and the lamb shall feed together,
> the lion shall eat straw like the ox;
> and dust shall be the serpent's food (Isa. 65.25).

Modern readers differ from the biblical writers and readers of these passages in that the latter no doubt believed that a violence-free creation had once existed and that it would return in some physical form – a belief which we reject. On the other hand, it is possible to exaggerate the difference between these two views. The importance for biblical readers of a violence-free world lay not in the *fact* of its supposed existence, but in the way in which it witnessed to a possible form of existence that was also a radical criticism of the actual world of human experience. The story of the original creation and the hope for its restoration were judgments upon the present state of the world, and imperatives for action to achieve as much of the vision as was humanly possible. For modern readers, the biblical passages can function in the same way. One of the traditionally telling arguments against theism has been the existence of natural evil, and my own view is that it is preferable to say, with the Old Testament, that natural evil is not the will of God (with all the problems that ensue) than to try to justify natural evil or to explain it away.

The raising of the question of the importance of passages such as Genesis 1.28, 9.3–4, and Isaiah 65.17–25 for modern readers has been a slight diversion. It is necessary to return to the question of the significance, for an understanding of animal sacrifice, of the Priestly view that the original creation was vegetarian.

In a series of articles of great technical detail, Norbert Lohfink has argued that the historical part of the Priestly source (P^g) deliberately tries to present a violence-free account of Israel's history.[12] In particular, he argues that P^g deliberately avoided any reference to Israel's warlike conquest of Canaan in order to occupy it. Following the theory of sacrifice of Girard, he believes that the writer of P^g envisaged a community from which violence between humans had been eliminated, because war between humans and animals had taken its place. This, states Lohfink, is the assumption behind P^g's view of the world and the role of animal sacrifice, and he supports this position by pointing out the similarity between the renewed mandate to the human race in Genesis 9.2 and the form known in the Old Testament as the war oracle. In particular the words 'the fear and dread of you' suggest a war context. What follows, while differing from Lohfink, is greatly indebted to him.

The starting-point for a different approach must be the distinction between wild animals and animals used for domestic purposes. No doubt the warlike language of Genesis 9.2 expresses the actual relationship between humans and wild animals in the world of Israel's experience, but it does not express the relationship between humans and their domesticated animals, especially when the Old Testament contained laws such as Exodus 23.12, which provides that the ox and the ass should rest on the sabbath, and Deuteronomy 22.10, which prohibits ploughing with an ox and an ass together. And it was *domesticated* animals that were used for sacrifice, not wild animals.[13]

How did Israelites use and relate to their domesticated animals? In the

first place, they rarely consumed them. In the advice given in Proverbs
27.25–7 about the wise use of animals, there is no mention of eating at all:

> Know well the condition of your flocks,
> and give attention to your herds;
> for riches do not last for ever;
> and does a crown endure to all generations?
> When the grass is gone, and the new growth appears,
> and herbage of the mountains is gathered,
> the lambs will provide your clothing,
> and the goats the price of a field;
> there will be enough goat's milk for your food,
> for the food of your household
> and maintenance for your maidens.

The reason for not consuming one's animals was that they were capital, in
that they provided wool, and milk that could be made into cheese.[14] For dry
farmers, which was what villagers living in the central highlands of ancient
Israel and Judah were, animals represented a resource that sustained them
during the dry summer (providing them with milk and cheese) and which
could be moved to more fertile areas in years of poor rainfall.

A consideration of the use of domestic animals in ancient Israel serves as
a warning against generalizations, and draws attention to how greatly their
availability differed in different parts of a small country. Although much is
unclear about the extent of livestock husbandry in the central highlands,[15]
it is not misleading to say that, in the biblical period, the valleys of the low-
lands to the west of Judah and the wilderness to its east, together with the
valleys that intrude into the northern highlands from Shiloh northwards,
were favourable places for sheep and goats. How far villages in the less
favoured parts of the highlands could maintain numbers of sheep and goats
will have depended on whether it was possible for them to move to more
fertile parts – possible in the sense of their being allowed to move by those
who controlled the valleys. The Old Testament also mentions oxen and
milch cows as animals used for domestic purposes,[16] most likely for heavy
work such as ploughing and threshing. Cows were not used, it seems, for
providing milk; and the actual availability of these animals was probably
much less than is suggested by passages such as I Kings 4.23 and Nehemiah
5.18, where roast ox as well as other animals was on the daily menu for
Solomon and Nehemiah and their guests. These exaggerated descriptions
of meat consumption point up vividly the difference in lifestyle between

privileged and powerful rulers and the ordinary subsistence farmers who rarely ate meat. But they also raise important questions about the availability of animals for sacrifice.

In books such as I Samuel there are descriptions of communal sacrifices for a town (I Sam. 9.12) or a large family group (I Sam. 20.6) at which the animal was consumed by those present. The animal or animals were no doubt provided either by the head of the ruling family in the town, or the head of the family group. Such provision would have been a duty or a privilege without economic implications. However, the matter is quite different if we consider the regular needs of the Second Temple and ask what sort of economic base could have existed to support it. According to Exodus 29.38–42, two he-lambs a year old were to be offered daily as sacrifices. (All the lambs in what follows are also he-lambs.) These were to be supplemented by two more year-old lambs each sabbath day, and on the first day of each month two bullocks, a ram, and seven lambs were to be offered. A particularly demanding period was the holy convocation of the seventh month (see Num. 29) where the extended festival required seventy-three bullocks, one hundred and nineteen lambs, and a small number of rams and he-goats. Some rough calculations suggest that, for these regular ceremonies alone, around one thousand lambs and nearly a hundred bullocks were required, and the numbers could be increased if added to them were the requirements for the passover (Num. 28.16–25) and festival of first fruits (Num. 28.26–31). And all this, as Numbers 29.39 reminds us, was in addition to freewill offerings, burnt offerings, and peace offerings.

Perhaps a temple organization that possessed suitable land could produce annually for its basic needs the thousand sheep and hundred bullocks estimated above. But as far as we know, the Jerusalem temple of the Persian period (515–323 BCE), during which time the Priestly legislation reached its final form, was supported by only a comparatively small area of the Judaean highlands, whose agriculture was devoted mainly to the production of olive oil and wine, since it was not suited to the growing of cereals.[17] No doubt the enlargement of the territory of Judah to include the much more fertile northern and eastern areas of Samaria, Galilee, and Transjordan during the second and first centuries BCE radically altered the economic base supporting the temple, but it is proper to ask whether the Priestly legislation regarding sacrifice was anything more than an ideal when it was finalized.

That there were difficulties, or at least reluctance on the part of the people to provide the necessary animals, is indicated in at least two parts of the Old Testament. In Malachi 1 the complaint is made against priests as well as laymen that they have despised God by offering blind, sick, or lame animals in sacrifice. The point is made that they would not think of doing such a thing to the (probably Persian) governor! We cannot be sure, of course, whether the complaint concerned animals offered as part of regular temple offerings or on a personal basis. Also, we do not know the exact reason for the offering of sick animals; but it is plausible that economic reasons were involved. To offer an animal for whatever reason was to lose part of one's capital, and the smaller the flock or herd from which it was taken the more severe the loss. A sick animal would be less of a loss. The second relevant passage is Nehemiah 10.32–3, where an assembly pledges itself to pay a tax to support the temple service, including providing the continual burnt offering. The fact that this has to be publicly agreed to implies that it has been neglected.

The aim of the preceding paragraphs has been to explore some of the complex issues involved when considering the Priestly material about sacrifice. Were the sacrifices prescribed actually offered, at any rate in the Persian period? How was such a potentially destructive economic practice related to the economic base on which the temple depended? If Israelite villagers valued their domestic animals and rarely consumed them, what was the attitude of priests to the animals that were offered (whether or not the full legislative programme was being carried out)?

Although certainty cannot be achieved in responding to these questions, the following suggestions are put forward for consideration. First, it is probably wrong to say that animal sacrifice constituted the institutionalization of violence against animals. While the Second Temple community was small, it probably lacked the economic base to support the sacrificial programme, which, in addition, was not congenial to the villagers. By the time that the territory of Judah had expanded to provide a sufficient economic base, it included many for whom the temple was remote and rarely visited. Second, it may be more accurate to describe the Priestly view of animal sacrifice not as something institutionalized but as an ideology. That ideology was no doubt deeply aware of the dimension of guilt, especially guilt for the wrongdoings that had led to the destruction of the First Temple and the indifferent situation of the Second Temple community. Primal feelings that atonement for guilt could be made, among other ways, by the offering of animals on which depended the material existence of the community also drove this ideology. And yet it was not the only viewpoint, as was indicated at the beginning of the chapter. And in the larger context of the Priestly work, this belief in the necessity of offering large numbers of domestic animals was set against a belief in an original conflict-free, and vegetarian, creation. In other words, it can be argued that, for some priests at least, the system of animal sacrifice symbolized the failure of humanity as represented by Israel to live in the world as God intended. Violence among humans, violence among animals, and violence done by humans to animals was not what creation was intended to be. Even if, as Lohfink has suggested, the view of P^g was that a society free from human conflict could be sustained by animal sacrifices, that community was encouraged to hope for a world completely free of conflict.

In the matter of trying to understand the meaning of sacrifice in the Old Testament, anthropology cannot take us the whole way, valuable as it may be. The last word rests with the stories in which the details about sacrifices are embedded,[18] and in the Old Testament the guiding narratives are those that speak of an original conflict-free creation (including no conflict among animals, or between animals and humans), and which look for its restoration.

2

What was the Meaning of Classifying Animals as Clean or Unclean?

Walter Houston

In European culture the Jew and the Muslim draw attention to themselves, and not infrequently incur ridicule and obloquy as well, by their distinctive scruples in the matter of diet. Why must they refuse to eat pork? Why do they insist on eating only meat slaughtered in an approved fashion, and one which is *not* approved by many advocates of animal rights? Why do Jews make themselves difficult by refusing to eat meat and milk or milk products in the same meal?

I cannot deal with all these rules, just with one particularly interesting aspect: the classification of animals as it is found in the Hebrew scriptures, in Leviticus 11 and Deuteronomy 14.3–20, which governs the diet of orthodox Jews to this day.

A well-known biblical story will illuminate for us the meaning of this classification in practice: Peter's dream in Acts 10.9–16, where he sees all kinds of animals and birds and creeping things and is told 'Kill and eat', and on his natural refusal as an observant Jew is told 'It is not for you to call profane what God has made clean' (v. 15).[1] In the sequel it emerges that this dream is not really about animals. When he is invited to speak to Cornelius and his household, Peter testifies (v. 28) that God has shown him (in the dream, obviously) that he is to call no *human being* profane or unclean. In the narrative of Acts the dream signifies the acceptance of Gentiles, as Gentiles, uncircumcised and Torah-ignorant, into the church alongside Torah-observing Jews.

Luke's symbolism is not arbitrary or idiosyncratic, because it is the precise converse of that in God's words in Leviticus 20.24–6: 'I have made a clear separation between you and the nations, and you are to make a clear separation between clean beasts and unclean beasts, and between unclean and clean birds . . . You must be holy to me, because I, Yahweh, am holy. I have made a clear separation between you and the nations, that you may belong to me.'[2] If the classification of some animals as not to be eaten makes Jews awkward customers in a Gentile environment, that is precisely its purpose according to this passage: to mark the chosen people out as distinctive, to preserve them from being dissolved in the multi-ethnic stew of a world empire or world civilization. Such calculated distinctiveness is characteristic of a minority group under pressure from the majority culture and determined to resist it.[3] Luke believes this purpose has been transcended in the emergence of the Christian church as a society embracing both Jews and Gentiles, and expresses this in the image of Peter's dream, which reverses the symbolism of Leviticus 20.

But this is only the beginning of an answer to our question. More interesting in the context of this volume are the questions: why should animals in particular be selected for this symbolic purpose; why is the boundary drawn in just the places that it is – why, for example, are pigs unclean and not cattle or sheep; and how does abstaining from unclean flesh make Israel *holy?* I have discussed these questions at length in my book *Purity and Monotheism*, which the reader should turn to for argumentation and points of detail.[4]

There have been many false starts in thinking about this problem, which has fascinated both Jew and non-Jew for centuries. For example, the answer which seems to be most popular in our modern culture, where 'science' has great prestige but where most people's understanding of science is as superficial as their understanding of human society, is that the dietary rules serve a hygienic purpose. There are several objections to this theory, especially its failure to realize that *all* animals may carry dangerous diseases. But, in any case, it is looking in the wrong place. It looks to microbiology to answer a question about human culture; it looks to facts about real animals to answer a question about animals as symbols. Two facts are essential to an understanding. The one is that the phenomenon is not unique: we are dealing with a widespread feature of human culture. All cultures have their taboos, and in most cases they include animals. Rationally we should expect similar reasons to lie behind similar phenomena. The main distinctive feature of the Jewish taboos is that they are recognized as commanded by the authority of the one God as a binding condition of the covenant with Israel.

The other point is that we can only understand this particular realization of the general tendency to taboo animals if we pay close attention to the biblical source in which it is embodied. This does not merely pick out certain species as unclean: it offers a *system* of symbolic classification which covers the entire animal kingdom. The text of Leviticus 11.2–23 and Deuteronomy 14.3–20 classifies animals into three groups according to their sphere of life, and a fourth is added in Leviticus 11.29–38, 41–3. So we have beasts on the land, creatures of the water, and winged creatures in the air; Leviticus 11 completes the classification by adding the 'swarming creatures' of the ground, a classification which covers everything from small rodents and reptiles to worms and non-flying insects. For the first and second groups criteria are offered by which the species that are permitted to be eaten may be identified and distinguished from others. In the third no criteria are offered for birds, but the species that are not permitted are named; for flying insects criteria are offered in Leviticus only. The fourth is declared impermissible *en bloc*.

The path to the correct understanding of these rules has been opened up by Mary Douglas.[5] Human societies have a tendency to symbolize their own concerns and tensions by representing them to themselves in the way they understand the outward, physical world: the temple, the human body, the animal world. Animals are well fitted to play this role by their variety and the close and complex relations between them and human society. This tendency varies in strength from one culture to another, but it is particularly strong in Jewish society as it is represented in the priestly rules of the Hebrew Bible. We have already seen how the distinction of clean and unclean animals serves to represent the distinction between the people of God and all others. But it is not an arbitrary distinction. It arises out of realities in the relationship between animals and human society in Israel.

I have argued that the three sets of criteria in Leviticus 11 defining groups of animals which are permitted to be eaten (vv. 3, 9, 21) are to be seen as derived from the characteristics of known and accepted food animals (as contrasted with others), rather than the other way round.[6] This is particularly evident in the fact that no criteria are given for the birds; it is only in post-biblical literature that the attempt to derive criteria is made.[7] So we can see the move to define criteria of 'cleanness' as a long-drawn-out process beginning in the (late?) biblical period and carrying on to Talmudic times, and at all times dependent on common custom. Clean beasts can be defined as cloven-hoofed ruminants because sheep, goats, and cattle had always been sacrificed and eaten: it is not the definition which made it permissible to eat the animals. And locusts had to be recognized as edible (Lev. 11.21–3, despite Deut. 14.19) because locusts were eaten.

Analysis of animal remains from archaeological sites in Palestine and the surrounding areas through the Bronze and Iron Ages shows that the food mammals are overwhelmingly sheep, goats, and cattle.[8] Little game was eaten, and what there is is mainly deer and gazelle, which are ruminant animals permitted by the Levitical rule.

The pig, however, is a special case, an animal raised for the table which is yet explicitly excluded by the rule. Most domestic sites in the Bronze Age show a modest proportion of pig bones, but in the Iron Age this generally drops to very low levels (although rarely to zero), even at most non-Israelite sites, if it is possible to make such an identification. It is difficult to keep pigs in a relatively waterless country, since they need to bathe to keep themselves cool in hot weather; and the drop in the Iron Age could be due to the settlement and coming to power of people with a pastoral-nomadic heritage who would have had no inherited experience of pig-raising, and quite possibly attitudes of contempt towards it.

But there is a broader background to such attitudes in the ancient Levant. So far as the beasts are concerned, and to some extent the birds as well, their use in sacrifice as well as for food affects the issue. As one might expect, only animals that were eaten could be sacrificed, as most sacrifices were in fact eaten. But there is also a reverse effect, in part because in traditional society it was rare to eat meat *except* in sacrifice. There was a tendency to restrict people's animal diet to those types of animals that were permitted to be sacrificed.[9] The significance of this emerges when we look at sites which can be identified as ritual centres, whether shrines or tombs: we are struck by the absence of pig bones everywhere and in all periods;[10] if there are exceptions, and this is doubtful, they belong to the realm of the private and perhaps clandestine worship of the powers of death.[11]

The evidence of the remains is supported by written evidence.[12] Porphyry (third century CE) tells us that the Phoenicians did not eat pork. Nor are pigs ever mentioned in the prescriptions for sacrifice among the thirteenth-century BCE texts from Ugarit on the Syrian coast, or in those at Carthage in the third. And there is some evidence that even in the Bronze Age the eating of pork was rejected by urban élites.[13]

This evidence suggests that the distinction between clean and unclean animals, at least so far as beasts are concerned, is much older and more widespread than its appropriation by the writers of the Torah round about the sixth century BCE. The way in which it was observed was perhaps different – perhaps not so different, if we allow for the problem of enforcement in cultures much less tightly knit than rabbinic Judaism. It is identifiable as primarily the attitude of priestly and urban élites, as well as of pastoral nomads; the peasants may not share it. But those who do, everywhere in the Palestine-Syria area, since at least the beginning of the second millennium BCE, find only the same narrow repertoire of species acceptable for sacrifice and increasingly for eating as well. Pigs were unacceptable, even if they happened to be raised and eaten in many places in the country where sufficient water was available. Deer and gazelles could be eaten and might be accepted on the altar (at Carthage and perhaps in early Israel)[14] – they could be seen as honorary cattle, as it were – but most wild animals were not.

These facts may be explained on the basis of a pattern of associations between human and animal life, which can be traced in sources such as the Hebrew Bible. The pattern is a binary one, opposing tame and peaceful creatures, which are identified with the order and justice of the human community, to the wild and bloodthirsty creatures of the natural world.[15]

The animals kept by a people who combined agricultural and pastoral activity in their economy tended to be seen as in some sense part of the human community, or at least analogous to it. This was as true of beasts of burden such as the donkey as of goats and sheep and cattle. But while the latter were kept for food among other purposes, the donkey was purely a labourer. As Porphyry notes in his argument for vegetarianism, 'we do not slaughter . . . any of those animals that share our labour but do not enjoy its fruits',[16] and even the animals of the flock and herd were traditionally only slaughtered under ritual conditions, and their blood offered to the deity (cf. Lev. 17.10).

Over against these animals, which shared in the blessing of the community, were the beings of the wild, who refuse the dominion of humankind, tend to be violent and dangerous, and may eat carrion and blood. A few wild animals, because of their close resemblance in morphology and diet to cattle, could be allowed to belong to the class of cattle, but all the rest were beyond the pale. This restriction of edible game to forms closely resembling cattle is found among a number of East African peoples who closely identify themselves with their cattle – not only strict pastoralists such as the Masai and the Nuer,[17] but also the agricultural Kikuyu.[18]

On the other hand, two domestic or semi-domestic creatures found themselves lined up with the wild beasts, principally because of their diet. The dog was the universal scavenger, a consumer of blood, dead flesh, and dubious things, and references to it in the Hebrew Bible are consistently unfavourable; its name is an all-purpose insult.[19] It was indispensable in the absence of modern waste-disposal systems, and yet it was despised for doing what it was needed for.

The pig seems likely to have found itself in the same unenviable predicament. We can guess that where it was kept it was likely to have been fed on waste, as pigs are in China and were at one time in Britain. This would put it in the same category as the dog, and would account for its rejection by people who considered themselves of superior breeding, and its absolute unacceptability for public sacrifice. In all probability only poor peasants will have eaten it, offering a very useful vehicle for urban contempt of the village-dweller. In a culture where meat was not normally eaten except as the sequel to sacrifice, it is likely that some gods would have been acknowledged when pigs were slaughtered, but these would not have been the publicly acknowledged gods of state or tribe; in Israel, not Yahweh. As the city, and in Second Temple Judah the temple especially, extended its political and market power, it would steadily have driven out the domestic pig from its remaining ecological and cultural niches. However, this process was put into reverse when Hellenistic culture with its different symbolic concerns gained power in the region; otherwise there could have been no Gadarene swine!

The distinction among water creatures in Leviticus 11.9–12 is probably based on custom, but we have no direct evidence to back up this conjecture. When we move to the birds, we find that the ones listed as 'abominable' in Leviticus 11.13–19, as far as we can identify them – and that is not easy – seem mostly to be predators and carrion-eaters; certainly this was the opinion of the editors of the Mishnah. This aligns them with the unclean beasts; yet unlike the beasts the great majority of wild birds are regarded as edible. We may guess that birds in general were felt to be less closely related to human society than beasts, and hence raised less tension.

We may suspect that the creeping things of the ground simply were not normally thought of as even conceivable food: they were unconsciously tabooed, to use Leach's term.[20] Leviticus 11 deals with them at first not as putative food but as threats to the purity of food (vv. 29–38). It is only as an afterthought in vv. 41–43 that they are dealt with as possible food. There may be a connection here with Isaiah 66.17.[21]

The priestly composer or editor of Leviticus 11 thus had a rich tradition to draw on. He was not an innovator, but took over existing practice and attitudes and gave them a distinctive meaning. The demand for purity in diet affects the whole life of Israel and is to be maintained in perpetuity because they are dedicated to one God alone. Deuteronomy (14.1–3) had reminded the people that they were holy to Yahweh, and had exhorted them to eat nothing which was unfitting to that status. Clearly anything (such as the flesh of pigs) which had traditionally been thought of as unsuitable for the service of the gods could not be eaten by a people who were permanently consecrated to Yahweh.

The priestly editor of Leviticus 11 puts it in a slightly different way. If the peroration in vv. 43–45 can be seen as his personal contribution, he is likely to be the same person as the editor of the so-called Holiness Code in

Leviticus 17–26. As there, Israel is exhorted *to be holy* to Yahweh who is holy. It is a state constantly to be struggled for, constantly to be guarded, and it is threatened by 'all creatures that swarm' and by all other kinds of unclean flesh, for, as has always been known, these are unacceptable to the service of God and, what is more – if we may take Isaiah 65.3–5 and 66.17 at face value – they may be used in the service of unclean powers. The rhetoric aligns such defilement with such breaches of Israel's faithful commitment to Yahweh's moral demands as incest (ch. 18), unneighbourliness (19), or the devotion of one's children by fire (20.1–7). Separation from unclean flesh symbolizes and to an extent actually entails separation from anti-social practices, from the service of strange gods, and – the point emphasized in Leviticus 20.24–6, as we have seen – from other peoples who do not serve Yahweh.

In the priestly historical work, the opposition that I sketched above between tame and wild, culture and nature, appears in the form of myth. In the creation which God pronounces 'good', there is no killing for food (Gen. 1.29–30) and humanity exercises a peaceful dominion. But this situation cannot endure in the face of the 'corruption of all flesh'. 'All flesh' is swept away in the Flood, but the world that arises out of the Flood is one of total war between humanity and all other creatures (Gen. 9.2),[22] and it is a world where God cannot abide with humanity. If there is no way back to the original utopia, short of the messianic age (Isa. 11.6–9), there is the mediating solution of a people called by God to be God's own, who observe a Torah including severe restrictions on the eating of flesh, among whom God is able to dwell and be their God. So the dietary laws mediate the contradiction between the ideal of a non-violent world and the fact of unrestrained violence against animals.

It is clear from our brief discussion that great resources of meaning lie in the law of animal classification in the Hebrew Bible. The opposition of clean and unclean represents and includes the opposition of wild and tame, of civilization and the desert, of social conformity and unconformity, of the divine and the demonic, of violence and non-violence, of the people of God and the nations. The Christian gospel in its early radical form brought some of these oppositions into question. In its Pauline, universal form it needed to abolish the last one, and hence abandoned the distinction of clean and unclean animals. Loss and gain may be recognized in this historically inevitable development. Christians need to recognize the loss. We would benefit by equally fruitful structures of meaning which would remind us of our calling 'both indoors and out of doors, when you lie down and when you rise'.

3

A New Testament Doctrine of Creation?

John Muddiman

It may appear that the New Testament, since it embodies the eschatological world view of the early Christians, lacks the material to provide a basis for an ethic of environmentalism. It may even appear to be hostile to such a project, since the standard assessment of early Christian teaching is that it preached rescue from imminent judgment for an elect few. On this view the natural world cannot be the object of particular ethical concern, but is merely the temporary and dispensable backdrop to the higher drama of salvation. I hope to show, however, that in order to understand what the New Testament says about the End it is necessary to take into account its assumptions about the Beginning, the Jewish doctrine of creation; and that, when read in this way, it lends no support to the sort of extreme other-worldliness that arose in the Christian church and contributed to Western Christianity's dubious record of indifference to the environment. From the second century onwards, the original assumptions of the New Testament were replaced with a different set, associated with a platonizing philosophy, in which both orthodox and heretic shared. When the New Testament is read in its proper setting, its understanding of salvation begins to look rather different – not individualist and escapist but historical, material, and corporate – and its understanding of human nature, focussed as it is on the person of Jesus Christ, not so much anthropocentric as theocentric and holistic.

We need to raise at the outset a general problem, which affects all aspects of New Testament interpretation: how much does the New Testament depend upon the Old? Is there a basic continuity between the Testaments? Under the influence of the later separation and hostility between Christianity and Judaism, the discontinuity has been exaggerated. Jesus did not often expound scripture in the manner of the scribes (cf. Mark 1.21), and Paul could write letters to several of his churches without quoting scripture at all. Nevertheless, we should remember that the New Testament writers were probably all Jews and had read little if any literature apart from the Hebrew scriptures; their education did not go beyond the resources of the synagogue, and so, even in the absence of direct quotation, we are probably right to discern, beneath the surface of their words, a vast web of allusion, and multiple echoes of biblical ideas.[1]

The New Testament may not have much to say explicitly about the doctrine of creation, but its silence is not the silence of dissent. It simply assumes without question the truth of what Genesis, Isaiah, Ezekiel, the Psalms, and the Wisdom writings say about creation. These assumptions might be spelled out in four main propositions:

First, the one true God made everything in the universe; creation of all that is is the defining characteristic of deity. The world is not an accident or the work of a demiurge or the devil, and it shares in a certain sense the perfection of its maker, including the ambiguous perfection of freedom.

Second, God made everything simply for God's own glory and not for any other reason, in particular not for the exclusive benefit or convenience of any one species. Thus, all created things serve God's purpose simply by being themselves.

Third, God freely enters into a covenant of care for the world, and orders everything with a special divine wisdom and providence.

Fourth, God made men and women in his (her) own image, which means at least that he (she) graciously shares with human beings his (her) own creativity and dominion and calls them to co-operate with it.

These are the unspoken axioms that come to the surface occasionally in the New Testament but are everywhere implicit.[2] Of course, the New Testament is for this reason a rather ambiguous book: it is possible to read it against the background of a very different set of assumptions, and the early church had quite quickly to deal with this problem in the rise of gnosticism, which could be characterized as a reading of the New Testament predicated on the denial of the four propositions outlined above.[3]

The dependence of the New Testament on the Old Testament doctrine of creation has been disputed, however. It is said to depart from the biblical tradition in three principal respects. It lays heavier stress than the Old Testament on the Fall and its catastrophic effects on both human beings and the environment; it sees the world no longer as God's good creation but as the occupied territory of Satan and the demons; and it brings into prominence an idea suppressed in the Old Testament, that creation is a not entirely successful attempt to impose order on a pre-existent chaos.

Let us look at these three qualifications in turn:

Has the world as God made it been so ruined by the sin of Adam that humanity has lost the image of God and creation itself has become corrupt and diverted from its original purpose? Is the picture painted in the early chapters of Genesis a lost dream, the description of a world which might have been, with little relevance to the way things now are since the Fall?

Broadly speaking, the evidence of first-century Judaism is against such a conclusion.[4] When Adam's sin is mentioned – which is not frequently – it is attributed to his immaturity (since he was created as a fully grown adult, he missed all the educational advantages of a gradual adolescence). Alternatively, his sin is explained as a typically male weakness, that of listening too much to his wife's advice. In a neat rabbinic speculation[5] the chief result of the Fall is that Adam shrinks: before he was one hundred cubits tall, now he is only three; and this shrinkage naturally affects his senses, including his sense of hearing, so that whereas previously God's voice was sweet and gentle afterwards it sounds harsh and booming. The world becomes a frightening and threatening place for the shrunken Adam, but not because *it* has changed in any way or because the Fall has altered his fundamental character – simply because he is smaller than he was intended to be. What this Jewish theodicy is effectively saying is that there is nothing wrong with the world as God made it: the problem is our human perspective on it, which has become too small and diminished. We were not meant to take the worm's-eye view, to which sin has reduced us.

The only exception to this rather mild treatment of Adam's disobedience is the so-called fourth book of Ezra,[6] in which Ezra the scribe is dramatically presented discussing with an angel the appalling consequences of the first sin. Although this pseudepigraphon is quite untypical, some scholars emphasize its importance because of Paul's apparent echo of it in his account of the Fall in Romans 5. However, we should remember that IV Ezra was in fact written fifty years later than the Epistle to the Romans, and in the gloomy aftermath of the Jewish war with Rome. Furthermore, Paul himself does not make the Fall as much of a catastrophe as might appear. The very word 'fall' sounds catastrophic to us, but in Greek it simply means a slip (*paraptoma*), normally of the pen or of the tongue. Nor does Paul say in Romans 5.12 – except in the Latin version – that Adam's offspring inherited his guilt and sin:[7] on the contrary, Paul says that every person is his own Adam. And the Apostle does not maintain elsewhere what he seems to suggest here, that universal death is punishment for Adam's disobedience. We should compare I Corinthians 15, where he deduces natural human mortality from the fact that Adam was created out of dust, and was bound eventually to disintegrate, whether he had sinned or not. This, rather than Romans 5, is what Paul the Jew really believed, for one simple reason which is so obvious that it is easy to overlook, namely that death in itself is not half enough punishment for sin.[8] One might live a life of cruelty and greed and then just slip away in old age and evade God's wrath (cf. Luke 16.19–31): the sting in the tail is not death but the dreadful prospect that one might not *stay* dead but might be resurrected for judgment.

So the Jewish and early Christian view is that the world is still basically as God made it. It has not been irretrievably corrupted by some ancient sin, though it is constantly corrupted by actual sins, which make human beings incapable of seeing in it the hand of the Creator (Rom. 1.20) and thus frustrate its original purpose (Rom. 8.20).[9] If only we could stop sinning, the created universe might start to recuperate, and recover its former glory.

The second qualification I referred to was that the world view of early Christianity was radically different from that of most of the Old Testament because of its belief that demons had invaded and taken possession of creation.[10] This is indeed a striking difference between the Testaments. The origins of Jewish demonology are very obscure. Some aspects of it develop from within the tradition – for example, by reflection on the myth in Genesis 6 that fallen angels raped human women and so produced a race of evil spirits. But for the full-blown notion of Belial and his angels ranged against Michael and the forces of light, scholars are probably right to posit some importation from outside the tradition, especially from Iranian dualistic mythology. However, what is clear is that, although the New Testament reflects these beliefs, it does not subscribe to the view that the world is under their power. Following Jesus himself, it made a strong stand against demonology. Jesus decisively defeated the evil empire, casting out demons by the spirit of God; and on the cross he defeated the principalities and powers, restoring creation to where it was before, and liberating people from fear of the demonic. In a sense, therefore, the New Testament speaks a lot about the devil, not because it has changed the Old Testament doctrine of creation but, on the contrary, because it wants to reclaim that monistic view against a prevailing first-century dualism. Admittedly, the more common opinion among interpreters is that the New Testament is distinctive in its departure from monotheism and its addition of one or two more persons to the Godhead. But this opinion ought to be challenged: the beginnings of the doctrine of the Trinity in the New Testament are precisely attempts to safeguard a monotheistic view of God and a monistic view of the creation against the prevailing alternatives in the Jewish and Hellenistic worlds of dualism, polytheism, and pantheism.

The third qualification arises from the theory that the New Testament reintroduces the notion of chaos. If the Babylonian myth of creation as the defeat of pre-existing chaos was known to Old Testament writers,[11] then they substantially modified it, in order to give Israel's God absolute priority. Thus the monster of the deep was turned into a mere 'waste and void' over which the spirit broods; the dragon of mindless destruction becomes a wily lizard up a tree; and Leviathan sports himself in the ocean for God's pleasure, like a large pet goldfish. When the Psalms speak of a God who rules the waves, they do not imply that the unruly waves were there before God was; the stormy sea stands for the most powerful force in nature, which is no rival to the transcendent power of God but a positive analogy for it. In the New Testament the Book of Revelation refers to an 'angel of the bottomless pit' whose name is Abbadon or Apollyon, the 'Destroyer' (9.11), but this is not chaos, a private domain where the Creator's writ does not run. Even the abyss has its place in God's plan. There is no sea in the New Creation (21.2), but there is a river of life (22.2) and water is a symbol of salvation, not an alien element in the cosmos. In the Gospels, the Lake of Galilee – usually referred to, with exaggeration, as the Sea – is a positive symbol, associated with successful preaching and mission. The only exception might be the episode of the stilling of the storm, but the suggestion that this miracle represents the messianic pacification of chaos is unconvincing: the scene is altogether too domestic, with the disciples afraid and Jesus asleep on a cushion, to carry such cosmic significance. Thus the New Testament no less than the Old resists the notion of chaos as a power that pre-exists God's creative order.

Incidentally, these three ideas, of the Fall, evil spirits, and chaos, are developed much further in later Christian thought. In particular, they give rise to three quite different conceptions of hell: hell as solitary confinement where one endures the just punishment of God; hell as a place of torment, where devils feast on the damned; and hell as a madhouse, where rational beings finally go to pieces. There seems, then, to be no consensus about hell in Christian symbolism: it is anybody's guess – from which I suppose one might draw a modicum of comfort!

To illustrate what I have been saying about the axiomatic character of the doctrine of creation in the New Testament, I want to look at the prologues to the Gospels of Mark and John.[12] Both are in effect meditations on the creation: Mark is more like the Yahwist account in Genesis 2, John closer to the Priestly version of Genesis 1. Both attempt to see the creation story fulfilled and reaffirmed in the coming of Jesus. In both the first word is 'beginning', which is the first word also of Genesis and provides its title. An informed audience would immediately start picking up such echoes.

In Mark's account, the beginning of the Gospel, which Matthew explicates as 'The book of Genesis of Jesus Christ', leads straight into the appearance of the prophet John as the herald of the Messiah. He is the voice of one crying in the wilderness, 'Prepare the way of the Lord.' Mark may well have referred to Isaiah by name – although part of the quotation is from Malachi, and he does not usually identify his sources – because he wanted the audience to take into account the larger context of the prophecy, which speaks of the restoration of creation: valleys will be lifted up and hills made low, uneven places made level and rough places plain, so that exiled Israel can regain the promised land. The Lord whose way is prepared is himself the restorer of creation: he will feed his flock like a shepherd and gather the lambs in his arms, and gently lead those who are with young. (We notice here how sympathy for a pregnant female crosses the barrier between species.)

John the Baptist is a 'green' figure in Mark. His dress and diet come to him straight from the desert. He is not quite a vegetarian, but someone who eats only locusts is probably the most ecologically benign type of carnivore. He preaches repentance and the coming of the Messiah as the restoration of creation. The baptism of Jesus confirms this interpretation, for it recapitulates the story of Genesis. The heavens are torn open, not sealed up; what descends is not an outpouring of divine anger as at the Flood but the creator Spirit who once brooded like a dove over the face of the water. And the gentle voice of God announces, as he did silently over his first creation, 'Thou art my only Child.' And just as God once declared everything to be very good, so now he says, 'with thee I am well pleased'. The serpent's temptation of the human couple in the garden parallels the temptation of Jesus by Satan. And a final echo of the creation story comes in the last brief reference 'he was with the wild beasts'. Being with the beasts implies that there is no threat from them; without suddenly changing their predatory ways,[13] they restrain themselves in the presence of a servant of God, and thus offer a foretaste of the return of God's kingdom of peace.[14]

It is worth noting at this point that the animals which figure in many of Jesus' parables and sayings all remain their natural selves. There is no anthropomorphism, there are no fables, everything is normal – sparrows drop dead, dogs scavenge and lick the wounds of beggars, and eagles gather over a carcass. Wolves can be expected to harass sheep – it would only be reprehensible if, like false prophets, they dressed up like sheep to do it. There is a certain realism here, and a respect for the way things are, since that is the way God has made them.

There are other motifs in the Prologue of Mark which are not relevant to our present purpose, but its basic assumption and the key to its interpretation is the Jewish doctrine of creation fulfilled in the coming of Jesus. It is surprising how many symbols of nature have been squeezed into its opening paragraph – desert, river, sky, camel, bee and locust, dove and wild beast. And within this interdependent ecosystem, this continuum of created being, true humanity is restored to its proper place. This is a theocentric and ecological vision of creation renewed and restored, anticipated in the person of Jesus Christ.

St John's Prologue uses a very different mode of expression – a cross between philosophy and poetry, where Mark gave us a folksy story – but the intention is the same. 'In the beginning was the word' clearly echoes God's words at creation, 'Let there be light'; all life emerges into the light, and this light and life are expressed also through the prophetic word to Israel and at last through the Word made flesh, God's only child, the true Adam.

The Fourth Gospel has special reasons arising from its own setting for making what seems at first sight the astonishing claim that a recently crucified Palestinian prophet was the agent of God in the creation of the world. First, we can tell from the Johannine Epistles[15] that there were schismatic and ascetic tendencies threatening the community from within, which conceived of salvation as a flight from the world of flesh. In response, the Evangelist says that the one who saves is also the one who, created in the beginning, came into the flesh which he had made.

Secondly, John's community had recently been expelled from the synagogue,[16] on the charge of disobedience to the law, as we can tell from the sharp exchanges between Jesus and the Jews in the Gospel, especially the incident of the man born blind in chapter 9. Rejecting this charge, the Evangelist proceeds to clothe the person of Christ with all transcendent functions of the law, in creation and redemption, so that while the words of the law may have come through Moses, its grace and its truth are seen to come through Jesus Christ (John 1.17).

Thirdly, the Prologue, by reflecting on creation,[17] offers an answer to the problem of how one can worship Christ as God for us, as Johannine Christians did, and yet still claim to be loyal monotheists. The answer is that there is a Word of God who is God with God, that Jesus is so transparent of God's will and goodness that to see him is to see the invisible creator, without any risk of infringing his unity.

The theology of John is easy to misunderstand if its Jewish assumptions are ignored.[18] Its focus on the person of Christ and its spiritualization of eschatology might be thought to justify the accusation with which we began, that the New Testament is anthropocentric and escapist, and hostile, therefore, to environmentalism. But viewed against the background of the doctrine of creation the Prologue begins to look very different. The Word did not merely become human: he became flesh, the term which defines the solidarity of humanity with the rest of creation in its bodiliness: 'All flesh is grass and its beauty like the flowers of the field; the grass withers and the flower fades, but the Word of the Lord remains for ever' (Isa. 40.6–8). And it is this incarnate solidarity in the flesh which promises for the future a restoration of the world which God created in the beginning.

The New Testament, then, takes the Old Testament doctrine of creation as axiomatic. To read it without this background or against another background is to distort its message. Adam's fall, the power of demons, and elements of random disorder may be used to explain perceived disruptions in the world, but they do not alter its basic structure as God's creation. The Prologues of Mark and John illustrate the theme of a new creation through the coming of Christ. Their understanding of salvation is not the rescue of isolated humans from the world but the restoration of true humanity in the world.

4

Jesus and Animals I:
What did he Teach?

Richard Bauckham

A cursory reading of the Gospels might well leave the impression that there is very little to be said about Jesus and animals. This impression would seem to be confirmed by the fact that modern New Testament scholarship has given virtually no attention to this subject. However, this chapter will show that there is in fact a good deal to be learned from the Gospels about Jesus' understanding of the relationship between humans and other living creatures. This will only be possible by relating Jesus and his teaching to the Jewish religious tradition in which he belonged. All aspects of Jesus' ministry and teaching, even the most innovatory, were significantly continuous with the Jewish tradition of faith, especially, of course, with the Hebrew Bible. Many features of this religious tradition Jesus presupposed. He did not argue, for example, that the God of Israel is the one true God, but everything he did and said presupposed this. Similarly, he presupposed the religious and ethical attitudes to animals which were traditional and accepted, both in the Old Testament and in later Jewish tradition. In his teaching, he adopts such attitudes, not for the most part in order to draw attention to them for their own sake, but in order to base on them teaching about the relation of humans to God. But this does not imply that he took them less seriously than other aspects of Jewish faith and religious teaching which he endorsed and developed. But it does mean that, in order to appreciate the full implications of Jesus' references to animals in his teaching, we must investigate the context of Jewish teaching to which they belong.

Compassionate treatment of animals

A duty to treat animals humanely and compassionately, not causing unnecessary suffering and whenever possible relieving suffering, was well established in Jewish tradition by Jesus' time, though it was applied largely to domestic animals – those animals owned by humans as beasts of burden, working animals, sources of milk and food, and therefore also offered in sacrifices to God. These were the animals for which humans had day-to-day responsibility. They were not simply to be used and exploited for human benefit, but to be treated with respect and consideration as fellow-creatures of God. Proverbs 12.10 states the general principle:

> A right-minded person cares for his beast,
> but one who is wicked is cruel at heart[1] (REB).

In later Jewish literature, an interesting instance is the Testament of Zebulon,[2] which is much concerned with the duty of compassion and mercy to all people, exemplified by the patriarch Zebulon himself, and understood as a reflection of the compassion and mercy of God.[3] Compassion is probably here an interpretation of the commandment to love one's neighbour (Lev. 19.18), taken to be the central and comprehensive ethical commandment of God and interpreted as requiring compassion for all people. In other words, the love commandment is interpreted much as Jesus interpreted it. But in Zebulon's general statement of the ethical duty of compassion he extends it not only to all people but also to animals:

> And now, my children, I tell you to keep the commands of the Lord: to show mercy to your neighbour, and to have compassion on all, not only human beings but also irrational animals. For on account of these things the Lord blessed me . . . (T. Zeb. 5.1–2).

Another interesting, if not perhaps very representative, passage from the Jewish literature of Jesus' time occurs in II Enoch (the Slavonic Apocalypse of Enoch) in a context of ethical teaching which again has many points of contact with the ethical teaching of Jesus. Chapters 58–59 deal with sins against animals. Uniquely, they teach that the souls of animals will be kept alive until the last judgment, not, apparently, for the sake of eternal life for themselves,[4] but so that they may bring charges, at that judgment, against human beings who have treated them badly (58.4–6). There seem to be three kinds of sins against animals: failing to feed domestic animals adequately (58.6),[5] bestiality (59.5),[6] and sacrificing an animal without binding it by its four legs (59.2–4). This third sin may seem at first sight to be purely a matter of not observing what the author understood to be the proper ritual requirements for sacrificial slaughter, and it is not obvious why it should be considered a sin against the animal. The reason may be that an animal not properly bound would struggle and die with unnecessary suffering. More probably, the idea is that if the animal struggled, the knife used to cut its throat might slip and damage the animal in some other way.[7] The animal would then not satisfy the ritual requirement that a sacrificial victim be without blemish, and could not be a valid sacrifice. In that case, its life would have been taken to no purpose. This passage of II Enoch is evidence that some Jews in Jesus' time gave serious thought to human beings' ethical duties towards animals.

Of more direct relevance to material in the Gospels (as we shall see) are Jewish legal traditions, in which the law of Moses was interpreted as requiring compassion and consideration for animals. Later rabbinic traditions understood a whole series of laws in this way (Ex. 22.30, 23.4–5; Lev. 22.27, 28; Deut. 22.1–4, 6–7, 10, 25.4).[8] In many of these cases, it is not obvious that the point of the law is compassion for the animals, and modern Old Testament exegetes often understand them differently.[9] Ancient Jews could also do so. For example, the law of Deuteronomy 22.6–7, which requires someone taking the young birds from a nest (for food) to let the mother bird go, was evidently understood (probably correctly) by the Jewish writer known as Pseudo-Phocylides (lines 84–85) as a conservation measure: 'leave the mother bird behind, in order to get young from her again'.[10] But it was also commonly understood as a matter of compassion for the bird (Josephus, *C. Apion.* 2.213; Lev. R. 27.11; Deut. R. 6.1). The rabbis deduced from such laws a general principle that all living beings should be spared pain (the principle of *sa'ar ba'aley hayyim*).[11] The rabbinic material, of course, post-dates the New Testament, but there are enough pieces of early evidence of the same kind of interpretation for us to be sure that this way of interpreting the law, as concerned with compassion for animals, was well established by Jesus' time. For example, Josephus, in a remarkable passage in which he is trying to represent the law of Moses in the ways most calculated to appeal to Gentile critics of Judaism, explains that Moses required that the Jews treat strangers and even national enemies with consideration, and then argues that Moses even required consideration for animals:

> So thorough a lesson has he given us in gentleness and humanity that he does not overlook even the brute beasts, authorizing their use only in accordance with the Law, and forbidding all other employment of them [cf. Ex. 20.10; Deut. 5.14, 22.10]. Creatures which take refuge in our houses like suppliants we are forbidden to kill.[12] He would not suffer us

to take the parent birds with the young [Deut. 22.6–7], and bade us even in an enemy's country to spare and not to kill the beasts employed in labour [perhaps cf. Deut. 20.19]. Thus, in every particular, he had an eye to mercy, using the laws I have mentioned to enforce the lesson (*C. Apion.* 2.213–14).[13]

Here the principle of compassion for animals apparently leads to the formulation of laws not to be found in the written Torah at all.

A very similar treatment, though restricted to laws actually found in the Torah, is given by Philo of Alexandria, who sees the gentleness and kindness of the precepts given by Moses in the fact that consideration is extended to creatures of every kind: to humans, even if they are strangers or enemies, to irrational animals,[14] even if they are unclean according to the dietary laws, and even to plants and trees (*Virt.* 160; cf. 81, 125, 140). He expounds in detail the laws which he understands to be motivated by compassion for animals: Leviticus 22.27 (*Virt.* 126–33); Leviticus 22.28 (134–42); Exodus 23.19, 34.26; Deuteronomy 14.21 (142–4); Deuteronomy 25.4 (145); Deuteronomy 22.10 (146–7).

This line of interpretation of the law cannot be explained merely as an apologetic for the law of Moses by diaspora Jews concerned to impress Gentiles. It can be paralleled in later rabbinic literature.[15] One striking instance, which almost certainly goes back to New Testament times, is found in the Palestinian Targum. It concerns the law of Leviticus 22.28, which forbids the slaughter of an animal and its young together. According to the Targum of Pseudo-Jonathan, which frequently preserves Jewish exegetical traditions from this period,[16] God, when giving this commandment, says to the people: 'just as I in heaven am merciful, so shall you be merciful on earth' (cf. Luke 6.36). Behind this statement probably lies Psalm 145.9: 'The Lord is good to all, and his compassion is over all that he has made.' God's compassion for all creatures is to be imitated by the people, and the laws requiring consideration for animals are given to this end.

The idea that compassion for animals is a general principle of the Torah explains why acts of compassion for animals were permitted on the sabbath, even though they involved what would otherwise be considered work. On three occasions in the Gospels Jesus refers to such generally recognized exceptions to the prohibition of work on the sabbath. He does so in the context of debate about his practice of performing healings on the sabbath, to which the Pharisees (Matt. 12.10–14; Luke 14.3) and others (Luke 13.14, 14.3) objected. In each case his point is to argue that, since his opponents agreed that relieving the suffering of domestic animals was lawful on the sabbath, how much more must relieving the suffering of human beings be lawful. The statements are:

> Suppose one of you has only one sheep and it falls into a pit on the sabbath; will you not lay hold of it and lift it out? How much more valuable is a human being than a sheep! So it is lawful to do good on the sabbath (Matt. 12.11–12).[17]

> If one of you has a child[18] or an ox that has fallen into a well, will you not immediately pull it out on a sabbath day? (Luke 14.5).[19]

> Does not each of you on the sabbath untie his ox or his donkey from the manger, and lead it away to give it water? And ought not this woman, a daughter of Abraham whom Satan bound for eighteen long years, be set free from this bondage on the sabbath day? (Luke 13.15–16).

Not all Jews would have agreed with Jesus' account of what it was permitted to do for animals on the sabbath.[20] The written Torah, of course, makes no such explicit exceptions to the sabbath commandment. Therefore the Qumran sect, whose interpretation of the sabbath laws was extremely strict, categorically forbade such acts of mercy: 'No man shall assist a beast to give birth on the Sabbath day. And if it should fall into a cistern or pit, he shall not lift it out on the Sabbath' (CD 11.12–14).[21] On this latter question, addressed in Matthew 12.11 and Luke 14.5, later rabbinic opinion was divided as to whether it was permissible to help the animal out of the pit or only to bring it provisions until it could be rescued after the sabbath (b. Shabb. 128b; b. B. Mes. 32b). We may take the Gospels as evidence that the more lenient ruling was widely held in Jesus' time. As to the example given in Luke 13.15, it is very much in line with the Mishnah's interpretation of sabbath law in relation to domestic animals, though not explicitly stated as a rabbinic ruling. The point is that tying and untying knots were defined as two of the types of activity which constituted work and were generally unlawful on the sabbath (m. Shabb. 7.2), but provision for domestic animals was one kind of reason for allowing exceptions (m. Shabb. 15.1–2; cf. b. Shabb. 128a–b; cf. also m. Erub. 2.1–4, where it is taken for granted that cattle are watered on the sabbath).

These exceptions to the prohibition of work on the sabbath are remarkable. They are not cases in which the lives of the animals were in danger, and so they cannot be understood as motivated by a concern to preserve the animals as valuable property. Rather they are acts of compassion, intended to prevent animal suffering. It was only because the law was understood as generally requiring considerate treatment of animals that the sabbath commandment could be interpreted as not forbidding such acts of mercy to animals on the sabbath. Moreover, it is clear that Jesus understood the issue in this way. His argument is that, since his hearers agreed that acts of compassion designed to relieve the suffering of animals are lawful on the sabbath, surely acts of compassion designed to relieve human suffering are also lawful. According to Matthew 12.12–13, rescuing a sheep from a pit on the sabbath is 'doing good', and so healing a man's withered hand on the sabbath is also doing good.

Of course, in all three texts, the law's requirement of compassion for animals is only the presupposition for the point Jesus is making. But his argument is certainly not merely *ad hominem*. He is arguing from a presupposition which is really agreed between him and his opponents. Jesus, in his recorded teaching, does not teach compassion for animals, but he places himself clearly within the Jewish ethical and legal tradition which held that God requires the people to treat their fellow-creatures, the animals, with compassion and consideration.

An apocryphal story

A little-known apocryphal story about Jesus is unique in showing Jesus engaged in an act of compassion for an animal:

> It happened that the Lord left the city and walked with his disciples over the mountains. And they came to a mountain, and the road which led up it was steep. There they found a man with a pack-mule. But the animal had fallen, because the man had loaded it too heavily, and now he beat it, so that it was bleeding. And Jesus came to him and said, 'Man, why do you beat your animal? Do you not see that it is too weak for its burden, and do you not know that it suffers pains?' But the man answered and said, 'What is that to you? I may beat it as much as I please, since it is my property, and I bought it for a good sum of money. Ask those who are with you, for they know me and know about this.' And some of the disciples said, 'Yes, Lord, it is as he says. We have seen how he bought it.' But the Lord said, 'Do you then not see how it bleeds, and do you not hear how it groans and cries out?' But they answered and said, 'No, Lord, that it groans and cries out, we do not hear.' But Jesus was sad and exclaimed, 'Woe to you, that you do not hear how it com-

plains to the Creator in heaven and cries out for mercy. But threefold woes to him about whom it cries out and complains in its pain.' And he came up and touched the animal. And it stood up and its wounds were healed. But Jesus said to the man, 'Now carry on and from now on do not beat it any more, so that you too may find mercy.'[22]

Since nothing is known of the source of this story, preserved in Coptic,[23] it is impossible to know whether it derives from an early Gospel tradition. However, it does seem to presuppose the Jewish legal tradition which we have discussed in the last section. Specifically, it relates to the commandment to relieve an animal which has fallen under its burden (Ex. 23.4; Deut. 22.4), interpreted as requiring compassion for an overburdened animal.[24] So the story may go back to a Jewish-Christian source in which Jesus' teaching that love is the overriding principle in interpreting the law was extended, as it is not explicitly in the canonical Gospels, to concern for animals as well as people. Jesus' final saying in the story extends to the treatment of animals Jesus' general principle that 'the measure you give will be the measure you get' (Matt. 7.2; Luke 6.38), as well as the thought of the beatitude: 'Blessed are the merciful, for they will receive mercy' (Matt. 5.7). If people do not show mercy to their animals, they cannot expect mercy from God.[25] Whatever its source, the story is at least a kind of testimony to the impression the figure of Jesus in the Gospels can make on their readers. This – we may agree – is how the Jesus portrayed in the Gospels would have behaved in such a situation.

God's provision for creatures

Look at the birds of the air; they neither sow nor reap nor gather into barns, and yet your heavenly Father feeds them. Are you not of more value than they? (Matt. 6.29).

Consider the ravens: they neither sow nor reap, they have neither storehouse nor barn, and yet God feeds them. Of how much more value are you than the birds! (Luke 12.24).

In this saying, as in the corresponding exhortation to consider the wild flowers (Matt. 6.28; Luke 12.27), Jesus adopts the style of a Jewish wisdom teacher, inviting his hearers to consider the natural world, God's creation, and to draw religious lessons from it (cf. Job 12.7–8, 35.4; Prov. 6.6; Sir. 33.15; I Enoch 2.1–3, 3.1, 4.1, 5.1, 3). What he asks them to notice – that

God feeds the birds/ravens – is drawn directly from the creation theology of the Old Testament, especially the Psalms, in which it is a commonplace that God the Creator supplies all living creatures with food. Psalm 147.9 is one example among several:

> He gives to the animals their food,
> and to the young ravens when they cry.[26]

It is probably impossible to tell whether, in Jesus' saying, Matthew's 'the birds of the air' or Luke's 'the ravens' is more original, but the latter gives a more precise Old Testament allusion to Job 38.41 or Psalm 147.9. The reason why both these Old Testament texts single out the ravens is that the cry of the young ravens, to which they both refer, was especially raucous. Young ravens 'squawk for food with louder and longer cries than almost any other species'.[27] In the context of Jesus' saying, it might also be significant that, according to the dietary laws, the raven is an unclean animal (Lev. 11.15; Deut. 14.14). The point would then be that God takes care to provide even for an unclean bird like the raven.[28]

The Old Testament creation theology, which Jesus here echoes, includes humans among the living creatures for whom God provides. The great creation Psalm 104, where humans are included among all the creatures who look to God for food (vv. 27–28), is notable for its depiction of humans as one species among others in the community of creation for which the Creator shares. Psalm 145.15, which echoes Psalm 104.27–8, does so, as the context makes clear, in order especially to highlight God's provision for humans. Like Jesus, the psalmist points to God's care for all living creatures in order to assure humans who turn to God in need that God provides for them. The same point is made, in dependence on these psalms, in a later Jewish psalm (from the first century BC):

> For if I am hungry, I will cry out to you, O God,
> and you will give me (something).
> You feed the birds and the fish
> as you send rain in the wilderness that grass may sprout
> to provide pasture in the wilderness for every living thing,
> and if they are hungry, they will lift their eyes up to you.
> You feed kings and rulers and peoples, O God,
> and who is the hope of the poor and needy, if not you, Lord?
> (Pss. Sol. 5.8–11).[29]

Clearly, in arguing from the Creator's provision for birds to provision for people, Jesus' words belong firmly within Jewish tradition. The point that is not from the tradition is Jesus' observation that birds do not sow or reap or store their food in barns. This observation has been variously interpreted. Jesus has sometimes been thought to contrast the birds who do not work with people who do: if God feeds even the idle birds, how much more will he provide for people who work hard for their living. He has also been thought to compare the birds who do not work with disciples who do not work either, but as wandering preachers depend on God's provision by way of receiving charity. It is improbable that either of these alternatives is the real point. Rather the point is that, because the birds do not have to labour to process their food from nature, their dependence on the Creator's provision is the more immediate and obvious.[30] Humans, preoccupied with the daily toil of supplying their basic needs by sowing and reaping and gathering into barns, may easily suppose that it is up to them to provide themselves with food, and neglect the fact that, much more fundamentally, they are dependent on the divine provision, the resources of creation without which no one could sow, reap or gather into barns. The birds, in their more immediate and obvious dependence on the Creator, remind humans that ultimately they are no less dependent on the Creator.

Once again, as in the sabbath healing discussions, what Jesus says about animals is a presupposition from which to argue something about humans. But it is a necessary presupposition. It is not, as some modern readers tend to assume, just a picturesque illustration of Jesus' point, as though the point could stand without the illustration. Rather Jesus' argument depends on the Old Testament creation theology evoked by his reference to the birds. Humans can trust God for their basic needs, treating the resources of creation as God's provision for these needs, only when they recognize that they belong to the community of God's creatures, for all of whom the Creator provides. Only those who recognize birds as their fellow-creatures can appreciate Jesus' point. It is noteworthy that, although the argument, like that in the discussions of sabbath law, is an argument from the lesser to the greater, it is not an argument which sets humans on a different plane of being from the animals. On the contrary, it sets humans within the community of God's creatures, all of whom are provided for. Apparently, they are regarded as particularly eminent members of that community (a point to which we shall return), but they are members of it, nonetheless.

God's concern for every creature

> Are not two sparrows sold for a penny? Yet not one of them will fall to the ground apart from your Father. And even the hairs of your head are all counted. So do not be afraid; you are of more value than many sparrows (Matt. 10.29–31).

> Are not five sparrows sold for two pennies? Yet not one of them is forgotten in God's sight. But even the hairs of your head are all counted. Do not be afraid; you are of more value than many sparrows (Luke 12.6–7).

Evidently sparrows were sold in the market, either in pairs or in fives (which for Jewish counting in tens would be equivalent to our half-dozen), as food for the poor, who would probably rarely be able to afford any other form of meat. That sparrows were the cheapest birds for sale in the market – and for this reason selected by Jesus to make his point – is confirmed by a decree of the emperor Diocletian (late third century AD) which fixes maximum prices for all kinds of items and lists sparrows as the cheapest of all the birds used for food.[31] The cheapness of birds, in general, is interestingly confirmed by a passage in the Mishnah relating to the law of Deuteronomy 22.6–7, which, as we have already noticed, forbids taking the mother bird together with her young from a nest. The rabbis were struck by the fact that, very unusually, this law specifies a reward for keeping it: 'that it may go well with you and you may live long' (Deut. 22.7). They concluded that if such a reward attaches to 'so light a precept concerning what is worth but an *issar*', then how much more will a similar reward be given for observing 'the weightier precepts of the law' (m. Hull. 12.5). The commandment is here considered trivial, compared with others,[32] because it concerns only a bird, which is worth only an *issar*. The issar is the same small copper coin as Matthew's and Luke's 'penny' (*assarion*).[33]

Thus Jesus has selected a creature which is valued very cheaply by humans, of course on the basis of its limited usefulness to them. Even a creature which humans think so unimportant is important enough to God for it never to escape caring attention. Matthew's and Luke's versions of the saying make the point in slightly different ways. Matthew's is the more specific and relates to the capture of sparrows for food. The sparrow's fall to the earth is not, as modern readers often suppose, its death,[34] but what happens when the hunter's throw-net snares it (cf. Amos 3.5).[35] It will then be sold in the market. The sparrow's capture cannot happen 'without *(aneu)* your Father' (Matt. 10.29), i.e. without God's knowledge and consent. There is a remarkably close parallel, not only to this point but also to the moral which Jesus draws from it with regard to God's care for the disciples, in a later rabbinic story, which must show that Jesus is drawing on traditional Jewish teaching. The story concerns Rabbi Simeon ben Yohai (mid-second century AD) who at the end of the second Jewish war spent thirteen years hiding in a cave with his son.

> At the end of this period he emerged and sat at the entrance of the cave and saw a hunter engaged in catching birds. Now whenever R. Simeon heard a heavenly voice exclaim from heaven, 'Mercy!' [i.e. a legal sentence of release] it escaped; if it exclaimed, 'Death!' it was caught. 'Even a bird is not caught without the assent of Providence,' he remarked; 'how much more then the life of a human being!' Thereupon he went forth and found that the trouble had subsided (Gen. R. 79.6).[36]

Rabbi Simeon realizes that his fate is in the hands of God, to whom he can therefore entrust himself, when he realizes that this is even true of each bird.

If Jesus drew on traditional Jewish teaching, this teaching was itself rooted in the Old Testament, which says that

> In his hand is the life of every living thing
> and the breath of every human being (Job 12.10)

and

> You save humans and animals alike, O Lord (Ps. 36.6).

It is God who preserves the life of each creature, animal and human, and who likewise allows that life to perish when it does.

Luke's version makes the more general point that not a single sparrow ever escapes God's attention ('forgotten in the sight of God' is a Jewish reverential periphrasis for 'forgotten by God'; cf. Matt. 18.14). But in both versions the point is God's caring providence for each individual creature. God is not concerned only with the species, but with each individual of the species. Nor does God simply superintend what happens to each without concern for the welfare of each: this would provide no basis for Jesus' assurance that the disciples need have no fear. The point is that since God actually cares about and takes care of each sparrow, how much more must

God care about and take care of Jesus' disciples. Of course, Jesus does not raise the problems of such a doctrine of providence:[37] Why does God let one sparrow escape and another be captured and killed? Why does God allow righteous people to suffer? Here Jesus is content to affirm that the disciples, like all God's creatures, are in the hands of God who cares for all God has made.

Humans are of more value than animals

All the references to animals in the sayings of Jesus which we have considered belong to a form of argument from the lesser to the greater (*a minore ad maius*, or, in rabbinic terminology, *qal wa-homer*). Since, it is stated or assumed, humans are of more value than animals, if something is true in the case of animals, it must also be true in the case of humans. If acts of compassion for animals are lawful on the sabbath, then acts of compassion for humans must also be lawful. If God provides for birds, then God can be trusted to provide for humans also. If not even a sparrow escapes God's caring attention, then Jesus' disciples can be sure they are in God's care.

This form of argument is used in rabbinic literature, and so we can probably conclude that it was already an established form of Jewish religious argument in Jesus' time. In addition to the passage quoted (from Gen. R. 79.6) in the previous section,[38] the following are examples of it:

m. Qidd. 4.14: R. Simeon b. Eleazar says: Hast thou ever seen a wild animal or a bird practising a craft? – yet they have their sustenance without care and were they not created for naught else but to serve me? But I was created to serve my Maker. How much more then ought not I to have my sustenance without care? But I have wrought evil, and [so] forfeited my [right to] sustenance [without care]. [39]

b. Qidd. 82b: R. Simeon b. Eleazar said: In my whole lifetime I have not seen a deer engaged in gathering fruits, a lion carrying burdens, or a fox as a shopkeeper, yet they are sustained without trouble, though they were created only to serve me, whereas I was created to serve my Maker. Now, if these, who were created only to serve me are sustained without trouble, how much more so should I be sustained without trouble, I who was created to serve my Maker! But it is because I have acted evilly and destroyed my livelihood, as it is said, your iniquities have turned away these things [Jer. 5.25].[40]

y. Ber. 9.3.13c: Elijah asked Rabbi Nehorai, Why had God created in his world tiny insects and worms? He replied, 'When human beings sin, He looks on the lower forms of creation and says: "If I sustain these tiny useless creatures, how much more must I preserve human beings who are useful."'[41]

Deut. R. 6.5: Another comment [on Deut. 22.6–7]: R. Hiyya said: If a bird that has neither ancestral merit nor covenants nor oaths to rely upon, can be atoned for by her children, how much more will the children of Abraham, Isaac, and Jacob who have ancestral merit to rely on, if any of them sin, be atoned for by their children in the time to come.[42]

All of these passages use the phrase 'how much more', which Jesus also uses in other examples of *qal wa-homer* argument in his teaching (Matt. 6.30 par. Luke 12.28; Matt. 7.11 par. Luke 11.13; Matt. 10.25: *posoi mallon* in all cases except Matt. 6.30). But this expression is not used in the arguments from animals to humans (except in Luke 12.24). Instead, expressions employing the verb *diapherein* are used:

How much more valuable *(posoi diapherei)* is a human being than a sheep! (Matt. 12.12).

Are you not of more value *(mallon diapherete)* than they [the birds of the air]? (Matt. 6.26).

Of how much more value are you *(posoi . . . mallon diapherete)* than the birds! (Luke 12.24).

You are of more value *(diapherete)* than many sparrows! (Matt. 10.31).

You are of more value *(diapherete)* than many sparrows (Luke 12.7).

It might be a preferable translation of *diapherein* to say that humans 'are superior to' animals. The reference is probably to the kind of hierarchical superiority which is implied in the Old Testament's notion of human dominion over the animals (Gen. 1.26–8; Ps. 8.5–8). Humans are of superior status in the sense that a king is superior to his subjects. At least in biblical thought, a king is not of greater value than his subjects. However, we cannot rule out the idea of a difference in intrinsic value. Certainly the law of Moses treats human life as more valuable than animal life. A human being or even a domestic animal that kills a human being is subject to death, but a human being who kills a domestic animal is required only to make financial restitution to its owner (Ex. 21.28–35; Lev. 24.17–21; cf. Gen. 9.5–6). In these laws animals seem to be treated only as property, but it should also be noted that the prohibition on eating meat with blood in it (Gen. 9.4; Lev. 3.17, 7.26, 17.10; Deut. 12.16, 23, 15.23) is a kind of recognition that animal life is valuable (it is the gift of God and must be returned), even though there are permissible reasons for taking it. Jesus' arguments certainly presuppose that animals have intrinsic value for God. Otherwise it could make no sense to say that humans are more valuable.[43]

Two observations on Jesus' arguments from animals to humans are appropriate. In the first place, they do not employ certain ideas that we find in some of the rabbinic passages quoted above. In the saying of Rabbi Simeon b. Eleazar (m. Qidd. 4.14; b. Qidd. 82b), animals are said to have been created only to serve humans. This non-biblical idea – which is certainly not implied in Genesis 1–2 and is clearly refuted by Job 39 – entered both Jewish and Christian thought from Aristotelian and Stoic philosophy.[44] There is no reason to think that it is presupposed in Jesus' sayings. The saying attributed to Rabbi Nehorai may well reflect the kind of discussions which the Stoic notion that all other creatures exist for the sake of their usefulness to humanity provoked. Many creatures seemed of no obvious use to humanity at all, and ingenious explanations of their usefulness had to be found.[45] Rabbi Nehorai admits that some tiny creatures are useless (presumably to human beings), but gives them a kind of use in reminding God to preserve human beings, who, by contrast, are useful (presumably to God). The only point at which Jesus refers to the value of creatures by the standard of their usefulness to human beings is when he cites the price of sparrows in the market (Matt. 10.29; Luke 12.6), but he does so in order to contrast this human estimate of the value of sparrows with their importance to God. Thus, if Jesus' sayings do imply a kind of hierarchical superiority of humans to animals, it is not the kind of hierarchy implied in these two rabbinic sayings, in which animals exist solely to serve humanity and humans to serve God. It is a hierarchy within the community of creation, in which humans and animals alike exist for God's glory, and in which there is a mutuality in fellow-creatureliness, such that, if some animals do serve humans, humans also have responsibilities of care towards those animals (Matt. 12.11; Luke 13.15, 14.5).

The second observation is very important. It is that Jesus never uses the superiority of humans to animals in order to make a negative point about animals. He does not argue, as some later Christian theologians influenced by Greek philosophy did,[46] that because animals are inferior to humans, humans have no ethical responsibilities towards animals. He does not argue that because animals are inferior to humans, God does not take as much trouble to provide for animals as in the case of humans. He does not argue that because animals are inferior to humans, God's providence does not extend to individual animals, but only to species.[47] On the contrary, in every case, his argument is that because such-and-such is true in the case of animals, it must also be true in the case of humans. The arguments actually depend more on the idea that humans and animals are all creatures of God than they do on the idea of a hierarchical difference between them.

Perhaps this is the appropriate point at which to mention the incident of the Gerasene (or Gadarene) swine (Matt. 8.28–34; Mark 5.1–20; Luke 8.26–39), since, at least since Augustine, this has often been understood to demonstrate that Jesus set little value on animal life. Augustine argues, against the Manicheans, that it is not wrong to slaughter animals, since Jesus himself did so when he sent the demons into the herd of pigs. But Augustine shows the presuppositions on which his reading of the story depends, when he says that Jesus did this 'on the ground that there is no community of rights between us and brutes'.[48] This is the Stoic doctrine that, because humans are rational and animals irrational, there can be no question of justice or injustice in human relationships with animals.[49] Animals have no rights which can affect human treatment of them. This Stoic principle was to have a long history in Christian thought,[50] but it would not have influenced Jesus.

We should observe that in the Markan and Lukan versions of the story Jesus permits the demons to enter the pigs, in response to their begging him to let them (Mark 5.12–13; Luke 8.32), and although Matthew makes the permission into a command of Jesus, it is still a command to do what they have begged to be allowed to do (Matt. 8.31–32). The story can only be properly understood in terms of the ideas of the demonic prevalent in Jesus' time. The demons fear being without a living being to inhabit, and would certainly not have remained without a habitation for long. According to contemporary Jewish ideas on the subject, if they could not readily find an alternative home, they would be liable to return to the one they had left (Matt. 12.43–45; Mark 9.25). Moreover, demons were thought to be associated with particular locations, and would naturally see the nearby pigs as a suitable refuge.[51] Their destruction of the pigs manifests the inherent tendency of the demonic to destroy whatever it possesses (cf. Mark 5.5, 9.22). Finally, although only Matthew's version attributes to the demons when they first encounter Jesus the alarmed question, 'Have you come here to torment us before the time?' (Matt. 8.29; cf. Mark 1.24), the thought underlying this question is certainly implicit in all three versions. It is that the eschatological 'time' – the day of judgment – when God will abolish all evil and destroy the demons has not yet come. Jesus' ministry of victory over evil anticipates that time; he can deliver people from the power of the demonic; God's destruction of the evil forces that oppress people has decisively begun (cf. Matt. 12.28); but nevertheless Jesus does not yet abolish the demons or send them back to the abyss (Luke 8.31). Until the end of history evil can be deflected and diminished but not abolished (cf. Matt. 13.24–30).[52]

Thus Jesus, in this story, permits a lesser evil. There is no reason at all to suppose that he sets no value on the life of the pigs or values it only for the sake of human beings. But the destruction of the pigs is preferable to the destruction of a human personality. The principle that human beings are of more value than other animals here operates to the detriment of the latter, in a case, unique within the Gospels, where a choice has to be made.

5

Jesus and Animals II:
What did he Practise?

Richard Bauckham

In the previous chapter we studied the evidence of Jesus' teaching in the Gospels. There remains the question of how Jesus related to animals in practice. The evidence to answer this question is even less extensive than his recorded teaching about animals, but still it is not negligible.

From Jesus' general teaching and its roots in the Jewish tradition, we should certainly expect that Jesus treated animals with care and compassion. In so far as Christians look to Jesus for an example of the ethical lifestyle which they should follow, Jesus' general practice of love and compassion is of great importance for their treatment of animals. Even though the Gospels do not record specific instances of Jesus exercising compassion for animals (the apocryphal story quoted in the last chapter is the only known instance of this in any ancient literature about Jesus), nevertheless readers of the Gospels find it hard to imagine him failing to do so. (This is why the incident of the demons and the pigs, discussed in the last chapter, seems to many readers problematic in that Jesus appears to act out of character.)

However, beyond this general point, there are two specific issues we can explore. The first is whether Jesus ate meat. The answer is not immediately obvious in the Gospels, but there are a number of indications and pieces of evidence which we can consider. The second issue is whether Jesus in any way brought animals within the scope of his messianic mission. Most of the acts of Jesus recorded in the Gospels are illustrations and examples of the healing and forgiveness and deliverance from evil which he brought to human life. But did the salvation he brought from God extend in any way beyond the human world to the other living creatures with whom we share God's world? One brief but decisive reference to animals in Mark's Gospel (1.13) provides, as we shall see, a richly significant answer to this question.

Sacrifices and meat-eating

We have seen that Jesus' attitude to animals belongs wholly within the Old Testament and Jewish tradition. In this tradition it was permitted to kill certain animals for sacrifice to God in the temple and for food. For Jesus to have rejected either of these practices in principle would have been a significant innovation. Of course, there were innovatory aspects of Jesus' interpretation of the law of Moses, but there is no evidence at all that he innovated in either of these two ways.

With regard to sacrifice, had there been any tradition of words of Jesus rejecting the sacrificial system, then the Gospels, probably all written by and for Christians who had abandoned the practice of sacrifice in the temple, would surely have recorded it. The so-called cleansing of the temple (Mark 12.15-17), which has sometimes been interpreted as a symbolic rejection of the system of sacrificial worship, would certainly not have been so understood by Jesus' contemporaries. Jesus objected to the way the priestly aristocracy who ran the temple were exploiting the sacrificial system as a means of financial profit, thus distorting the real purpose of sacrifices as a vehicle of prayer.[1] Matthew twice attributes to Jesus, in his debates with the Pharisees, a quotation from Hosea 6.6: 'I desire mercy, not sacrifice' (Matt. 9.13, 12.7). In neither context is a reference to sacrifice as such especially relevant. Sacrifice must be taken here as representative of the ritual aspect of Jewish religion, which the Pharisees are seen as giving precedence over the ethical demand of God's law. But the sharp antithesis is not really intended, any more than it is in its original context in Hosea, to mean that sacrifice is not God's will. The meaning is that mere ritual observance is of no value in God's sight. We can be sure that Matthew does not understand Jesus to be rejecting the sacrificial system, because in Matthew 5.23-24 he preserves a saying of Jesus which takes it for granted that his hearers, like almost all Jews, would be following the practice of offering sacrifice in the temple.[2] It seems clear that, despite his criticism of the way the priestly hierarchy ran the temple, Jesus did not go as far as the Qumran sect, who rejected the legitimacy of the worship in the temple (while not rejecting sacrifice in principle). We must also take it as virtually certain that he himself participated in sacrificial worship, both in attending the prayers that accompanied the regular sacrifices in the temple, and in offering sacrifices himself (which were not of course only offered in atonement for personal sin, but also for purification from ritual impurity and as offerings of praise and thanksgiving).[3] His attendance at the regular annual festivals in Jerusalem (Luke

2.41–42, John 2.13, 7.1–10, 10.22–23) would have involved this. If the impression the Synoptic Gospels give that the last supper was a passover meal is correct (Mark 14.12–16; Luke 22.14; but contrast John 18.28, 19.14, 31), then Jesus ate with his disciples the passover lamb which had been sacrificed in the temple that afternoon.

Eventually most early Christians came to believe that the sacrificial system, or at any rate sin-offerings, had been rendered redundant by the sacrificial death of Christ (see especially Hebrews), while the principle of the Pauline mission to the Gentiles was that Gentile converts to Christianity were free from all the ritual requirements of the Mosaic law. But there is no suggestion in any of the New Testament writers (not even in Stephen's speech in Acts)[4] that God had not really commanded Israel to offer animal sacrifices.[5] However, this does seem to have been the view adopted by the later Jewish Christian sect of the Ebionites (to be distinguished from the majority of Jewish Christians, who were known as Nazarenes), doubtless in reaction to the destruction of the temple and the end of the temple cult in AD 70.[6] Accordingly, in the Gospel of the Ebionites, which is based on the three Synoptic Gospels,[7] they attributed to Jesus the saying: 'I came to abolish sacrifices, and if you do not cease from sacrificing the wrath will not cease from you' (*ap.* Epiphanius, *Pan.* 30.16.5). In the account of the preparation for the last supper, this Gospel borrowed from Matthew 26.17 the disciples' question to Jesus, 'Where do you want us to prepare for you to eat the passover?' For Jesus' answer the words of Luke 22.15 ('I have eagerly desired to eat this passover with you') were used, but turned into a question expecting the answer 'no': 'Have I eagerly desired to eat meat with you this passover?' (*ap.* Epiphanius, *Pan.* 30.22.4). The addition of 'meat' to the words taken from Luke probably indicates not only that the Ebionites could not accept that Jesus would have eaten a sacrificial animal, but also that they thought Jesus was vegetarian. To the latter point we shall return below. But it is clear that these features of the Gospel of the Ebionites are late adaptations of the Gospel tradition, designed to bring it into line with the particular views of the Ebionite sect and of no historical value.

Just as we can scarcely doubt that Jesus participated in the sacrificial system, so we can scarcely doubt that he also ate meat other than that of sacrificial animals. It is true that meat was a luxury in Jewish Palestine (cf. Sir. 39.26–7).[8] Jesus would not have eaten it regularly. But the meals to which he was invited in the houses of the wealthy (Mark 2.15; Luke 7.36, 11.37, 14.1, 19.5) are likely to have included meat. Jesus does not seem to have disapproved of the employment of those of his disciples who had been

fishermen (see especially Luke 5.3–10). In the feeding miracles, he multiplied fish, along with loaves, to provide food for the crowd (Mark 6.38–43,
8.7), while after his resurrection he not only cooked and served fish for the
disciples (John 21.9–13) but also ate fish himself (Luke 24.42–43). Even
though the historical value of some of these passages in the Gospels is
widely disputed, it is hard to believe that if Jesus had been vegetarian such
traditions could have arisen in the early church.

Some Jews in Jesus' time did practise abstention from meat, for two main
reasons.[9] One was the need, in a Gentile context, to avoid the defilement
which eating Gentile food might incur (Dan. 1.5–16; Tob. 1.10–13; Judith
10.5, 12.2). Red meat would not have been correctly slaughtered and
drained of blood. Especially there was the probability that Gentile meat had
been offered to idols in pagan temples before being sold in the market. This
is almost certainly the reason why some Jewish Christians in the church in
Rome were vegetarian (Rom. 14.2). But such problems did not occur in
Jewish Palestine where Jesus lived.

The second reason for abstention from meat was as an ascetic practice of
self-denial. As such, it was relatively unusual. Jews regularly practised
fasting, which meant complete abstention from food and drink for short
periods. The traditional form of long-term self-denial was the Nazirite
vow, which required abstention from alcoholic drink but not from meat
(Num. 6.3; Judg. 13.4, 7, 14). According to Luke 1.15 John the Baptist, like
Samson, was a Nazirite from birth, which did not therefore prevent him
from making locusts part of his ascetic diet in the wilderness (Mark 1.6).
However, because meat was regarded as a luxury, the practice of abstaining
from wine and meat was sometimes adopted as a kind of semi-fast which,
unlike true fasting, could be maintained over a long period. It was considered a form of mourning (Dan. 10.2; T. Reub. 1.10). It might be
practised for a few days or weeks (Dan. 10.2; IV Ezra 9.23–26, 12.51) or,
exceptionally, for several years (T. Reub. 1.9–10) or a lifetime (T. Jud.
15.4). The Therapeutae, a Jewish community who lived a kind of monastic
life in Egypt, never drank wine or ate meat (Philo, *Vit. Cont.* 73–4).
Apparently, after the destruction of the temple in AD 70, many Jews
abstained permanently from wine and meat, as a form of mourning for the
temple (t. Sot. 15.11–15). In an account of James the Lord's brother, which
is largely legendary but probably does derive from second-century
Palestinian Jewish-Christian tradition, in which the memory of James
was revered, Hegesippus represents him as, in effect, a Nazirite who
augmented his vow by abstaining from meat as well as from wine. Since he
is also said to have been constantly in prayer for the forgiveness of the

Jewish people, his asceticism is probably to be understood as a form of mourning for their sins (*ap.* Eusebius, *Hist. eccl.* 2.23.5–6).

In the Gospel of the Ebionites, John the Baptist's diet in the wilderness is said to have been, not locusts (Greek *akris*) and wild honey (as in Matt. 3.4; Mark 1.6), but wild honey that tasted like a cake (Greek *ekris*) in oil (*ap.* Epiphanius, *Pan.* 30.13.4). Clearly the change is designed to make the Baptist the kind of ascetic who abstained not only from wine but also from meat. Probably, in representing Jesus also as vegetarian (as we noticed above), this Gospel was making Jesus also into this kind of ascetic. Perhaps the Ebionites took the Jewish Christian tradition about the asceticism of James the Lord's brother as the model to which they conformed both John the Baptist and Jesus. It does not necessarily follow that the Ebionites themselves were all lifelong vegetarians.

However, we can be sure that Jesus did not practise this form of asceticism. A reliable Gospel tradition strikingly contrasts him with the ascetic figure of John the Baptist:

> For John the Baptist has come eating no bread and drinking no wine; and you say, 'He has a demon'; the Son of man has come eating and drinking; and you say, 'Look, a glutton and a drunkard, a friend of tax-collectors and sinners!' (Luke 7.33–34; par. Matt. 11.18–19).

Moreover, Jesus' vow of abstention from wine taken at the last supper (Mark 14.25) implies that he had not previously abstained from wine, and abstention from meat without abstention from wine is unknown in Jewish or early Christian ascetic practice. When Jesus was asked why his disciples did not follow the normal Jewish practice of regular fasting, he compared his ministry with the festivities of a wedding celebration in which it is inappropriate to fast (Mark 2.18–20). With this view of his ministry, we cannot imagine Jesus adopting a practice which symbolized mourning.

According to Genesis, both meat eating (Gen 1.29, 9.3) and wine drinking (Gen. 9.20–21) began after the Flood. So it is possible that the ascetic practice of abstaining from both was associated with a return to the practice of early humanity, before divine concessions to human corruption. But there is no evidence for this, and it is not easy to relate this notion to the fact that abstention from meat and wine symbolized mourning. Nor is there any evidence of any Jews or early Christians adopting vegetarianism out of a desire to return to the paradisal condition of humanity.[10] We might think this would have been appropriate in Jesus' case (especially in view of Mark 1.13, to be discussed in our next section), but the evidence is entirely against it. We must conclude that Jesus neither adopted vegetarianism for reasons which other Jews had for doing so nor adopted it for innovatory reasons of his own. Of course, it does not follow that there cannot be any kinds of valid Christian arguments for vegetarianism,[11] but an argument that meat eating is absolutely wrong would clearly contradict the Christian belief in the sinlessness of Jesus. It would also cut Christianity's roots in the Jewish tradition of faith to which Jesus so clearly belonged.

The messianic peace with wild animals

Mark's account of the forty days Jesus spent in the wilderness following his baptism (Mark 1.13) falls into a different category from most of the material in the Gospels which we have studied so far, and for this reason has been left till last. In the first place, whereas we have so far been concerned for the most part with Gospel traditions which we can be fairly sure preserve accurately the teaching of Jesus, it is much more difficult to assess the historical character of Mark 1.13. Even if Jesus did spend a period alone in the wilderness before the commencement of his public ministry, which is likely enough, many scholars would regard the details of Mark's account of this as not so much a historical report as an early Christian attempt to express the theological significance of Jesus and his messianic mission. So we shall here be content to understand the significance Mark and his readers would have seen in the statement that Jesus 'was with the wild animals', without attempting to decide the historical question. But, secondly, Mark 1.13 differs from the other Gospel material we have studied in that, whereas other references to animals are incidental, in the sense that they take for granted a well-established Jewish attitude to animals in order to make a point which is not primarily about animals, in Mark 1.13 the evangelist, as we shall see, understands Jesus' mission as designed to make a difference to the human relationship with wild animals.

Mark 1.13 reads: Jesus 'was in the wilderness forty days, tempted by Satan; and he was with the wild beasts; and the angels waited on him.' The statement that Jesus was with the wild animals[12] is a mere four words of the Greek text, but we should not be misled by its brevity into thinking it insignificant or merely incidental. In Mark's concise account of Jesus in the wilderness no words are wasted. Each of the three clauses has its own significance.

Mark's prologue (1.1–5), in which this verse occurs, presents Jesus as the messianic Son of God embarking on his mission to inaugurate the kingdom of God. Following his anointing with the Spirit at the baptism, the Spirit drives him into the wilderness (v. 12) for a task which evidently must be fulfilled before he can embark on his preaching of the kingdom (v. 14). The wilderness had gathered rich symbolic associations in Jewish tradition, but we should not be distracted by the symbolism it carries in the fuller Matthean and Lukan accounts of the temptation (Matt. 4.1–11; Luke 4.1–13). Nor should we describe Mark 1.13 as Mark's temptation narrative: the testing by Satan is for Mark only the first of three encounters, all important. In Mark 1.13 the wilderness carries its most fundamental biblical and natural significance: it is the non-human sphere. In contrast to the cultivated land, where humans live with their domesticated animals, the wilderness was the world outside human control, uninhabitable by humans, feared as it threatened to encroach on the precarious fertility of the cultivated land and as the haunt of beings hostile to humans.[13] It was the natural home not only of the wild animals but also of the demonic. Hence Jesus goes into the wilderness precisely to encounter the beings of the non-human world: he must establish his messianic relationship to these before he can preach and practise the kingdom of God in the human world. Significantly, none of the three non-human beings he encounters in the wilderness – Satan, the wild animals, the angels – subsequently appear in Mark's narrative of Jesus' activity in the human world.

The order of the non-human beings in Mark 1.13 – Satan, the wild animals, the angels – is not accidental. Satan is the natural enemy of the righteous person and can only be resisted: Jesus in the wilderness wins the fundamental victory over satanic temptation which he can then carry through against the activity of Satan's minions in the human world later in the Gospel (see especially Mark 3.27). The angels, on the other hand, are the natural friends of the righteous person: they minister to Jesus as they did to Elijah in the wilderness (I Kings 19.5–8) and to Adam and Eve in paradise (b. Sanh. 59b). Between Satan and the angels the wild animals are more ambiguous: they are enemies of whom Jesus makes friends. This is the point that we shall shortly establish.

We must first ask: Which animals are designated by the word *theria* ('wild beasts') in Mark 1.13? The word usually refers to wild animals in distinction from animals owned by humans, and usually to fourfooted animals in distinction from birds, reptiles, and fish, though snakes can be called *theria* (e.g. Acts 28.4–5). However, the word can also have the more limited sense of beasts of prey or animals dangerous to humans. Though sometimes supplied by the context or an adjective, this sense of 'dangerous beast of prey' seems quite often required by the word *therion* alone.

This linguistic phenomenon corresponds to an ancient tendency, at least in the Jewish tradition, to consider wild animals primarily as threats to humanity, either as direct threats to human life (e.g. Gen. 37.20, 33; Lev. 26.6, 22; II Kings 2.24, 17.25–26; Prov. 28.15; Jer. 5.6; Lam. 3.10–11; Ezek. 5.17, 14.15, 34.25, 28; Hos. 13.7–8; Amos 5.19; Rev. 6.8) or, by attacks on flocks and herds, as threats to human livelihood (Lev. 26.22; I Sam. 17.34–37; Hos. 2.12; Amos 3.12; John 10.12). The sense of wild animals as threatening belongs to the prevalent conceptualization of the world as conflict between the human world (human beings, their animals, and their cultivated land) and wild nature. Not many wild animals (as distinct from birds and fish) were hunted for food in Jewish Palestine, and so interest in them tended to be limited to those which were threats to humanity. Seeing these animals purely from the perspective of sporadic human contact with them could produce a distorted and exaggerated view of their enmity to humans, as is shown in a remarkable passage by Philo of Alexandria (*Praem.* 85–90), who portrays wild animals, meaning the dangerous beasts of prey, as engaged in a continuous war against humans, constantly waiting the opportunity to attack their human victims. That Philo, living in Egypt, thinks this is true of the Indian elephant is only mildly surprising, but that he considers the Egyptian hippopotamus to be a man-eater shows the level of paranoia involved. Alien and excluded from the human world, wild animals had human fears projected on to them. It is also worth noting that the staging of conflicts between people and wild animals in the Roman amphitheatres, in which of course the animals were provoked into antagonism, would have heightened first-century people's sense of the enmity of wild animals. Of course, ancient peoples who perceived wild animals primarily as a threat did not notice that they themselves were also a threat to wild animals by steadily reducing their habitats as they extended the area of cultivated or deforested land.

The Jewish tradition, in the context of which Mark 1.13 should be read, saw the enmity of the wild animals as a distortion of the created relationship between humans and animals and the result of human sin. In creation God established human dominion over the animals (Gen. 1.26, 28; Ps. 8.6–8; Sir. 17.2–4; Wisd. 9.2–3), which should have been peaceful and harmonious, but was subsequently disrupted by violence. The Noahic covenant (Gen. 9.1–7) takes account of the violence. But that humans should live in fear of animals should not be the case even by the terms of the Noahic covenant, which promises that animals shall go in fear of humans (Gen. 9.2). In fact, wild animals were perceived as menacing. Jewish literature therefore envisaged two ways in which the true relationship of humans and wild animals might be restored: one individual, one eschatological. In the first place, it could be thought that the truly righteous person should enjoy divine protection from wild animals as from other threats to human life: as Eliphaz told Job: 'At destruction and famine you shall laugh, and shall not fear the wild animals of the earth . . . [They] shall be at peace with you' (Job 5.22–23). In later Jewish literature the idea is that the truly righteous person exercises the human dominion over the animals as it was first intended, as it was given at creation (b. Sanh. 38b; b. Shabb. 151b; Gen. R. 8.12).[14]

Secondly, Jewish eschatological expectation included the hope that the righting of all wrongs in the messianic age would bring peace between wild animals and humans. The classic scriptural expression of this hope is Isaiah 11.6–9:[15]

> The wolf shall live with the lamb,
> and the leopard shall lie down with the kid,
> the calf and the lion and the fatling together,
> and a little child shall lead them.
> The cow and the bear shall graze,
> their young shall lie down together;
> and the lion shall eat straw like the ox.
> The nursing child shall play over the hole of the asp,
> and the weaned child shall put his hand on the adder's den.
> They will not hurt or destroy in all my holy mountain;
> for the earth shall be full of the knowledge of the LORD,
> as the waters cover the sea.

This has often been misunderstood by modern readers as a picture simply of peace between animals. In fact, it depicts peace between the human world, with its domesticated animals (lamb, kid, calf, bullock, cow), and the wild animals (wolf, leopard, lion, bear, poisonous snakes) which were normally perceived as threats both to human livelihood (dependent on domestic animals) and to human life. Peace between all animals is certainly implied, both in the fact that the bear and the lion become vegetarian (11.7) and the snakes harmless (11.8), and in the cessation of all harm and destruction (11.9), which must also mean that humans are to be vegetarian. The picture is of a restoration of paradise ('my holy mountain' is Eden, as in Ezek. 28.13–14) and the original vegetarianism of all living creatures (Gen. 1.29–30), but it is presented from the perspective of ancient people's sense of threat from dangerous wild animals. That threat is to be removed, the enmity between humans and wild animals healed. Later Jewish literature, down to the New Testament period, continued the same expectation, primarily inspired by Isaiah 11.6–9 (see Isa. 65.25; Sib. Or. 3.788–95; Philo. *Praem.* 87–90; II Bar. 73.6). In such passages, the dominant notion is that the original, paradisal situation, in which humans and wild animals lived in peace and harmony, will be restored in the messianic age.

We need not limit the wild animals (*theria*) of Mark 1.13 to the somewhat dangerous animals that might be encountered in the wilderness of Judaea: bears, leopards, wolves, poisonous snakes (cobras, desert vipers, and others), scorpions. The word does not prohibit well-informed readers from thinking also of other animals: hyenas, jackals, caracals (the desert lynx), desert foxes, fennec foxes, wild boars, wild asses (the onager and the Syrian wild ass), antelopes (the desert oryx and the addax), gazelles, wild goats (the Nubian ibex), porcupines, hares, Syrian hyraxes, and so on.[16] But both the use of the word and the habits of thought which went with it would be likely to bring especially the dangerous animals to mind.

Mark's simple but effective phrase indicates Jesus' peaceable presence with them. The expression 'to be with someone' (*einai meta tinos*) frequently has the strongly positive sense of close association or friendship or agreement or assistance (e.g. Matt. 12.30, 26.69, 71, 28.20; Luke 22.59; John 3.2, 8.29, 15.27, 16.32, 17.24; Acts 7.9, 10.38, 18.10; Rom. 15.33), and in Mark's own usage elsewhere in his Gospel, the idea of close, friendly association predominates (3.14, 5.18, 14.67; cf. 4.36). Mark 1.13 depicts Jesus enjoying the peaceable harmony with wild animals which had been God's original intention for humanity but which is usually disrupted by the threat of violence.

Apart from the context, we might class Jesus, in terms of the Jewish traditions we have outlined, simply as the individual righteous person who is at peace with the wild animals. But Jesus in Mark's prologue is no mere individual. Just as he resists Satan not as merely an individual righteous person but as the messianic Son of God on behalf of and for the sake of others, so he establishes, representatively, the messianic peace with wild animals. He does so only representatively, in his own person, and so the objection that a restoration of paradise should not be located in the wilderness is beside the point. More to the point is that all the wild animals of Isaiah 11 would be most easily encountered in the wilderness. Jesus does not restore the paradisal state as such, but he sets the messianic precedent for it.

If Mark's phrase 'with the wild animals', indicating a friendly companionship with the animals, would certainly evoke, for his original readers, the Jewish expectation of the age of messianic salvation, it also contrasts with some aspects of the way the restoration of the proper human relationship to wild animals was sometimes portrayed in the Jewish literature. There the animals are portrayed as fearing humans (a reversal of the present situation of human fear of the animals and no doubt thought to be the proper attitude of respect for their human rulers: T. Napht. 8.4; T. Benj. 5.2; Philo, *Praem.* 89; cf. Sir. 17.4; Ap. Mos. 10.3; Gen. R. 34.12) and the expectation is that they will serve humans (II Bar. 73.6). In other words, they too will become domestic animals. The human dominion over them is conceived as domination for human benefit. Such ideas of the ideal human relationship to the wild animals as one of lordship over subjects or domestic servants did continue in Christianity, but they are very notably absent from Mark 1.13. Mark says nothing of that sort at all. Jesus does not terrorize or dominate the wild animals, he does not domesticate or even make pets of them. He is simply 'with them'.

The context to which Mark 1.13 originally spoke was one in which wild animals threatened humanity and their wilderness threatened to encroach on the human world. The messianic peace with wild animals promised, by healing the alienation and enmity between humans and animals, to liberate humans from that threat. Christians who read Mark 1.13 today do so in a very different context, one in which it is now clearly we who threaten the survival of wild animals, encroach on their habitat, threaten to turn their wilderness into a wasteland they cannot inhabit. To make the point one need only notice how many of the animals Jesus could have encountered in the Judaean wilderness have become extinct in Palestine this century: the bear, the onager, the desert oryx, the addax, the ostrich, and no doubt others. Others, such as the leopard and the gazelle, would not have survived without modern conservation measures. But Mark's image of Jesus' peaceable companionship with the animals in the wilderness can survive this reversal of situation. Its pregnant simplicity gains a new power for modern Christians in a world of ecological destruction. For us Jesus' companionable presence with the wild animals affirms their independent value for themselves and for God. He does not adopt them into the human world, but lets them be themselves in peace, leaving them their wilderness, affirming them as creatures who share the world with us in the community of God's creation. Mark's image of Jesus with the animals provides a christological warrant for and a biblical symbol of the human possibility of living fraternally with other living creatures, a possibility given by God in creation and given back in messianic redemption. Like all aspects of Jesus' inauguration of the kingdom of God, its fullness will be realized only in the eschatological future, but it can be significantly anticipated in the present.

PART TWO

Wrestling with the Tradition

Introduction

Andrew Linzey

'Much of the history of theology has been characterized by forgetting as well as by learning, with the result that instead of an accumulation of knowledge and understanding we see only the replacement of one partial insight by another equally partial.' These words, from *Christian Believing*, issued by the Doctrine Commission of the Church of England, seem especially relevant to the subsequent growth of the Christian tradition and its relation to some of the biblical insights explored in our last section. For whilst it cannot be argued that the biblical material is unequivocally positive about the status of animals, it cannot be denied that it does contain significant positive insights. How, then, are we to understand the emergence of mainstream theologies apparently heedless of these very insights?

'Augustine is interested in the spiritual struggles of human beings,' maintains Gillian Clark – and there is nothing remarkable about that in a great Christian writer, we might think. But it is when this concern for human beings is coupled with an apparent *unconcern* about animals that we should begin to ask questions, as Clark herself does. Why is it that Augustine 'does not seem to be concerned with the exploitation of animals, or with the impact of human beings on the natural world in which they live'? Part of the answer given by Clark is that while concern for animals was on the agenda, then as now (although hopefully a little more now) philosophers concerned for animals were in a minority. Even so, Platonism was not universally indifferent to other creatures, and outstanding Greek philosophers such as Plutarch, Porphyry, and Theophrastus were strong advocates for animals. It is not sufficient to blame Greek philosophy for the apparent indifference of some mainline Christian theologians – as some of us have done in the past.

Nevertheless, there are some key ideas in Hellenism which when used in particular ways buttress speciesist tendencies. The first is obviously the notion that animals are inferior in, or devoid of, reason, and the second that 'it is right for reason to rule over unreason'. When these two ideas are joined with a reading of the 'image of God' *as consisting in* the possession of a rational soul, then we have that fateful and self-justifying combination which has come so to dominate scholastic thinking about humanity to the detriment of 'brutes'.

Of course it needn't have been so. The idea that the human logos can apprehend the Divine Logos does not necessarily lead to unconcern for, or even a disparagement of, those creatures intellectually less capable. Quite the reverse. It could be claimed, and by some undoubtedly was, that such is the privilege of rationality that its blessings should be expressly shared with those less well endowed. But, tragically, it was not to be. As Clark explains, according to Augustine, the 'implications of the rule of reason' are that 'animals, animal behaviour, and animal suffering are all for the physical or spiritual benefit of human beings'.

Aquinas – to take another giant of the tradition – appeals directly to Augustine's formulation that 'by a most just ordinance of the Creator, both their [i.e. animals' and plants'] life and their death are subject to our use'. Such a line tends to squash the theological meaning of animals as existing for themselves as creatures of God, and, as Dorothy Yamamoto wryly observes, this view could only be practically sustained by ignoring the evidence of our eyes. 'By restoring strangeness to [animals]', she argues, 'we have begun to draw them away from the clutches of unthinking instrumentality.'

If Thomist thought is vulnerable on this level, it is even more so when it comes to the central idea of a unique human rationality, since by positing 'humanness as the *possession* or the *exercise* of some quality we have also [simultaneously] generated the possibility of *losing* that quality, or having it taken away from us'. The rational boundary, therefore – if it is to be convincingly maintained – requires constant and frequently anxiety-making attention and repair. Claiming rationality for men, less for women, and none for animals arguably fixes not superiority but vulnerability. 'Can it be that declaring ourselves to be "rational beings" in the Thomist sense', asks Yamamoto, 'has become more burdensome than enabling?' The question is raised whether our own theological self-definition has been truly self-serving, even on its own terms. Perhaps the key Hellenistic ideas as developed by Christian theologians have fostered a false – or at least a faulty – anthropology in which animals are not the only victims.

The Reformers reinforced the boundary of rationality, and Luther, in particular, tied the Augustinian scheme more firmly to the exercise of dominion – so much so that animals became almost invisible: 'for Luther the non-human creation is a *function* of anthropology,' Scott Ickert maintains. Created with the divine image – constituted by their capacity for reason – humanity is given 'unconditional dominion' over the non-human. Luther's reading of Genesis places extreme emphasis on the Fall, with animals as the hapless, innocent victims. The destruction of animals is a divine punishment for (purely human) sin. The animals now suffer 'a more oppressive form of bondage', argues Luther, because they are 'subjected to man as to a tyrant who has absolute power over life and death'. In Genesis 9.1–2,

> God sets himself up as a butcher: for with his word he slaughters and kills the animals that are suited for food, in order to make up, as it were, for the great sorrow that pious Noah experienced during the flood.

Although not part of the original arrangement, the world now becomes by God's gracious design 'a kitchen with all kinds of meat'. The Augustinian notion that animals should be ruled by reason, even the fallible rationality of fallen humanity, is taken to its most grotesque limit, whereby

> Human beings, though they do not deserve it, are thus provided for well beyond basic sustenance, in order that a difficult existence in a fallen world might be not only bearable but pleasant. Thus 'dumb' animals and 'brute beasts' carry out a recognizable 'Christ-like' function as they sacrifice themselves for the sake of an endangered and sinful humanity.

Such a scenario is plainly heartless and barbaric. One wonders what kind of redemption could be sufficient for the crucifixion that animals have to undergo. Luther's doctrine is the ultimate outworking in biblical dress of the Augustinian notion that animals are here for nothing else but our physical and spiritual benefit.

In the light of this dismal record, one might wonder whether any mainline theology, Catholic or Protestant, can adequately make space for an ethical appreciation of animals. James Gaffney offers a welcome piece of Catholic self-criticism, acknowledging that the tradition has failed at critical junctures to lend support for animal protection. He cites papal opposition to the setting up of a Society for the Prevention of Cruelty to Animals in Rome in the nineteenth century as the decisive moment of moral blindness – occasioned, it should be noted, by a pope for whom 'liberalism' (including, of course, zoophily) was 'a term of execration'. Of the textbooks which inhibited Catholic sympathy for animals none was more influential than Joseph Rickaby's *Moral Philosophy* (1901), which took

Thomism and Augustinianism to their extreme limit, declaring the world to be divided into 'persons' and 'things'. 'Brute beasts not having understanding and therefore not being persons, cannot have any rights . . . we have no duties of charity or duties of any kind to the lower animals, as neither to stocks and stones.'

If there is to be a recovery of Catholic sensitivity to animals, argues Gaffney, it needs to begin with a thoroughgoing theological – nay, christological – rejection of cruelty focussed on the Christ-like innocence, and suffering, of animals. He uncovers a remarkable sermon of 1842 by Cardinal John Henry Newman which posits the moral equivalence of cruelty inflicted on innocent animals with that inflicted on Christ himself. Gaffney is optimistic that such an identification could lead to an enriched spirituality based on the belief that 'in Christ's Passion incarnate divinity participates in a common victimhood of tormented animality, both human and non-human'.

Here the 'Christ-like' function of animals described by Luther is given its proper christological interpretation. If the cross is God's own identification with all innocent suffering both human and animal, then we have here the christological criterion with which to both develop and critique all existing theologies of animals. Far from being the 'dumb brutes' of creation made available for human service, their very logos reflects the Eternal Logos made available to all on Calvary.

6

The Fathers and the Animals:
The Rule of Reason?

Gillian Clark

It is no longer standard church practice to look to the early Fathers for an authoritative, and if possible collective, response on questions of doctrine. Interest has shifted from their (supposed) consensus to their individuality in a specific social and intellectual context. This context, the interrelation of Graeco-Roman culture and Judaeo-Christian scripture in late antiquity (approximately the third to the sixth centuries), is fascinating in itself. But what the Fathers say is still worth hearing, and not only as a piece of cultural history or for their influence on European Christian thought. Because their context is different from ours, they ask questions differently, and the questions they do not ask are also important.

This chapter focusses on Augustine, but makes no claim to construct an 'Augustinian' account of animals. Augustine's provisional or exploratory arguments have too often been taken out of their context and made into dogma, sometimes with disastrous results for human beings. He never (and this in itself is important) engaged in sustained theological argument about the nature of animals and their relationship to God and to humans. He made assertions about animals, sometimes when expounding a text of scripture, often in the context of argument or exegesis on quite different questions. The main concerns of this chapter are what Augustine takes for granted about animals, why it seems obvious to him, and why he did not question it further.

I

Augustine resigned his chair of rhetoric at Milan in 386. He soon moved back to North Africa, where, first as ascetic and then as priest and bishop, he lived in a small community of like-minded men; it was probably the first North African monastery. They raised questions of theology and philosophy, and some of his answers are recorded in the *83 Questions on Various Topics*.[1] One question was perhaps inspired by a long-running philosophical debate on anthropocentrism: 'what proof is there that human beings are superior to animals?'[2] Augustine replied: 'Among the many ways in which it can be shown that human beings surpass animals in reason, this is obvious to all: beasts [*beluae*] can be tamed by human beings, but human beings cannot be tamed by beasts.'[3]

In this brief reply, Augustine did not think it necessary to defend his interpretation of 'superiority' as a higher level of reason, to discuss whether animals have a lower level of reason or none at all, or to justify the taming of animals by humans. Underlying his response are two standard assumptions of Graeco-Roman philosophy, inherited from discussion going back at least to Plato: that human beings are distinctively rational animals, and that it is right for reason to rule over unreason. 'Reason' means not just intellectual capacity, but the aspect of human beings which is closest to God, so it is both an intellectual and a spiritual force. When a Greek philosopher says that humans have *logos*, this means both that we can make sense of the world and that we can express our understanding in words; and our understanding includes awareness of God and of the choices we should make in our own best interests. Animals do not use words, and it was assumed that they lack *logos* in other ways and have a soul, *psuchê* (Latin *anima*), only in that they are alive and sentient; they do not have a rational or spiritual soul as humans do.[4] They were often referred to as *aloga zôa*, 'living creatures without *logos*' or, in the common translation, 'irrational animals'.

Augustine's vocabulary reflects both this distinction and the general perception of animals. He rarely uses the neutral term *animalia*, a Latin equivalent of the Greek *zôa*, 'living creatures', which could in principle include humans. Instead, he uses words for animals as seen by humans: either tame flocks and herds for human use, or wild beasts which war against humans and (it was believed) each other. His most common word is *pecus*, 'cattle' in the general sense, but he also uses *belua*, which connotes monstrosity, and *bestia*, which connotes ferocity.

The question of animal reason is treated more fully in Augustine's dialogue *On Free Choice*, which arose from discussions in Rome (377/8) before his journey back to Africa, and was finished during the years before he was consecrated bishop (395/6). The speakers are conventionally identified with Augustine and his friend Evodius. Book 1 moves from the ordering of society by God's eternal law to the ordering of the individual human being. Augustine then asks, unexpectedly, whether everything that is alive knows that it is alive, and when Evodius says he does not know, replies 'How I wish that you had knowledge, as well as belief, that beasts [*pecora*] lack reason!'[5] The taming of animals is essential to the argument which follows. Animals (*bestiae*) are tamed by humans, so that not only the body but the soul (*anima*) of the animal is subject to the human and obedient to the human's will. But animals do not tame humans, although animals surpass humans in physical strength. It must, then, be reason or intelligence in which humans surpass animals; and Evodius moves, without discussion, from the claim that humans surpass animals in reason to the claim that animals lack reason. Augustine then argues that what we know is what we have perceived by reason, and since animals lack reason, they do not know that they are alive.[6]

Eventually it becomes clear why the question was asked. Knowledge that you are alive is superior, Augustine and Evodius agree, to being alive; and a human being is most ordered if 'that, whatever it is, by which humans surpass animals – whether it is more correctly called mind or spirit or either, for we find both used in scripture – rules over everything else that constitutes a human being'.[7] So what is it by which we surpass animals? We share sense-perception and physical activity with them: 'indeed, all the activity of animal life is to seek the pleasures of the body and avoid distress'. Animals do not laugh or make jokes, but that is not the highest human activity; nor do animals seek fame and glory and power, but our desire for these does not make us better than animals. The difference is in reason. A human being is ordered when reason rules over the irrational movements of the soul.[8]

This discussion of animal reason does not arise from concern for animals. Its purpose is to establish, by contrast with animals, what it is to be properly human, and that is to have reason in control. Similarly, in book 2, it is argued that animals have the 'inner sense' which perceives the five senses: an animal must be aware, for instance, that its eyes are closed, or it could not open its eyes to look. But the animal is only aware that it perceives, it does not know that it perceives, because it does not have reason.[9] Again, the point of this argument is to move from the inner sense, which humans share with animals, to the judgment of reason on the inner sense, and from reason to knowledge of God. The sequence reappears in a famous passage of the *Confessions* (which were begun, and perhaps finished, in 397, and which draw on work that Augustine had done in his early African years) on the 'ascent of reason'.

I asked myself, then, why I approved the beauty of bodies either heavenly or earthly, and what helped me to make a firm judgment of mutable things, saying 'This should be so, and that should not be so'. Asking how I made this judgment, I found the immutable and true eternity of truth above my mutable mind. Thus step by step, from bodies to the soul which senses through the body; thence to its interior power, to which bodily sense reports external things, *which is as far as the beasts can go*; thence again to the reasoning power, to which is referred for judgment that which is taken from the senses of the body; and this power too, realizing that in me it is mutable, raised itself to the level of its understanding and led thought away from its usual habits, withdrawing itself from the contradictory swarms of appearances, so that it might discover by what light it was flooded when it proclaimed, without the least hesitation, that the immutable is to be preferred to the mutable, and how it knew immutability – for if it did not know in some way, it would not certainly prefer it to the mutable – and it attained to that which is, in the flash of a trembling look.[10]

Augustine here assumes, as he does in *On Free Choice*, that animals can co-ordinate the reports of the senses, but cannot theorize about them or make value-judgments about them, still less reflect upon the activity of making judgments and thereby discover eternal truth.

II

The superiority of humans was reinforced in one obvious context for talk about animals, namely the providence of God as displayed in the creation. The 'argument from design' has a philosophical history going back to the students of Socrates, and the use of animal behaviour as moral example was also well established.[11] Augustine may have heard Ambrose preach, at Milan, a series of sermons on the *Six Days of Creation* (adapted, without acknowledgment, from Basil of Caesarea). It might at first appear from Ambrose's examples that animals are morally better than humans: crows, for instance, are devoted parents, whereas human parents wean too early, use wet-nurses, or even abandon their children, that is if they allow them to be born at all.[12] But animals are not a serious challenge to humans, because animal behaviour is not presented either as a conscious choice to do right or (as in Plutarch's dialogue *Gryllos*)[13] as an effortless and uncorrupted instinct. It is simply a reproach to humans, who should do better because they have superior abilities. Human reason can outclass any animal skill (the fifth-century bishop Theodoret tells his audience not to envy spiders)[14] and tame any animal strength. The climax of Ambrose's account is the astonishing size and strength of the elephant, but his concluding sentence is 'yet this huge beast is subject to us and complies with our commands'. Elephants, lions, and tigers can be trained by humans.[15]

Ambrose goes on to discuss Genesis 1.26: 'God said, Let us make man in our image and likeness.' The image of God in human beings, he says, is the rational soul, not the bodily form. His main concern is to show the error of thinking that scripture ascribes human characteristics to God, and he does not comment on the second half of Genesis 1.26: 'let them have dominion over the fish of the sea, the birds of the air, the wild beasts and all the creeping things that crawl upon the earth'. Augustine, in his *Literal Commentary on Genesis* (written in the early years of the fifth century), argues that the second half of the verse explains the first. 'Let us make man in our image and likeness' is, he says, followed by

> let him have power over the fish of the sea and the birds of the air and the other animals which lack reason, so that we should understand that man is made in the image of God in that respect, in which he surpasses the irrational animals. And that is reason, mind, intelligence, or any other word that says it better.[16]

'The other animals which lack reason' is, of course, Augustine's paraphrase of the biblical text. If humans are in God's image in the sense that they, and they alone, have reason, it follows (for him) that they must rule over non-human animals which lack reason. It also follows that non-human animals, lacking God's image, are not in contact with God, and that God's concern for them is restricted to their survival.

> 'And He gives the cattle their food.' By these cattle he means the flocks of God. God does not cheat his flock of their food through men, for whose service He made plants grow. That is why the Apostle says [I Cor. 9.7] 'Who feeds a flock and does not take milk from the flock?' 'He who gives their food to the cattle, and to the raven chicks which call on Him.' Shall we suppose that ravens call on God to give them food? Do not think that an irrational animal calls on God: no soul except a rational soul knows how to call on God. Take it as a figure, lest you should think, as some impious people say, that human souls return to cattle, dogs, pigs, ravens. The human soul was made in the image of God: He did not give His image to dogs and pigs.[17]

Augustine is here expounding a verse (Ps. 147.9) which, taken at its face value, affirms God's concern for the non-human creation. He promptly appropriates it for humans, so that the raven chicks turn out to be Christians, who unlike their raven parents know that they must call to God. Even the young lions who seek their prey from God (Ps. 104.21) are reinterpreted as spirits of wickedness.[18] Augustine agrees with Paul (I Cor. 9.9) that God is not concerned for oxen – or, at least, agrees that 'You shall not muzzle the ox that treads the corn' is to be interpreted as 'Fair pay for the clergy'.

> Listen! God did not make only the heaven and the earth and the sea: 'He made heaven and earth and the sea and all that is in them'. 'All that is in them' includes you. And not just you: sparrows, locusts, worms, He made them every one, and His concern is for all. His concern is not to give them instruction, for He gave instruction only to humans. The psalm says [Ps. 35.7–8] 'You will make people and cattle safe, Lord, in accordance with the greatness of Your mercy, O God'. . . And the Apostle says [I Cor. 9.9] 'Is God concerned for oxen?' . . . Are these contrary? . . . Where the instruction is 'You shall not muzzle the ox that treads the corn', is God not thinking about oxen? He wanted the oxen to symbolize certain people. God is not concerned to tell you how to treat oxen: human nature includes that. Man is so made that he knows how to look after his cattle: he has not received instruction on this from God, but God put it into his mind that he can do it without instruction; God made him like that. But, as he rules cattle, so he must be ruled by another, and he receives instruction from the one who rules him. So as regards the retention of instruction, God is not concerned for oxen, but as regards the universal providence by which he created all things and rules the world, 'You shall make people and cattle safe, O Lord' . . . Let us listen to the Lord himself, the ruler and teacher of apostles. 'Look at the birds of the air: they do not sow or reap or gather in barns, and your heavenly Father feeds them.' So, besides man, these animals do pertain to God's concern, so that they should be fed, not so that they should receive the law.[19]

There seem to be several unsupported leaps of interpretation here. How does Augustine know that animals are not rational, cannot pray, and receive only physical support from God? His conviction of human superiority leads him to argue that even the struggle of animals to survive is both appropriate and edifying. He envisages a reader of Genesis asking not just why there are animals which harm humans – obviously, because they punish sin or develop virtue – but

> why then do beasts harm each other, when they commit no sins to prompt such a penalty, and acquire no virtue by such a struggle? No doubt because some are food for others. We cannot rightly say: let there not be some on which others feed. All things, so long as they exist, have measure, number, rank.[20]

The efforts of animals may not do them any lasting good, but they offer an example to humans: Augustine's reader learns

> how much he must do for spiritual and eternal salvation, in which he surpasses all irrational living creatures, when he sees them all, from the greatest elephants to the smallest worms, do what they can by resistance and avoidance for their bodily and temporal survival, which is their lot in accordance with the inferior rank of their kind.[21]

III

In *City of God*, Augustine develops the argument that the rule of reason over non-reason is part of the natural order, as distinct from the social hierarchy which is necessary in a fallen world. His concern is for human hierarchies, but it is clear why he did not think he needed to argue further for human rule over animals.

> Those who take thought for others rule over them, as a man does for his wife, parents for their children, masters for slaves. And people obey those who take thought, as wives do their husbands, children their parents, slaves their masters. But in the house of the just man who lives by faith, and is still on a journey from that heavenly city, even those who rule are the servants of those whom they appear to rule. They do not rule in the lust for power, but in the duty of taking thought, nor in the pride of being first, but in the mercy of taking care. The natural order prescribes this; that is how God made man. For 'Let him rule' Scripture says 'over the fish of the sea and the birds of the air and all creeping things which move upon the earth'. God did not want man, made rational in His image, to rule over any but the irrational, not man over man but man over cattle. Thus the first men were created as righteous shepherds of flocks rather than kings of men, so that God might also

suggest in this way what the order of created things requires, and what has been made necessary because sinners deserve it.[22]

It might be expected that Augustine would somewhere go on to ask what exactly is the difference in rationality between humans and animals, and what kind of human rule over animals it implies. He was never satisfied with standard answers, and the choices he made about his lifestyle confronted him with the problem. He had given up his worldly career to become a celibate Christian living a deliberately simple and disciplined life. Such a change would usually entail vegetarianism, because meat was both a luxury and a morally suspect food, linking meat-eaters to the life of passion and violence which was ascribed to carnivorous animals. Athanasius' *Life of Antony* was an important factor in Augustine's decision, and Athanasius thinks it hardly needs saying that when Antony renounced his property to lead a life of solitary prayer, he also gave up meat and wine.[23] Augustine's diet in his community was austere, but not vegetarian. The basic Mediterranean diet was bread, or cooked or soaked grain and pulses, accompanied (just as pasta or pizza is now) by small amounts of whatever was available to add relish: meat, fish, cheese, olives, vegetables, or just oil and herbs. Augustine's biographer Possidius says he sometimes had meat or vegetables on the table because there were guests, or because someone had been ill, and his community rule advocates fasting when health allows but does not restrict types of food.[24] In *Confessions* 10 Augustine worries that he still enjoys satisfying hunger, whereas eating should be like taking necessary medicine, but it is not the kind of food which concerns him.

> I do not fear the impurity of the food but the impurity of desire. I know that Noah was permitted to eat every kind of flesh which was of use as food, that Elijah renewed his strength by eating meat, that John, endowed with wonderful abstinence, was not polluted by eating animals, that is, by the locusts which were his food; and I know that Esau was deceived by his strong desire for lentils, and that David blamed himself for wanting water, and that our King was tempted not by meat, but by bread. That is why the people in the desert also deserved rebuke, not because they wanted meat, but because in their wish for food they murmured against the Lord.[25]

There is a special reason why Augustine makes this point so strongly. When he wrote the *Confessions*, in his first years as bishop of Hippo, many people in North Africa suspected that he was still a Manichaean. That is, they thought he still belonged to a sect which held that our spirits are fragments of the divine, trapped in a material world which is not God's good creation. Manichaeans were morally and politically suspect. They were also notorious for food rules and excessive fasting.

Manichaeans believed that fragments of the divine were dispersed through the material world, including plants, so that even picking fruit or harvesting grain was an injury to God. The Manichaean 'elect' avoided guilt by leaving the preparation of food to their followers, whom they rewarded by praying for them.[26] Augustine insists, against the Manichaeans, that scripture authorizes the eating of meat.

> Some people try to extend this precept [Do not kill] even to beasts and cattle, so that it would not be permitted to kill even one of these. Why not plants too, and whatever is anchored to the earth by its roots and nourished by them? This kind of thing, although it does not feel, is said to live, and consequently can die – and even, if force is applied, be killed. So the Apostle says, speaking of such seeds, 'What you sow cannot live unless it dies', and it is written in a psalm 'He kills their vines with hail'. Are we then to think, when we hear 'Do not kill', that it is a crime to dig up a bramble, and do we assent, in utter folly, to the Manichaean error? So, leaving these ravings aside, when we read 'Do not kill', if we do not accept that it is said of plants because they have no sensation, this applies also to irrational living creatures – flying, swimming, walking or creeping – because they are not linked to us by reason. Reason has not been given to them to have in common with us, and so, by the most just ordinances of the Creator, both their life and their death is subject to our use. It remains that we must understand 'Do not kill' to apply to human beings: not another, and not yourself, for whoever kills himself kills nothing other than a human being.[27]

Once again, the treatment of animals is a parenthesis within the main argument, and is justified by the distinction between rational and irrational. Why does Augustine not question the distinction, or ask what behaviour is licensed by human dominion?

IV

Augustine had raised the question of animal reason and knowledge in an early dialogue, *On the Magnitude of the Soul*. Animal knowledge is not a primary concern, but it is relevant to the central question of how knowledge relates to reason and sense-perception. Evodius instances Ulysses' dog, who knew his master after twenty years' separation; Augustine remarks that he can see why people wonder whether elephants have knowledge.[28] But Evodius and Augustine agree that animals simply cannot have knowledge, or they would be better and happier than humans – which is obviously wrong.

Why? Augustine does not explain in this dialogue that he thinks animals incapable of happiness or unhappiness. This is, in part, a matter of definition. Latin *passio* and Greek *pathos* are usually translated as 'emotion', but Augustine (like most Greek and Roman philosophers) regards them not as movements or responses from within, but as invasive disruptions of the soul. In *City of God* he defines such disturbance, *perturbatio*, as 'a movement of the soul opposed to reason', and says (in parenthesis) that comparable experiences in animals are not disturbances because they cannot be contrary to reason, which animals lack.[29] The absence of reason would, of course, rule out for him any possibility that animals can experience true happiness, namely the love of God, or true misery, namely its absence.

To return to Ulysses' dog, Augustine does not accept that the dog had knowledge of his long-lost master.

> What do you suppose this is, but a power of sensing, not of knowing? Many beasts surpass us in sensing – this is not the place to ask why – but in mind, reason, knowledge God put us before them. Their sense-perception can discern the things in which such souls take pleasure, reinforced by the great power of habit; and the more easily, because the soul of beasts is more attached to the body.[30]

Later, in his *Genesis* commentary, Augustine does weaken the distinction between rational and non-rational. His text of Genesis 1.20, in the Old Latin Bible, read: 'and God said: let the waters bring forth creeping things of living souls, and flying creatures above the earth under the firmament of heaven'. Readers who (like Augustine) knew no Hebrew were puzzled by the difference in wording from 1.24, 'let the earth bring forth a living soul in its kind, beasts of burden and creeping things and the beasts of the earth'. Since Augustine works on the principle that everything about scriptural language is important, he offers an explanation.

> Some think that fish are called not 'living soul' but 'creeping things of living souls' because they have no memory or any life which is, so to speak, close to reason: but they are misled by their lack of experience.

Authors have written remarkable accounts of what can be seen in fish-ponds; and even if what they wrote happens to be wrong, it is certain that fish have memory. There is a large pool near Bulla which is full of fish. People look in and throw them something, and either they converge swimming and snatch it first, or they tear it to pieces in their struggle. They have grown accustomed to being fed, and when people walk along the edge of the pool, they swim with them in a shoal and return, waiting where the people, of whose presence they are aware, would throw them something . . . And if the absence of memory, or slowness of perception, denied the name of 'living soul' to the fish, it would surely be given to the birds. Their life is before our eyes: they have memory, they chatter, and they are very skilled at building nests and raising young.[31]

It is clear from the *Confessions* that 'memory' for Augustine includes not just remembrance of the past, but all the furniture of the mind, including the ability to form concepts.[32] Animal memory may be different from human memory, as in the case of Ulysses' dog, but here Augustine's point seems to be that fish and birds do have a life 'close to reason'.

Unfortunately, Augustine seems not to have encountered the fullest collection of arguments on this subject, Porphyry *On Abstinence from Animate Food*, though he read several other works by this third-century Platonist.[33] Porphyry offers examples of rational and social behaviour in animals (including a friendly partridge) and poses a dilemma. If animals are irrational, and therefore inferior to humans, then humans should not behave like their inferiors by hunting and killing; in fact, humans behave worse, because wild animals are driven by hunger and necessity, whereas humans do not need to kill for food. But if animals show signs of rationality and therefore are like humans, it is clearly unjust to kill kindred beings unless we are actually endangered by them – and though killing in self-defence may be justified, it does not follow that we can eat our kill.[34]

But reading Porphyry would not have been decisive. He allows that animals are less rational than humans, and Augustine regards it as part of the natural order that the weaker in reason should be ruled by the stronger. What, then, may the ruler justly do to his subjects? In *City of God* Augustine uses the familiar analogy of the ruler as shepherd. The political ruler may authorize the killing of a criminal or an enemy for the protection of his other subjects, just as the shepherd's duties include the defence of the flock against predators. But what could authorize the shepherd to kill one of the flock? Augustine's answer would probably be that the shepherd needs no authorization to kill sheep, for the rule 'Do not kill' applies only to humans. The example of Antony influenced Augustine's choice of a committed religious life, and the stories of Antony and of other Desert Fathers might have given him a different model of human authority over animals, namely friendly coexistence in a restored Paradise.[35] If they did, he made no theological use of it.

V

So the implications of the rule of reason are, according to Augustine, that animals, animal behaviour, and animal suffering are all for the physical or spiritual benefit of human beings; that God's providence is concerned (within limits) for the physical survival of animals, but animals are not in spiritual contact with God, lack knowledge, and cannot experience happiness. These questions are discussed briefly, and usually in relation to a different argument. Augustine is just not very interested in animals unless they supply a moral lesson or an image of God's love. Attention to animals for their own sake is a distraction:

> When I am sitting at home, a lizard catching flies or a spider trapping them as they rush into its web often fascinates me; it cannot make any difference that these are little creatures. I go on to praise You, the wonderful creator and orderer of all things, but that is not why I began to be fascinated.[36]

Augustine is interested in the spiritual struggles of human beings. He is concerned about the food they eat because it can help or hinder their progress, and he wants them to be aware of this world in so far as it will help them to recognize the greatness and the loving concern of God. He does not seem to be concerned with the exploitation of animals, or with the impact of human beings on the natural world in which they live.[37]

Why not? The question whether the world and everything in it was made for us, or for other creatures just as much as us, or for its own order and beauty, was certainly on the philosophical agenda. But it was a minority of philosophers, then as now, who were seriously concerned for animals. Platonism, the dominant philosophy of late antiquity, discouraged attention to this complex and mutable world. Natural beauty should prompt us to look inwards, to reflect on what beauty is and on the power of the human mind which perceives it (as in the 'ascent of reason'). But Platonism does not require indifference to the creatures with which we share the world: Porphyry, and his contemporary Iamblichus, are outstanding examples of

Platonist philosophers who affirmed that animals are akin to humans and should be treated with justice.[38]

Perhaps Augustine simply accepted, and to some extent justified, the ordinary practice of his time. Farming followed the same pattern as in the Judaeo-Christian scriptures. Livestock was an important capital investment, killed not as a matter of course, but selectively and for special occasions. Wild animals were a real threat in some regions, and one specific social practice reinforced – or required – the belief that wild animals are savage. Huge numbers were slaughtered for entertainment in 'the games', pitted against each other or against humans (condemned criminals or trained hunters), or just massacred.[39] No one thought in terms of 'endangered species', but it was difficult to keep up supplies for these expensive and prestigious entertainments. Augustine deeply disapproved of 'the games', but what worried him was the swamping of human reason by the collective blood-lust of the spectators.[40] The mass slaughter of animals for food, in hunting, or for entertainment was the exception not the rule. It was not an inescapable part of human society, as slavery was then and intensive farming is now, and it did not thrust itself on Augustine as a manifestation of the institutionalized sin which enmeshes all humans. It was a specific manifestation of cruelty or greed, and Christians could simply be told not to attend wild-beast shows or give extravagant banquets. The reasons they were given were concerned with human, not with animal, needs.

These facts of late-antique social and intellectual life go some way to explain Augustine's lack of interest in animals. We do not know why it did not occur to him, or (apparently) to any other patristic writer, to question Christian treatment of animals and the assumptions on which it rested. But any television programme on the natural world – the modern equivalent of Ambrose's or Augustine's sermons to a mixed-ability audience – imports assumptions about human and animal behaviour which need at least as much defence as the rule of reason. We can still learn from the exegesis of scripture which was produced in the late fourth century by very intelligent and committed Christians. Inevitably, they interpreted it in accordance with their leading concerns, found that it reinforced some of their central beliefs, and did not ask some questions about it which other people might want to ask. The same is true of late twentieth-century exegesis: what are we taking as obvious truth?

7

Aquinas and Animals: Patrolling the Boundary?

Dorothy Yamamoto

St Thomas Aquinas' view of animals is, at first glance, an unambiguous and uncompromising one. In the Thomist scheme, creation is a hierarchy, with creatures ranked according to their degree of participation in the divine nature. Humans, who have reason, are placed above animals, who lack it. Since the lower parts only exist to serve the higher, it is entirely right that, just as plants, vegetable life-forms, are used by animals for their food, so animals in turn should be used by humans.

> According to the Divine ordinance the life of animals and plants is pre-served not for themselves but for man. Hence, as Augustine says (De civ. dei i, 20), 'by a most just ordinance of the Creator, both their life and their death are subject to our use'.[1]

Therefore, there is no sin in killing animals. In fact, to refuse to eat meat is to spurn the careful provisions which God has made to sustain human life on earth.

The Thomist view of animals and their role has exerted enormous influence on Christian tradition, particularly in the Roman Catholic church. My purpose in this chapter is not to trace this influence, or to place Aquinas' arguments about animal nature in the wider context of his theology. It is to take up two particular points he makes and explore the repercussions that these had within mediaeval culture. I hope to demonstrate that the responses aroused show up some of the fissures within the Thomist argument, and reveal it to be more problematic than might at first appear.

'The truth as in a mirror'

Of course in mediaeval times, as at all other times in human history, animals were used for a host of practical purposes. However, practicalities were not the limit of their usefulness to people – in fact, these come last in Aquinas' list:

> Now we see that in the course of nature the intellectual substance uses all others for its own sake: either for the perfection of the intellect, which sees the truth in them as in a mirror; or for the execution of its power and the development of its knowledge, in the same way as a craftsman develops the conception of his art in corporeal matter; or, again, to sustain the body that is united to the intellectual soul, as is the case in man.[2]

So, looking at animals, humans behold 'the truth in them as in a mirror'. That is to say, in the words of Claude Lévi-Strauss, they are not just *bonnes à manger* – they are *bonnes à penser*. But what exactly does this mean?

Extracting morals from animal behaviour is an old-established practice. 'Go to the ant, thou sluggard; consider her ways and be wise,' wrote the author of Proverbs (6.6). In the Middle Ages, however, the truth that could be learnt from animals was not limited to personal rectitude or even wisdom: instead, in the tradition of the Bestiary and related texts,[3] animals were understood to hold within themselves God's determinate scheme of how everything ought to run – the actual blueprint of creation. Many animals, for instance, are said to reflect the ordering of the natural world in their bodily forms and in their behaviour. The ostrich does not lay her eggs until she can see the Pleiades appear in the sky, while the liver of the mouse grows bigger and smaller with the waxing and waning of the moon.[4] In other cases animals show humans how they ought to live by providing models of perfect communality. Fish, for example, the Bestiarist says, maintain bonds with each other of absolute purity and fidelity. They preserve an untainted descent ('pura et inviolata successio') and are never, ever, guilty of adultery with strange fish. When danger threatens their offspring, fish open up their mouths so that the young fish can swim inside and shelter there, absorbing them, for the while, back into their own bodies.[5] The deepest human embrace is shallow by comparison! Fish are also ideally attuned to their appointed environment, the sea – in fact, if they are taken away from it, they die at once. Birds, too, provide patterns of ideal social behaviour. The hoopoe cares for its parents when they grow old, preening their feathers, keeping them warm, and cleaning their eyes.[6] Crows accompany their young when they learn to fly, and take care to lay in a store of food for them.[7]

Are animals, then, moral paragons? Not so, for they do not *choose* to act the way they do. Rather, it is the bodily identity of each creature, God's imprint upon it at the moment of creation, that determines its behaviour. And the animals themselves have no awareness of the ideals they embody – they simply show forth their text to the privileged reader, 'man'. We might think of each as a computer diskette containing vital information. Two diskettes side by side on a table cannot trade that information, any more than two mice can speak to each other about the special properties of their livers – instead, the programs on the diskettes have to be run inside a computer. So the secrets which God has encrypted in the bodies of God's creatures can only be accessed by the human intellect.

So far, so good – it might appear that there is nothing yet to challenge the Thomist view. However, uncertainty enters once we begin to suspect that some of the 'truths' that animals are supposed to embody are *not* necessarily immutable parts of the divine plan but have a decidedly sub-lunary origin. The lessons we draw from animals in fact always reflect modes of thought within our own milieu, and as such must be contingent rather than essential. For example, the popular author and television presenter David Attenborough transmits a version of Richard Dawkins' 'selfish gene' theory when he writes that 'All organisms are ultimately concerned to pass on their genes to the next generation. That, it would seem to a dispassionate and clinical observer, is the prime objective of life.'[8] Brian Klug's chapter in this book deals nicely with the myth of the 'dispassionate and clinical observer': I merely point out here that the promise of totality in Attenborough's series title *Life on Earth* is an illusory one. Current intellectual fashions shape and constrain his project – as they must shape and constrain all of our thinking about animals. In the mediaeval period, the 'lessons' humans were being asked to draw from animals were often primers for a particular political agenda – and some people were beginning to be aware of this.

The Thomistic universe is an orderly and a hierarchical one. Every element within it has its own, divinely appointed place. This is true of animals too – in the Bestiary tradition, each is unalterably associated with a particular way of life. Thus, if the template of animal society is held up to the human one, it can be seen that the precepts extracted from the former will be those that favour order, stability – in other words, the *status quo*. It is a fact, too, that, while animals do modify their behaviour in response to changes in their environment, over the long term their modes of social organization do not change. Mediaeval bees – for example – lived in the same way as modern bees do (among other sources, the Bestiary tells us this). There has been no flirtation with democracy in bee society, no attempt by the worker bees to change their lot. Nor, in general, do animals change their habitat – in fact, many are so well adapted to a particular ecological niche that they are unable to survive in another, apparently similar, one. So it can be seen that if animals are presented to humans as social exemplars a heavily weighted message is likely to emerge. It is one which will privilege things as they are and will censure nonconformity or attempts to change old practices for new ones. So, we are told by the Bestiarist that

> The coot is a clever and very intelligent bird, which . . . does not fly about aimlessly, but lives in one place, remaining there all its life and finding its food there. If all believers behaved themselves and lived in this way, and did not wander off on strange paths as the heretics do, and did not seek secular desires and pleasures, but stayed in one place and rested in the Catholic Church, where the Lord makes them dwell together in harmony, they would have their daily sustenance, the bread of immortality, and the precious blood of Christ would be their drink.[9]

In other words, the Thomistic model of consonance between animal and human affairs cannot cope with dissent, change, or development. It is irredeemably wedded to the *status quo*. That is fine, as long as the *status quo* continues to satisfy. However, the late Middle Ages was a time of ferment: the structures of feudalism, which, in their delineated hierarchies, replicated the Thomist world-view, were breaking down, to be succeeded by new relationships founded on economic considerations, and by an ever-increasing degree of social mobility.

One of the challenges to the old system comes from one of Chaucer's Canterbury pilgrims – the Monk, who escapes from his monastery as often as he can so he can enjoy his favourite pastime of hunting.[10] The failure of members of the religious orders to observe their vow of stability of place was a common complaint against them in Chaucer's day – and among the artillery deployed by their accusers was the argument that, in leaving their monasteries or convents, they were behaving like 'fishes out of water'. The conservative moralist (and friend of Chaucer) John Gower fulminated against vagabond monks in his Latin work, *Vox clamantis* ('The voice of one crying'):

The sea is the proper habitat of a live fish, and the monastery is the right home for a monk. . . . A fish ought not to be out of the water, nor ought a monk to be away from his cloisters . . . If there were a fish that forsook the waters of the sea to seek its food on land, it would be highly inappropriate to give it the name of fish; I should rather give it the name of monster. Such shall I call the monk who yearns for worldly delights and deserts his cloister for them. He should not rightly be called a monk but a renegade, or what God's wrath brands as a monster of the Church.[11]

Chaucer's pleasure-loving Monk does not bother refuting this argument – he simply brushes it aside. In his opinion, it's 'not worth an oyster'. Of course, his portrait is a satirical one, and one could argue that he *should* adjust his behaviour to the model provided by the fish, and get back inside his monastery. Typically, Chaucer conceals his own thoughts on the matter, taking cover behind his persona of the naïve pilgrim Geoffrey, who is full of admiration for the energetic, macho Monk and eagerly endorses what he says ('And I said his opinion was good . . .'). Nevertheless, there is a hint of slyness in the way 'cloister' is made to rhyme with 'oyster', a knife-blade cunningly inserted to prise the whole structure apart. All right, monks ought to stay in their monasteries. But what about lay people who want to change their station in life (as Chaucer himself did)? Are they also to be told 'Stay where you are.' And, if so, on whose authority?

Once it becomes apparent that, looking at animals, we do not see in them 'the truth as in a mirror' but rather a reflection of our own worldly concerns, the other elements in the Thomistic formulation begin to show signs of strain. To loosen the tight consonance between animal and human ideals is to admit that their lives may differ from ours in ways we have not yet imagined – it is to liberate them into their own, idiosyncratic ways of being. Perhaps it is even to entertain the glimmerings of a possibility that they might be there for their own sake and not merely as tools for the 'intellectual nature'. Of course, it could be argued that we have not breached the central stronghold – the fact of animals' practical subordination to humans and human needs. But, by problematizing one aspect of the relationship presented by Aquinas, we have started to insist upon animals' ontological distinctiveness. By restoring strangeness to them we have begun to draw them away from the clutches of unthinking instrumentality. Perhaps the truth goes even further. Perhaps, in important ways, we cannot 'think' animals at all. Wittgenstein famously said that if a lion could talk, we could not understand him.[12] Such questions, however, go far beyond both my philosophical competence and the limits of this chapter. I turn instead to another crux of the Thomist scheme: the *nature* of the difference between animals and humans.

The boundaries of the human

It is a cornerstone of Aquinas' scheme that there is an absolute difference between animals and humans. Humans have reason, 'intellectual nature'; animals have none, and are guided purely by instinct.

> Now it is clear from what has been said that God is the last end of the universe, Whom the intellectual nature alone obtains in Himself, namely, by knowing and loving Him, as was proved above. Therefore the intellectual nature alone is requisite for its own sake in the universe, and all others for its sake.[13]

The difference between humans and animals is not one that we can see or hear or touch – it can only be established by exercise of the quality which is itself its essence, rational thinking. *How* animals – or humans – actually present themselves to our corporeal senses is irrelevant to the Thomist scheme. This opens up the unsettling possibility that a creature which *looks* like a human might actually be an animal. And vice versa.

This may not appear to be a problem for *us* (although films like *Invasion of the Body-Snatchers* show that the theme is still a live one – with aliens playing the animals' role), but it certainly was for mediaeval people, whose world contained many more 'possible forms', in the shape of half-known, or unknown, variations of being, than ours does today. Not only were there animals which people knew actually existed but had (most probably) never seen for themselves (lions, tigers, elephants), the Bestiary itself contained a further array of fabulous beasts which might also exist if travellers' tales were to be trusted (manticores, basilisks, centaurs), while beyond these again there lurked the mysterious members of the 'monstrous races' – man-like creatures with the heads of dogs, with single, umbrella-like feet, with faces in their chests, or with other gross deformities.[14] Were the latter group 'human'? Augustine had pondered the problem in his *De civitate dei*. He was careful not to say that he absolutely believed in the existence of such creatures (he was particularly doubtful about the dog-heads), but, *if they did exist*, he saw no reason why they should not be human, have descended from Adam, and be included in God's providential scheme for humankind. After all, Augustine argued, human beings may be born with more or less serious deformities – extra fingers or toes, or both male and female sexual organs. This does not lead us to question their humanity. In fact, in our fallen state, we are unable to pronounce on the physical parameters of 'humanness' since, unlike God, we only see a very small part of the picture.

> For God is the creator of all, and he himself knows where and when any creature should be created or should have been created. He has the wisdom to weave the beauty of the whole design out of the constituent parts, in their likeness and diversity. The observer who cannot view the whole is offended by what seems the deformity of a part, since he does not know how it fits in, or how it is related to the rest.[15]

Augustine's 'inclusive' view is illustrated in a story told by the mediaeval author of *Mandeville's Travels*. In this, St Antony, travelling across the Egyptian desert in search of an even more reclusive saint, the holy hermit Paul, is met by a strange creature who is like a man above the waist (although he has two horns sprouting from his forehead) and like a goat below. Antony asks him who he is, and receives the reply that he is 'a deadly [i.e. mortal] creature such as God had formed and dwelled in the desert in purchasing his sustenance; and besought the hermit that he would pray God for him, the which that came from Heaven for to save all mankind, and was born of a maiden, and suffered passion and death'.[16] Through his familiarity with the essential 'story' of God's dealings with humankind, and his eagerness to receive the benefits of intercessory prayer, this 'monster' proves that he is unquestionably human, and part of the Christian community – despite his weird body.

The dissociation of humanness from outward appearance increases the difficulty of patrolling the boundary. But there is also something in the very nature of a boundary that seems irresistibly to attract human speculation. Given that a boundary exists, is it the case that some animals – or humans – are closer to it than others? Or, to put it another way, all humans are rational, but *are some humans more rational than others?*

The answer that a mediaeval respondent would give is 'Yes, and they comprise half the human race.' The tradition that women were intellectually as well as physically and (usually) morally inferior to men was a venerable one. For Philo of Alexandria, the female represented the world of sense perception while the male represented the rational soul.[17] Aquinas himself argued that the man's greater wisdom naturally entitled him to be the head of his family:

For good order would have been wanting in the human family if some were not governed by others wiser than themselves. So by such a kind of subjection woman is naturally subject to man, because naturally in man the discretion of reason predominates.[18]

If women were generally seen as less rational than men, and thus as closer to the borderline, one group was propelled right across it. Several mediaeval theologians argued that Jews could not really be human since, in failing to understand the way in which two natures, divine and human, are present in Jesus, they show that they are unable to transcend the world of sense-perception and aspire to rationality – which is the *sine qua non* of humanness.[19]

We can see that the boundary-line between humans and animals is beginning to blur. Humanness may not be our birthright but may depend upon the exercise of a particular faculty. If such a faculty is *not* exercised, does it then cease to exist? And do we lose our purchase upon humanness as a result? The mediaeval imagination played around with the possibilities that this suggested, generating (for instance) the figure of the 'wild man' who stands on the borderline between humanness and animality.[20] In many romances the hero goes through a period of living like a beast in the wilderness, usually after suffering a traumatic disappointment in love.[21] Such characters are explorers at the edge, testing out for us how similar to an animal a person can become without forfeiting their essential humanity. Also popular was the biblical story of King Nebuchadnezzar, whom God turns into a beast as a punishment for his inordinate pride in his own achievements:

The same hour was the thing fulfilled upon Nebuchadnezzar: and he was driven from men, and did eat grass as oxen, and his body was wet with the dew of heaven, till his hairs were grown like eagles' feathers, and his nails like birds' claws. And at the end of the days I Nebuchadnezzar lifted up mine eyes unto heaven, and mine understanding returned unto me, and I blessed the most High . . . At the same time my reason returned unto me . . . (Dan. 4.33–6, AV).

What exactly happened to Nebuchadnezzar during this period of his ordeal, when, according to God's command, 'his heart [was] changed from man's' and 'a beast's heart [was] given unto him' (Dan. 4.16)? With the loss of his 'reason', did he step over the borderline and really become the animal his outward appearance suggested? In which case, in what sense could the ox-like creature still *be* Nebuchadnezzar? The king, relating the events in retrospect, seems to confirm the survival of some degree of personhood and subjectivity in his words, 'I Nebuchadnezzar lifted mine eyes unto heaven . . .', but such evidence is hardly conclusive. In Gower's retelling of the story in his major English work, the *Confessio amantis* ('The lover's confession'), after Nebuchadnezzar has lived for seven years as an ox, participating, it seems, solely in an ox's world of immediate sense-impressions (the water he drinks out of wells and puddles seems to him 'good enough'), he is suddenly granted self-awareness and stares in horror at his beastly body with its clawlike nails. He starts to weep and lifts his face to heaven, but although he has regained human affectivity his powers of language have not returned, and he is forced to 'bray' out a wordless plea to God (who, fortunately, understands him). At which precise point are we to think of Gower's Nebuchadnezzar as becoming human again? It is hard to say![22]

These mediaeval examples show that the Thomist assertion of a boundary-line – an essential difference – between humans and animals did not put an end to debate about what it meant to be really human. In fact, it even encouraged it, as both theologians and writers of imaginative literature toyed with the possibilities of approaching the borderline, or even of crossing it.

Such questions, and such enterprises, are not, of course, peculiar to the mediaeval period. In the eighteenth century, for instance, writers and thinkers pondered the cases of so-called 'wild children', who had apparently grown up without any human contact at all. Was there some inalienable human characteristic which had survived in these children? Or were they truly indistinguishable from the animals which were sometimes thought to have reared them?[23] Today the debate goes on, although the grounds have shifted. Now our attention has turned to the great apes who are our nearest relations in biological terms. Numerous experiments have been carried out to discover whether or not chimpanzees can 'talk' – that is, manipulate linguistic counters or use a gestured code such as American Sign Language. The jury is still out: some researchers express disappointment at the chimps' inability to progress beyond the level of a two-year-old human child, while others find evidence of genuine creativity in their unprompted 'signing'. 'Before they can fly, apes must jump, insist commentators who believe that the linguistic gulf between man and beast has already begun to vanish. To jump is not to embark on flight, the doubters retort . . .'.[24]

All these examples suggest that proclamation of our 'humanness', our identity as rational beings, which Aquinas saw as empowering us over against the rest of creation, inevitably runs into all kinds of problems. In fact, *no* single factor indisputably distinguishing us from the rest of the animal kingdom has been discovered, despite the best efforts of philosophers over the centuries.[25] The search is starting to look futile – like the mediaeval quest to find the philosophers' stone, or, perhaps, like attempts to pinpoint the moment when an unborn baby acquires a 'soul'. It has also given rise to deep anxieties – for by positing humanness as the *possession* or the *exercise* of some quality we have also generated the possibility of *losing* that quality, or having it taken away from us. Can it be that declaring ourselves to be 'rational beings' in the Thomist sense has become more burdensome than enabling? Is our drumming on about *difference* merely the knell of an outdated anthropocentricity that refuses the ampler view illustrated by the passage from Augustine I quoted earlier, which is open about our 'creatureliness' and our consequent inability to see the whole picture?

These are awkward questions on which to end – but I would like to add a further one, also unanswerable. Suppose (in a parallel universe) *Homo sapiens* was the only animate species on a planet. What sense of their 'humanity' would the people on that planet have?

8

Luther and Animals:
Subject to Adam's Fall?

Scott Ickert

Martin Luther (1483–1546) was not interested in animals *per se* as a theological topic but only as they relate to the doctrine of creation, in which the human community is said to have dominion. Therefore Luther considers animals primarily, although not exclusively, in the context of his lectures on Genesis. For the most part, Luther's views represent a traditional, mainly Augustinian, perspective on the relative status of animals in the order of creation.

Lectures on Genesis 1

When Luther considered the role of animals in his lectures on Genesis (1535–45) he did so in terms of human dominion over them (Gen. 1.26). Thus one might say that for Luther the non-human creation is a function of anthropology as anthropology is a function of the doctrine of God. A manifest hierarchy exists. Animals are subordinate to human beings as the latter exist to glorify – and exemplify – God. Therefore, the dominion that human beings exercise over the non-human creation is a part of the divine ordering of creation. Consequently, human dominion is not merely advised but is expressly commanded by God.[1]

Moreover, men and women are commanded to exercise this dominion because they alone among God's creatures are created in the image of God: 'man is the noblest creature, not like the rest of the animals but according to God's image'.[2] Adam and Eve rule over the earth, the sea, and the air because the human being is God's 'most beautiful creature, who knows God and is the image of God, in whom the similitude of the divine nature shines forth through his enlightened reason, through his justice and wisdom'.[3] As Augustine had maintained, rationality – here 'enlightened reason' – is the *conditio sine qua non* of the divine image, a quality which human beings alone possess.[4] Animals are 'brute beasts'.[5] Thus Adam and Eve originally had perfect knowledge of God and nature, which the animals never possessed. The animals 'do not know their creator, their origin, and their end; they do not know out of what and why they were created. Therefore they certainly lack that similitude of God.'[6] The animals' lack of knowledge, however, does not mean that they enjoy no positive or enduring relationship to their creator. Though not created in the divine image, the animals are the 'footprints of God', an idea which Luther derives from Peter Lombard.[7]

Created in the divine image, humanity is given unconditional dominion over the non-human creation. Human beings were created for eternal life (further evidence of the divine image in them), animals principally for temporal existence. 'Man' 'is to have knowledge of God; and with the utmost freedom from fear, with justice and wisdom, he is to make use of the creatures as he wishes, according to his will. Nothing is lacking. All these things have been created in greatest abundance for physical life.'[8] Animals are thus subordinate in order to sustain and promote human well-being. Enhancing human life in its worldly existence, they are a sign of God's favour. 'The beasts of the field and the birds of the heaven were created for mankind; these are the wealth and the possessions of men.'[9]

Still, despite this stress on the basically temporal function of animals, when asked whether dogs – in particular his own dog, Tölpel – would inhabit heaven, Luther is reported to have said, 'Certainly, for there the earth will not be without form and void. Peter said that the last day would be the restitution of all things. God will create a new heaven and a new earth and new Tölpels with hide of gold and silver. God will be all in all; and snakes, now poisonous because of original sin, will then be so harmless that we shall be able to play with them.'[10]

But this pertains to the eschaton. Sadly, at present all the good things relating to the original creation, including dominion, have been 'lost through sin; and we, who have kept hardly a shadow of this realm, are today like a corpse of that first human being'.[11] The Fall has tainted the divine image and has compromised the exercise of dominion. For example, Luther says that human beings can no longer fathom the disposition of the animals: we lack insight

into that fullness of joy and bliss which Adam derived from his contemplation of all the animal creatures. All our faculties today are leprous, indeed dull and utterly dead. Who can conceive of that part, as it were, of the divine nature, that Adam and Eve had insight into all the dispositions of animals, into their character and all their powers? . . . Among the saints there is evident in this life some knowledge of God . . . But knowledge of nature – that we should know all the qualities of trees and herbs, and the disposition of all the beasts – is utterly beyond repair in this life.[12]

Prior to the Fall, 'when Adam and Eve knew God and all the creatures',[13] there was a substantial distinction between the human and the non-human creation. This distinction existed within a condition of evident harmony,[14] for the image of God in human beings was bright and clear and dominion was exercised benevolently as palpable evidence of God's rule over creation. But after the Fall, when the image is tarnished by sin, what humans accomplish in this life – i.e. catching and trapping birds and fish and taming animals – they achieve not by dominion but by industry and skill. Original dominion, therefore, was not exercised in terms of the hunting and taming – and eating – of animals. This came later as a result of the Fall, and the eating of animals was instituted after the Flood. Nevertheless, this employment of ingenuity and industry has positive significance in that it gives the *appearance* of dominion and, in a fallen world, persists as a trace of the way dominion was once properly exercised.

> But it is extremely small and far inferior to that first dominion, when there was no need of skill or cunning, when the creature simply obeyed the divine voice because Adam and Eve were commanded to have dominion over them. Therefore we retain the name and word 'dominion' as a bare title, but the substance itself has been almost entirely lost. Yet it is a good thing to know these facts and to ponder them, so that we may have a longing for the coming Day when that which we lost in Paradise through sin will be restored to us.[15]

The original dominion has been compromised by the Fall to the extent that it is hardly visible any more, and survives only as a 'bare' title. After the Fall the human treatment of animals only passes for dominion – 'the substance itself has been almost entirely lost'. Thus one must strive constantly to re-establish creation's originally intended harmony, *including* human dominion over animals, a dominion jeopardized and reduced by sin. Therefore, although it is a part of the original created order dominion can never be taken for granted, but must be continually reconsidered and re-evaluated in the light of the word and command of God, and over against human corruption.

Moreover – and this point is crucial – any ongoing reconsideration of dominion is intensified by an eschatological urgency, whereby creation's original harmony is transferred into the realm of expectation and hope. The original command to have dominion is now an eschatological promise. For the creation exists in the interim between the first creation and the new creation, between Fall and final judgment. Because human beings live in the interim, their dominion retains only a vestige of its original scope; and animals, originally created for enjoyment in a situation of concord, are now required for sustenance. The exercise of dominion, however poorly and inadequately administered in the interim, nevertheless preserves traces of its intended purpose. More importantly, it now becomes a sign of the time when perfect harmony will be restored. Thus, in a positive sense, human dominion over the animal creation, despite its evident defects after the Fall, plays an important eschatological role by anticipating the *coming* harmony of humans and animals adumbrated in creation's initial ordering.

Lectures on Genesis 6–9

Genesis 6 deals with the corruption of the earth, which God was about to destroy with a flood. Luther points out that the animals also bore the punishment of sin and perished together with humankind. This was not the animals' fault, but was effected 'because God wanted to destroy man completely, not only in body and soul but also with his possessions and the dominion with which he had been created'.[16] Here we are reminded that the animal creation, after the Fall and with respect to the dominion to which it is subject, exists to sustain human life in its worldly aspect. Therefore, the destruction of the animals was a divine punishment for sin.

Nevertheless, God preserved some of the animals in a gracious act which serves the purposes of human beings. After the Flood, as creation is restored, God repeats his original blessing along with the charge to have dominion (Gen. 9.1–2, cf. 1.28). Only this time 'the fear of you and the dread of you shall be upon every beast of the earth . . . into your hand they are delivered'. Luther remarks on the changed situation after the Flood. The original harmony, already fractured after the Fall, has now been shattered. After the Flood animals fear people. 'The reason is that until now the animals did not have to die in order to provide food for man, but man was a gentle master of the beasts rather than their slayer or consumer.'[17] Up until this time, Luther reminds us, animals were not used for food. Now, however, they have to endure 'a more oppressive form of bondage' and human beings exercise 'a more extensive and oppressive dominion', because 'the animals are subjected to man as to a tyrant who has absolute power over life and death'.[18] Yet even though this power is absolute, it is not arbitrary. 'God wants not even an animal killed except in a scrupulous manner, that is, either for sacrifice or for human consumption.'[19] Moreover, with this increase of human authority over the animals which is far more than the patriarchs exercised, 'God gives a special indication that he is favourably inclined and friendly toward man.'[20] It is 'an extraordinary gift, of which the heathen, who are without the word, have no knowledge'. Thus,

> In this passage God sets himself up as a butcher; for with his word He slaughters and kills the animals that are suited for food, in order to make up, as it were, for the great sorrow that pious Noah experienced during the flood. For this reason God thinks Noah ought to be provided for more sumptuously now.[21]

The gift also serves a practical purpose. In Noah's time there were fewer human beings and a superabundance of the fruits of the earth. Now, without this gift, there would not be enough food to go round.

Clearly for Luther this arrangement is not part of the original order of creation, hardly a constituent part of the nature of things. Still, it did not come about merely by chance, as the heathen assume – they think the custom always existed – but was established 'or rather permitted by the word of God'. 'An animal could not have been slain without sin unless God by his word had clearly given permission to do so.' There is no law to forbid the eating of animals, 'and consequently there can be no sin in their use'. The 'villainous popes', however, 'have wickedly imposed burdens on the church [i.e. rules of fasting and abstinence] in this matter too'.[22] The eating of animals, therefore, is given by divine permission and should not be restricted arbitrarily; otherwise a false legalism, or even idolatry, is introduced.

Thus the killing and eating of animals is expressly permitted, in a fallen world, in the interim before the final judgment, for the practical purpose of preserving and sustaining human life – and it is a gift and a sign of God's compassion. All this happens according to God's word. The new practice is an augmentation, made necessary by the remarkable extent of human sinfulness, to the original dominion. Yet it is also an act of compassion, a reward to pious Noah, and a provision for future generations. These blessings, however, do not mitigate the reality that were it not for the Fall animals would not have to be killed; and the original harmony between humans and animals would not have been further compromised. It is a factor of the interim nature of the creation that the animals' misfortune and the further restriction of the original harmony can become a remarkable act of grace for fallen humanity. In the interim animals serve human beings in this new way. Through their service and sacrifice fallen humanity's table is supplied and Noah's posterity is secure. Still, this new arrangement is accompanied by certain limitations, for neither blood lust nor the arbitrary restriction of the use of animals for food or sacrifice (as was imposed by the popes) is permitted or sanctioned by God's word. Within these limits, however, human beings are free to exercise their new form of dominion.

> In this passage [Gen. 9.2] the dominion of man is increased and the dumb animals are made subject to man for the purpose of serving him even to the extent of dying. They fear and shun man because of this regulation, which was now and hitherto had not been observed in the world. For Adam it would have been an abomination to kill a little bird for food; but now, because the Word is added, we realize that it is an extraordinary blessing that in this way God has provided the kitchen with all kinds of meat. Later on, when He shows man how to cultivate the vine, He will also concern Himself with stocking the cellar.[23]

The new situation is a sign of God's benevolence.

> These are reliable and excellent proofs that God no longer hates man but is kindly disposed toward him. Accordingly, this historical account gives examples of both facts: just as God's wrath is unbearable when He has begun to be incensed, so his compassion is boundless and without measure after it begins to shine again. Therefore his compassion is more abundant because it is a part of God's nature, since wrath is truly God's alien work, in which He engages contrary to His nature, because He is forced into it by the wickedness of man.[24]

Thus animals are given to humankind for food as a demonstration of God's mercy and kindness, highlighting the contrast between God's wrath (God's alien work) and compassion (reflecting God's essential nature). Therefore the animals live a sacrificial existence at the service of the human creation both with regard to God's wrath – which though aimed at human sin affected the animals as well in order to increase human misery – and God's compassion, which after the Flood made provision for a sinful humanity.

In the midst of this discussion Luther reminds us that animals also serve as instruments of God's wrath and punishment. They naturally fear human beings. As sin increased, however, this fear became a vehicle for God's anger. 'I have no doubt,' Luther said, 'that at the time of Noah and of the fathers close to him this terror [of human beings] in the animals was greater, since righteousness flourished and there was less sin. When saintliness of life declined and sin increased, this blessing also began to wane, and wild animals began to be a punishment for sin.'[25]

After the Flood, therefore, God increases the servitude of animals, while augmenting the oppressive nature of human dominion, by giving some animals for food. Here God sets himself up as a butcher. On the other hand, animals are also agents of God's wrath. The interim nature of creation is clearly the context for this new situation, in which animals become both blessing and curse for human beings, living together with them in an ambiguous and temporary sort of 'harmony' until the final true concord is established.

The reality of human nature in the interim: animale corpus *and wild beasts*

In his discussion of I Corinthians 15 Luther says that Paul uses the word 'animal' to denote the human being's natural or fleshly nature. In scripture the term *animale corpus* designates a natural body. Luther explains:

> a body such as is born on earth, which for its natural preservation or sustenance requires meat and drink, clothing, fire, water, air, wood, iron . . . a natural body is nothing other than physical life as it is lived by every animal. In good clear German we might call it *einen viehischen Leib* [a beastly body] . . . for in point of physical life there is no difference or very little difference between us and the animals . . . the only difference is that they have no reason.[26]

In this context Luther contrasts earthly physical life with eternal life. Christian faith makes an important distinction between the two. Pagans, however, regard human beings only in their external aspects: according to them a human being dies 'like a cow or a pig'. They were not 'wise enough to differentiate . . . between a man and any animal'.[27] Animal existence is earthly existence – Augustine claimed that the image of God is found in the immortality of the rational soul[28] – and therefore it is not in the strict sense a matter of the gospel or of eternal life, but pertains merely to what is of this world.[29]

However, the application of the term 'animal' to human beings also pertains to God's provision for the ordering of society. In his *Sermon On Keeping Children in School* (1530) Luther contrasts human society, which is governed by God's law, with the society of wild beasts, which, though preserved by God, is not regulated in the same way.

> As it is the function and honour of the office of preaching to make sinners saints, dead men live, damned men saved, and the devil's children God's children, so it is the function and honour of worldly government to make men out of wild beasts and to prevent men from becoming wild beasts . . . Protection of this sort does not exist among the beasts, and if it were not for worldly government there would be none of it among men either; they would surely cease to be men and become mere beasts.[30]

Apart from God's law human beings live and act like wild beasts.

> When the theologians disappear, God's word also disappears, and nothing but heathen remain, indeed, nothing but devils. When the jurists disappear, then the law disappears, and peace with it; and nothing but robbery, murder, crime, and violence remain, indeed, nothing but wild beasts.[31]

Human beings share animal existence to the extent that they live in the world, in temporal as opposed to eternal existence. In this regard, then, animal existence symbolizes the human situation after the Fall when the divine image has been forsaken, and humans behave irrationally, disorderly, and venally – like wild beasts.

Conclusions

What implications may one draw from Luther's comments, and what consequence does his thought have for our current concern for animals?

1. Animals were not created in God's image, and thus they lack rationality. Their purpose, therefore, pertains more to this world than to eternal life. As 'footprints of God' animals embody a certain dignity within the realm of God's creation, a status which demands our ongoing atten-

tion and concern. Also, precisely as a crucial element of the creation, which God promises to redeem and renew, they can be expected to share in the anticipated restitution of all things. Our mistreatment of animals, therefore, has eternal significance, because, as with the survival of all our victims in a redeemed creation, their presence and 'forgiveness' will be for us a kind of judgment.

2. Human dominion is inadequate and defective because of sin; nevertheless, this dominion continues with the command and sanction of God. This means that human beings are given an unequivocal responsibility to care for and protect the non-human creation. Though they are free to employ it for their own benefit, humans must be wary of the divinely ordained limitations within which their freedom over against animals never ceases to operate.

3. Animals were created to serve human beings even to the point of being sacrificed for their welfare. Human beings, though they do not deserve it, are thus provided with a generous sustenance, in order that a difficult existence in a fallen world might be not only bearable but pleasant. Thus 'dumb' animals and 'brute beasts' carry out a recognizable 'Christlike' function as they sacrifice themselves for the sake of an endangered and sinful humanity.

4. There is no blanket restriction on eating animals and thus no compulsion towards vegetarianism. Meat is a sign of God's compassion and favour, not merely a necessary provision. For that reason, and however displeasing it may be to some, one must acknowledge that animals have been given to humans for their consumption and pleasure. Therefore, arbitrary and mandatory restrictions on the eating of animals compromise God's freedom and deny God's good will. However, this does not *exclude* vegetarianism as a response of the individual conscience, or as an act of self-discipline, or as a testimony against cruelty to animals. Vegetarianism cannot advance or realize the coming harmony between the human and the non-human creation, which God the Father will establish in the fullness of time through Christ and in the Spirit, but it may be freely embraced as an anticipation of that harmony.

5. The arbitrary killing of animals (for example, for sport) is not sanctioned here. Humans must still act prudently and circumspectly even when confronted by 'wild beasts'.

6. Wild and dangerous animals are God's agents of wrath against human wickedness, a sign of God's absolute and perfect rule over the creation in which human beings exercise a defective dominion. Clearly animals have a distinctive role to play in the creation which awaits its ultimate fulfilment.

Even dangerous animals are 'sacred' (especially?) when they threaten human existence.

7. In the original ordering of the creation there was a certain harmony in which dominion was exercised. With the Fall that harmony vanished and dominion was irreparably compromised. Animals fear human beings and shun them because of the augmented, and tyrannical, form of dominion that humans may now exercise. Notwithstanding this arrangement, even such ambiguous vestiges of dominion are indicators of a future in which God will establish perfect concord between humans and animals. Luther seems to suggest, therefore, that the significance of the original paradisal harmony lies in its anticipatory function, pointing forward to the final great and perfect fulfilment of God's promise and intention for everything created and called good. Thus our treatment and use of animals must be set against the hope for the new creation where Christ will be all in all.

9

Can Catholic Morality Make Room for Animals?

James Gaffney

The modern movements for animal protection and animal liberation that have by now taken firm hold in most of the world's civilized nations arose during the nineteenth century as one of a number of humanitarian reform movements of compassion and social justice that were popularly viewed as components of the broad cultural phenomenon called the rise of liberalism. Unhappily, these developments occurred at a most inopportune time in the history of Roman Catholicism, when that church was ruled, in an extraordinarily autocratic manner and for a remarkably long time, by a pope, Pius IX, for whom 'liberalism' was a term of execration, and by whom virtually every social movement identified with the liberal agenda tended to be deplored and denounced. The astonishing fact that the Vatican actually opposed the establishment by the city of Rome of a Society for the Prevention of Cruelty to Animals finds its main explanation in that spontaneous, indiscriminate resistance to anything and everything bearing the stigma of liberalism. Among the unfortunate results was an effective closing of the church's official mind to arguments and appeals by animal protectionists. Accordingly, the church's semi-official moral teachers, the clerical authors of approved seminary textbooks in moral philosophy and theology, submissively put forth a uniform doctrine that discouraged sympathetic interest in the whole subject among the church's ministers. Textbooks published around the turn of the century, which inhibited Catholic sympathies for decades afterwards, can be fairly typified by the very popular *Moral Philosophy* of the English Jesuit Joseph Rickaby, which went through many editions and was widely adopted by seminaries in the United States as well as Britain.

'Brute beasts,' Father Rickaby assures his readers, 'not having understanding and therefore not being persons, cannot have any rights.' What is more, and in my own view considerably more indefensible, he goes on to say that we can have 'no duties of charity or duties of any kind to the lower animals, as neither to stocks and stones'. In drawing practical conclusions from these premises, he introduces the curious distinction that although 'it is wanton cruelty to vex or annoy a brute beast *for sport*', there is nevertheless 'no shadow of evil resting on the practice of causing pain to brutes *in sport* . . . Much more, in all that conduces to the sustenance of man may we give pain to brutes, as also in the pursuit of science. Nor are we bound to make this pain as little as may be.' 'Brutes are', Father Rickaby concludes, 'as things in our regard.'[1]

This blunt doctrine of the English Catholic moralist found no contradiction or criticism among other Catholic textbook writers who condescended to deal with the subject at all. Whether or not they did deal with it was largely determined by the strength of animal protection movements or the liveliness of related controversies in their respective regions. The literature abounds in tragi-comic ironies, such as the tendency of Spanish moralists who find nothing objectionable in patronizing bull-fights to impose severe cautions on farm workers assisting the stud activities of a bull on a cattle ranch. There is something in the notion that viewing a bull's copulation is morally hazardous while viewing a bull's torment is innocent entertainment that brings out all that is most atrocious in this area of Roman Catholic thought. International fairness obliges us to recall that the moralists of every nation tend to be least critical of the types of mistreatment of animals that enjoy most prestige in their own lands. Thus, recent accounts of British foxhunting (which could easily be duplicated in the USA) hardly warrant superciliousness in commenting on the *corrida*. Nevertheless, the Catholic church's general reluctance to criticize bull-fighting in lands where it is the predominant religious community is consistent with the ethical position typified by Father Rickaby.

It will be helpful to summarize the main tenets of that position. Non-human animals can be neither the subjects of any rights nor the objects of any duties. There is nothing wrong with inflicting pain on non-human animals in sport, for human sustenance, or in the pursuit of science, and it is unnecessary to bother about minimizing the pain that is inflicted for those purposes. Indeed, the only thing regarded as objectionable is to torment animals not 'in sport' but 'for sport' – presumably, therefore, out of an extraordinarily rarefied sort of sadism. And it is hard to see how even that minimal objection can be reconciled with the conviction that animals are 'as things in our regard'. The objection is not really to treating animals abominably, but to fostering in oneself a particularly hideous sort of emotion, and it would be equally applicable if the stimulus were a fantasy or a photograph instead of an actually suffering animal.

In addition to these main lines of argument, it is sometimes alleged that predatory behaviour, with all that it entails, comes naturally to human beings, and therefore enjoys the sanction of moral law. The same is said of carnivorous eating habits, with all that they entail. Although abstinence from flesh meat is an honoured tradition in Roman Catholic religious life, it has always been regarded as a penitential practice, and therefore as a self-deprivation of wholesome, natural gratification, rather than as the abandonment of behaviour that is in any way intrinsically reprehensible. Even the several biblical passages that appear to imply compassion and enjoin restraint with regard to animals have frequently been interpreted allegorically, rather than literally, in ways that effectively abolish their relevance to the treatment of animals. A very powerful precedent for this latter procedure derives from the New Testament itself, where, in I Corinthians 9, St Paul cites the text of Deuteronomy 25.4, 'You shall not muzzle an ox when it is treading out the grain', only to explain that the text is not really about animals at all, but a figurative way of insisting that religious ministers, like Paul and Barnabas, are entitled to material support from the communities they serve. Perhaps the severest blow dealt by the Bible to religiously grounded concern for animals is the almost flippant way that St Paul disposes of the literal meaning of that Deuteronomic text: 'Is it for oxen that God is concerned? Does he not speak entirely for our sake?' How firmly this plainly erroneous Pauline interpretation took hold in early Christianity is made clear by a passage in a slightly later New Testament document. Thus we read in I Timothy 5, 'Let the elders who rule well be considered worthy of double honour, especially those who labour in teaching and preaching; for the Scripture says, "You shall not muzzle an ox when it is treading out the grain."'

It was for many centuries a common practice among Christians, confronted with biblical passages whose plain import conflicted with their own notions of what a divine revelation might decently contain, to resort to allegorism. Every passage that appears to take the interests of animals sincerely to heart was often dealt with in this way. An especially far-fetched instance is in Deuteronomy 22: 'If you chance to come upon a bird's nest in any tree or on the ground, with young ones or eggs, and the mother sitting upon the young or upon the eggs, you shall not take the mother with the young; you shall let the mother go, but the young you may take to yourself.' I assume that any of us, coming upon such a passage, would recognize it as an early example of practical environmentalism aimed at preserving animal species, perhaps mixed with a little tenderness towards a hapless individual animal. And we might well be astonished to learn from a centuries-long tradition that really it has nothing to do with birds at all. Instead, leaving the nest and mother bird means abandoning the Jewish synagogue, while taking the young means bringing Jewish converts into the Christian church. The fact that Martin Luther is among those who offer the latter interpretation is a reminder that such misleading exegetical habits lasted into the Reformation and among the Reformers. Nevertheless, it must be conceded that allegorical interpretation was favoured much longer in Roman Catholic than in Protestant churches, thus perpetuating a Catholic presumption that concern for animals finds no direct support in the Bible. Even more than Protestants, Jewish readers of the Bible generally admitted the plain sense of its words on behalf of animals, and the Talmud accordingly recognizes a religious duty to prevent or alleviate what it refers to in general terms as 'the pain of living creatures'. Thus in Judaism the Bible's particular injunctions and exhortations on behalf of animals are seen not only as authoritative in themselves but as exemplifying a general duty of compassionate care.

Jews have also been more inclined than Christians to draw moral conclusions from biblical passages, of which there are many, referring to God's providential care for animal creation, seeing in this a divine disposition that should be imitated in the life of a righteous person. This way of thinking is not only constructive in itself, but is an effective deterrent of ruthless interpretations of the authority over lesser creatures that is assigned to human beings in the creation narrative. Thus Psalm 8.6, 'Thou hast given [man] dominion over the works of thy hands; thou hast put all things under his feet, all sheep and oxen, and also the beasts of the field, the birds of the air and the fish of the sea' proclaims indeed the animals' dependence on human beings, but on human beings whose closeness to God involves seeing these creatures as manifestations of divine glory and dealing with them as co-operators in divine providence. The negative implication is to exhibit negligent and abusive treatment of dependent animals as not only unseemly, or even cruel, but as inherently irreligious.

Thus, among the obstacles to improved Catholic attitudes towards animals must be included certain ways of reading the Bible, whereas among Catholicism's current opportunities is its increasing adoption, partly on the basis of improved critical scholarship, of interpretations hitherto more common among Protestants and especially among Jewish readers. It is a familiar fact that interpretations of the Bible tend to harden in the shape of existing social practices, whereas conscientious reappraisals of the *status quo* often suggest the arbitrariness of such interpretations and the plausibility of quite different ones. Thus animal liberation has been impeded by the Bible in much the same way that the abolition of slavery and the equalization of women's rights have been impeded by it, but in the long run all of those liberation movements have assisted Christians to read the Bible with more acute moral vision, and to draw from it inspiration to assist those very movements. Our ways of living and our ways of reading influence one another, reciprocally and progressively, for good or ill.

I have emphasized the obsessive and indiscriminate anti-liberalism of nineteenth-century official Catholicism because that seems clearly to have been the time when a kind of doctrinaire paralysis settled over the church which only in recent decades has begun to relax. Prior to that time, among Christians, Catholic attitudes towards animals show little distinctiveness. During the Enlightenment, cruelty to animals was deplored by Puritans, Pietists, and Wesleyan Methodists especially. Generally, their moralizing was opposed by a cynicism well epitomized by Macaulay's quip, that Puritans hated bear-baiting not so much for the pain it caused the bear as for the pleasure it gave to the human spectators. Contemporary Puritan criticism of hunting was often satirized in similar terms. Actually these Protestant critics based their objections on grounds that had been occupied by Catholic critics since centuries before the Reformation, namely that cruelty is a vice established by practice, and that habits of cruelty developed by abusing animals would find expression in the treatment not only of animals but of human beings as well.

Although the ethical point of view here is undoubtedly anthropocentric, it should not be overlooked that the very notion that moral vices derive from immoral actions implies, in this instance, that immoral actions can be perpetrated on animals. To say that one was cruel to a horse and cruel to a child is not to mean two quite different things by 'cruel'. Such reflections on our ordinary moral language remind us of how unreal a world appears to be implied in a moral position of the kind I have cited from Father Rickaby. It is a world of rather dismaying simplicity, occupied, at least for the practical purposes of morality, by only two categories of beings, namely, human persons and – things. It takes a profound submissiveness to the theoretical to identify such a view with the enormously various daylit world that meets our eyes when we look up from the desk and out of the window. It is a view of the world that should never be adopted without trying it out on persons who look at the world eagerly and often, and with eyes unclouded by theory. Such persons are readily available in every community that has not abolished childhood. Tell a normal, intelligent child that ponies and dogs and cats, the bird in the hedge and the toad underneath it, and even the trees and the flowers are all, morally speaking, just

'things' and that our duties to them all are the same as to 'stocks and stones'
and the child will doubt either your seriousness or your sanity. Most of us
probably were told something like that at some point in our development,
and had our incredulity dissolve only gradually as we were immersed in a
culture in which stale theories count for more than fresh observations.
Naïve realism reappears, however, in our recognition that 'cruelty to
animals' means exactly what it says, whereas 'cruelty to stocks and stones'
is nonsense. But if 'cruelty to animals' means what it says, so also must
'kindness to animals' mean what it says. And if those phrases mean what
they say, then we do recognize animals as moral objects, and our treatment
of animals as subject to conscientious norms.

It has been interesting to observe, during the current international debate
over the morality and legality of abortion, how often moral critics of
abortion have appealed, through photographs or vivid descriptions, to an
intuitive recognition of inflicted suffering as indicating that cruelty has
been exercised on a human foetus in the process of aborting it.[2] The implication is that such cruelty has a moral atrociousness of its own that may
elicit a moral indignation that even the prospect of death does not. Given
the capacities of a human foetus, what is actually perceived as cruelty in
such cases is not different in kind, or, necessarily, in degree, from what is
perceived in cases of cruelty to animals. Regardless of whether or not one
considers the killing of a human foetus to be in any way morally comparable
to the killing of a non-human animal, it is hard to deny the moral com-
parability of tormenting a human foetus and a non-human animal. Without
wishing to deny that distinctions are often appropriate and sometimes
extremely important in comparing the sufferings of different victims and
kinds of victims, there remains a basic sense in which cruelty is cruelty.
And cruelty occurs whenever avoidable pain is inflicted for reasons that are
disproportionate or indifferent to the interests of the sufferer. Weighing
suffering against benefit in a moral scale is not, of course, an exact science,
and honest differences of estimate must be respected and may demand
compromises. It is an effort to make such estimates carefully, in the light
of all relevant data, that demonstrates the inclusion of animals within a
civilized ethic.

The easiest way for Roman Catholicism to begin building a place for
animals within its moral philosophy and theology is by simply retaining its
traditional moral understanding and estimate of cruelty while avoiding the
illusory flight from common sense and common perceptions, exemplified
by Father Rickaby's pretence that cruelty is applicable to animals only in
some fanciful or equivocal sense. That comparisons of cruelty to human

victims with that inflicted on animals are admissible on even the highest
planes of Christian religious discourse may be persuasively suggested by
the following passage by the contemporary theologian whom Father
Rickaby most admired. Indeed, I was aided in finding the passage by its
inclusion in Father Rickaby's *Index to the Works of John Henry, Cardinal
Newman.* The following is from Newman's Good Friday sermon, on the
passion and death of Christ, preached at Oxford in 1842.

He was as defenceless, and as innocent, as a lamb is. Since, then,
Scripture compares him to this inoffensive and unprotected animal, we
may without presumption or irreverence take the image as a means of
conveying to our minds those feelings which our Lord's sufferings
should excite in us. I mean, consider how very horrible it is to read the
accounts which sometimes meet us, of cruelties exercised on brute
animals. Does it not sometimes make us shudder to hear tell of them, or
to read them in some chance publication which we take up? At one time
it is the wanton deed of barbarous and angry owners who ill-treat their
cattle, or beasts of burden; and at another, it is the cold-blooded and
calculating act of men of science, who make experiments on brute
animals, perhaps merely from a sort of curiosity. I do not like to go into
particulars, for many reasons; but one of those instances which we read
of as happening in this day, and which seems more shocking than the
rest is, when the poor, dumb victim is fastened against a wall, pierced,
gashed, and so left to linger out its life. Now do you not see that I have
a reason for saying this, and am not using these distressing words for
nothing? For what was this but the very cruelty inflicted upon our Lord
. . . Now what is it moves our very hearts, and sickens us so much at
cruelty to poor brutes? I suppose this first, that they have done no harm;
next, that they have no power whatever of resistance; it is the cowardice
and tyranny of which they are the victims which makes their sufferings
so especially touching . . . There is something so very dreadful, so
satanic in tormenting those who have never harmed us, and who cannot
defend themselves, who are utterly in our power, who have weapons
neither of offence nor defence, that none but very hardened persons can
endure the thought of it . . . Think then, my brethren, of your feelings
at cruelty practised on brute animals, and you will gain one sort of
feeling which the history of Christ's Cross and Passion ought to excite
within you.[3]

The implication of such preaching, that in Christ's Passion incarnate divinity participates in a common victimhood of tormented animality, both human and non-human, enlarges the scope of Christianity's central belief, and points the way to an enriched spirituality.

As already ruefully observed, Roman Catholicism during most of the past two centuries has been less ready to regard animals as moral objects than have many Protestant and most non-Christian religious communities, including those sharing a biblical heritage, notably Judaism and Islam. As a result, the increasingly ecumenical and interreligious sympathies of Roman Catholics, encouraged especially by and since the Second Vatican Council, have served incidentally to foster wholesome second thoughts about the moral status of animals. In my own experience, Catholic students, at least as much as others, are nearly always pleasantly surprised and positively influenced by their discovery that in the moral wisdom of most of the world's great religions, especially those of Indian origin, strictures against inflicting death and pain are not usually confined to human victims. A strong current interest in Taoist values, often initially inspired by Taoist esteem for characteristically feminine dispositions, is readily extended to the Taoist appreciation of human beings rather as members than as masters of the natural world. Likewise tribal religions, no longer denigrated by ecclesiastical and colonial imperialists as demonic or barbaric, are increasingly admired for their delicate responsiveness to and reverence for the natural world.

Given the strong emphasis in Roman Catholic moral tradition on conformity with the 'natural law', understood as a revelation of divine purpose through regularities and spontaneities of unspoiled nature, the understanding of nature itself has moral implications, and plausible revisions of that understanding hold potentialities for ethical reform. As a result, the increasing awareness, through ecological education, that human beings are integral parts, at once powerful and vulnerable, of an ecosystem, rather than its detached observers and managers, has served to dispel the illusion that it is natural, and therefore legitimate, for human beings to deal capriciously and voraciously with their animal neighbours. In at least some circles there is also developing an educated scepticism about the hyper-Darwinian vision of nature as essentially a field of ceaseless combat that delivers its spoils to the survivors. In our modern world belief in the wholesome naturalness of untrammelled competition is hard to sustain in face of the environmental, social, economic, and military horrors that such beliefs have supported. I recall that during my own youthful involvement in New York with the 'Catholic Worker', Dorothy Day's radical movement for international peace and social justice, a book we were all required to read and frequently discussed was the Russian Prince Kropotkin's *Mutual Aid*, the study by a field naturalist of the place of co-operation, rather than competition, in the animal world.[4] Now, thirty-five years later, that book and others like it can be found in the hands of many Catholics of all ages, in many languages.

Having said so many words of apology for Roman Catholicism's contribution to a moral obtuseness about animals, I should like to add a few compensatory considerations. For one thing, I have been happy to observe that, now the anti-liberal obscurantism of the nineteenth-century papacy has receded, a Christian spiritual resource found most abundantly in Catholic churches, Roman, Eastern, and Anglican, is contributing in all those churches to a renewed reverence for the non-human components of nature. Often referred to as sacramentalism (related to but distinct from actual doctrines of sacramental theology), it is a disposition to discern in all material created things an authentic reflection of the presence and power of God, and to value the diversity of material creation for its suggestion of divinity's inexhaustible richness. It is compactly summarized by Dante's famous opening verses of the *Paradiso*, 'The glory of Him who moves all things penetrates throughout the universe, in one place more resplendent, in another less . . .'. In a material world so envisaged, every material thing becomes, so to speak, an icon, and the more intricate and exquisite are material creatures, the more transparent are they to the glory of their Creator. In such a scheme of things, animals must occupy an especially hallowed place, and become, not merely legitimate objects of Christian care and compassion, but incentives to awe and devotion. Recently, my wife and I had the pleasure of spending two weeks in the Galapagos Islands, and we were struck by how frequently the very secular and cosmopolitan group of people we shared a boat with referred to the experience of that world of unintimidated animals as a 'religious' experience.

This sacramental view of nature is closely associated with a certain kind of mysticism, wherein the worshipper's mind is drawn progressively towards contemplation of divinity, from level to level of creation. It has been abundantly evident in recent years that Catholicism's nurturing of mystical traditions, even when most Protestant churches repudiated or ignored them, has provided a deep foundation for sympathetic understanding between many Catholics and the meditative religions of the East as well as tribal nature mysticisms. It can be said with some fairness that, even during those recent decades when Catholic officialdom, along with the semi-officialdom of approved philosophers and theologians, took so dim a view of animal nature, Catholic poets and mystics tended to remain faithful to older and better insights. It is agreeable to recall that when, despite the Vatican's original disapproval, Rome did create its Society for the Prevention of Cruelty to Animals, it was dedicated to the protection of animals under the patronage not of some upstart modern reformer but of St Francis of Assisi. That dedication has always brought together in my mind two of the most famous images of St Francis, both immortalized in Giotto's marvellous frescoes. In one he stands among the animals, preaching playfully to the birds. In the other he stands over a sleeping pope, propping up a church that leans dangerously off balance. The current pursuit among Catholics of a spirituality that befriends, rather than enslaves, nature testifies to an enduring power for restoring balance to the church, of a tradition that St Francis proclaimed and personified.

Roman Catholic tradition can also point, in its earlier history, to evidence of misgivings among the Renaissance humanists about accepted ways of dealing with animals. The most striking evidence of this is provided by another man whom Catholics venerate as a saint, Thomas More, in his *Utopia*. It is important to bear in mind the peculiar nature of that work. It begins with a conversation among learned friends touching upon a number of the more notorious abuses and scandals in contemporary civic and ecclesiastical life. It then introduces a traveller who is persuaded to describe life as he once observed it in a remote land called Utopia, where the problems under discussion were almost unheard of. The distinctive thing about Utopia is its confident and exclusive reliance on human reason; it has no supernatural revelation or authoritative dogma. As a result, More's account of a fictional place, attributed to a fictional narrator, enables him, without uttering a disloyal syllable about church or state, to whimsically challenge the assumed reasonableness of many aspects of national and ecclesiastical life. It is noteworthy that among the many objects of this prudent satire are the acceptance of hunting as a recreation, butchering as a regular occupation, and also the dogmatic assertion that non-human animals are soulless and ephemeral beings. The Utopians' objection to hunting anticipates by two centuries that which was taken up by a number of Enlightenment thinkers, including perhaps the most influential of all modern moral philosophers, Immanuel Kant. It is essentially humanistic. The sport of a hunter 'results, in the opinion of the Utopians, in a cruel disposition. Or, if he isn't cruel to start with, the hunter quickly becomes so through the constant practice of such bestial pleasures.'[5] More's spokesman assumes his most mocking tone in rejecting the notion that a hunter's enjoyment has little or nothing to do with the violent outcome. 'Is there any more real pleasure, they ask, when a dog chases a rabbit than there is when a dog chases a dog? If what you like is fast running, there's plenty of that in both cases . . . But if what you really want is slaughter, if you want to see a living creature torn apart before your eyes, then the whole thing is wrong.'[6] With butchering, too, it is the occupation's capacity to generate callousness in the face of pain and death that persuades the Utopians that it is no proper occupation for respectable citizens. A more theoretical passage is that in which the Utopians are said to be mostly persuaded, on strictly rational grounds, that human beings should anticipate life after death. Some, however, do not believe in an afterlife, while still others suppose 'that animals too have immortal souls, though not comparable to ours in excellence, nor destined to equal felicity'.[7] Although the Utopians make efforts to correct those who disbelieve in any afterlife, those who would extend immortality to animals 'are not considered bad, their opinion is not considered altogether unreasonable, and so they are not interfered with'.[8] Without pretending that speculations of this kind were representative of Roman Catholicism in any age, it is nevertheless gratifying to find among thinkers of this calibre a readiness to acknowledge at least mysterious possibilities in the souls of non-human animals. With regard to recreational hunting and butchering, Thomas More was undoubtedly aware that, although not morally disapproved, the church's law did, ironically enough, prohibit these activities to 'sacred' persons, namely clergy and religious.

The tendency of traditional Roman Catholic ethics to look to nature and naturalness as an index of morality has already been noted in connection with ecological insights into the place of human beings in the living world. By the same token, the long-standing assumption that human beings are 'naturally' hunters has been placed in a new light by findings and speculations in evolutionary biology.[9] Those who read at least popular summaries of palaeo-anthropology, the scientific investigation of humanity's evolutionary origins, will probably have noticed in recent decades the emergence of a theory that is sometimes interestingly referred to as a biological counterpart of original sin. It is the theory that a particularly fateful turn taken by our ape-like ancestors launched them on to a course of development that entails all that is most impressive but also all that is most repulsive in the material events of human history. Put very simply, certain typically vegetarian apes became, in certain fortuitously favourable circumstances, meat-eaters, and eventually predatory carnivores. This new way of life succeeded in a world of natural selection, despite physical inferiority to such fanged and four-footed predators as wolves and leopards, in virtue of mental developments that made possible verbal communication and the construction of artificial weapons. From that point on, the so-called 'killer-ape' continued to improve communication and weaponry, becoming as a result ever more dangerous and collectively almost invincible – except, of course, by other killer-apes similarly equipped. As an early British proponent of the theory, Harry Campbell, writing against the sobering background of the First World War, described the historical consequences of this evolutionary development, man 'in the matter of slaughter, leaves all other animals far behind. He is the arch-slaughterer – *facile princeps*. Since the time the pre-human ape took to hunting he and his human descendants have wrought ruthless havoc among the lower animals, and at the present day man not only hunts them but breeds them for the express purpose of destroying them, partly for food, partly for amusement . . . In his upward march he has left behind him one long trail of blood.'[10] The 'feel' of the forces unleashed by such an evolutionary development is marvellously evoked by William Golding's extraordinary novel *The Inheritors*, in which the lethal rise of our terrible new species is seen through the eyes of its peaceful vegetarian predecessors during the course of their own destruction.[11] The theory itself has gone in and out of fashion among modern scientists, but in recent decades it is not lightly dismissed, and there are many who share the opinion expressed by the ethologist Valerius Geist: 'Whether we love hunting or hate it, eulogize its blinding passion or condemn it, hunting was the force that shaped our bodies, molded our souls, and honed our minds.'[12]

Theories of this kind take on a special poignancy for Bible readers, who have often noted that in the first chapter of Genesis where divine provision is made for human needs, the only menu envisaged appears to be vegetarian. Apparently the concept of a sinless paradisal world is of a world that is not carnivorous, presumably because it is non-violent. The same implication is found in the well-known prophetic vision of a healed and restored world where 'the wolf shall dwell with the lamb . . . and the lion shall eat straw like the ox'. It is only after sin has brought in alienation and disorder that we find mention of the first herdsman, and later still the prototypical hunter appears on the scene. Linked to the former is the story of the first homicide, introducing a narrative from which cruelty and violence are never again long absent.

The theory that our species' great productivity and great destructiveness, our rise to power and our fall from grace, are alike rooted in the evolutionary transformation of a vegetarian gatherer into a carnivorous hunter is, of course, only a theory, even if a rather ingenious one. A curious thing is that so many alternative theories have been aired in recent years that are evidently much less provable or plausible. Some scientists have suggested that what this seeming contest of rival scientific theories really represents is a struggle to establish a mythology to assist humanity in escaping from the destiny implied in the character of a killer-ape. What the struggle is thought to express is a deep revulsion for the bloody history of our species combined with a deep fear of where our slaughtering propensities now threaten to lead us. The 'naturalness' of hunting, as supposedly rooted in our evolutionary beginnings, has become for many a frightening thought.

Whether or not our species got its start as predators, it seems less than reasonable to assume that predatory habits must haunt us eternally in the form of excessively cruel thoughts and compulsively violent deeds. Mental capacities originally developed in the service of hunting are not thereby disqualified from criticizing hunting. Attributing to evolution an all-determining development in the remote ancestral past distorts the very idea of evolution as a continuing process. What adaptation to one environment can do, adaptation to another can undo or redo, and patterns of behaviour pursued when they ensured survival may be abandoned or modified when they threaten it. Whether or not we began, in some sense, as killer-apes, killer-apes are not the best we can hope to be. 'Evolution made me do it' is as fatuous an excuse for irresponsibility as 'the devil made me do it'.

Sometimes the possibilities encompassed by natural selection are best brought home to us by those we observe under artificial selection. From those who tell me I am stuck with the character of a killer-ape I turn for reassurance to one of our family's dogs. Chaser is a boxer, and a beautiful one, lean and graceful, yet massively muscled, with a brow like granite and jaws like steel, clever, alert, eager, and dauntless. And we all know how he got that way. Artificial selection by the breeders of his ancestors in France and Germany built into them, and through them into him, the physique of a perfect dog for – bull-baiting. But Chaser does not bait bulls or show any inclination to do so. He has found lots of other things to do with his strength and courage and alertness. Tireless companion, protector, playmate, clown, given to eating with a pigeon perched on his dish and sleeping with a cat between his paws, his origins have empowered him but not enslaved him. Good animals can teach us to be good animals, and killer-apes can, like boxers, turn their evolved talents to better pursuits in a better environment!

PART THREE

Disputed Questions

Introduction

Andrew Linzey

Far from being a minor or secondary issue in theology, animals pose fundamental questions about the justice of God, the nature of creation, the reality of evil, and the scope of redemption. In this section we bring together some of the divergent views under three overlapping heads in order to give some account of what MacIntyre calls the 'continuities of conflict'.

Nature and providence

The first concerns the status of the natural world and its relationship to God. A significant number of environmentalists as well as animal advocates argue that what is urgently needed is a reappraisal of the worth of nature itself as a means of preventing its wanton exploitation and destruction. The reason we exploit nature, including the creatures, it is argued, is because we have de-sacralized it. What is required is a vision of nature as coterminous with God, or at least a vision of God-with-nature as the ideological fortress against further intrusion and exploitation.

Stephen R. L. Clark begins by setting his face against this tendency, especially against all forms of pantheism. Nature is not God. While there is good in nature, not all nature is unambiguously good. If God is unambiguously identified with nature, then nature is inevitably seen as the embodiment of God's moral will. 'If Nature's Way is to be our guide, it is pointless to complain of mass extinctions, or pollution.' Again: 'If nature is unambiguously God's will, God apparently wants us to be predatory nepotists.' Once it is grasped that there is 'a way things could be that does not depend upon mutual competition', there is that 'distinction between Nature and the Divine' that environmentalists have (erroneously) 'blamed for twentieth-century mistakes'. What is required, according to Clark, is the reawakening of a full-blooded traditional theism. Clark advances the 'Christian answer' that Christ was 'divinely indestructible' and that all things are taken up and renewed in him as a microcosm of all creation.

Thomas Hosinski, on the other hand, argues that an evolutionary perspective requires us to modify our traditional ideas of God. God should be seen as the Creator who endows all creatures with real freedom, which means that God cannot be, as traditionally understood, omniscient, or indeed omnipotent. God is radically affected by the world, 'vulnerable to it, though not entirely or finally captive to it'. Hosinski takes up Whitehead's philosophy in which God is conceived of as 'acting on the world by organizing and presenting potentials or possibilities' and endowing each creature with the freedom to respond to the divine 'lure' present within creation itself. God's providence for animals consists not only in the lure to self-realization (even at the expense of other creatures) but also in a 'higher' form in which suffering is redeemed 'and taken into God's own experience'.

The underlying issues appear to be these. First, what is the moral status of nature? Is it as God intended and therefore perfect? Is it ambiguous, containing both moral good and natural evil? If the latter, can it at the same time be both as God intended and *in process* towards some divinely appointed goal? Secondly, how transcendent can God be without appearing indifferent (or a cause of indifference) to the daily sorrow of God's creatures? Conversely, how immanent can God be within creation without ceasing to be God – at least a God who is sufficiently omnipotent to be able in the last to redeem the suffering and misery of the world? From the standpoint of animal theology, which doctrine of God most adequately recognizes the moral gravity of animal suffering and best offers the hope of individual redemption for suffering creatures?

The Fall and predation

The problem here is how to *account for* evil in the world and how to reconcile it with belief in an all-loving God. Michael Lloyd is clear that one of the chief manifestations of evil is the parasitical nature of the created world. Such a world is not the kind of place we would envisage an almighty, loving God to have created. Lloyd rejects two common sets of answers, the first that predation is not actually evil and the second that 'it is bad but necessary and worthwhile'. If, then, evil has come into the world, by what means has it done so? The first candidate is the notion of the 'world-soul' – a 'collective fall of the race-soul of humanity in an indefinitely remote past'. The second is that favoured by process thinkers represented (in varying degrees) by Hosinski and McDaniel. According to this view, the agency of fallenness is (at least in part) nature itself, specifically the free will of the creatures who are able to 'deviate from the divine will for them'. The third candidate is the fall of the angels, nothing less than 'a moral revolt within the spiritual dimension of the created order' prior to the creation of humankind. This last candidate is, in Lloyd's view, the most plausible. To the challenge that there is no direct supporting evidence, Lloyd replies: 'the hypothetical assertion that natural evil is the result of the distortion of creation brought about by the Fall does not need evidential support at this precise point if it can be shown that it is organically related to a world-view which is coherent and carries evidential support at other key points. I submit that this is the case.'

Jay B. McDaniel, on the other hand, is adamant that the notion of the Fall is no longer plausible. 'We cannot follow this route, for we have to acknowledge that there never was a time when life on this planet was free from violence. Predator-prey relations existed long before the early hominids appeared.' How, then, is God to be envisioned in relation to the violence and apparent evil in creation? McDaniel opts for a panentheistic model in which the universe is 'immanent within the divine Life, even as the divine Life is more than the universe'. In any given predator-prey relation God is immanent within *both* creatures – even, 'God *is* inside each creature'. As Whitehead remarks, 'God is a fellow sufferer who understands.' From a process perspective 'things happen in the universe which God does not will, but which are nevertheless part of God's life'. Process thinkers may discern a 'fallen' dimension in predator-prey relations, 'but they also see God as partly responsible for their existence in the first place'. In short: 'The "fall" into carnivorous existence was lured by God, with co-operation of creatures. It was a "fall *upward*".'

Both contributors begin their chapters with a memorable account of predation: in Lloyd's case, a savage killing in the woods, in McDaniel's, orcas battering a grey whale to death. Both chapters attempt to recognize and account for 'natural evil'. The question is: which has best succeeded? The weakness in Lloyd's case is the lack of evidential support so that there remains some doubt as to whether we are dealing – at worst – with an empty hypothesis. The weakness in McDaniel's, on the other, is its apparent acceptance that God is at least partly to blame (with the co-operation of creatures) for the evil and suffering in the world and, if so, is surely a morally compromised God hardly credible as a means of liberation and redemption. At the very least, it is worrying that Christian theology should have devoted so little time and attention to a problem which poses a *prima facie* – if not insuperable – challenge to the plausibility of an all-loving God.

Souls and redemption

Christian theology has frequently been hesitant about the possibility of individual redemption for sentients, and even more so about the idea that animals may possess immortal souls. Yet the issue of suffering and evil endured by animals makes the question central to theodicy. However we may construe the origins of evil in the world, a just and loving God must in the last analysis be able to offer recompense and redemption commensurate with the evil that has been endured.

John B. Cobb, Jr. begins by protesting at the traditional christological preoccupation with individual human souls. He offers two ways of correcting the imbalance. The first is through the realization that the Logos as understood by the Johannine Prologue is immanent within the whole creation 'enlivening all living beings'. The second is through the Pauline metaphor of the indwelling Christ which, whilst focussed on individual believers, has a wider reference which includes all created beings enlivened by his life. All creatures have an eschatological fulfilment in Christ: 'In Christ they are all reconciled – slaughtered and slaughterer, tortured and torturer – to one another and to God.' This paradigm releases us from narrow humanocentric perspectives and provides the necessary stimulus for ethical reappraisal. 'A creature in whom we see Christ cannot be *only* a commodity to be treated for our gain or casual pleasure,' he maintains. That may well be true, but is reconciliation in Christ sufficient recompense for the suffering and futility to which creation has been subject? If we must not 'sentimentalize' nature, and predation remains God's will, what is the moral or theological basis for positing redemption? Why would God want to redeem what God actually created?

Paul Badham, on the other hand, justifies the traditional concentration on the immortal souls of humans. 'One might well agree', he argues, 'that animals are not machines but are feeling, thinking agents with purposes, wills, and rights which should be respected, without wanting to commit oneself to the view that they possess an eternal destiny beyond bodily death.' But why, exactly? Badham's answer appears to be that animals 'live very much in the present . . . [and] without a complex language it is hard to see how it would be possible to have a developed, reflective life and a fully developed power of reasoning such that one could identify one's selfhood in that capacity'. On the other hand, a list of criteria dreamt up by dolphins might include various complexities of language and spiritual experience that humans would similarly fail to meet. Badham concludes that 'We have no means of knowing whether or not animals partake in any of these [human] experiences and therefore no basis on which to extend the Christian hope to our animal cousins.' Could the dolphins claim the same?

Against Badham, Petroc and Eldred Willey maintain that the issue is not *whether* animals will be redeemed but *how*. They sketch out the weaker and stronger possibilities of redemption, ranging from the notion that animals may be saved in, or through, humanity, to the possibility that their individualities will be redeemed analogously to ourselves. The idea that animals do not constitute individualities, as some have presupposed, is sharply rejected: 'We may often regard animals as substitutable repetitions of a type, but it is clear that animals themselves do not.' Animals are 'unique individual selves, each living and dying with its own life experiences arising out of its individual substantial being'.

I suggest that there is something theologically odd about all discussion of immortal souls – the plain absurdity, no less, of humans deciding for themselves which essential or substantial qualities qualify them for eternal life and which may or may not exclude animals. In that sense, despite the colossal weight placed upon these discussions and the distinctions to which they have given rise within the tradition, I suggest that they are all theologically a false trail. Eternal life is God's own gift; it is not something which we can merit. The divine prerogative is total and absolute here. Instead of reducing immortality to theological anthropology or even theological animality we should concentrate our vision on how the Christian God is *simultaneously* Creator, Reconciler, and Redeemer. If full weight is given to God's gracious and wide-ranging activity in creation, then it is inconceivable that the God who redeems will be *less* than the God who creates. In this sense the issue of animal immortality is wholly integral to the view that God does actually care not only for the whole world but for each and every individual being within it, including – of course – sparrows.

That said, there is not a weaker but a stronger case for animal redemption that must be drawn from the nature of God revealed in Christ, for that God is pre-eminently a God who has taken sides with the weak, the vulnerable, and the innocent. All redemption is moral redemption or it is nothing. In that sense animals *do* merit redemption in a way in which wicked, sinful, and violent human beings never can. The moral character of redemption, precisely because it follows from the moral integrity of God, is inseparable from the establishment of justice. Whatever other things animals may have to fear, divine justice is not among them.

Nature and Providence

10

Is Nature God's Will?

Stephen R. L. Clark

A religion for the times?

The social and environmental problems that we face at this tail end of twentieth-century progress require us to identify some cause, some spirit that transcends the petty limits of our time and place, that gives us something to work for that is not just 'our own profit'. Fortunately for the future, and our children's fortunes, many of us do identify with our posterity, plant woodlands that we shall not see, and seek to save our children's children from disaster. But our willingness to sacrifice our own present interests for the general good of humankind or of the world is feeble: advising others not to cut down rain forests or pollute the seas is easy enough; preserving our own wetlands or cutting back on burgers is another matter. Only a 'religious spirit', a willed and eager commitment to a larger whole, can easily sustain us through adversity, let alone through prosperity. The question is: what spirit shall that be?

Arnold Toynbee, conversing with Daisatsu Ikeda in the early 1970s, declared:

> a right religion is one that teaches respect for the dignity and sanctity of all nature. The wrong religion is one that licenses the indulgence of human greed at the expense of non-human nature. I conclude that the religion we need to embrace now is pantheism, as exemplified in Shinto, and that the religion we now need to discard is Judaic monotheism and the post-Christian nontheistic faith in scientific progress, which has inherited from Christianity the belief that mankind is morally entitled to exploit the rest of the universe for the indulgence of human greed.[1]

Toynbee went on to concede, under pressure from Ikeda (himself a Buddhist working for the moral regeneration of his country), that such pantheism has often led to nationalism, 'the worship of collective human power', but continued to disparage the anthropomorphic, anthropocentric tendencies of theism. Was he correct?

A 'pantheistic' religious sensibility, whereby the divine is sensed or worshipped in what happens by nature, has considerable influence on other folk than Toynbee. It may issue in nothing more radical than a romantic love of 'unspoilt countryside' as being more 'natural' than the town. Sometimes, and with greater emotional intensity, it is the image of the Whole Earth, seen from orbit, that reminds us of a real beauty that is likely to outlast us all – unless we deform and destroy it. Some such enthusiasts pass beyond a love of 'country walks' or a verbal appreciation of the Living Earth to regulate their own behaviour by asking, 'How may we live so as to sustain the fragile beauty of the earth in which we have our being?' To that question many more than Toynbee have replied with a vigorous rejection of 'theism' in its familiar Jewish, Christian, or Islamic guise, and also of 'post-Christian humanism'. Theism, it is supposed, denies the intrinsic value of the natural world, and leads us to overestimate the value of those powers and characters that we share with a god made in our image. What follows from the alternative doctrine, that we should worship what is manifested in nature at large, not only what is manifest in human culture? Toynbee would say (and so would others) that we would thereby save ourselves from destructive acts of a kind that must eventually ruin us. If we continue to believe that it is only humankind that enshrines divine value, the world of nature suffers.

Devotees of this budding 'religion of the Living Earth' often suggest that we must put aside our older reliance upon 'reason' in favour of a more emotional and empathetic insight into things. But they are also glad to welcome what seems like a kind of endorsement from within the scientific framework. Television documentaries have predisposed us to believe that 'things make sense', that what exists, however baroque or convoluted, has been 'chosen' by the invisible hand of Nature. Mainstream biologists would of course deny that Nature has any providential purpose, but the moralistic thesis is still clear: if it's 'natural' we ought to think it good. 'Gaia' or the Living Earth is represented as a self-maintaining, self-repairing system that deserves our reverence. What might have turned out to be a mere collection, hodge-podge, or muddle of living creatures without any common goal or good, appears instead to be a unified, adaptive whole, grounded in the shifting bacterial populations that store or produce the substances that they and their dependants need.[2] The living Earth is a homeostatic (or, rather, a *homeorhetic*) system rather like a living organism: James Lovelock called it 'Gaia' (and has since wished that he had not used the capital).

Lovelock also follows Lynn Margulis, one of his most eminent collaborators, in emphasizing the problems posed by eukaryotic cells and multi-cellular organisms (as well as hives and societies) for a sheerly competitive theory of evolutionary change. Eukaryotes have incorporated sometime independent entities as endosymbionts: instead of all-out war different entities co-operate in sustaining a larger whole. Chloroplasts descended from Archaean cyanobacteria power cabbages and redwood trees; our own cells require the constant co-operation of sometime alien organisms with their own genetic lifeline. As a larger whole is formed, destructive competition at a lower level is restricted: or, putting it differently, every individual contributor to the next generation's gene-pool can increase its own 'genetic fitness' by co-operation (and has good reason to enforce such co-operation upon others). The 1980s ideology of individualist competition – fuelled even against their personal intentions by writers like Dawkins and Wilson[3] – needs to be severely modified to acknowledge the real abiding force of Mutual Aid, and the real organisms that arise from that co-operation.

Both the theory and mainstream reaction to it suggest to some, and especially to those already disenchanted with modern technocratic civilization, that there are other forms of knowledge than the merely rational or objective. We know the world best when we *feel* with it, when we recognize it from within, as part and parcel of a multi-millionfold experiment in being. Its most enthusiastic supporters see Gaia as a counter-example to the neo-Darwinian notion that providence plays no part in things, and also to the merely anthropocentric fantasy that it is our advantage that such a providence provides. In that sense the 'Television Documentary Syndrome' (that all is for the best in this best of all possible worlds) does have a part to play in the acceptance of the hypothesis: not that the world is the best there is for us, but that we should reorganize our moral perceptions so as to think that what is good for Gaia is the only or pre-eminent good. So Gaia either is itself the thing most worth admiring or it is the best available image of co-operative, synergistic life, the Mother.

Embarrassing associations?

But before we accept the Living Earth and Nature as our guide, in the guise of Gaia or the Mother Goddess, we should consider the historical associations of that creed. The charge against traditional religion, that it has inhumane or destructive associations, can, unfortunately, be turned round: this century (as Ikeda hinted) saw the rise and fall of a movement that actually shared a great many of the doctrines and evaluations typical of Toynbee's pantheistic environmentalism, namely Nazism. Consider the following compendious account of modern 'naturism' (a term now associated with high-principled nudism – whose roots are not so far from the ideology I aim to describe). The 'natural' (which is to say the living) world is perfect in its beauty, not to be disparaged or renounced in the name of any other or transcendental world. There is a 'balance of nature' which can be momentarily upset but which will (with more or less inevitability) swing back. 'Human beings', as a class, are no more than one temporary – and heterogeneous – species amongst the many strands that make up the biosphere. The 'technological fix' is to be distrusted partly because it favours the delusion that 'no man need pay for his sins', and partly because technology in the modern manner is founded on the assumption that the world can be managed 'mechanically' rather than 'organically' and with due attention to the 'spirit within'. Some human beings have been misled – usually by Jews and Christians, but sometimes by Hellenists – into thinking that they have special rights or dignities, but our best image of the 'Divine' is not human, but either the Earth herself, Gaia, or the multitudinous spirits of wood and river, spring-time and leaf-fall, sex, death and affection. For similar reasons merely legal or official authority, the kind of authority that depends on office or abstract law, is of less significance than charismatic or national authority. The 'real' person, and the 'real' world, are ones stripped of all 'merely cultural or historical' significance, so that nakedness is indeed of more than 'hygienic' or 'aesthetic' importance.

Let me emphasize the most embarrassing association. The humankind that is most deadly to the world – so pantheistic environmentalists will often say – is individualistic, capitalistic, deracinated and influenced by the dreams of human grandeur purveyed – supposedly – in the Jewish scriptures. As Toynbee said: we must discard Judaic monotheism, and prefer the sort of rooted love of earth and its spirits that pantheism or paganism stands for. Instead of treating land as real estate to be transformed to abstract capital we must live within our limits, acknowledging the ties of kinship and the love of earthly beauty. The real cause of plague lies in the Jewish heritage of civilized humanity: we must root out its causes – *which is just what Hitler said*. It would not take much for the notions that humankind is, as presently constituted, a plague, and that it is all – some-how – the fault of the Jews (deracinated intellectuals and capitalistic usurers), to merge in anti-semitism of Hitler's kind. The Nazis did not treat Jews (and Gypsies) as animals (Hitler disapproved – though, as usual, incoherently – of hunting, flesh-eating, and vivisection), but – exactly – as bacterial infections. Popular environmentalism of the kind purveyed in television documentaries continues, despite a hundred refutations, to blame 'Christianity' or 'the Jewish scriptures' for our arrogance in neglecting the rightful claims of nature.

The fact that there have been pantheists, or anti-theists, who have been guilty of atrocious crimes is not, of course, enough to refute those versions of environmentalism, or neo-paganism. So after all have Christians, Marxists, pagans, and 'postmodernists'. 'Just because something happens to have been emphasized by people as despicable as the Nazis does not make it wrong.'[4] But we clearly need to ask whether pantheism offers a viable alternative to more humanistic ideologies: how naturist can good Christian theists be?

A good many such theists are very sympathetic to naturism. Non-Christian naturists regularly blame 'the Judaeo-Christian patriarchalist tradition' for Western assaults on nature. Christian naturists prefer to blame 'the Greeks'. All insist that true doctrine rejects any split between Spirit and Nature, the Eternal and the Here-and-Now. Many suggest that we are wrong to distinguish 'substances' and 'processes'.[5] Jewish or Christian stories and doctrines that seem to imply otherwise must be interpreted 'metaphorically' if they are to be acceptable: notions like 'Original Sin', 'Fallen World', 'the World to Come' are suspect (unless they refer to capitalist corruptions of human nature, and the classless future). Christian naturists may retain some notion that there is an Outside, and that Humanity is a crucial link between this World and God ('the world's High Priest'), but worship of that Outside is – in the modern style – generally to be equated with 'love of the neighbour', action in the world, and not any 'flight of the Alone to the Alone'. All too often even that 'neighbour-love' amounts only to an insistence on 'togetherness' and 'socializing the economy'.

If Gaia, the Whole Earth, is a living organism, 'the Earth Mother', are we tissues, or organs, necessary to its survival or integrity? Or must we be considered something like a bacterial infection, an alien intrusion or cancerous growth? According to some versions, humankind is the mind and voice of Gaia, the 'growing point of evolution', the grand experiment to try out conscious thought as a mechanism for Gaia's future life. Pierre Teilhard de Chardin convinced some that evolutionary history was headed towards the increased 'complexity' of intellectual and social life, that it would culminate in the 'noosphere' – and lesser forms of humankind would be only failed experiments, perhaps to be disposed of.[6] Gaia, wild nature, was to be fulfilled by being fully understood and tamed in human civilization. Modern pantheistic environmentalists think de Chardin's vision unduly anthropocentric – as mainstream biologists always thought it unduly optimistic in imagining that 'evolution' had a fixed direction. But some would still suggest that human beings are justified by the contribution they can make to Gaia – and condemned by their failure to contribute.

Popular versions of evolutionary theory suggest, like Irenaean theodicies,[7] that there is a direction to evolution, and that God's creation of so terrible a world is justified by the impossibility of creating 'persons' (like us) by any less tortuous or tortured route. Such a defence of God requires a radical revision of divine 'omnipotence' (since the God of our tradition could have raised up people from the very stones without requiring them to struggle 'up' through many million years of random change). If the world is only good because, by providence or random change, it leads to *us*, then anthropocentric moralists are right to conclude that we should use the world of nature instrumentally. If we should not, because (as tradition also says) the world was already good, was what God wanted it to be, before there were any human persons, then there is much less reason to suppose that evolutionary change has a direction. The tapestry, and not only our own thread of it, is what God wants. But does God want it in the shape that it has had so far?

Pantheism vs. nihilism?

There is certainly good reason to reject the converse creed, that 'only man is vital', and the rest of creation devoid of anything but instrumental value. Unless, as Hans Jonas has pointed out,[8] we accept a thoroughly Gnostic account of being (for which we are intruders from the Great First Light upon an alien world) we cannot live with a wholly alienated universe. A merely mechanical universe, without real ends or real requirements, one that we cannot 'animate' or cannot find any 'common cause' with, is one that could never have produced such beings as we think ourselves to be. If human beings are valuable then either they are intruders on a universe they have no hope of understanding or need to admire, or else the world is one already animated, valued. As Plotinus, greatest of late antique philosophers, said to the Gnostics: 'if God is absent from the world, he will be absent from you, and then you would have nothing to say about him or the beings which come after him'.[9] If nothing 'worldly' were of any value, then our own 'natural responses', cognitive and affective, would have no value.

So there is at least some sense to the claim that we do not inhabit a mechanical or 'value-neutral' world, that Spirit and Nature are not deathly opposites, and that our technophiliac enthusiasms might justly be restricted by reborn respect for 'Nature's Way'. 'If the earth is holy then the things that grow out of the earth are also holy. They do not belong to man to do with them as he will. Dominion does not carry personal owner-ship . . . nor commission to devastate.'[10]

But can that be all? Is Nature's Way just God's Way? Is our religious duty just a duty to accept our passing place within the overarching whole, the Earth? Nature's Way, after all, is the Way of Predation, a way that is indeed compatible with co-operation, symbiosis, organic unity, but which as frequently sets one organism, one cluster against another. Social Darwinists saw more of direct, face-to-face competition in the record than they should, and Kropotkin was right to insist that 'the fittest' (who survive to breed) are not simply the strongest and most self-willed.[11] Nor are the most successful genes, *pace* Richard Dawkins, the most 'selfish' ones.[12] But there are limits on the kind of co-operative ventures that can be expected. Humanity is no more than an abstract or ideal unity: the really available syntheses are tribes, nations, cults. The only altruism that Neo-Darwinian theorists can expect to last is nepotism. Even if there is eventually to be Point Omega, the Terrestrial Monad in which all smaller co-operatives co-operate, 'one far-off divine event, To which the whole creation moves',[13] the way to that imagined whole is littered with the victims of evolutionary process. And what is to be done with those who resist amalgamation, or prefer their own transcendent ideal to the 'reality' of a healthy folk? If it is the future that will vindicate the past, then we must expect that all manner of 'failed experiments' will perish. If the world is perfect just as it is, irrespective of its future, there still seems little reason to resist species-extinction. There have been many occasions when the number of species, and kinds of species, has been drastically cut. That is as much a feature of the world as individual death. As Tennyson realized, types are no more eternal than individuals:

> 'So careful of the type?' But no.
> From scarped cliff and quarried stone
> She cries 'A thousand types are gone:
> I care for nothing, all shall go.'[14]

If Nature's Way is to be our guide, it is pointless to complain of mass extinctions, or pollution. In a mechanistic universe terms like 'pollution' (which implies that there are preferred states, or real goals) are out of place: there is only biochemical change. But 'pollution' is also out of place in a pantheistic world: there are only openings up of new ecological niches, the testing of old-established kinds against new challenges. It is the office of each kind, each 'separate' organism to maintain its own as best it may, so that the glory of the whole be made richer through the war of its parts. So the worship of Nature which has been so popular a response to environmental catastrophe bids fair to explain such things away. Think of it – and of genocide – as evolution in action, to no human end. Environmentally-minded theologians often suggest that it is 'natural' (and so commendable) that gangs of dogs, for example, should pull down, kill, and disembowel their prey. Human predators are just as 'natural', and it is quite unclear what limits they should put upon themselves, or what would count as an 'unnatural' greed. If nature is unambiguously God's will, God apparently wants us to be predatory nepotists.

Pantheism is not only a response to rumours of environmental catastrophe: it is a reaction against the 'objectifying gaze' that turns nature into mere material, emptying it of any sacred value so as to possess it fully. Empty the world of its significance and it is only a step onward to empty human beings of all significance as well. 'The notion of the world as indifferent stuff open to manipulation has been formed by expelling moral order from nature and lodging it in the human subject.'[15] The world of matter-in-motion, stripped of all emotional affect, without intrinsic goals or inner spirit, is an ideological fiction, intended to release the human spirit from slavery to any powers of this world: Cartesian ego and Cartesian mechanism stand opposed, and the ego may do just as it pleases. Those who followed Descartes in thinking that the human subject, unlike any other thing in the world, was a real subject of experience, an intruder upon the merely mechanical motions of those stuffs studied by physicists and biologists, could consistently declare that human beings derived their value from a supernatural source. But those heirs of the Enlightenment that went on to say that the human self has no transcendent source thereby committed themselves to the view that there can be no real value in the human subject either, and that all things, including us, were manipulable material. Dogmatic humanism, for which nothing but human selves are valuable, easily sinks into nihilism: material motions cannot explain subjective being, nor allow any content to the notion of objective value. ' "Man's power over Nature" is really the power of some men over others, with Nature as their instrument.'[16] In a world without intrinsic values or immanent (moral) laws, the naked will must rule, for arbitrary ends and without hope of any lasting success. If there are no obligations there cannot even be an obligation to accept a valid argument with true premisses.

There are indeed plenty of nihilists around, at least among the chattering classes. There are those for whom ideals of justice and of truth alike are only bourgeois illusions: 'really', there is no reality beyond the patterns that 'we' make; 'really', we ourselves are only characters in a bad novel, without beginning, middle, end or discernible plot. It is a source of constant astonishment to me that some theologians imagine they must take this stuff seriously, as more than an intellectual aberration, or a piece of devil worship. Turning from that postmodernist abyss we may find comfort in a living earth: 'there is no inorganic nature, there is no dead, mechanical Earth. The Great Mother has been won back to life.'[17] The great German philosopher Heidegger, whose rhetoric is also influential in environmentalism, believed that National Socialism offered a real spiritual rebirth, in opposition to technocratic nihilism: in later life the only error he confessed was in not seeing the nihilistic, technocratic aspects of Nazism. Nazism, it turned out, was part of the disease, and not its cure.

But was that not to be expected? Is pantheism a genuine alternative to nihilism? Nihilism is the doctrine that there are no real values in nature, not even the values of reason or humane companionship: our (whose?) goals are simply those that evolution has equipped us with (and other creatures will have other goals and ways). There is no natural kind, humankind, that the word 'we' must name: 'we' means me and mine; even 'I', for many really modern thinkers, means nothing very much. Even if 'we' decide to mean 'all humankind' by 'we', the world acknowledges no debt to us and to our values.

We were talking of the Universe at tea, and one of our company declared that he at least was entirely without illusions. He had long since faced the fact that Nature had no sympathy with our hopes and fears, and was completely indifferent to our fate. The Universe, he said, was a great meaningless machine; Man, with his reason and moral judgements, was the product of blind forces, which though they would so soon destroy him, he must yet despise. To endure this tragedy of our fate with passionless despair, never to wince or bow the head, to confront the hostile powers with high disdain, to fix with eyes of scorn the Gorgon face of Destiny, to stand on the brink of the abyss, clenching his fist at the death-pale stars – this, he said, was his attitude, and it produced, as you can imagine, a powerful impression on the company. As for me, I was carried away completely. 'By Jove, that is a stunt!' I cried.[18]

Pearsall Smith's gentle mockery (probably of Bertrand Russell)[19] does not wholly subvert that heroic image. We who live on the other side of the century may be more suspicious of such fantasized heroics in a dying world. But perhaps there is something right about it: how can we take our cue from Nature? Pantheists insist that we should take our place within the living world, with no higher hope than to maintain things so. Heroic fantasists defy the Prince of this World to do his worst: they will maintain, they say, their human dignity, their 'reason and moral judgements', even if the Prince is unimpressed. Nihilists see more clearly, maybe, that the Prince has arranged the seeming heroism, that this is just as much a pointless product of an indifferent world. If nothing matters how can our heroics? If our integrity does matter, then the world must matter. We seem to be faced with a choice between nihilism and pantheism: but don't they amount to the same thing? Either nothing at all has value (and destruction is as welcome as creation), or everything does (and destruction is as welcome as creation).[20]

Pantheism is invoked to remedy the ills we have caused to Gaia: pollution, population crashes, destruction of habitats. But 'pollution' is a biochemical change, an opening up of ecological niches; population crashes are quite usual in evolutionary history; habitats shift back and forth, and always will. Even a nuclear winter will probably be less destructive than past episodes in Gaia's history that the *bacteria* have survived. Why then struggle against the Goddess? Think of it as evolution in action.

A vision of peace?

It is still, obviously, true that many would-be pantheists are environmentalists – but is that not because they are *not* pantheists? Even if 'only man were vile', that would be a sufficiently large exception to demonstrate that not all naturally occurring things embody the Divine. Environmentalists hold an image in their hearts of the true, the paradisal land, which human greed and conceit has maimed. They believe that every thing is lovable – but not that everything that happens should.

And where does this little image of a land intended for all its creatures come from? Whence the idea that human greed can maim the world, but that it is constantly re-called to life? What are the historical roots of the wild suggestion that there is a pattern of right-living that is appropriate to the way things are, even if it is not now how things are?

Chesterton's 'The Ballad of the White Horse', first published in 1911, attempted to identify a different sort of rebel from the 'spirit of laughing ecstatic destruction' that Yeats saw unleashed on Europe (to our cost).

For riseth up against realm and rod,
a thing forgotten, a thing downtrod,
the last, lost giant, even God,
is risen against the world.[21]

Chesterton himself shared all too much of that anti-capitalistic, nationalistic contempt for what he thought Jews were (and was, therefore, a Zionist in hopes that Israelites would not be 'jews').[22] But his praise was of the Jewish God, who has blessed creation and set us in a garden, within a larger world, to tend and keep it on the mere condition that we not take everything as if it were our own. Only those who share that faith, that the Lord is God (which is to say, that the demands of justice and fair-dealing lie at the foundations of the world), can have much reason to expect that those demands will in the end be met.

In brief, the doctrine that there is a way things could be that does not depend simply on mutual competition, a way that serves us as a guiding light, amounts to that distinction between Nature and the Divine that Toynbee and others have blamed for twentieth-century mistakes. What we emphatically do *not* need is a new pantheistic religious sensibility, but a reawakening of something very like theism in its Jewish, Christian, and Muslim guise. We need to believe that there are rules of good behaviour over and above those that godless brigands might devise for their own immediate security.[23] The Jewish scriptures, even as they have been interpreted by Christians, insist (1) that there is something of value in the natural world, whether or not it serves our passing purposes; (2) that we are allowed our modest use of parts of nature explicitly upon condition that we leave it at peace, that we not take all of it; (3) that we are not to imitate what we imagine we see in 'nature' when that conflicts with the demands of love and justice; (4) that merely emotional identification should not be a substitute for careful reasoning, nor reasoning be allowed to subvert the foundations of our life as moral beings; (5) that the spirit of fair-dealing whereby we identify with a wider world than our own life will sustain us through the years that the land, neglected by us in the past, enjoys its sabbaths.[24]

The spirits of wood and stream were not banished merely to release wood, water, earth, and air from any ban upon their usefulness. They were banished because they were no fit models for the human heart. Less poetically: how things currently are is no sure guide to how they should be.

So much is indeed obvious. Although one charge against traditional theists is that they disparage Nature, and ought instead to find the Divine Here-Now, another is that no god worthy of worship could be supposed responsible for so vile a universe. Theists are wrong because they disparage the World but reverence its Creator. Moderns are 'right' because they can conceive no higher standard than Nature's Way, and simultaneously denounce that standard.

> Are God and Nature then at strife,
> that Nature lends such evil dreams?[25]

The only sensible answer would seem to be: yes. What should happen and what does are no closer in the world of non-human nature than in human history, despite the readiness of pantheists to see 'beauty' in the subtle ways of death devised by parasite and predator. But there must be something in the world that is as it should be (or else 'what should be' is an unknown, a figment, of no causal or moral effect). Something like theism is a necessity of thought: the only question is, where are we to find 'what should be'? The standard must be both natural (part of the causal network that is Nature) and supernatural (standing in judgment over against the rest of that Nature). Which is yet another, and familiar, story.

Pantheists, whether they call themselves that or not, regularly insist that what happens 'naturally' is right and proper. We should admire the elegance and splendour of a world where wild dogs tear deers' bellies open while they live, larvae breed in living flesh, and vampire bats spread AIDS. It is more difficult, no doubt, to admire such pests as we ourselves may suffer from, and even those who insist that human beings are only natural organisms like the rest may feel a little differently about multiple murderers than about over-excited mink. Trying to see the good in things is no ignoble policy, and an understandable reaction against the view that saw the non-human world as nothing but the Devil's handiwork. But seeing it all as evil and seeing it all as good amount to the same thing: if it is all good, then our acts in it are good as well (whatever they are); if it is all evil, then our own affective responses are unreliable, and those we think are wicked (and who work to destroy the world) are the true Lord's envoys. Either way we lose our grip on good: either those who throw babies into furnaces in honour of Moloch are an approved part of Nature's Way ('everything is good'), or else our own heartfelt rejection of such practices is only a further twist of the knife ('everything is bad').

Traditional Judaism, Christianity, and Islam all insist both that there is a standard of Righteous Conduct that is bound in the end to be victorious because everything that is draws its strength from that standard, and also that things as they are for us here-now are not such as that standard would require ('there is good *in* everything, but not everything does good'). Those who would arbitrarily remake the world (if they could) and those who think it perfect 'as it is' are alike mistaken. In traditional language: God wills that we should inhabit a world always on the verge of self-destruction, so organized that there can be no competition without co-operation, no lasting success for any individual or kind without a real attention to the equal needs of aliens. We are, as it were, in receipt of a divine revelation in the natural universe, but that revelation is obscured and twisted by the effects of some primaeval sin. Without a clue to what the message must be we would have little chance of reading it; but if there were no message at all 'in nature' there could be none by grace.

And what is that message? When God spoke to Job out of the whirlwind it was not to proclaim the harmonious, man-centred parkland of the humanistic dream, but the wild glory of a universe where no single kind or entity can serve as the sole image of the Divine – apart, perhaps (or so Christians have contended), from that Jewish *ḥasid* who walked in the wilderness with the wild beasts, the late-born Adam through whom the world was made.

The questions remain: how 'naturist' can Christians be, and how much can their mere Christianity contribute to the issue? It is my conviction that there is a distinctively Christian answer, and one that some modern theologians, modernist in their overt concern for the environment, have unnecessarily neglected. Our doctrine has long been that there is someone in the world whose speech and life is God's, and that in him our nature was taken up into the Godhead. That human nature suffered torture, death, and degradation, but he who bore our nature was and is also divinely indestructible, forced – by his permission – 'new strange shapes to take', but as clearly divine in torment (to the eye of faith, the eye that has already caught the clue) as he will be in glory. What we have neglected, but which is implicit in the tradition from the very beginning, is that the whole world was also taken up in him (for there can be no human life without a cosmos to sustain it, nor any clear division between the *human* being and the myriad cells and mitochondria of one human body, and the swarming life-forms of the terrestrial biosphere needed to sustain that body), and that the whole world was founded in him. Conversely, one of the many oddities of modernist theology is that tradition is abused both for neglecting bodily matters and for insisting on the crude materialism of a physical resurrection. If the body (and its attendant biosphere) should not be immortal, neither should it be given much importance.

According to one rabbinic tradition the Lord created the world begin-

ning with Mount Zion. Christian tradition narrows the beginning down
still more: it began with Calvary.[26] Was that God's will? Apparently so: or
at any rate that is the form God's will and wisdom (which is to say, the
Word) takes when acted out in time. It does not follow that we are
commanded to repeat such crucifixions. The Lamb who was slain 'before
the foundation of the world' is the very type of all self-giving, but this is no
excuse for butchering lambs.

To believe in the God and Father of our Lord Jesus Christ is to believe
that all things take their life from one source, however cruelly distorted
their lives may be, and that all may return to table-fellowship with God.
Nature, like Calvary, is what we do to God: but Christ is risen. The
awakened love of Gaia, and the creatures that share the world with us,
requires us to believe both that there are 'natural values' and that not everything that actually or imaginably happens is what should. There are real
resources of good will and imaginative insight in traditional religion and
philosophy that make it unnecessary for us to tread the dangerous route
through pantheism even if we also acknowledge, as we should, that there
are also truths that pantheistic environmentalists have brought to light, and
that some spokesmen for what is generally a sounder doctrine have themselves often given very bad advice. 'The moral consequence of faith in God
is the universal love of all being in him . . . This is [faith's] requirement:
that all beings, not only our friends but also our enemies, not only men but
also animals and the inanimate, be met with reverence, for all are friends in
the friendship of the one to whom we are reconciled in faith.'[27] It is that
Judaic faith which issues more reliably in a conviction of the infinite worth
of *all* those whom God has chosen from infinity, and that ceaselessly
reminds us that there are real things, real values outside the merely social
nexus. And by the same token it is that Judaic faith which should serve to
remind us that oppression does not go unavenged. Those who will not
grant the land her holidays, will find that they have lost her. 'We can
ravage the ecology, suppress the poor, murder prophets, adulterate the
gospel, shake our fists defiantly at God and declare the world a mechanism
and human beings machines. But the System of systems remains the ultimate arbiter, and we can no more secede from its jurisdiction than we can
stop breathing air.'[28]

How does God's Providential Care Extend to Animals?

Thomas E. Hosinski

As an undergraduate I majored in geology, with a special interest in palaeontology. One day towards the end of the basic palaeontology course, deeply awestruck by my professor's summary of the different types of animals that had lived and gone extinct, I asked him why all those animals had lived and died. Most palaeontologists then and now would simply have told me that there is no reason other than evolution's ceaseless exploration of any possible form of life and every possible niche for its survival. But I was studying at a Catholic university and my professor was a man of deep religious faith; he told me that my question was theological in character, not scientific, and that he was not competent to give an answer beyond his conviction that there is some deeper meaning to the history of life.

I narrate this incident because for me it expresses several points which I wish to discuss. First, the question of how divine providence may be bestowed upon animals must be addressed in the broad context of the evolutionary history of life on this planet, not just in the restricted context of animals presently living. Whatever position we come to must take into account and test itself against that evolutionary history, in which contingency, chance, and the operation of blind natural forces apparently play a large role.

A second point we must address is the undeniable ambiguity of nature. If there are experiences of beauty and harmony that lead a William Paley to affirm that 'it is a happy world after all',[1] there are also experiences of pain, suffering, and horrible deaths that lead a Charles Darwin to exclaim 'What a book a devil's chaplain might write on the clumsy, wasteful, blundering, low, and horribly cruel works of nature!'[2] Part of the motivation for my question to my palaeontology professor was a feeling for the magnitude of the suffering and death represented by the evolutionary history of life. Any answer we give must deal with this problem of suffering and evil.

Another subject that any proposed answer to the question must consider is the relation of human beings and our history to animals and the evolutionary history of life. Evolutionary theory discloses that we humans are but one of countless animal species, that we are creatures of the evolutionary development of life on earth, that we are related to all other forms of life and consequently are squarely within nature, not above it. We can no longer assume that there is some immense gulf separating humans from animals, some ontological difference of status lifting humans outside the world of nature so that God's providence for us can be understood differently from God's involvement with the rest of creation. Any position on God's providence for animals must be consistent with our position on God's providence in human life and history, and vice versa.

At root the difficulty confronting us is finding some persuasive way of understanding how God can act in a universe such as science and our own experience reveal to us. Ultimately we need an ontology of nature and history that will enable us to construct a theological cosmology: a vision of how God interacts with the world, a vision that is at once compatible with what science reveals about the nature of reality and with what our religious faith holds about reality based on the revelatory 'event' of Jesus Christ. I offer here a few of the considerations a theological cosmology must take into account, and provide an outline of how God's providential care for animals might be understood.

A useful place to begin is to call attention to the history of life on our planet as we presently know it. We do not know exactly when life emerged, but there is evidence of life in rocks 3.75 billion years old.[3] For 2.4 billion years after the earliest evidence (approximately two-thirds of the entire history of life on earth), all organisms were single-celled creatures of the simplest kind: prokaryotic cells (possessing no organelles, no nucleus, no paired chromosomes, no mitochondria, and no chloroplasts). Eukaryotic cells (with all the complex features lacking in prokaryotic cells) appear in the fossil record approximately 1.4 billion years ago; but for over 700 million years after their appearance, there apparently were no multi-cellular organisms. Multi-cellular organisms emerged approximately 570 million years ago and their development into the multitude of extinct and presently living species of plants and animals occupies only one-sixth of the entire history of life on earth. This represents a veritable explosion of experimentation in forms compared to the massive stability of single-celled organisms for five-sixths of the history of life.

What is more, instead of presenting us with a gradual evolution of many forms out of an original few (the classic 'tree trunk' model of evolutionary history), the fossil evidence for multi-cellular organisms seems to indicate a profusion of initial forms (more like a bush having many shoots emerging from the ground), which were subsequently 'pruned' by mass extinctions so that only a few of the initial phyla survived. These surviving phyla diversified into many orders, genera, and species, which were themselves severely 'pruned' by the periodic occurrence of mass extinctions.[4] One of the leading contemporary theorists of evolution, Stephen Jay Gould, has argued that this evolutionary history of life is fundamentally contingent in character.[5] He means that science can offer no reasons for the actual course of life's history other than the facticity of the history itself. The history of life appears to be exactly like human history, composed entirely of contingent events that might easily have been otherwise.

All this appears to indicate that we would not be wrong to affirm a great deal of freedom in the natural order, a great deal of flexibility. Instead of being a realm of determinism, in which natural laws dictate all outcomes, the natural world appears to be a large-scale experiment in the pursuit of possibilities, in which the outcomes are largely a result of freedom, contingency, and even chance. Just as the actual course of human history is the result of a combination of chance and what humans in fact choose to do in their freedom, so too the history of life seems to have just this sort of contingent character. Contemporary physics, particularly quantum theory and the physics of dynamic systems, leads to similar conclusions concerning even 'non-living' matter and the world of sub-atomic particles.[6]

Our view of providence, of how God acts in the universe, must be able to deal with the freedom that seems to be pervasively present in nature. It must be compatible with the apparently contingent character of the history of life (and perhaps of universal history). Most importantly, our view of providence must have some way of reconciling a God of goodness and love with the horrendous suffering to which life on earth has always been subject and which manifests itself most strikingly in the periodic mass extinctions that punctuate the history of life.

To most theologians addressing these and related issues, it has seemed clear that an understanding of God and God's action that is compatible with what science is revealing and implying about the nature of reality will involve several important revisions of the traditional idea of God. Coming to the question with different approaches and utilizing widely different resources, theologians have achieved a remarkable degree of consensus on the general outlines of such a revised understanding.[7] The major points can be summarized swiftly.

　1. God as Creator is understood to endow all creatures, not just human beings, with genuine freedom.

2. In order to understand the world's freedom as truly genuine, we must affirm a limitation on God's power, whether it be self-imposed by God for the sake of the creature or an inherent feature of reality to which God is subject.[8] In either case God can no longer be understood to be omnipotent in the classic sense.

3. Respect for the freedom of creation also requires us to understand the future to be truly open, for God as much as for the world; and this requires us to hold that God does not know the future, for the simple reason that the future does not yet exist to be known. Thus although God's knowledge of past and present is perfect and God grasps all future possibilities, we cannot affirm God's omniscience in the classic sense.

4. God must also be understood to be receptive to and influenced by what is done in the world's freedom. God is consequently affected by the world, vulnerable to it, though not entirely or finally captive to it.

5. God must be understood as somehow experiencing time, as well as being transcendent to it.

In short, while maintaining many aspects of the traditional understanding of God's transcendence, a contemporary idea of God consonant with the view of reality revealed by modern science must also affirm God's immanence in the world in a new way: we must conceive of God being influenced by the world and interacting with it.

A view of God developed along these general lines implies an understanding of how God acts in the universe, which is the crucial problem in working out a contemporary notion of providence. Different approaches are possible. But in my own reflections on this topic I have found Alfred North Whitehead's analysis of God's relation to potentiality or possibility most helpful. Of all the philosophers with whom I am acquainted, Whitehead took most seriously the fact of the occurrence of novelty in the world and sought to deal with the underlying philosophical problem of potentiality or possibility. In Whitehead's philosophy, God acts on the world by organizing and presenting potentials or possibilities.[9] God creates the world by making it possible, by endowing each agent in creation with its potentials and the freedom to create itself on this divinely-given ground. Each agent is free to actualize any of the potentials or possibilities open to it in its situation. The only way God can influence the free self-actualization of each agent is by 'luring' it towards those possibilities God values as most beautiful and good. Thus God acts in the world through persuasion, not through coercion. What actually happens is finally in the hands of the causal agents of the world.

At each moment God experiences what each agent in the universe has chosen to do in its freedom and responds to it by presenting to each agent in the next moment new possibilities for good. In this way God seeks to overcome whatever evils or tragedies have resulted from the exercise of freedom by all agents in the universe. Thus, apart from the persuasion towards the best possibility (which is an unconscious experience even in those agents capable of consciousness), God can exert no direct causal influence on the world. Anything we might want to consider divine action can occur only with the co-operative action of causal agents within the world.

Before employing this philosophical view to address the specific question of how God's providence is bestowed on animals, we must test it to determine whether Christian theology can adopt such a theory of divine action. I would argue that this view of God's action on the world is in conformity with what we witness in the life of Jesus Christ. When we examine Jesus' life, we do not see him acting with coercive power, or the power of force. Instead we see Jesus acting by teaching and living God's 'kingdom', acting with the persuasive power of ideals, with the 'lure' of beauty and value and holiness. We see him unresisting at his arrest, trial, and execution; we see a deliberate rejection of violent means. We see him suffering and dying, 'powerless' in the hands of those who opposed him and used coercive force against him. Yet the tragedy and evil of his death was overcome and transformed in his resurrection, which gave new possibilities and new hope to his followers for ever after.

If Jesus Christ is our strongest clue to how God acts in the world, then what we see is a God who acts through the presentation of possibilities, ideals, and values; a God who must suffer what the world chooses to do with its freedom; and a God who overcomes and transforms the suffering and evil in the world with healing and new hope in redemptive love.

This view of how God acts does not demean God or render God ineffectual. Persuasion can be a very powerful force, as we know from our own experience. And our minds cannot begin to plumb the infinite wealth of possibility. The resurrection of Jesus Christ is for Christian theology the firmest sort of evidence that God can bring about the wholly unexpected. As Jesus himself is reported to have said, 'With God all things are possible' (Matt. 19.26). Thus we must not underestimate what God can bring about in the world through the power of divine persuasion.

With this view of how God acts, we can affirm that in a metaphysically general sense God extends providential care to animals in the same way God extends it to human beings: at each moment God endows each creature with its possibilities and seeks to 'lure' each animal to actualize in its freedom the best of the possibilities open to it given its situation. God cherishes the beauty of each creature and through the divine 'lure' seeks to bring about the best for each creature. Whitehead's philosophy suggests this way of understanding God's presence to, and care about, each creature in the world.

To recognize the foundational implications of the doctrine of creation, as Whitehead's metaphysics does, is an important part of any understanding of how God's providence is extended to animals. There would be no universe at all without God's role as Creator, making the universe possible at each moment. In Whitehead's philosophy, each causal agent in the world (each 'actual entity') begins its self-creative becoming in each moment by taking into itself the creative endowment it receives from God: its possibilities and its drive to make something of itself in that moment. As Whitehead once said, 'The world lives by its incarnation of God in itself.'[10] When one reflects on the implications of this position, one can conclude that it is not naïve to believe that God cares for animal life, that God 'feeds the birds' of the air. This belief is expressing a religious intuition of the underlying religious dimension of our universe; it is grasping God's involvement and immanence in making our universe possible, and grasping as well that all good things can rightly be traced back ultimately to God's creative action.

For a variety of reasons, however, the divine lure towards the good and the beautiful will not always be followed. Creatures choose for themselves, and in their freedom may actualize any of the possibilities open to them, even the one God values least. There is nothing in the nature of freedom itself that determines it will always be exercised for the best. Thus we are not faced with having to say that God intended the actual course of evolutionary history or all the experiences of any individual life. Because of the exercise of freedom in the entire natural universe, many things can and do happen to bring suffering to animals. There is conflict of purposes pursued by different agents exercising freedom and this will result in great suffering, especially when animals are acted upon with coercive power they cannot avoid. God can act in the world only through persuasive power and through the co-operation of the causal agents in the world. The very freedom of all creatures in the world acts as a limit on what God can do; freedom cannot be coerced without destroying it. Thus God can only seek to persuade the creatures of the world along the best path. The coercive power exercised by causal agents in their freedom can ignore and trample upon persuasion and resist co-operation with the divine lures. All God can do in such situations is to suffer with suffering creatures and seek to bring the best out of bad situations. This view of God's action and the limitations on what God can do takes seriously the contingent character and ambiguity of the evolutionary history of life and of the experiences in any individual life and offers a solution to the problem of evil.

There is one difference between God's providential care for animals and God's providential care for humans that we must recognize. Human beings, so far as we know, are unique in their ability to bring things to reflective consciousness. We humans are capable of grasping God's 'lures' to the good and the beautiful quite consciously, whereas for all other animals the experience of these divine lures is an unconscious one (as it is even for us most of the time). One can argue that what the great religions teach is precisely this, the conscious recognition of God's lures for us. In Christianity, for example, the symbol 'kingdom of God' presents to us in all its richness God's vision of what is possible for us and the world if we follow God's lure. We must recognize, then, our own capability of acting as instruments of God's providence for animals, exercising our freedom in co-operation with God's lures toward a universal 'kingdom' of peace and harmony.[11] We can, to some degree, alleviate the suffering of animals, at least that which we ourselves inflict on them; and in this way we act as co-operative agents of God's providential care.

But Whitehead's philosophy also allows us to affirm a higher kind of providence: an ultimate redemption of the suffering, fragmented, disharmonious world. In Whitehead's philosophy, each moment of experience in the world affects God, is taken into God's own experience, and lives everlastingly in God. Although I do not have space here to explore the technical aspects of his argument, Whitehead affirms that in God's developing experience all creatures are not simply received into God, but are transformed, 'purged', and harmonized in the everlasting unity of God's own life.[12] What is ambiguity in the temporal world is redeemed and harmonized in God. The sufferings and evils are still quite real, but they are healed and redeemed in God's own life and find some ultimate meaning and harmonization in relation to God's eternal vision of value and beauty. This seems to me to give philosophical expression to the promise expressed in Isaiah's vision of a peaceable kingdom where the lion and the lamb lie down together (Isa. 11.6–7. 9).

This vision and promise allows us to hope that the highest aspect of God's providential care – ultimate redemption and inclusion in the everlasting life of God's 'kingdom' – will in fact be extended to all God's creatures.

The Fall and Predation

12

Are Animals Fallen?

Michael Lloyd

> Not long ago I was sleeping in a cabin in the woods and was awoken in the middle of the night by the sounds of a struggle between two animals. Cries of terror and extreme agony rent the night, intermingled with the sounds of jaws snapping bones and flesh being torn from limbs. One animal was being savagely attacked, killed and then devoured by another. A clearer case of a horrible event in nature, a natural evil, has never been presented to me. It seemed to me self-evident that the natural law that *animals must savagely kill and devour each other in order to survive* was an evil natural law and that the obtaining of this law was sufficient evidence that God did not exist.

So writes Quentin Smith at the outset of 'An Atheological Argument from Evil Natural Laws'[1] – an argument which he believes justifies the conclusion that 'the horror I experienced on that dark night in the woods . . . was a brief and terrifying glimpse into the ultimately evil dimension of a godless world'.[2] His argument, in outline and shorn of its philosophical sophistication, runs as follows: some animals are, by nature, carnivorous, but there is no necessary reason why this should be so. Tigers, for example, have in fact evolved as carnivorous animals, but there is no logical reason why an animal should not have evolved instead of the tiger which is identical to the tiger except that it has the property of being nourished by vegetables instead of meat. A world tigered by such vegetarian tiger-counterparts would be a better world than one tigered by the carnivorous tigers which we know in our world, and therefore an omnipotent, omniscient, and omnibenevolent God would have created tiger-counterparts instead of tigers, and the fact that our world has tigers in it is thus an argument against the existence of such a God. The same goes, *mutatis mutandis*, for all the other carnivores. A world in which one species has, for its survival, to prey upon and destroy another is not one that you would expect a good God to create.

The recognition that nature is red in tooth and claw and that this is difficult to square with theistic belief is an ancient one to which Smith has given new and rigorous expression, and it constitutes a serious problem for theistic believers. In responding to it, I want to begin by intensifying it. For theists who believe in the omnipotence, omniscience, and omnibenevolence of God, the problem is bad enough. For Christians, the problem is even more pronounced, not just for the usual reason that the more one emphasizes the love of God the more of a problem suffering becomes, but also because of other aspects of the distinctively Christian vision of God: a world in which one species has to devour another is not the world that one would expect a good God to create. It is *certainly* not the sort of world which one would expect the God we meet in Christ to have created. The cross reveals God as the one who lays down life that others might live. The natural world is one in which animals kill others that they themselves might live. The movement of the one in reckless self-giving is in a totally different direction from the movement of the other in ruthless self-preservation.

I begin here because that protest against the predatory character of nature springs precisely and most profoundly from a christological conception of God. In the cross of Christ, Christians have an ontological basis for their instinctive abhorrence of the conflict and violence which characterize the animal world. We may in passing question whether atheists have any such basis for the protest that they rightly feel and articulate against the terror and agony to which the animal world is subjected. If God sets the norm, then we have a yardstick by which we may measure the cruelty of nature and assess it to be evil, but if there is nothing beyond nature with which to compare it and by which to assess it, then on what basis might we make such a judgment? However, counter-attack constitutes no defence, and we must attend to the contradiction between the nature of nature as revealed in the cries of terror and extreme agony which so disturbed Quentin Smith that dark night in the woods, and the nature of God as revealed in the agonized cries that came from the wood of the cross that dark afternoon.

First set of answers: 'It is not bad'

Christian theologians have responded to this problem in one of three ways. First, some simply deny that there is a case to answer. Either they argue that animals do not in fact experience pain, despite all appearance to the contrary,[3] or they accept that animals do experience pain, but deny that fact any moral significance.[4] The former claim is hard to assess. Whilst allowing for the dangers of anthropomorphic projection of human feelings on to animal symptoms, it is hard to accept that there is *no* correlation between what looks like pain in animals and what we experience as pain in ourselves, and most will feel that any theodicy which depends upon the absolute denial of animal suffering thereby loses plausibility and moral credibility. However, even if it were established that no pain afflicted the animal creation at all, the Christian theist would not be out of the woods, for, as we observed earlier, the whole direction of animal predation seems contrary to the movement of Christ's self-offering. Even without pain, predation does not seem unambiguously to declare the glory of God, and theodicies which seek to justify predation as part of the creational purposes of God tend to adopt anti-Christian attitudes in the attempt. Austin Farrer, for example, praises eloquently 'that enormous vitality of force' which causes 'every physical creature to absolutize itself, so far as in it lies, and to be the whole world',[5] which seems almost Nietzschean in its approval of the will to power. Farrer asks: 'if the several systems are to occupy just as much free space each as they need, without crowding their neighbours; if none is ever to incorporate any part of another in itself, except in such fashion that it preserves or even enhances the self-being of that other; then what sort of a world shall we have?'[6] The answer would seem to be, 'one which reflects the vitality and love of our triune, servant-minded, self-sacrificial God'. Why should a Christian theodicy adopt a definition of vitality which includes the will to power, and a denigration of service, love, and respect as 'slave morality'? Yet that would seem to be the implication behind Farrer's value judgment here. If the characteristics of God's triune nature are fellowship, love, and grace, should we rejoice in the desire of God's creatures to absolutize themselves at the expense of one another? That desire seems completely at odds with a God who, far from seeking to be the whole world, created a world which is genuinely contingent and 'other' and made creatures which are free to act in ways that oppose God's will;[7] the God we see in Jesus Christ, who, far from absolutizing himself, emptied himself and took the form of a servant; who, far from rooting out the weak or imposing his will upon them, sought out the weak and asked them what they would have him do for them; who, far from killing others that he might live, gave up his life that others might live; who, in the incarnation, resurrection, and ascension, incorporated creaturehood into himself precisely in order to preserve and enhance the self-being of that creation. As for the denial of moral significance to the pain of animals and the predatory pattern of their interlocking teleologies, it is frankly hard to square this indifferent god with the God who made both killer and victim, who 'hatest nothing that thou hast made', whose omniscience and providential concern extend to the single sparrow which falls or is sold, and whose purpose is to unite all things in Christ in such a way as to restore all creation to that peace and harmony which, I shall argue below, were always God's intention for it. The question remains how such a God made such a world. There is a case to answer.

Second set of answers: 'It is bad but necessary and worthwhile'

The second response is to acknowledge that there is a case to answer, to accept that God has made a world which in this significant respect fails to reflect the goodness of God's character, but to argue that this is a necessary price to pay for some other feature of what remains essentially a good world. For some, that feature of a good world which necessitates and justifies a divided and predatory natural order (and the suffering which ensues from it) is aesthetic – that although the pain of the part is bad, it contributes overall to the good of the whole. In Augustine's image, adopted from Plotinus, the dark parts of the canvas are necessary to the artistic integrity and beauty of the total picture. Or in Barth's musical analogy, discords are necessary to the music of Mozart, but ultimately they find their resolution. In the context of the whole, they find their proper place and their utterly essential role, and so it is with the shadow side of creation, characterized as it is by suffering. And, in response, I have to say that if God requires God's creatures to suffer for the sake of some artistic design, if God gets some sort of aesthetic pleasure out of predation and pain, then what we are dealing with is a cosmic sadist, and not the God that we meet in the face of Jesus Christ. If God as composer has written cries of pain into the score of human history, then it is not a work of art, it is the work of a sick mind.

The other main candidate for the feature of a good world for which we have to pay the necessary price of natural evil is human free will. Without natural evil, says John Hick, we would not have that epistemic distance from God which alone establishes our independence and freedom. Without natural evil, says Richard Swinburne, we would not know how to carry out evil acts, and without that knowledge we would not possess significant freedom. Smith subjects both these positions to severe and, I believe, successful criticism. What I want to do here is not to rehearse arguments against particular positions but to show that this whole set of answers is vulnerable to one trenchant theological objection. What they have in common is that they are all *instrumental*. On each of these readings, God is responsible for the suffering involved, but not culpable, because God is using it as an instrument in the pursuit of some greater good, be it aesthetic richness or human freedom. These instrumental accounts of suffering seem to me to be open to a number of generic criticisms. First, they tend to be anthropocentric.[8] Hick does not mention animal suffering at all in his statement of 'An Irenaean Theodicy'. Indeed, he ignores it in his very definitions: 'A morally wrong act is, basically, one which harms some part of the *human* community . . .'.[9] And when forced to address the issue by one of the other contributors to the symposium, he first dismisses 'the traditional doctrine of the perversion of the natural order as a consequence of the Fall' and then suggests that 'The question, then, is not why animals feel the kinds of pains that they feel, but why there should be a realm of animal life at all.'[10] So anthropocentric is Hick's position that not only can he offer no theodical account of animal suffering, he can see no reason for animal existence unless it be to add to the epistemic distance at which humanity is set. As Smith rightly points out, it is hard to see how this is consistent with a Christian conception of God: 'No omnibenevolent creator would use animals as a mere means to the end of human welfare, treating them as if they had no value or rights by themselves and could be tortured with complacency on a mass scale for the sake of "spiritual benefits" to the human species. Animals are sentient creatures capable of suffering and as such are moral ends in themselves; the failure to treat them as such is a sign of selective benevolence and callousness and is inconsistent with the definition of God.'[11]

Secondly, instrumental views leave God directly responsible for suffering. If predation and animal suffering are logically necessary to God's purposes for the world, then they obviously have a more direct place in the divine will than if they are seen as a strange and unwanted aberration, and the distinction between God allowing evil and God deliberately creating evil is correspondingly blurred. Yet I want to argue that this is an important distinction and that the instrumental readings ignore it to their great disadvantage. Let me explain this claim by reference to the parent analogy. Hick himself suggests that

Men are not to be thought of on the analogy of animal pets, whose life is to be made as agreeable as possible, but rather on the analogy of human children, who are to grow to adulthood in an environment whose primary and overriding purpose is not immediate pleasure but the realization of the most valuable potentialities of human personality. Needless to say, this characterization of God as the heavenly Father is not a merely random illustration but an analogy which lies at the heart of the Christian faith . . . And so it is altogether relevant to a Christian understanding of this world to ask, How does the best parental love express itself in its influence upon the environment in which children are to grow up?[12]

Yet that analogy seems to me to count against Hick's position and any which sees natural evil as necessarily built into creation. For, though one might understand parents deciding not to shield their child from some potentially painful experience on the grounds that the child may grow and develop and deepen in and through the experience, it is hard to imagine any loving parents deliberately arranging some painful experience for their child to go through. Yet this is what the instrumentalists would have us believe of God – that God deliberately created a world including pain, for the good that it would do us.[13]

Thirdly, the instrumental answers diminish the praise-worthiness of God. It is one of the privileges of the church that 'you may declare the praises of him who called you out of darkness into his wonderful light' (I Peter 2.9). It detracts from those praises if it was God who put us in that darkness in the first place. Could we muster wholehearted praise for a God who rescues us from a situation God had deliberately created from the out-set? The prophetic promise that the wolf will lie down with the lamb (Isa. 11.6–9) is seen as one of the grounds and causes of universal proclamation and praise (Isa. 12.1, 4–6). But if it were God who set up the structures of predation and violence originally, how genuine would be the gratitude of creation? Austin Farrer speaks of God as 'our rescuer from that whirlpool, in which all things, whether good or evil, senseless or sentient, are sucked down'.[14] Yet if God created that whirlpool and placed us within it, how fulsome will be our praise? T. F. Torrance can speak similarly of how 'The purpose of the Incarnation . . . was to penetrate into the innermost centre of our contingent existence, in its finite, fragile and disrupted condition, in order to deliver it from the evil to which it had become subjected, healing and re-ordering it from its ontological roots and entirely renewing its relation to the Creator',[15] because he believes that we should not 'regard evil and disorder in the universe as in any way intended or as given a direct function by God in the development of His creation'.[16] What the instru-mentalists have in common, however, is a belief that natural evil *does* have a direct function in the development of God's creation. They cannot there-fore speak in the same way of God rescuing God's creatures, and our praise of God the Redeemer must correspondingly be weaker.[17]

Fourthly, the instrumental answers drive a wedge between creation and redemption. Either predation and pain were, and remain, God's eternal purpose for creation, in which case redemption is unnecessary, undesirable, and impossible; or they were part of God's *temporary* purpose for creation, in which case creation and redemption seem to point in worryingly different directions.[18] C. W. Formby draws out the problem with this latter position: it implies, he says, that 'God, having continued the organic process as a purely constructive method for countless ages, upon the self-centred principles of ruthless competition and instinct-control, sought in later stages to unmake what He had made, by spiritual influences, by recourse to the moral teaching of the Bible, and by the power of the Incarnation.' 'Thus,' he concludes, 'the method attributed [by this position] to God amounts virtually to self-contradiction.'[19] There are three areas, one theological and two pastoral, in which the wedge thus driven between creation and redemption is particularly damaging. Theologically, the seemingly different directions of creation and redemption, which gnosticism accounted for by attributing one to a demiurge and one to the good God, here become absorbed into the one God, placing disintegrative tensions within any systematic conception of the nature of the Godhead. Pastorally, we are still required to operate with a more direct understanding of the place of natural evil within the purposes of God than is appropriate within a pastoral context. And pastorally again, at the human end of the spectrum, such a view requires us to speak of the 'gulf that lies between humanness and what religion calls redemption',[20] whereas I suggest that it is pastorally important to insist that salvation in Christ does not detract from our humanness but restores it. If, theologically, we see creation and redemption pulling in different directions, then, pastorally, we shall ourselves be pulled in different directions. If, however, we see redemption as precisely *re*demption of the created order, then we shall see, and experience, redemption as becoming ourselves. Christ at his ascension did not abandon or jettison his humanity, and we, by being in him, do not leave ours behind either. Thus there is no gulf between humanness and redemption, and if the instrumental views require such a gulf, as they seem to do, that correspondingly weakens their case.

Fifthly, the instrumental answers tend to justify the *status quo*. The ministry of Jesus, however, and (I would argue) the human vocation and (therefore) the mission of the church is not so much to justify the *status quo* as to challenge and change it. And even where we cannot change it, we must not dignify it with the status of normality.

Sixthly, the cross acts as God's protest against the divisions and disorder of creation. As Torrance writes:

The Cross of Christ tells us unmistakably that all physical evil, not only pain, suffering, disease, corruption, death and of course cruelty and venom in animal as well as human behaviour, but also 'natural' calamities, devastations, and monstrosities, are an outrage against the love of God and a contradiction of good order in His creation. This does not allow us to regard evil and disorder in the universe as in any way intended or as given a direct function by God in the development of His creation, although it does mean that even these enormities can be made to serve His final end for the created order, much as He has made the dastardly violence of men in crucifying Jesus to serve His healing purpose for mankind, without in any way justifying our human evil and guilt that brought Jesus to the Cross.[21]

The logic behind this statement has to do, partly, I suspect, with the diametrically different direction of Christ's self-offering from that of self-preservational predation, as discussed above. It may, however, have to do also with the salvific scope of the cross. The cross challenges that which it seeks to heal. The very fact of healing implies the need for healing. The very fact of reconciliation implies an intended harmony that has been broken. If salvation is cosmic in its scope,[22] then it is cosmic too in its challenge, critique, and protest. That which is healed is thereby revealed as fallen. It is not the healthy who need a doctor, but the sick.

Lastly, all the instrumental answers are particularly vulnerable to the challenge which Ivan Karamazov makes to his devout brother, Alyosha, in Dostoyevsky's *The Brothers Karamazov*:

'Tell me yourself, I challenge you – answer. Imagine that you are creating a fabric of human destiny with the object of making men happy in the end, giving them peace and rest at last, but that it was essential and inevitable to torture to death only one tiny creature – that baby beating its breast with its fist, for instance – and to found that edifice on its unavenged tears, would you consent to be the architect on those conditions? Tell me, and tell me the truth.'

'No, I wouldn't consent,' said Alyosha softly.[23]

Instrumental approaches to the problem of evil are particularly vulnerable to this challenge because they see suffering as essential to the divine edifice, and therefore as directly willed by God. The only question that remains is whether the end justifies the means.[24] Ivan's instinct, and I think it is a sound one, is that suffering cannot adequately be addressed from one end alone. Eschatology by itself is not sufficient; however great the happiness, peace, and rest on offer, they do not justify the means. The problem must be addressed at the other end as well. We need an account of evil in which God is not only victoriously against it at the end but is also resolutely against it at the beginning. In other words, we need a doctrine of the Fall as well as an eschatology. With a doctrine of the Fall, suffering and violence, and ruthless self-assertion, are no longer seen as essential or inevitable, no longer seen as having any direct place in the creational intentions of God; in fact they are not therefore 'means' at all. They are deprived of the status of normality, and we are mandated to fight them and to alleviate their effects and to work for their eradication without any fear that in so doing we may be opposing the will and purpose of God or depriving our world of any good that is essentially dependent upon them. The only possible defence for God against the charge of making a world riddled with suffering and violence is that God didn't. And that is what the doctrine of the Fall tells us.

Third set of answers: 'It is bad, and not the work or will of God'

The third set agrees with Smith that 'the natural law that *animals must savagely kill and devour each other in order to survive*' is an evil natural law, but denies that God set up creation with that evil natural law in place. Predation is part of the way things are now, but 'from the beginning, it was not so'. This answer suggests that there has been a hiatus on the line from the way God intended things to the way things are now, a Fall away from God's creational purposes. It sees that Fall as being cosmic in its scope and not limited to human sin. In the particular terms of the question at issue here, it believes that animals are part of the fallen creation, that despite their status as creatures, their current characteristics and interactions cannot be unambiguously equated with the will of their Creator. 'If nature is fallen, then there is no straightforward line to be drawn from present reality to the purposes of God.'[25]

Those who hold thus to the fallenness of the whole of creation do so not primarily to get faith out of an apologetic hole, but for intrinsic theological and christological reasons which they see embedded in the revelation of God in Christ and scripture. Some of these reasons we have already explored indirectly in our critique of the first two sets of answers; we shall look briefly at three more. First, the cleanness and uncleanness laws: as George Caird put it, 'Among creatures which the Levitical code declares to be unclean . . . are all beasts and birds of prey . . . are we not dealing here with a naïve expression of the idea that nature red in tooth and claw has in some measure escaped the control of the divine holiness?'[26] Secondly, in the person of Christ, that control was being re-established, and natural evil was being undone. Not only did the blind receive their sight and the lame walk, the lepers get cleansed, the deaf hear, and the dead get raised up, but storms were stilled and disorder in the natural world was turned to order and peace. Here at last is a human being doing what human beings were called to do – subduing[27] all that resists God's rule and dislocates creation. And that which resists God's rule extends beyond the confines of humanity. Thirdly, there are the prophetic visions of creation at peace.[28] If, in Christ, the control of the divine holiness, the mediated rule of God over creation, the kingdom of God (in fact) was being re-established, then what we have in Christ is a glimpse of the eschaton present and incarnate in the midst of human history, an anticipation of creation healed and restored. And what we have in the prophets is the promise that that re-establishment will be completed, that eschaton ushered in, and that kingdom unambiguously co-extensive with the whole of creation. Now, if the wolf is to lie down with the lamb and the leopard with the goat, and if we are not to drive a wedge between creation and redemption nor leave God guilty of self-contradiction, then we must see the mutually harmful and destructive interactions of the animal realm as originally inimical to the creational intention of God, as historically assaulted by the recreative, restorative, and reconciliatory ministry of Christ, and as ultimately to be swept away by the oceanic knowledge of God in the messianic age.

The question must now be faced as to how that which was inimical to the creational intention of an omnipotent God could have come to be. Granted that the whole of creation is fallen, how did it fall? Granted that the divisions of creation are not a design fault of the Creator but the result of free decisions by free creatures, what account may we give of the volitional process or processes which brought about that Fall? Since Darwin, it has not been possible to characterize all the divisions of creation as the effects of the human Fall, because the evidence suggests that predation, pain, disease, and death pre-dated the emergence of human beings. Those who have sought to retain the notion of a fallen creation in modern times have therefore looked elsewhere for the agency which occasioned that fallenness, and three candidates have been presented.

The first is the 'World-Soul'. In 1927, N. P. Williams published his still standard work on *The Ideas of the Fall and of Original Sin*. His starting-point was the unequivocal acceptance of the necessity of fallenness:

If savagery and cruelty are the expressions of a fundamental law, how evil must be that law, and how deep its discordance with the will of the all-loving Creator revealed by Christ, Who clothes the lilies of the field, and without Whom not one sparrow falls to the ground. If we face the facts candidly, we must admit that no one of us, if he had been in the position of Demiurge, would have created a universe which was compelled by the inner necessity of its being to evolve the cobra, the tarantula, and the bacillus of diphtheria. How, then, shall that God, the infinite ardours and pulsations of Whose love bear the same relation to our weak emotions of sympathy and fellow-feeling as the infinity of His wisdom does to our dim and limited knowledge, have done so? The answer can only be that He did not do so; that He did not create such a universe; that, in the words of the most ancient Scriptures of our monotheistic faith, in the beginning 'God saw everything that He had made, and, behold, it was very good.' To explain evil in Nature, no less than in man, we are compelled to assume a Fall – a revolt against the will of the Creator, a declension from the beauty and glory which God stamped upon His work at the beginning.[29]

As to who it is that thus falls, revolts, and declines, Williams rejects human beings as the ultimate culprits 'because we know that the strong preyed upon the weak, that "tooth and claw" were "red with ravin", and that the "dragons of the prime . . . tare each other in their slime," millions of years before our race was born'.[30] Against Kant and Hegel, however, he insists that the Fall must have taken place in time, 'for any attempt to lift the ultimate origin of evil out of Time plunges us into the gulfs either of dualism or of unmoral monism'.[31] Instead of the human Fall, he suggests the 'conception of a collective fall of the race-soul of humanity in an indefinitely remote past'.[32] He draws on the Platonic and Plotinian category of the World-Soul, or, rather, he redraws it, insisting that it should be seen as a created being and not a necessary emanation of God, that it fell away voluntarily from conformity with the will of its Creator, and that it constituted, in personal but collective form, the totality of (not just human but) all organic life. It is difficult to assess this hypothesis. Clearly, at the time that Williams wrote, the idea of a collective cosmic entity was in its heyday – witness Bergson's Life-Force and Jung's collective unconscious – and Williams is justified in his claim that 'This conception of the Life-Force permeates much of the cosmological speculation of modern times.'[33] The weakness of this position in terms of its continuing explanatory power is two-fold. First, it is, as Williams admits, speculation. Now, that is not fatal to his case; up to a point, any suggested answer to this question is bound to involve speculation. However, since he rejects the hypothesis of the Fall of the angels being the cause of the fallenness of nature because of 'the total and utter absence of any sort of serious evidence',[34] then to postulate the notion of a World-Soul being responsible for the divisions of the natural order would seem to leave him vulnerable to his own criticism. At least the claimed agency of the former has some grounding in the biblical narratives and in the teaching and ministry of Jesus. The claimed agency of the World-Soul has none. Angels are part of traditional Christian discourse and theology in a way that the World-Soul is not. Secondly, whilst the concept of a collective entity was part of cosmological speculation in Williams' day, it is not in ours, and few are likely to find it compelling now. However, it is a coherent position and has the strengths, first, 'of relieving God from responsibility for the origin of evil',[35] and, secondly, of embracing 'our modern view of man as organic to Nature'.[36]

The second candidate for the agency whereby the fallenness of nature was brought about is nature itself. Process theodicy, based upon the 'neo-classical metaphysics' of Whitehead and Hartshorne, attributes to every level of reality[37] some degree of freedom and therefore believes that 'all creatures great and small have some power with which to deviate from the divine will for them . . . Accordingly, if God has always worked with materials that were not necessarily in a perfect state, and which have some inherent power to deviate from God's aims and to influence their successors forevermore, there is no reason to infer that cancer, polio, tornadoes, and earthquakes exist because God wanted our world to have them.'[38] Thus, process theodicy too works on the assumption that nature is fallen, and it traces that fallenness to the myriad occasions[39] on which God's suggested course of action has been rejected. In its stronger expositions, process theodicy knowingly and willingly sacrifices the omnipotence of God[40] in such a way as to make it difficult to square with biblical theism in general and with any eschatological hope in particular.[41] Some writers,[42] however, have tried to use the categories of process theodicy without embracing a full process metaphysic. The problem with this more modest position is that it still ascribes the agency of fallenness to that which is less than personal. This raises questions both about the plausibility of such a schema (i.e. whether sub-personal agents can be said to make anything even analogous to a moral decision),[43] and about its worthwhileness (i.e. whether the freedom of such sub-personal agents is a good great enough to justify the suffering that it allows).[44]

The third suggested candidate for the event(s) which vitiated the creative process is the Fall of the angels. C. S. Lewis,[45] E. L. Mascall,[46] Dom Illtyd Trethowan,[47] Hans Urs von Balthasar,[48] Alvin Plantinga,[49] and Stephen Davis[50] all take seriously the biblical language of angels and demons, and argue that, if there is substance to such language, and if there has been a moral revolt within the spiritual dimension of the created order, then 'it seems reasonable to suppose that defection and rebellion in the angelic realm will drastically disorder the material world, and that, while its development will not be entirely frustrated, it will be grievously hampered and distorted'.[51] Within this view, death, disease, division, and predation are seen as symptoms of this distortion, consequences of the angelic Fall rather than part of the good order of creation. Creation is thus already fallen before ever human beings evolve – there are already aspects of creation which need to be subdued (Gen. 1. 28), there is already created reality (the serpent) which works against the divine purpose, and the apparently harmonious environment into which God places humanity (Eden) is only a garden, not the whole of creation. So when human beings emerge, they are given the task of healing that which has already fallen, of subduing that which is already distorting and disfiguring the good creation of God.[52] Humanity, however, did not respond to that vocation, but joined in the rebellion and exacerbated the divisions. Thus to blame the angelic Fall for the origin of natural evil is not to evade all responsibility for its continuing occurrence. Nor is it to leave all hope in merely human hands. For there has been One who did not join in the rebellion, who accepted the human vocation, and who therefore exercised that redemptive dominion over creation to which humanity had always been called. Thus victims of natural evil were healed, death was undone, and nature's destructiveness defused. So the nature and healing miracles of Christ are both glimpses back to the forfeited potentialities of faithful humanity in the creation purposes of God, and glimpses forward to the future restoration and renewal of heaven and earth.

Quentin Smith is aware of this third answer, at least in the philosophical formulation given it by Plantinga. He admits 'that it is possible that all instances of E [the evil natural law that animals must savagely kill and devour each other in order to survive] are effects of free decisions of fallen angels and that the positive value of the free activity of these angels outweighs the negative value of the instances of E', but he insists that this is not actually the case. How does he know this? 'I would explain that I have probabilistic knowledge that there are no fallen angels who cause the instances of E. *There is no evidence* that there are free non-human creatures who cause the instances of E and this fact justifies the belief that there are probably no such creatures.' However, it is not clear that such an evidentialist challenge is sufficient to damage the plausibility of a hypothesis. In any package of beliefs, the weight does not have to be borne equally by all of the elements. A relatively unsupported assertion may be 'carried' by more supported assertions if it bears some organic link with them. In a scientific hypothesis, deductions may be made from more grounded and established conclusions, and these deductions need not have any evidential support at all to be accepted as valid and plausible components of the hypothesis. Landau's assertions about neutron stars are a case in point; they were not verified evidentially until Jocelyn Bell discovered one in 1967, but remained a perfectly valid hypothesis throughout the intervening period. Similarly, the hypothetical assertion that natural evil is the result of the distortion of creation brought about by the angelic Fall does not need evidential support at this precise point if it can be shown that it is organically related to a world-view which is coherent and carries evidential support at other key points. I submit that this is the case. Belief in the existence of such personal agents is 'carried' by the much more supported package of beliefs of which it (arguably)[53] forms an intrinsic part.

It seems to me, therefore, that Smith's moral intuition is sound and that predation is an evil phenomenon both in the sense that it is something which our universe would be better off without, and in the sense that it is at odds with the sort of God in whom Christians believe. For reasons which are intrinsic to a Christian understanding of God and of the world, focussed as they both are in Christ, we should see animals, their interaction, and the natural world in general as no longer the way God created them to be. Smith's conclusion that there is probably no God depends upon the premiss that 'If God exists, then there exist no instances of an ultimately evil natural law.' That premiss itself depends upon the unfallenness of creation and upon seeing God as the sort of dictator who insists on getting their own way. I suggest that there is good evidence for rejecting both those assumptions. On the contrary, the doctrine of the Fall implies that creation *is* fallen, that it does not reflect the self-giving love of God that we meet in Christ, and that the God we do meet in Christ is the sort of God who gives creatures that freedom to reject God's purposes without which love is meaningless. If we understand 'godless' to mean 'having turned away from God', then Smith's experience that dark night was indeed a veridical insight into the deeply evil dimension of a godless world. But where his position offers no hope, the doctrine of the Fall offers the hope that, if suffering was not the first word about our world, it need not be the last.

13

Can Animal Suffering be Reconciled with Belief in an All-Loving God?

Jay B. McDaniel

'Life in the wild is not just eating berries in the sunlight.'[1] So writes Gary Snyder, one of the most gifted nature writers in the United States. Deeply influenced by Zen Buddhism, Snyder recommends that we look at wilderness with Zen eyes, seeing it as it is, not as we think it ought to be. To be sure, Snyder says, there is much in the wilderness that rightly elicits our appreciation. There are Douglas firs and Ponderosa pines, red-tailed hawks and mountain lions, softly rolling rivers and awe-inspiring mountains. But this is not the whole story. There is also the 'ball of crunched bones in a scat, the feathers in the snow, the tales of insatiable appetite'. Life 'is not just a diurnal property of large interesting vertebrates; it is also noctural, anaerobic, cannibalistic, microscopic, digestive, fermentative: cooking away in the warm dark'.[2] Furthermore, as a friend and fellow environmentalist reminded him, even the large interesting vertebrates have their moments of sheer horror:

> Jim Dodge told me how he had watched – with fascinated horror – Orcas methodically batter a Gray Whale to death in the Chukchi Sea.[3]

The Chukchi Sea is just north of western Alaska; and orcas are 'killer whales'. If we want to be honest about the natural world, Snyder seems to say, we must imagine ourselves inside the skin of the grey whale as she is being battered and then eaten by the orcas.

For Christians, such imaginative empathy is difficult. Not only is it painful to open ourselves to the suffering of other living beings, it is also troublesome to reflect on their suffering in the light of our claims concerning an all-loving God. Where is this God, we ask, when the grey whale suffers her terror? And why must there be so much suffering and violence in life on earth, if life itself was called into existence by this God's love?

Earlier generations of Christians would have explained the violence in creation by reference to a Fall that occurred in the distant past, itself initiated by human sin. But we cannot follow this route, for we have to acknowledge that there never was a time when life on our planet was free from violence. Predator-prey relations existed long before the early hominids appeared. Millions of years before human sin, there was a 'dark side'.

My purpose is to offer one way of envisioning God in relation to this dark side, through the model of 'process theology'. Before I proceed, however, a word about the word 'animals' is in order. In the biological sciences, the word names creatures ranging from single-celled organisms through multi-celled insects to complex organisms such as grey whales and human beings. The ordinary use of the word is more restricted, however, referring to complex organisms, particularly mammals, other than humans. I find the latter usage problematic, for it suggests that we humans are of an order different in kind from other creatures of the flesh. Too often this suggestion has itself functioned to sanction human abuse of animals. Thus I prefer the biblical word 'creature', precisely because it can remind us of our continuity with other creatures – at least if we recognize that we are creatures ourselves. Still, as a concession to ordinary language, I will use the word 'animal' to name mammals other than human beings, and will refer to human beings in other ways. At points when I seek to refer to humans and other mammals together, I will use the term 'mortals'.

Let us turn, then, to the grey whale. What did she *feel* as she was surrounded, beaten, and then eaten by her fellow cetaceans? A few might argue that she felt nothing at all, since only humans have feelings or sub-jective experiences. But most of us would realize the speciousness of this anthropocentric bias. It would be odd if we alone, out of all the mammals with complex nervous systems, enjoyed pleasure and suffered pain, while all the rest were mere automatons devoid of sentience. It seems much more likely that other mammals, with nervous systems analogous to our own, have experiences analogous to our own, and that their capacities for feeling, like our own, emerged as evolutionary adaptations to environmental contexts. Biological science suggests as much.

Biological science also suggests, of course, that the death of the battered whale, including the subjective experiences leading up to it, served a valuable role in the marine ecosystem of which she was a part. In dying as she did she contributed to the lives of orcas and many other sea creatures who fed off her remains. She was an instrument for larger ecological ends, a subroutine in a larger evolutionary process.

Still, we cannot help but wonder how things felt from her own, individual point of view. As she was being attacked by the orcas, did she like what was happening? Was she pleased when their jaws ripped into her skin? Did she find consolation in the fact that she was contributing to the good of others? Jim Dodge did not think so, and neither should we. He took her attempts to flee at face value. Like other mortals she wanted to live rather than die, with a minimum amount of pain and a maximum amount of satisfaction; and, like other mortals, her desires were frustrated, at least at the end of her life. In the end, prior to unconsciousness, she felt pain and terror, not satisfaction.

And this, it seems to me, is the heart of any concern for animal well-being. We are concerned with their well-being because we realize that they, like us, have projects, aims, and interests of their own. Generally speaking, these aims, like ours, are *to survive with satisfaction, moment to moment, relative to what is possible in the situation at hand.* One of the tragedies of biological life, then, is that, so often, the aims of different animals to 'survive with satisfaction' are incompatible. For the orca such an aim meant eating the grey whale; for the grey whale it meant escaping the orca. For one to succeed, the other had to fail. As Snyder puts it: 'Wild systems are in one elevated sense above criticism, but they can also be seen as irrational, moldy, cruel, parasitic.' The 'cruelty' does not lie in the motivation of the orca, but in the tragedy of the whole situation, the incompatibility of legitimate aims.

Which takes us back to the original dilemma. Why do we live in a world with such cruelty, if in fact it was called into existence by an all-loving God? To approach an answer to this question, let us consider another. Let us assume that God is in fact Christ-like, and hence all-loving, and ask: As the orca was chasing the grey whale in the Chukchi Sea, whose side was God on?

The answer must be that God was 'on the side' of both creatures, to the exclusion of neither. At least this is the case if we assume that God's love, like human love, involves a desire that the interests of living beings, in surviving with satisfaction, be realized. Schubert Ogden, a leading theologian in the United States, puts the point this way: 'Because God's love itself is subject to no bounds and excludes nothing from its embrace, there is no creature's interest that is not also God's interest and, therefore, necessarily included in the redeeming love of God.'[4]

Ogden is influenced by process theology, as am I. Process theology has at least two sources, and the first is the cosmology of the late Alfred North Whitehead, particularly as developed in his *Process and Reality*. Whitehead is one of the very few philosophers in recent centuries to argue that animals as well as humans have – or, better, are – souls. In a Whiteheadian context, the word 'soul' points to the inner dimension of a mammalian life, to what otherwise might be called the 'psyche' or 'seat of awareness' or 'mind' of that mammal. As Whitehead sees it, this 'soul' or 'psyche' is distinguishable from, yet deeply influenced by, that mammal's brain. The interiority of a 'soul' consists of a series of experiential moments, the successors of which inherit from predecessors with peculiar immediacy, such that the mammal at issue has a subjective history, a biographical story. Thus a mammal, non-human or human, is not just an object in the world but also the subject of a life. When we imagine ourselves inside the skin of the battered grey whale, we are imagining ourselves inside her own distinctive point of view, inside her 'soul'.

A second source of process theology is the Bible.[5] Along with most biblical authors, process theologians in what is called the 'speculative' tradition of process thought envision God as a self-conscious Life – a Thou – to whom we can pray, in whom we can place our deepest trust, and who can guide us, if we are open, into the very fullness of life. Moreover, just as the Bible often pictures God as responsive to events in history as they occur, not before they occur, so process thinkers picture God as responsive to events after not before they happen. At least in this sense, the God of process thought is temporal rather than non-temporal, a God of *history* – which encompasses biological, geological, and cosmic as well as human history. This 'God of history' is related to the whole, as well as to each part, and the whole itself is an unfinished process.

In process theology, the relation between the unfinished creation and God is understood pan*en*theistically. Panentheism refers to the view that the unfinished universe is in God in some way, even as God is more than the universe. Often this is illustrated by a circle in which is enfolded a spiral. The circle represents God: the One in whom, according to Paul, the universe 'lives and moves and has its being' (Acts 17.28). The spiral represents the unfolding universe in its galactic, geological, and biological phases. The point is that the unfinished universe is immanent within the divine Life, even as the divine Life is more than the universe.

What is not clear from the circle diagram, but which is nevertheless the case, is that panentheism offers a distinctive way of understanding God's connection with the animal soul. To understand this solidarity, an analogy often used in process theology to explain God's relation to the world – that of the soul and the body – is in order.

What does it mean to say that the unfolding universe is *in* God?

According to the process model, it means that the universe is present to God, and immanent within God's own life, in much the same way that events within our own bodies are present to, and immanent within, our own minds or souls. Just as what happens in our bodies happens in and to us, even though, as souls, we are more than our bodies, so what happens in the universe happens in and to God, even though God is more than the universe. The universe is the body of God, so process thinkers aver, and God is the Soul of the universe.

To be sure, analogies between mammalian souls and the divine Soul are not exact. When, as living souls, we feel events in our own bodies, we often feel them in vague and collective ways. Thousands of cells in our bodies may suffer injury, for example, but we feel them only as a single, dull pain. By contrast, God feels each 'cell' in the universe as a life of its own, even as God also feels each 'cell' in its intimate relation to every other cell. In this context, a 'cell' would be any creature, anywhere in the universe, that has reality for itself. The grey whale being battered by the orca would be one cell in the body of God, and the orca doing the battering would be another. Moreover, these animals would not be felt by God from the outside, as if God were an external observer, but rather from the inside, as if God were inside the skin of each creature, co-indwelling its own perspective, and feeling the presence of the surroundings from its own unique point of view. Indeed, process thinkers would say that God *is* inside each creature.

Here again our own capacities are quite different from God's. Where we must only *imagine* what it might be like to be inside the grey whale and the orca, separated as we are from the two animals by the boundaries of our own skin, God has no skin that separates. God is best conceived not as above or outside the universe but rather as everywhere and nowhere. God is 'everywhere' in the sense of being coextensive with each and every creature, experiencing the world from that creature's point of view, and yet God is 'nowhere' in the sense of being beyond any attempts to 'locate' divine reality in one region of the universe as opposed to others. We can meaningfully speak of the universe as the 'body' of God precisely because God has no body of God's own, save the universe itself. All things are as close to God as, say, our own jugular veins are close to us.

Still more important than the spatiality of God, at least for religious purposes, is the love of God. From the vantage point of the process model, it is not simply the case that God 'feels' what it is like to be inside the skin of each and every creature, it is also the case that God 'shares in' and 'sympathizes with' what is thus felt. This means that as the grey whale is being battered by the orca, God shares in her aim to escape the orca, and also in her pain and terror. The pain and terror belong to God even as they belong to her. It also means that, as the orca seeks to satisfy his own hunger, God also shares in that hunger, and understands the distinctive delight of eating the whale. As Whitehead puts it, God is 'a fellow sufferer who understands'.

This is not to say that God necessarily approves or takes delight in what is understood. But it is to say that God identifies with the legitimate interests of each and every creature in surviving with satisfaction, not just with those that we might favour from a human perspective. Whereas our love is partial, God's is impartial, or, perhaps better, omni-partial. God is on the side of each and every life, on its own terms and for its own sake. This means that there is tragedy, heartbreak, even in the Soul of the universe. For Christians, of course, this is the truth of the cross. The tragedy of worldly violence is shared by God.

Why, we might ask, does God not simply eliminate the tragedy that causes such harm? Here again the soul-body analogy is helpful. Just as things happen in our own bodies which we do not will but which become part of our lives, so, from a process perspective, things happen in the universe which God does not will, but which are nevertheless part of God's life. Thus the universe has creative power of its own, incarnate in each and every living being in some measure, which cannot be reduced to, or equated with, divine power. Each cell in God's body has some capacity for agency, for power, which cannot be reduced to divine power. There are things that happen in the world that even God cannot prevent.

This takes us to a second way in which God can be imaged as loving animals. The first way is through empathy. The second way is through inspiration. God loves animals not only as one who shares in their sufferings but also as one who seeks to guide them into that ideal satisfaction which, at a given moment, would be 'the best for the impasse at hand'. The guidance itself comes through what process thinkers often call 'initial aims' or, to use more biblical terminology, 'divine calls'.

To illustrate how 'initial aims' or 'divine calls' play a role in the lives of ensouled creatures, I offer an example from feminist theology. Imagine a woman who suffers from self-hatred due to years of abuse from a dominating husband. He has told her that she is not worth very much, and she has come to believe it. Most moments of her conscious life are hounded by a voice that tells her she is a nobody, a nothing, that she is not meant to be anything except a doormat to her spouse. But imagine as well that, at a still deeper level of lived experience, she feels the presence of an inner call to break out of her self-doubt and to assert herself to her husband and to the world. Sometimes she hides from this call, because it seems dangerous to respond to it. Still, in an almost bodily way, she feels compelled to say 'I am somebody' and to challenge her husband's abusive behaviour. From a process perspective, the call she feels deep within her comes from God. It is the presence of the Holy Spirit in her life. Of course, the woman need not be a Christian or even believe in God in order for the Spirit to be present within her as an object of desire, a possibility for life's fullness, relative to the situation in hand.

Process theologians suggest that the Spirit just described is present in all creatures, albeit in different ways. In animals who enjoy a sense of personal history, 'initial aims' would take the form of possibilities for surviving with satisfaction, relative to what is possible in the situation at hand. Sometimes 'the best for the situation at hand' is itself promising. In the life of a young whale, for example, it may be to learn a particular skill in swimming, to enjoy rich forms of social relations with other whales, or to discover a new method of finding food. We can see the struggle of the whale to realize these ends as a response to God within her. At other times, however, as when that adult grey whale is being circled by orcas, it will be nothing more than making the best of a bad situation, as far as is possible. It will be to escape the orcas as they are encircling her, to fight them as they attack her, and, finally, to give in to the inevitable.

This, of course, is at the micro-level, the level of individual organisms. It is also possible to speak of the guidance of God at a macro-level, that is, at the level of evolutionary history itself. Here, process thinkers are inclined to see the guidance of God as a lure towards ever richer capacities for sentience and creativity. The general drift of biological evolution, they argue, has been towards creatures with ever richer capacities for feeling. Richness itself is measured in terms of two qualities, 'harmony' and 'intensity'. They would argue that mammals, for example, can experience their bodies and surroundings with more complex harmonies, and more vital intensities, than single-celled organisms, which came earlier in the evolutionary process. In the movement from single-celled to multi-celled organisms, they propose, we see the very hand of God.

And yet, as in the case of the individual organisms, God's hand is invitational rather than coercive. The particulars of evolution cannot be seen as the result of divine will alone, or of creaturely powers alone, but rather as the outcome of the interaction of the two. This means that, over the long run of evolution, things could well have happened that diverged from the will of God; routines could have emerged that violated divine intentions for creation. Were predator-prey relations among them?

It is tempting to say 'yes', and to imagine that the violence we see in creation is itself a 'fallen' routine that emerged at some point in the history of life on earth, with which God must now work in the ways suggested above but which runs counter to the original intentions of God in luring the world towards sentient forms of life. Indeed, this is the direction in which the Bible points. According to the first creation story in Genesis, the original intentions of God were for non-violence between higher animals.

Generally speaking, however, process thinkers take a different approach. They do indeed see a 'fallen' dimension in predator-prey relations, but they also see God as partly responsible for their existence in the first place. They speak of the very emergence of animal life as ambiguous, containing both good and evil. The 'fall' into carnivorous existence was lured by God, with co-operation of creatures. It was a 'fall upward'.

Does this mean that God is 'guilty'? Not really, at least for process thinkers. Their argument runs as follows. Built into the very nature of bio-logical life are necessary correlations among the capacities (1) to enjoy rich forms of sentience, (2) to suffer, (3) to inflict harm upon others, and (4) to contribute to the well-being of others. If any of these capacities increase, the others increase as well. These correlations are necessary rather than contingent, which means that they are not dependent upon choice, even divine choice. As God lured advanced forms of life into existence, there was a risk involved, even for God. It was that creatures would evolve into manners of interaction that would be tremendously painful to one another, even as they would also enjoy opportunities for harmonious and intense experience that were tremendously rich. Should those modes emerge, as we now know they did, both in human and non-human life, even God would partake of the suffering.

Was the divine risk worth it for the mortals themselves? Is it better to have lived and suffered than not to have lived at all? We can answer the question for ourselves, but it is not easy to answer it for other people, or for grey whales. However, the process perspective offers one final image of divine love, in addition to empathy and guidance. It is divine love as redemption.

In process thought, redemption itself is conceived in one or both of two ways. On the one hand, it can be understood as contribution to the experience of God. Recall that, from the vantage point of the process model, God shares in the joys and sufferings of each and every mortal, the grey whale and the orca included. As the grey whale suffered her terror, the terror was shared by God; and as the orca enjoyed his food, the enjoyment was shared by God. From our point of view as observers, these two feelings were in profound tension. Process theologians imagine that there was also tension from God's point of view. The Soul of the universe knows tragedy. But they also imagine that God seeks to unite the feelings into a single whole that gives meaning to each, inasmuch as is possible, without blocking out the tragedy. There is, in the divine experience, a kind of experiential reconciliation, a beauty, that is certainly invisible to our eyes, but for which we can nevertheless hope. As we see suffering and tragedy in non-human life, we can hope that, in some way beyond our understanding, the violence in creation is reconciled in a divine Life. This is to say that the terror of the grey whale and the enjoyment of the orca are harmonized in God's own experience, but not in a way that eliminates the tragedy suffered by the whale. The grey whale and the orca are brought together in God's experience, as they never were in their own, and they are, in this way, 'redeemed'.

The problem with this first view of redemption, however, is that the victims do not themselves enjoy the reconciliation achieved in God. Nor, for that matter, do the victimizers. This takes us to the second understanding of redemption offered in process theology, namely redemption as life after death.

Earlier I spoke of animals as well as humans as having – or, rather, being – souls. I said that the 'soul' or 'psyche' is distinguishable from, yet deeply influenced by, the brain. Given this view, and given the fact that the universe itself may contain planes of existence far different from our own three-dimensional plane, process thinkers find it possible, but not metaphysically necessary, that souls might survive bodily death, entering into other planes of existence where the journey of life continues, either indefinitely or for a certain extended period of time. In process theology such continuation is called 'subjective immortality', though 'immortality' is something of a misnomer since the survival itself can be of a finite duration. 'Subjective immortality', which involves the survival of the *experiencers* themselves, is distinguished from 'objective immortality', which is understood as the survival of *experiences* in the ongoing Life. Some process thinkers argue for 'redemption' in both senses, subjective and objective, while others argue only for the objective type, believing that human and animal souls perish with their bodies.

As a Christian, I find myself hoping, with John Wesley, that subjective immortality is a reality for all animals. Wesley hoped for a 'general deliverance' in which, after death, animals will be compensated for the suffering they underwent, and liberated from the rages of which they partook.[6] Hopes of this sort can be criticized as overly unrealistic and sentimental. Still, I cannot but hope that the grey whale's life did not end with her terror. It seems to me that, as we mortals struggle to survive with satisfaction, we are drawn by a still deeper desire for wholeness, for completeness, for a peace that surpasses understanding. Most of us, animal and human alike, die without enjoying this ultimate wholeness for which we yearn. The problem is not death, it is incompleteness. The grey whale's death was a vivid instance of the kind of incompleteness that many other mortals no doubt suffer. Thus, with Wesley, I find myself drawn to the possibility that the grey whale's journey did not end with the last moment of horror. My hope, as a process theologian myself, is that all mortals, grey whales and orcas included, partake of the resurrection in their own ways. This is not to say that, immediately upon death, all their suffering is redeemed. Rather it is to say that, as their journeys continue even after death, the Soul of the universe continues to draw them, inasmuch as is possible, into a still deeper form of satisfaction that represents union with the Soul itself. Once this union is realized, death would occur. Their souls would be merged into the divine Soul, their yearnings would themselves be realized. It seems to me that, only if they so partake, was the risk of life itself worth it, even for God.

Of course, what I am suggesting is immensely speculative. In some respects it may resemble Buddhist and Hindu points of view rather than Christian. Still, I submit, it is deeply Christian to hope that all living beings, in one way or another, find that peace for which their hearts yearn. Process theology, as amplified by the speculation just made, offers one way of envisioning this peace.

In sum, the process understanding of God offers three ways to affirm God's love for animals: empathy, guidance, and redemption. The process model is but one of many that need to be offered by Christians sensitive to animal suffering, none of which are entirely adequate. In any case, the best judge of their adequacy, in the last analysis, is the battered whale herself, the one who died in the Chukchi Sea. The truth lies in her own unique relationship with God, and also in the orcas' relationships with God, however mysterious to us those relationships might be.

Souls and Redemption

14

All Things in Christ?

John B. Cobb, Jr

Christology, taken as a whole, has been preoccupied with the saving effects of God on human souls. For example, Calvin accentuates this as the focus of the whole of Christian theology in the opening sentence of his *Institutes*: 'Nearly all the wisdom we possess, that is to say, true and sound wisdom, consists of two parts: the knowledge of God and of ourselves.'[1] (Although Calvin does not speak of the soul, the human self is here primarily viewed as the soul.) In focussing on God and the human soul, Calvin did not think of himself as in conflict with Catholic teaching, nor as differing from Luther. He was simply thematizing what he took to be the heart of Christian teaching. For much of this teaching the remainder of creation appeared only in the background or as a source of knowledge of God and the soul. There was little incitement to interest oneself in it for its own sake.

When christology is understood in this way, the question of the relation of Christ to animals other than human beings can hardly arise. And indeed this question *has* rarely arisen in the mainstream of Christian theology and church life. Those Christians who insist on the importance of other animals and connect this interest with their understanding of Christ have usually been viewed as eccentric, or worse. St Francis, John Woolman, and Albert Schweitzer have been loved, but they have not been followed. Their ideas have been treated with charitable condescension, and are rarely studied in theological schools.

My thesis is that this rejection of interest in animals other than the human species is not warranted by the Bible or by fundamental christo-logical doctrines. It involves a narrowing of focus that has been harmful even to the understanding of the relation of God and the human person. It has been disastrous ecologically, now threatening the healthy survival even of the human species. And it has been profoundly unjust to the other animals created by God who share this planet with us.

The first two of these three criticisms have now been widely accepted. A focus on the human soul that tends to separate it from the human body reflects Greek influences that lead to an anthropology different in significant respects from the Hebraic one that is expressed in the Bible. Many theologians in this century have tried to recover the holistic view of the human being that takes embodiment seriously.[2] The focus on the human soul, or even on the human psychophysical organism, that separates humanity from the remainder of the created order is now widely acknowledged to have blinded Christians to the effects of human action on that larger order. Christians were not the first to notice the harmful consequences and the threat to ourselves. Indeed, as a group we resisted this recognition longer than others. But today most of our churches have acknowledged that this *was* blindness, that we as Christians should concern ourselves with the well-being of the whole created order in relation to which God gave us special responsibility.

But the church as a whole still resists attention to the third criticism. It recognizes that other living things play an important role in the life of the planet, on which human beings depend for our well-being and even for our survival. It recognizes that the whole creation is good. But it is not willing to think of our relations to other animals, especially to individual animals, in terms of what justice and mercy require of us. Christology is still associated with the salvation of human beings, and of us alone.

We must acknowledge that this focus on human beings is shared by the biblical writers. They too are preoccupied with human sin and wretchedness and proclaim the good news that God loves us and acts for our salvation. The celebration of God's role in the whole of nature that still appears through the Jewish scriptures (Psalm 65 is a vivid example) is muted in the New Testament. Therefore the anthropocentrism of subsequent Christian theology is not an abrupt aberration from an earlier faith that showed deep sensitivity to other creatures.

Nevertheless, a narrowing *is* involved in the move from primitive Christianity to later doctrines. Jesus is depicted – rightly, I believe – as affirming God's providential care for wildflowers and sparrows. His point, it is true, is that God cares even more for us human beings. But the way he formulates his message would be meaningless if God did not also care for the plants and animals for their own sake. The narrowing process left this assumption behind. The heart of Jesus' message was his proclamation of the kingdom of God. What implications has this for the relation of human beings to the other animals?

Scholarly debates about how we are to understand the kingdom of God will continue indefinitely. I am not qualified to enter them seriously. But at least part of the meaning is given us in the prayer that we have learned from

Jesus and which is so central to the piety of the church. We understand our petition for the kingdom of God to come in the light of the petition that parallels and explains it: that God's will 'be done on earth as it is in heaven' (Matt. 6.10, NEB). We often interpret this to mean moral obedience, and we assume that such obedience is possible only for human beings. The petition may include, implicitly, a request for strength to live in accord with God's purposes. But, in this text, that request is indirect and tangential. The petition is for a different world order from the present one.

It may be that, in thinking of an earth that conforms to God's intentions, Jesus thought especially of the way human beings would relate to one another. But there is no reason to limit attention in this way. If we ask the question 'Is the existence of creatures other than human ones part of God's purpose?', no reader of the Bible can say 'No'. And if we ask, 'Would continuing human cruelty towards these other creatures belong to God's ideal intentions?', again the answer would have to be 'No'.

It is the failure to ask these questions, rather than a dispute about the answers, that has enabled Christians through the centuries to separate their relations with other animals from their recital of the Lord's prayer. If this failure is not justified by Jesus' own message, is it justified by that of Paul? Certainly Paul's focus on the salvation of human beings is even more intense than that of Jesus, and hence his contribution to the process of narrowing must be acknowledged. Yet Paul's vision of that for which we hope cannot be supposed to omit the rest of creation. In his fullest statement (Rom. 8.18–25) he makes more explicit than did Jesus that it is the whole of creation that now suffers and is to be redeemed. It is hard to say whether, when Paul thought of the groaning of all creation, he had in mind specifically the suffering of other animals. But at the very least there is no reason to suppose he excluded that, or to suppose that he would consider the eager expectation of creation fulfilled in a world order that included continuing human cruelty towards other animals. Although this recognition has been peripheral to Christianity as a whole, it has not been wholly absent even in the Western tradition. There is, for example, the outstanding sermon mentioned in the last chapter by John Wesley, based on this Pauline passage, entitled 'The General Deliverance' that deals extensively with the present suffering and eschatological salvation of all animals.[3]

Thus far, it could be argued, the discussion has been only about incidental opinions of Jesus and Paul, not about christology. Christology is about the person and work of Jesus. These, so the argument may go, are about how God has acted to save human beings, and that alone. The ignoring of other animals has been more determined by christological emphases than by the study of Jesus and Paul. At the same time, those who emphasize, rightly, that christology cannot be simply identified with what the New Testament says about Jesus as a historical figure also affirm that what the church came to say christologically is responsibly grounded in what the canonized writings tell us about Jesus.

The most influential bridge from the message of Jesus to the church's credal teaching about Jesus is found in the prologue to the Gospel of John. There, and in the creeds, Jesus is understood to be the incarnation of the Word that was with God from the beginning and was, indeed, God. In the title 'Christ' the church, from an early time, heard more clearly that Jesus was the incarnate Word than that he was the Jewish Messiah. The fulfilment of the messianic expectation must await the second coming. But the fundamental message of the gospel was that the eternal Word had already come and dwelt among us.

In the Johannine prologue the Word that became flesh in Jesus is involved in the whole of God's creative activity. Nothing has come into being apart from it. Above all, it is found in life, and all creaturely life participates in it. This life is also the light that illumines every human being, a light that is incarnate in Jesus. A definite difference is asserted between the way that the Word is present in Jesus and the way it is present in other human beings. The light that enlightens all human beings becomes flesh in Jesus. But, despite this difference, there is also continuity. For the light to enlighten all people means that it is somehow present with, to, or in all. My own judgment is that 'in' is not too strong. Certainly the way in which the Word was thought of in the general culture of the time suggests this relation, and there is nothing in the text to count against it. Similarly there is a difference between the light that enlightens all human beings and the life that enlivens other parts of creation. But here the continuity is even more strongly expressed. 'All that came to be was alive with his life' (John 1.4, NEB). The light *is* the life, or rather the life *is* the light. Perhaps the best understanding is to think of the presence of the Word as enlivening all living things and at the same time enlightening all that are capable of being enlightened. In other words, the Word is immanent in the whole of creation with differentiated results.

The Eastern church retained a clearer sense of the immanence of God in the world. The Western church obscured it in a more externalistic view of the creative act. Only in the West could the image of the watchmaker and the watch be taken seriously as expressive of the relation between the Creator and creation. When this deistic vision declined in the West and a sense of God's immanence in the world was recovered, there arose a sacramental or even an incarnational view of how God is present in the world – a view warranted by the Johannine prologue, and by other biblical texts as well. To perceive the incarnation of Jesus as revelatory requires not only that we see God's presence in him but also in others as well. And the 'others' include the flowers of the field and the sparrows as well as, most importantly, the 'least' among our sisters and brothers.

The Western church has feared this sacramental or incarnational view as moving toward pantheism. But pantheism only follows if we take a view of the incarnation from which the Church Fathers tried to protect us in their credal formulations. If the incarnation means that the humanity of Jesus is only an appearance, or only the bodily form, or only subordinate aspects of the psychic life – indeed, if the humanity of Jesus is curtailed in any way for the sake of making the divine presence predominate – then the extension of the idea of incarnation to the way God is in the sacraments, or the church, or the creatures in general, *does* lead toward pantheism. But if incarnation refers to the true presence of the true God in the truly human Jesus, co-constituting with the human the concrete actuality of the one person, then to find a less full incarnation of God in other creatures as well certainly does not lead towards pantheism. God's transcendence of the world in no way precludes God's constitutive immanence within it as its life, as the light that enlightens all women and men. By 'Christ' I mean the Word in its presence, immanence, or incarnation in the world. This Word takes on unique form, is 'made flesh', in Jesus. But it is present in every creature. It is the life of all that lives. To reverence Christ is to reverence life in all its forms.

There is no basis here for sentimentalizing. Life feeds upon life. We human beings are part of this system. There is no other creaturely possibility. We have come to be what we are in competition with other species of living things as well as in interdependence with them. Without the early death of myriads of animals there would be no space for those who survive. We could stop the suffering of wild things only by ending their wildness. In fact, however, our impact upon them has not been to lessen suffering but to increase it vastly. Domestication has also been degradation. We have reduced living, sentient beings to economic commodities considered only as they contribute to monetary gain. We routinely torture millions of animals, usually for inessential human purposes. To think of all things, and especially of all living things, as embodying Christ must give us pause. A creature in whom we see Christ cannot be *only* a commodity to be treated for our gain or casual pleasure. An animal that incarnates Christ cannot be *only* a specimen for our cruel experiments or an object forced to do unnatural things for our amusement.

Paul speaks of Christ in us (Rom. 8.10). By 'us' he has in mind chiefly Christian believers. Certainly Christ is *in* the believer in a way in which Christ is not in others, and in other human beings in a way that goes beyond the presence in other creatures. We noted the difference in John's language here between 'light' and 'life'. We noted also that there is a close connection as well as a distinction. I defined 'Christ' as the Word in its presence, immanence, or incarnation. But 'Christ' also means the eternal Word as it comes to be known through its revelation in Jesus. Of course these meanings flow into one another. More often than Paul speaks of how Christ is in us, he speaks of how we live 'in Christ' (see Rom. 6.5–11 and I Cor. 1.30). This, too, applies primarily to the human believer. Yet aspects of its meaning can apply beyond this central use. The cosmological possibility is developed in Colossians: 'In him everything in heaven and on earth was created . . . and all things are held together in him' (1.16–17, NEB).

This idea fits well with the teaching of Jesus that what we do to the least of these, our sisters and brothers, we do also to Christ. If all are in Christ, then in some way our treatment of creatures is also a way of treating Christ. Christ rejoices with us in our joys and suffers with us in our suffering. There is no reason to restrict this vision to the human creatures. It is indeed right to emphasize the importance of treating those human beings who are least able to demand justice for themselves as persons in whom we see Christ and through whom we injure or serve Christ. But we should not suppose that caring for other animals reduces caring for people. On the contrary, those persons who are most sensitive to others are often sensitive to *all* others, and those who restrict the range of their caring often care less for any. It is a mistake to restrict 'the least of these' to the human in the interest of ensuring concern for the human 'least ones'. To harden oneself against the suffering of other animals does not heighten sensitivity to fellow human beings.

Let us acknowledge, then, that all creatures are in Christ, and that Christ rejoices with all in their joy and suffers with all in their suffering. The realization of this with respect to human beings does not make it possible to avoid inflicting suffering upon other people. Much more, the realization that this applies to all creatures will not make it possible for human beings to become harmless. But our recognition that other human beings are *in* Christ does lead us to wrestle with the problems related to their suffering and especially with what we do that causes that suffering. It is a similar concerned wrestling about our impact on other animals that must follow from a vision of how we are all together *in* Christ.

'Christ' is our central symbol for Christian cosmology and Christian ethics. But we noted at the outset the narrowed focus of 'Christ' on salvation. Does this broadened understanding of Christ lead to the view that other animals also are 'saved'? The greatest difficulty in answering this question is that the word 'saved' has so many meanings both in the Bible and in ordinary language. A species may be 'saved' from extinction. And surely Christ's life is enriched. Animal rights activists may 'save' some rabbits from torture. And surely Christ suffers less as a result. But in ecclesiastical usage, 'save' also has been narrowed in its meaning. A species that is saved from imminent extinction will, nevertheless, someday become extinct. The rabbits saved from torture will probably be killed. In contrast, to be 'saved' in the ecclesiastical imagining of the term is something final, unsurpassable, and irreversible.

The closest the New Testament comes to this thought is in the passages from Romans and Colossians to which reference has already been made. Paul writes that 'the universe itself is to be freed from the shackles of mortality and enter upon the liberty and splendour of the children of God' (Rom. 8.21, NEB). In Colossians we read that through Christ 'God chose to reconcile the whole universe to himself . . .' (1.20, NEB). The logic is inescapable: all animals must be included in such statements about the universe. But *how* this eschatological freedom and reconciliation are to be understood is left very much to the reader to envisage.

One way of imagining this eschatological fulfilment connects closely to what has been said about all things being 'in Christ'. To be 'in Christ' can mean that all that happens fleetingly in the world is not only felt in the eternal Word but remains there forever. In Christ it is redeemed, not only in the sense that it is forever preserved, but also in the sense that it receives what meaning it can have, and plays what positive role it can play. Perhaps as Christ holds all things together, these things are held together cumulatively and forever. The lives of other animals as well as humans participate in forming the everlasting life of Christ. In Christ they are all reconciled – slaughtered and slaughterer, tortured and torturer – to one another and to God.

Recovery of the broader and richer christology from which the tradition narrowed its focus will not in itself 'save' millions of animals from loss of habitat and cruel exploitation by human beings. The steps needed to save animals have to be worked out in detail. They involve changes in our economic practice and curtailment of the growth of human population as well as attitudinal changes and compassionate actions. But although the practical changes needed will not follow from an enriched christology alone, they may not occur without it. The energies that are required to effect these changes are those that historically have been elicited only at the religious level of existence. A fundamental conversion is needed, both individual and social. Enlightened self-interest will not suffice. More and more those concerned for change look to the religious communities. In our Christian community thus far, our most precious symbol has been of little help in evoking the needed conversion. Yet the potential is there for realizing a truer and fuller meaning of 'Christ', a meaning through which Christ can rally the devotion of believers for the salvation of the whole world.

15

Do Animals have Immortal Souls?

Paul Badham

According to historic Christian tradition there is a clear answer to this question, and it is negative. St Thomas Aquinas in his *Summa theologiae* has no hesitation in endorsing the teaching of Gennadius' *Church Dogmas* that 'We believe man alone to have a substantive soul; the souls of animals are not substantive.'[1] Canon 1366 of the Catholic church's legal code prescribes that 'Catholic theology and philosophy be taught according to the method, principles and doctrine of the Angelic Doctor (viz. St Thomas Aquinas)'.[2] Consequently, traditional Catholics usually assume that Aquinas' views represent 'the mind of the church' except where otherwise stated. So let us start by examining the grounds on which Aquinas reached this conclusion.

In the understanding of reality which Aquinas inherited from Aristotle there is of course no doubt that animals have souls. The Latin word 'anima' means 'soul'. Hence animals are actually defined as creatures with souls. However, the kind of souls that animals have were thought to be only mortal sentient souls, as distinct from the immortal rational souls that characterize the human species. This difference is of crucial importance to Aquinas. For, as he puts it, 'Aristotle established that understanding, alone among the acts of the soul, took place without a physical organ . . . So it is clear that the sense-soul has no proper activity of its own, but every one of its acts is of the body-soul compound. Which leaves us with the conclusion that since souls of brute animals have no activity which is intrinsically of soul alone, they do not subsist . . . Hence though man is of the same generic type as the other animals, he is a different species.'[3]

The concept of the soul being employed here is one where the soul is perceived as a 'vital force' or 'animating principle' essentially distinguishing all living things from all inanimate objects. Since plants grow and develop they cannot be thought of as wholly inanimate, but must possess some kind of purposive force which stimulates their upward growth. This came to be described as 'a vegetative soul'. Animals not only grow and develop, but also move and feel so they must possess a 'sense soul'. Humankind, however, has the additional capacity to think and reason and for this an intellectual or 'rational soul' is required. The rational soul, being immaterial, can survive the death of the body, whereas the sense soul of the beasts is purely physical and as such perishes with the animal it animates.

The greatest problem that faces this traditional view is that the 'vitalist' understanding of souls, which it presupposes, is no longer tenable. Science is committed to the simplest and most economical solution of any problem, and where natural explanations are possible these are always to be preferred to the positing of hypothetical entities. Biology has made very significant advances this century and there is no longer any function to be served by positing a 'motivating' force to account for the fact that plants, animals, and humans grow and develop. Archbishop John Habgood, who was a research fellow in physiology before taking holy orders, writes that 'what must be absolutely rejected is the notion that at a certain point in the study of living things one comes upon a mysterious something which no longer obeys recognisable physical or chemical laws. To believe that this might happen is to retreat into mystery and to put a stop to science . . . A "vital principle" which is not sharply defined and cannot be submitted to ordinary scientific tests explains nothing.'[4] In fact the last serious biologist willing to defend vitalism was Hans Driesch and he did his creative work around the turn of the century. According to Theodosius Dobzhansky in 1967, 'The all but unanimous consensus is that vitalism is useless as a working hypothesis in biological research . . . It has been pretty nearly a dead issue in biology for about half a century.'[5] Sir John Eccles goes even earlier and claims that the untenability of the Aristotelian-Thomist view 'was already recognised by Descartes'.[6]

This raises the issue of whether Descartes' understanding of the soul, which Eccles champions, fares any better than the Aristotelian-Thomist understanding, which he rejects. According to Descartes our physical growth and development is a function of the human 'bodily machine', and to be explained solely by natural causes. Consequently Descartes totally repudiated any vitalist understanding of the soul and insisted that the study of human beings as physical organisms should proceed without any reference to metaphysical concepts. Descartes established a comparison 'between a sick man and a badly made clock' and a 'healthy man and a well made clock', comparing the 'wheels and counter weights' of the clock with the 'bones, nerves, muscles, veins, blood and skin' of the human being.[7] Descartes saw the soul as something quite other than the body even though it interacts with the body throughout life. The Cartesian picture of the soul is that it is the subject of consciousness. That we think is the essence of our identity. We can in imagination or dream think of ourselves in other bodies, and yet the dreamer never doubts his or her own mental continuity. I remain the subject of my dream experiences even if such experiences appear to locate me in another embodiment or even another space.[8]

Descartes' total identification of the soul with the mind led him to an absolute rejection of vitalist concepts of vegetative or sentient souls. He saw animals as simply complex machines without thoughts or feelings. Their actions, as indeed the actions of the human body, were to be explained in mechanistic terms. The only kind of soul there could be was the soul as the subject of human experiencing. And this, as an immaterial thinking substance, owes its creation directly to God, is enclosed within a body during earthly life, but on the death of the body continues to exist without it.

Whether or not any part of Descartes' theory is true, one aspect of it seems certainly false, namely his view that animals are mere automata without consciousness. As Charles Raven comments: 'for us in this country the native love of birds and beasts . . . ensured the speedy repudiation of the Cartesian doctrine'.[9] It would seem impossible for anyone to live in daily contact with an animal, such as a family dog, and not to become aware that it had feelings. The complex legislation that now exists to prevent cruelty to animals presupposes that they are sentient. Hence, even if a line can be drawn between humans and animals, it cannot be drawn in the place that Descartes drew it.   Descartes was able to make a clear distinction between human beings and all the rest of the created order because he believed that human beings were unique in possessing sentience and rationality. He assumed that animals cannot feel and that machines cannot think. Hence the human soul is utterly distinctive and forms our true identity. As Descartes put it, 'I thereby concluded that I was a substance of which the whole essence or nature consists in thinking, and which in order to exist, needs no place and depends on no material thing; so that this "I", that is to say the mind, by which I am what I am, is entirely distinct from the body, and even that it is easier to know than the body, and moreover even if the body were not, it would not cease to be all that it is.'[10]

A difficulty for Descartes' theory is that today modern science can not only explain the workings of the human 'bodily machine' but can show that almost every facet of our mental life is actually dependent on the physical features of our genetic inheritance, the nutritional quality of our diet, the correct functioning of our glands, and the working of our brains.[11] In theory this should not constitute a problem for Cartesianism, for on Descartes' theory of continual mind-body interaction one should expect a physical co-relate for all our mental states. The problem is, however, that if everything can be fully explained without the notion of the soul, what does talk of the soul actually add? William of Ockham laid down as a basic principle of science that 'entities are not to be multiplied beyond necessity'.[12] If there is no necessity to invoke a concept of the soul to give a full account of human character, consciousness, thought, and feeling, then can we not employ 'Ockham's razor' to shave away the notion of the soul altogether?

A further awkwardness for the concept of the soul arises from evolutionary theory and from what is now known of the development of the human foetus in the womb. It is now apparent that human beings are the product of an immensely long evolutionary development, and that there is no clear dividing line separating humankind from their hominid ancestors. For about three million years human beings co-existed on the African savannah with other hominid species who subsequently became extinct. For a further million years human beings continued to live a life virtually indistinguishable from that of other animals since all the cultural and technological artifacts which now distance us from other species are all of very recent origin. Taking evolution as a whole it seems impossible to make sense of the claim that at some point in the process one of our hominid ancestors acquired an immortal soul and thus became a full human being. There simply is no sharp intelligible dividing line. This might lead us to consider the possibility either of dispensing with the notion of the soul altogether, or of extending the concept to all animals with a sufficiently complex nervous system to provide a physical substratum for the soul to interact with. This does not solve the problem of the absence of a sharp dividing line, though it does perhaps alleviate the problem in that it ceases to be an issue on which we should expect to be competent to make a decision.

This may also help us with the other problem for the concept of the soul, namely, if a soul exists, at what point does it enter and inform the developing foetus? Since 70% of zygotes fail to be implanted, one cannot intelligibly place ensoulment at conception. Implantation will not do either, since the cell may split into identical twins or triplets weeks after implantation, and one can hardly postulate single souls subsequently becoming double or triple! 'Quickening' in the womb reflects a subjective report by the mother of her experience of movement inside her which different mothers may report at different stages. So once again there simply is no single non-arbitrary point at which one could place human 'ensoulment'. However, St Thomas Aquinas might be reconsidered at this point. For, according to the Catholic philosopher Michael Coughlan, on Aquinas' view ensoulment was not possible until the foetus possessed the physical organs, including brain matter, requisite for taking advantage of the potential which the soul is capable of activating.[13] On this view the fact that one could not actually say when the foetus was ensouled would not matter. As Cardinal Mercier points out, 'as to what precise moment the embryo reaches the degree of organisation required for being informed by the rational soul, is of course quite impossible to determine'.[14]

Let us temporarily set aside the question of the meaningfulness of the concept of the soul, and explore the implications of accepting both that evolution is true and that ensoulment of the foetus takes place when a sufficient physical substratum exists for the rational soul to interact with. Accepting evolution means recognizing that human beings are part of the natural order and have developed from earlier forms of life. Accepting that ensoulment takes place when the neuronal capacity of the foetus is sufficiently developed implies that the level of complexity necessary for a soul to be present does not exceed that of an unborn child. Both these positions have a profound bearing on the question of whether animals could have rational souls. If human beings have evolved from earlier forms of life then humankind cannot be radically different from other animals, and there can be no doubt that a very large number of mature animals possess far greater intellectual ability than unborn children.

According to David Hume, 'animals undoubtedly feel, think, love, hate, will and even reason, though in a more imperfect manner than men: are their souls also immaterial and immortal?'[15] We do not necessarily have to agree wholly with Hume's premises to see the strength of his argument. The relatively new science of animal ethology, in which researchers devote themselves to constant observation of how animals behave in their natural habitat, has made it increasingly difficult to think of the higher animals as creatures governed wholly by instinct. According to Professor W. H. Thorpe, 'no one who has worked for a long period with a higher animal such as a chimpanzee . . . is justified in doubting [their] purposiveness . . . Such purposiveness is also clear to the experienced and open-minded observer with many of the Canidae [dog family],) with some, probably many, other mammals and with certain birds.'[16] Experiments in teaching chimpanzees sign language suggest that their inability to speak has more to do with the shape of their larynx than with their intelligence, while their ability to recognize themselves in mirrors and photographs suggests that they possess self-awareness. Elephants not only have proverbially good memories of what has happened to them but also seem to be aware of death, in that they have been reported as covering their dead with branches and leaves. Dolphins have brains which are proportionately larger than our own, and the ease with which they not only learn circus tricks but volunteer new tricks of their own suggests some intelligence. Such facts about animals are now not merely known to the dedicated observer but, through the medium of television and the popularity of nature programmes, have become a part of our general consciousness. Descartes' confidence that 'brutes not only have a smaller degree of reason than men, but are wholly lacking in it'[17] now seems to exhibit ignorant chauvinism and almost inevitably raises the issue of whether animals too possess immortal souls.

However the word 'immortal' must give us pause. The religious importance of belief in a substantive rational soul is that it provides a vehicle for personal continuity between this life and the life of the world to come. This is a somewhat different issue from the question of the extent to which rationality can be ascribed to non-human animals, or the question of when in the development of a human being it becomes plausible to attribute the status of a person to it. One might well agree that animals are not machines but are feeling, thinking agents with purposes, wills, and rights which should be respected, without wanting to commit oneself to the view that they possess an eternal destiny beyond bodily death. Likewise one might well wish to attribute full legal status to a foetus at an advanced stage in its development so that it may enjoy greater protection against abortion as its time of birth draws nearer, without supposing that having got this far it will actually live for ever! Much of the desire to claim souls for animals or foetuses ignores the question of whether it is actually intelligible to suppose that they could live apart from their bodies.

According to Pope John Paul II's encyclical *Man's condition after death*, 'The Church affirms that a spiritual element survives and subsists after death, an element endowed with consciousness and will, so that the "human self" subsists, though deprived for the present of the complement of its body.'[18] In the case of spiritually sensitive, mature and rational human beings it seems just possible to speculate what this existence might be like. We can think of the disembodied soul existing in a mind-dependent state, aware of its own selfhood, remembering its past life, and contemplating the vision of God. But can we think thus of 'The condition of animals after death'? As far as we can judge, animals appear to live very much in the present and their thoughts and purposes concern their immediate needs. Indeed, without a complex language it is hard to see how it would be possible to have a developed, reflective intellectual life and a fully developed power of reasoning such that one could identify one's selfhood with that capacity. Yet unless the subject's selfhood can validly be identified with its capacity for reflective reasoning it would not be possible to say that that 'self' could exist in a disembodied state. Consider, for example, the suggestion that a dog's soul subsists after the death of its body. The question that has to be asked for this notion to be intelligible is whether a dog actually has the kind of mental life which alone could make sense of the suggestion that its soul could survive the dissolution of its body as the bearer of the canine personality. Though one cannot any longer accept the clear-cut distinctions of the Aristotelian-Thomist tradition, there does seem to be a point in its judgment that a soul which was only sentient would be mortal whereas a rational intellectual soul could enjoy immortality.

Turning to the religious dimension, Marx may well have been right to include religion as one of the features that distinguish human societies from animal societies.[19] At least what we can say is that some kind of ritual directed towards the transcendent has been observed to exist in every known human community but such behavioural evidence appears to be lacking from our observations of animal behaviour. Such evidence may not be completely lacking in that I remember being told that dolphins turn towards the sun in a characteristic way at sunrise and sunset. I cannot find documentation for this anywhere, so I do not know if this is fact or fancy. But even if this were both true and significant it would only extend the issue to dolphins. The general point remains valid that, as far as we can see (with the possible exception of dolphins!), animals do not worship. Hence a mode of existence which was given intelligibility by the thought that in it God would become the most real feature of our experiencing would not be a mode of existence which would ensure continuity of identity for animals.

In other words I conclude that although there are problems with both the Aristotelian-Thomist and the Cartesian concepts of the soul, and although we have evidence of both thought and feeling in many higher animals, it still remains the case that the concept of an animal possessing a substantive immortal soul capable of surviving the death of its body may not really be an intelligible concept if one explores its implications.

Most contemporary philosophers would agree with that judgment, but would go further and insist that humans also be regarded as unequivocally mortal and 'like unto the beasts that perish'. So is there any evidence for supposing that human souls could conceivably 'survive and subsist after death'?

First I suggest that the human soul be understood as a product of the developing life of the human brain. We have already noted the immense difficulties which arise if one tries to see the soul as infused at some point in the development of the foetus as the church has traditionally taught. These difficulties are lessened if like John Hick one thinks that 'distinctive human mentality and spirituality emerges in accordance with the divine purpose, in complex bodily organisms'.[20] The idea is that what we call the soul is not something we come into the world with, but something that we develop in the course of life. This view may derive from John Keats' suggestion that the purpose of our present lives is 'to school an intelligence and make it a Soul'.[21] Richard Swinburne argues that 'the process of evolution so arranged the atoms and molecules as to bring about creatures with a life of conscious experience, which is something altogether new . . . [for though] the mental life of thought, sensation and purpose may be caused by physico-chemical events in the brain, it is quite different from those events . . . our thoughts and feelings are not just phenomena caused by goings on in the brain . . . they are causally efficacious'.[22] Swinburne insists that we must fully accept all that modern biology teaches concerning the place of human beings in the natural order and that 'under normal mundane conditions the functioning of the soul requires the functioning of the body'.[23] Nevertheless, though 'the mental life of thought, sensation and purpose may be caused by physico-chemical events in the brain, it is quite different from those events' and the soul 'acquires some independence of the brain'.[24] Keith Ward adopts the same position: 'Of course the soul depends on the brain . . . but the soul need not always depend on the brain, any more than a man need always depend on the womb which supported his life before birth.'[25]

On this hypothesis the soul is an emergent property that comes into existence in the course of life. Throughout life it interacts with the body, but in principle it is separable from it and perhaps this separation occurs at death. This hypothesis appears to be supported by the claims made by many resuscitated persons that at the moment their hearts stopped beating they found themselves outside their bodies looking down with interest on the attempts made by the medical teams to revive them. What makes these claims evidential is that their observations seem to be extraordinarily accurate, and to accord with what would have been seen if they genuinely were looking down from above.[26] Such people never have any doubt that 'they' are most truly the subjects of the 'looking-down experience', rather than the comatose bodies they think of themselves as having 'left'. In almost all cases the experience leads to a sense of total conviction that their souls would have survived bodily death.

A second supporting argument for the emergence of the human soul is the development of rational thought. This argument is a very old one and we have already noted Aquinas' endorsement of Aristotle's view that understanding alone takes place without a physical organ. The argument is that rational thought, scientific enquiry, and responsible decision-making all depend on the view that human persons are genuinely free agents, and that a materialist understanding of the mind threatens that freedom. The human brain is a physical organism – as such it is subject to the laws of physics and chemistry. And one of these laws is that physical causes always precede physical effects, and that teleological kinds of explanation – that is, explaining natural phenomena by reference to future goals – are inappropriate. But almost all human researchers think of their own work as responsible and goal-directed, and when a person presents a rational argument he or she thinks she is doing something more than simply giving a report on his or her own past brain states. When Jacques Monod declared that his goal in writing *Chance and Necessity* was to show that there was no such thing as purpose, his argument depended on exempting himself from its remit.[27] For purposive activity is basic to all rational argument, and genuinely purposive activity is incompatible with physically determined activity. Only an immaterial soul can guarantee the freedom that human rationality requires.

A third argument for the immortality of the human soul is the claim that human beings can enter into a relationship of love and fellowship with God, and that God will wish to sustain this relationship through death. The evidence of prayer and worship is that experiential knowledge of God is central to living faith. Yet God is not apprehended through the senses, so if divine-human encounter is real it must be that God makes the reality of divine presence felt other than through neural pathways: direct to the mind and not via sensory stimuli. This can only happen if the soul exists as a substantive reality.[28]

The grounds for believing in the reality of the human soul are therefore the experience of separation from the body near the point of death, the experience of reflective rational thought, and the experience of divine human encounter in ways that transcend the physical. We have grounds for thinking that these are real human experiences. We have no means of knowing whether or not animals partake in any of these experiences and therefore no basis on which to extend the Christian hope to our animal cousins. On the other hand, if some of the higher animals do participate in such experiences there would be no theological problem in rejoicing that God's embrace of eternal love is wider than the Christian tradition has hitherto supposed.

16

Will Animals be Redeemed?

Petroc and Eldred Willey

Let us begin by making two points. First, *central to Christianity is a concern with redemption*, both from death and from sin, from a destructive pattern of relationships with God, with one another, with ourselves, and with creation. Secondly, both scripture and tradition agree that *the Christian understanding of redemption involves the whole of the created order* – and therefore animals – in *some* sense. Any Christian theology of redemption must do justice to the basic Christian belief that the whole creation will be transformed by God (as St Paul expresses it: Rom. 8.19–22), or succeeded by a new heaven and a new earth (II Peter 3.11–13; Rev. 21.1). In the Catholic tradition this belief is clearly stated in the documents of Vatican II, where it is stressed that the entire world will be fulfilled in Christ.[1] The difficulty, then, is not in establishing these general points, but in understanding just what can be *meant* by redemption in the case of animals.

Scripture and the early Christian tradition

Early Old Testament writings focus on the Spirit which God breathes into both humans and animals to give them life, and then withdraws from them so that they die (Gen. 2.7; Ps. 104.29–30). The belief in 'immortality' made a late appearance in Judaism, in the late post-exilic period. Wisdom, the last of the Old Testament books, written in the last half of the first century BC, does clearly look forward to immortality for *human beings*. Here it is synthesizing older hints and hopes (cf. Pss. 49.16, 73.23–4; Isa. 26.19; Dan. 12.2; II Macc. 7). For the Lord Jesus, however, the kingdom of God meant a time when God would rule all creation – 'heaven and earth, man and beast'.[2] On this point he was at one with prophetic hope, which had a wide understanding of the scope of redemption, often involving the idea of the earth's restoration.[3] The important point to establish, then, is that in the biblical tradition, taken as a whole, redemption is inclusive of animals.

No definitive understanding of the meaning of animal redemption is given in the early Christian tradition. But the doctrine that the whole world (and not just human beings and angels) is to be saved in *some* fashion occupies a key position in the theologies of many of the early Fathers, such as Justin, Irenaeus, Hippolytus, Mileto, Commodian, and Lactantius.[4] For instance, in his impressive scheme of creation and redemption, Irenaeus understands the historical process from the Fall until the incarnation as a narrowing of the locus of salvation: after the Fall only one nation was chosen to carry the message and task of salvation, and then one person was chosen to represent that people. But from the single point of the incarnation, an ever-widening transmission of Christ's redemptive life has begun as the church grows to include all nations. This movement, Irenaeus believed, will not be completed until the whole universe has been 'recapitulated' and transformed.[5]

In agreement with Irenaeus the early church established a firm link between protology and eschatology: any theological position which tried to drive a wedge between creation and redemption (e.g. gnosticism and Marcionism) was declared heretical. There was to be continuity and also transformation. God would make the 'last things like the first things' (*Epistle to Barnabas* 6.13), but this was not simply the restoration of an original perfection, an identity between beginning and end, as in the Origenist scheme. Paul stresses the superiority of the coming incorruptible state over the first things (I Cor. 15.35 ff.).

Animal redemption: the 'representative' and the 'non-representative' views

Given the prevalence of the notion of animal redemption in some form, there are two ways of construing its meaning: a 'representative' and a 'non-representative' view.

The first understands animal redemption taking place 'in' humanity, not as individual creatures, but as characteristics of the created order which are summed up in humanity. 'The remembered shapes of our evolutionary ancestry are recapitulated in every human embryo.'[6] On this view, the redemption of even a single human being would entail the redemption of the whole of creation. Since Christ is risen from the dead the animal kingdom is already redeemed in him.

According to this view, the history of the world and of evolution might be compared to a vast alchemical process. Alchemists held that all metals are living substances in the process of growth towards gold, which is their true goal. If there were no exterior obstacles, nature would always complete this process, since she longs only to make gold.[7] In the same way, the world could be viewed as aimed at giving birth to the children of God, which is its main purpose (cf. Rom. 8.18 ff.). In the alchemical process the metals are, ideally, transformed into gold. It might be argued that in this way they achieve 'salvation'.

In a similar way, animals might be understood to be undergoing a process of transformation into humanity, thereby achieving their redemption. Buffaloes will not be saved as buffaloes: in the alchemical process iron is not saved as iron, but only as gold. Animals will be saved by being incorporated into humanity. How might this happen?

First, through the resurrection of the human body. In the resurrection of the human body all of nature participates, since it is of the stuff of nature that the human body is composed. The human body is restored at the last because it participates in the realm of grace, and in this body the whole of nature, including animals, finds its looked-for transformation.

Secondly, through the consciousness or vision of the redeemed person. Here, the redemption of animals would be a matter of their being known and loved as they truly are, of their forms being taken into our consciousness and delighted in. Rilke's beautiful meditation in the *Duino Elegies* on the relationship between the human spirit and nature offers us such a picture.

> Isn't the earth's
> > hidden strategy
> > > when she so slyly
> > > > urges two lovers on
> > that each and every thing
> > > should be transformed
> > > > by the delight
> of sharing their feelings?. . .
>
> They want us to change them
> > completely
> inside our invisible hearts
> > into – oh endlessly –
> > > into ourselves! . . .
>
> Earth, isn't this
> > what you want:
> > > rising up

> inside us invisibly
>> once more?
>>> Isn't it your dream
>> to be invisible someday?
>>> Earth! invisible!
>>>> what is it
> you urgently ask for
>> if not transformation?
>>> Earth, my love
> I will do it.[8]

Thirdly, through the unique capacity of the human soul. This is supported by a theological understanding of the human person as a synthesized creature, a union of body and spirit. So Nicolas de Cusa, for example, said that the human soul assumes the capacities of all inferior creatures within its own unity.[9] The human person is nature's representative in the spheres of both creation and salvation. When a person adores God, then, the whole of nature adores God in and through that person. Each element of the created order can praise God separately, according to its proper mode, but each remains limited because of its own nature. The human person alone, as a representative being, can unite the praises of all creation.[10]

What is it exactly that the human person is representing? No single answer has been given in the Christian tradition. For example, within a Christian Platonist picture of the cosmos, it would imply the representation not of individuals but of general aspects or types: I do not represent Tabitha, but the Feline nature; not Leo the lion, but the Leonine nature. So, although the Feline nature will be saved, Tabitha will not. A related way of understanding the representation of animals is to conceive of this as being of general characteristics of the created order rather than of particular animal forms. What is lost in these notions of representation is a sense of the worth of animals as individuals in redemption.

The second, 'non-representative' view of animal redemption sees animals redeemed as individuals, just as, according to Christian theology, humans retain their full individuality when redeemed. This view may still be understood as redemption 'in' humanity, in the sense of stressing the inseparability of humanity from the rest of the created order, and the centrality of humanity in Christ to the created order. What is different, however, is the insistence that animals, as subjects of individual lives, cannot be incorporated as 'aspects' of humanity without a loss of their essential selves.

One of the arguments in favour of immortality for animals in this fuller sense is the fact that they suffer. Historically, part of the appeal of the Cartesian view of animals as automata, and so as incapable of experiencing pain, was that this removed the theological problem of animal suffering. For, argued numerous Cartesians, if animals are not destined for happiness in an afterlife, it would be an injustice on God's part if they were to suffer. From this they drew the rather startling conclusion that they do not suffer. For metaphysical reasons it was judged that the appearance of pain in animals must be deceptive, an unjustified inference from our own experiences of pleasure and pain and the physical signs that habitually accompany them. But if we reject the idea that animals are non-sentient, then by an application of *modus tollens* we can see that since animals do suffer it would be an injustice on God's part if they were not destined for happiness in some future life.[11]

A number of contemporary theologians consider, and reject, such arguments. John Hick, for instance, rejecting the suggestion of individual animal immortality, justifies animal suffering on the grounds that animals provide part of the present 'setting' for the making of human souls.[12] They are part of the environment within which human souls can develop and mature. Hick can adopt this line of argument because he does not believe that animals are subjects of lives in any significant sense so that, while God is Kantian in respect for human life (treating each as an end in itself), God can treat animals as members of a wider utilitarian whole.[13]

A second argument that might be advanced to support the non-representative view of animal redemption appeals to the notion of God's 'memory'. The idea of immortality through being held in public honour in perpetuity was much prized in antiquity. This notion has now fallen into disrepute since it is recognized that we can only count on this form of immortality in so far as we are able to trust the integrity of those who give it. An immortality which relies upon one's being remembered by the human community is a vulnerable immortality indeed. Moreover, on this basis the evil have as assured an immortality as the good.

Not so, some Christian thinkers have argued, if one is immortalized in the 'memory' of God. If God is outside time, then God's 'memory' is unlike ours in that it is not a matter of recalling something long past. Since God is beyond all categories of past, present, and future, God's 'memory' is equivalent to knowledge. God's 'remembering' of creatures is the same as God's knowledge of them. Now if this is what is meant by immortality – to be known by God – then it is clearly shared by the whole of creation. Trees, rocks, and computers, as well as humans and animals, exist eternally in

God's consciousness. In this sense Rahner can write of the whole history of the world entering eternal life.[14]

We need to clarify this idea, for if eternal life is an unchanging and exact transcription of this life, then the suffering millions will be suffering eternally. There is no change ensuring that the first will be last and the last first: the last will be eternally last. The Christian concept of the afterlife has always been linked to the idea of *transformation*. It is, precisely, a redemption *from present suffering and sin*, not a fixing of it in eternity. Hope in God would lose its meaning if the only prospect were that God would keep alive our present experiences in his ample memory. In fact, the scriptures seem to suggest that redemption is more about amnesia than about remembering. God 'forgets' our wickedness, by virtue of the redemptive act of Christ. It is a *new* earth which we can expect:

> Behold I will create new heavens and a new earth
> The former things will be remembered no more,
> Nor will they come to mind (Isa. 65.17).[15]

The situation is different if it is a case of God remembering not a series of experiences, not a transcript of this earthly life, but *us*. This would be closer to Berkeley's understanding of our existing archetypally in the mind of God.[16] Once more, then, we are led back to the issue of the notion of the *animal self*, for the strongest argument against the view that animals will be redeemed as individuals is that they have no enduring selves which could either benefit from immortality or sensibly be said to survive death.

The animal self

The traditional Christian concept of the animal self is a rich and rewarding one. For example, according to the Aristotelian metaphysics which was adopted by the central Christian tradition, each animal is a unique individual substance; each possesses an enduring self which is a living principle of unity, operation, and organization. Animals share with humans emotion, memory, imagination, and even rudimentary forms of thinking, in the degree which is appropriate to the complexity and depth of interiority of each particular species. They are not, then, mere examples of some general type, but are unique individual selves, each living and dying with its own life experiences arising out of its individual substantial being.

Modern discussions of the nature of the self – both human and animal – emerge from a context very different from this *philosophia perennis* and have lost much of the metaphysical sense of the interiority or depth of *being*. The focus has moved instead on to a consideration of *consciousness* and *self-consciousness* and so, for example, it has been argued that only those creatures who have a degree of self-consciousness could possibly share the life of the immortals. Though it might seem that those creatures who lack self-consciousness are thereby deprived of a great gift, this is held not to be the case, for they entertain no concept of a self which could be deprived. Humans are self-conscious and their lives constitute 'stories';[17] animals, on the other hand, though they live individuated lives which are extended through time, are not selves but (to use Hume's terminology) 'bundles of perceptions'.[18]

Hume, of course, doubted whether *we* are more than this – the change and flux of mental dispositions with no enduring self to whom they could be said to belong.[19] There is no empirical evidence, he held, for the existence of a single, permanent self underlying either human or animal perceptions. If we introspect, all we are aware of is a continuous sequence of changing mental states, never of any self which 'has' them.

Hume, however, was wrong. It is true that the self can never be the direct object of empirical knowledge, but it is counter-intuitive to presume that perceptions could exist without inhering in something: their existence lies, surely, in being perceived. But in that case there must exist individual subjects who do the perceiving. Perceptions inhere in the self in just this simple sense, that the self perceives them. When we talk about self-consciousness we do not necessarily mean an awareness of some transcendent 'I' but rather the ability to recognize certain acts and dispositions as belonging to me rather than anyone else.

It is this ability which many argue that a human possesses, while a cat does not. A cat's life would thus be considered as a series of sensations without any accompanying consciousness that they belong to one and the same creature, itself. Even if redeemed, this cat would not be able to identify itself with a particular animal who once lived on earth. By this argument, for it to make sense to speak of a creature being redeemed as an individual it has to be self-conscious. But animals are not self-conscious. So they will not be redeemed as individuals.

Can anything be said in answer to the self-consciousness argument? One response would be to accept the premiss that self-consciousness is crucial for redemption as an individual, but to contest the denial of self-consciousness to animals. Gallop, for example, has developed a procedure which exploits the interest displayed by the great apes in their own mirror images.[20] The sort of evidence we might look for, in trying to assess whether or not a given animal is self-aware, would be its ability to place itself in a social world. In particular we might ask whether the creature was able to recognize other creatures as individuals, since this would seem a necessary condition for understanding oneself as such.

We do not even need elaborate experiments with apes and mirrors. Consider the following common sequence of events: a single young male animal enjoys the freedom of bachelorhood and only has to feed himself. After he has paired and produced young, however, his behaviour changes. Even though he may be out of sight and earshot of his family, and therefore cannot be responding to a perception of them, he exerts himself to gather food for them. His understanding of himself has changed: he is conscious that he is not the male he used to be, that he has developed, that his 'story' has moved on. (Or is he? An opponent would argue that whilst his behaviour has changed this need not be accompanied by any self-reflective process.)

A second response would be to argue for the weaker thesis that, even if each member of an animal community is not self-conscious, we can still speak of the community as a whole being, in some *analogous* sense, self-aware. Just as we human beings gain a sense of self through being members of a community in which we can identify other selves, so animals, in being aware of each other, can be conscious of the one Community Self acting in and through them. Animal societies would thus be conceived rather as monistic systems where the whole is a single self-conscious being. There is one Ego self-conscious in every act of consciousness. It is the animal *community* which will be raised, and which will be able to recognize itself at the moment of resurrection as identical with an earthly society.

What would be the place of individuals in such a community? Is it important that the *same* individuals are raised to constitute the redeemed community, or is each individual essentially replaceable, so that the Dolphin Ego will recognize itself as identical with earthly dolphins whoever the individuals are who make up its resurrected form?

We may often regard animals as substitutable repetitions of a type, but it is clear that animals themselves do not. One important learning function in birds and mammals is the development of personal recognition of specific individuals. The ability to respond differently to specific creatures is an essential prerequisite for two of the fundamental features of closed animal societies: the distinction between members and non-members of the group, and the internal hierarchy prevailing among group members. Hen Agatha learns to act in one way towards hen Betty and in another way towards hen Clarissa. Each has her own place in the pecking order and in this way finds her identity in the community. If Betty or Clarissa were replaced by another hen she would have a different place in the whole and to that extent a different identity. So if Agatha is to be raised, Betty and Clarissa will have to be raised with her. The social relations between members of animal communities indicate, then, that animals are not simply replaceable and any account of animal redemption will need to take account of this. And they will have to be raised not as mere relations or objects of consciousness, because relations only exist between real subjects and because consciousness is an attribute of being.

Thus we return to the traditional understanding of the animal self as a unique individual substance.[21] This still offers the most satisfactory basis from which to consider the question of the redemption of animals. The tradition has, in fact, typically held that animals, while possessing selves which endure through time, do not survive the disintegration of death. But perhaps we can be agnostic on this point. *That* animals will be redeemed is certain: that was our starting point and can be our conclusion also. *How* that redemption is to be conceived – and especially whether it is to be thought of in terms of representative or non-representative models – turns on this question of the nature of the animal self. This is a matter on which scripture and tradition give us no *definitive* answer, and neither do the judgments of contemporary science. If the whole of what animals are can be incorporated into humanity then this suffices for their redemption. If the interiority and individuality of animals is such that they cannot be adequately represented in and through humankind then redemption will feature animal selves in their own right.

Tailpiece: Redemption from sin

Let us turn finally to the question of the transformation of relationships amongst members of the animal kingdom and between human beings and animals. Isaiah 11.6–9 and 65.25 present us with pictures of natural harmony in the redeemed creation:

> The wolf and the lamb shall feed together, the lion shall eat straw like the ox;
> and dust shall be the serpent's food.
> They shall not hurt or destroy in all my holy mountain, says the Lord.
> (Isa. 65.25)

Are these pictures to be taken merely as a figure for human relationships, or to be understood literally? Let us assume that they do refer to animals. Of course, we have to be careful that we are not being sentimental in supposing that there is something wrong with lions and wolves eating lambs. Predation and the suffering which goes with it is clearly built into the natural world. As Blake reminds us, God created the tiger as well as the lamb. Indeed, there is a predator-like aspect in God's nature which is reflected in his creatures:

> But ah, but O thou terrible, why wouldst thou rude on me
> Thy wring-world right foot rock, lay a lion-limb against me . . .[22]

We may – at least in the present aeon – be wanting both God and the natural world to be less than they are by wishing to eliminate killing for food. But we should not exaggerate the extent to which nature is red in tooth and claw: nature is not uniformly violent any more than the human race is. An alpine flower is as much part of nature as the lion and the wolf. However, it is clear that at present the lion cannot eat straw with the ox, not least because his alimentary canal is too short to digest it. In the present dispensation we should not prevent lions from attacking lambs – it would be cruel to lions to attempt this and it should be remembered that Jesus did not expect the human race to disentangle sin and virtue in the present order; he counselled his followers to let the wheat and the tares grow together.

On the other hand, let us consider the thesis that at least *some* of the violence of nature is associated with human sin. The biblical picture is of an 'intimate association of man and nature in their relation to the mystery of iniquity'[23] and to the mystery of redemption (cf. Rom. 8.18 ff.). When Israel sins, the land is laid waste, and when she returns from exile the land blossoms anew (see Isa. 41). In support of this picture we might point to the obvious visible causal links between some kinds of human behaviour and some kinds of domestic animal behaviour: we can breed dogs like retrievers, which play with children, or dogs like rottweilers, which savage them. Going further, we should remember that the saints among us, like St Francis, can apparently persuade wolves at least not to attack people.[24]

We can, then, unite ourselves to the Lord's redemptive work and to the healing of the relationship between humanity and the animal kingdom. Many relationships in nature are not mutually destructive, but symbiotic: they benefit both parties involved. A beech tree provides food for squirrels, and the squirrels help the beech tree to propagate by burying stores of beechnuts and forgetting some of them. Succulent fruits are designed to be eaten by animals so that the seeds, which are not digested, can be spread. If human beings were to move towards (and rediscover) these kind of relationships with the animal kingdom then Isaiah's vision of harmony would at least begin to become a reality.

PART FOUR

Obligations to Animals

Introduction

Andrew Linzey

The failure of the tradition to ask serious questions about animals has led to theologians, church leaders, and spokespeople being effectively embarrassed when it comes to public debate over issues in animal protection. Again and again, Christian spokespeople who are given the opportunity to engage in debate through the media either refuse or, even worse, accept and offer little more than platitudinous comment. The tragedy of this is that there are a range of pressing practical issues where a thoughtful Christian voice could, and should, be heard but rarely is. The neglect of creative theology has rendered the Christian voice almost silent. The result is that people come to believe that there really *are* no theological issues involved in how we clone animals in laboratories, genetically manipulate them in farming, trap them for fur, hunt them for sport, or patent them as inventions.

Just one example may suffice: some years ago the moderator of a paper in ethics I happened to be teaching circulated his judgment that the examination should more adequately cover issues in sexuality and marriage, and, since some students who were taking the paper were also preparing for ordination, he added the comment that ordained ministers would be expected to be 'experts' on marriage and not on the ethics of modern livestock systems. I couldn't help making the point that this presupposed a rather limited view of modern 'husbandry' – but I was nevertheless taken aback by the prejudice and the parochialism which the comments represented. I certainly hope that ordained ministers will be able to engage thoughtfully with issues relating to contemporary sexual morality, but it is an unhelpful and unwholesome caricature of Christian ministry to suppose that this should be the main or exclusive subject of ethical 'expertise' among the clergy. Almost by sleight of hand, the ethical issue about animals is pushed to one side.

In my view, work needs to begin in earnest to discern those Christian principles and insights at stake in public discussion about animals. Here is an agenda for every seminary, theological college, university department of theology, parish study group, weekend conference, evening discussion group, not to mention national church boards, councils, and synods. The aim must be to create as many Christian contexts as possible for informed and reflective discussion of the moral question about animals. There really is little hope for the Christian community until ethically concerned Christians refuse – volubly and persistently – to allow any further side-stepping and marginalization of the animal issue.

But would we know a moral question about animals if we saw one? The question is addressed by Brian Klug, who is disturbed by the way in which we allow other, non-moral questions to usurp the ethical one. There is a lesson here for all animal users and practitioners: the otherwise admirable single-minded attention to one particular aim, whether it be in research, farming, sport, trade, or commerce, can easily blind us to the moral issue just before our eyes. Recognition of this moral dimension is not an issue *per se* for experts, scientists, officials, academics, professionals, and the rest, but for all human beings simply because seeing the moral issue is an inescapable (or mostly inescapable!) part of being human. 'Calling a question moral is to call attention to this fact: to the fact that we are human beings first, whatever the particular angle of our professional interest,' maintains Klug. All of us who have any dealings with animals (and that means all of us) need to prize our status as moral 'lay people', that is, people who can see a moral issue for ourselves, with or without the help of the 'experts'.

That there is some glimmer of hope for theology and the churches is shown by the three remaining chapters, which indicate how major traditions – Evangelical, Anglican, and Catholic – are finding ways of thoughtfully addressing the animal issue. The first, by Huw Spanner, takes issue with the all-too-common acceptance among evangelicals that human life is infinitely more precious than animal life. He finds much in the Bible to challenge arrogant human supremacism. While humans are undoubtedly special, they are not God's sole concern. He draws explicit support from the biblical concept of servant-kingship, an idea fully realized in Jesus. 'If we have dominion over God's other creatures', he argues, 'then we are called to live in peace with them, as good shepherds and humble servants.'

An Anglican perspective is provided by Paul Brett, who has spent a lifetime addressing issues of social responsibility in the Church of England. He reviews the wide range of practical work by governmental and voluntary organizations in the United Kingdom, and notes the emotionally charged nature of the current debate – a feature which frequently causes church-people to dismiss a concern for animal welfare as sentimentalism. While emotion is an uncertain basis for ethics, Brett also recognizes that 'fellow feeling [is] an appropriate response'. But, in his view, emotionalism and compassion point beyond themselves to a stronger obligation – one that is now increasingly recognized by those involved in animal welfare – namely, justice. '[T]o attribute a right to a creature is to recognize its existence whether human beings find it convenient or not. It is to build on the sense that animals have a claim on us, and a claim that needs to be stated and protected in case it is overlooked.' Brett concludes that these rights have their 'origin both in natural law and in the divine will expressed in creation'.

Our final chapter, by the Catholic theologian John Berkman, relates the animal issue to the 'consistent ethic of life' movement in the United States. He questions the consistency of such an ethic that does *not* include animals. Since reverence for animal, as well as human, life is implicit in recent papal teaching, it is now only logical to apply this principle to the question of killing for food. Catholic thought has gradually broadened the range of its pro-life position to include almost total opposition to capital punishment. It is not inconceivable that future Catholic teaching will be extended further to include opposition to the non-necessary killing of animals, especially for food. In Berkman's view, confronting the 'culture of death' requires prophetic action as a form of witness to the peaceable kingdom. 'Some no doubt will argue that it is inappropriate to draw any connection between the goodness and dignity of the lives of animals and humans on Death Row,' he acknowledges. But he concludes that 'the goodness of both kinds of lives are due respect and protection'.

These final chapters enable us to end our collection on an upbeat note. Of course there are formidable difficulties in the churches confronting the animal issue. But are these difficulties any more insurmountable than those which the tradition has had to face on other issues – for example, biblical support for slavery, or traditional teaching justifying the subordination of women? Despite the heated debates, the threats of schism, and the fearfulness of many believers, churches can and have changed their minds and found themselves enlarged and revivified as a result. Of course, not all so-called 'progress' is good: there can be – and frequently is – regression in moral awareness. But since the heart of the animal issue is an advocacy for peace rather than violence it is difficult to believe the Spirit has not some hand in it – a hand which, according to tradition, leads us on to the fully realized peaceable kingdom.

17

Can we See a Moral Question about Animals?

Brian Klug

Consider the following question: May we ever perform experiments on animals that cause them harm or suffering, or kill them, or otherwise prevent them from living their lives? By 'we' I mean human beings in general and research scientists in particular. By 'animals' I mean, well, animals. But what is an animal? And do we know one when we see one? The answer to this last question depends, I think, on the frame of mind in which we look – on what Thoreau calls the 'intention of the eye'.[1] I am interested in the bearing that 'the intention of the eye' has on the question I formulated in the first sentence, a moral question about the use of animals in scientific research. I am concerned, in particular, with a certain kind of tunnel vision in science which subverts the question altogether, preventing it from being seen for what it is: a *moral* question about *animals*. My purpose is to save the question, not to answer it; to ensure it is on the agenda. (So I shall not discuss the pros and cons, the rights and wrongs, of using animals in scientific research.) I shall pursue this aim by examining the logic of the frame of mind that is blind to this question. To this end, I shall utilize excerpts from two works written in the second half of the nineteenth century which give expression to this frame of mind, one by a popular writer of science fiction, the other by a celebrated figure in the history of scientific research. I shall begin with the fictional Dr Moreau.

In *The Island of Doctor Moreau*, a novel by H. G. Wells published in 1896, Edward Prendick is marooned on a remote island somewhere in the Pacific. The island is uninhabited except for two Englishmen and a small population of malformed individuals who seem, to Prendick's eye, not entirely human. One of the two Englishmen is the 'prominent and masterful physiologist' Dr Moreau.[2] Moreau, a 'notorious vivisector', who was 'howled out of the country' on account of his experiments on live animals, continues to pursue his research in a laboratory he has built on the island.[3]

One day Prendick, hearing cries of excruciating pain coming from the laboratory, barges in, only to recoil from the sight of 'something bound painfully upon a framework, scarred, red, and bandaged'.[4] It is an animal – a puma – upon which Moreau has been operating. Several bizarre chapters later, Moreau divulges the secret of his research to Prendick. He explains that the humanoid creatures on the island are (or originally were) animals that he has surgically altered. He exclaims, 'To that – to the study of the plasticity of living forms – my life has been devoted.'[5] Warming to his subject, and calling himself 'an investigator', he gives eloquent expression to the 'intellectual passion' that motivates his work:

> You cannot imagine the strange colourless delight of these intellectual desires. The thing before you is no longer an animal, a fellow-creature, but a problem. Sympathetic pain – all I know of it I remember as a thing I used to suffer from years ago. I wanted – it was the only thing I wanted – to find out the extreme limit of plasticity in a living shape.[6]

When Prendick protests, describing his work as 'an abomination', Moreau responds by saying, 'To this day I have never troubled about the ethics of the matter. The study of Nature makes a man at last as remorseless as Nature.'[7] What Moreau means by this is unclear. Is he saying that, given the scientific nature of his work, ethics is not his business? Or is he saying that he operates on a plane that is higher than mere morality; that he is, so to speak, beyond good and evil? The latter seems to be implied by the way he describes himself. He calls himself 'remorseless'. Now, remorselessness is not a morally neutral state. (The fact that it is not morally neutral is one reason why the simile 'as remorseless as nature' is fatuous.) Normally, to describe someone as remorseless is to make a moral judgment: it is to say that they lack compassion, or that they fail to feel regret when they should. However, this cannot be what Moreau means when he calls *himself* remorseless, since he derides compassion ('Sympathetic pain'), referring to it as something he used to *suffer* from – as though it were a weakness or an affliction. So, rather than judging himself, he appears to be judging remorse: he appears to be saying, in effect, that such feelings would be a failing in an 'investigator' (in other words, a research scientist). It is not clear, then, whether he is saying that he is indifferent to 'the ethics of the matter' or that he is above them. But, either way, this much is clear: he is saying that the moral question of whether he should or should not pursue his research (or pursue it in the way that he does) does not concern him, because he is an 'investigator'.

Although the plot of the novel is pure invention, Dr Moreau is not necessarily – or perhaps simply – a figment of Wells' imagination. Wells, like his fictional character Edward Prendick, had studied under T. H. Huxley when he was a biology student in London.[8] He was certainly aware of the controversy surrounding the use of live animals in scientific research.[9] And Moreau's speech to Prendick is strikingly reminiscent of this passage from *Introduction to the Study of Experimental Medicine* written by Claude Bernard and published thirty years earlier, in 1865:

> The physiologist is not a layman, he is a scientist; he is a man gripped and absorbed by the scientific idea that he pursues: he no longer hears the cries of animals, he no longer sees the blood that flows, he sees only his idea, and perceives only organisms that conceal from him the problems he wants to solve.[10]

The frame of mind or point of view is essentially the same as that expressed by Moreau – even some of the words are the same (allowing for the difference between Bernard's French and Moreau's English). Where there might seem to be a divergence is in connection with what Moreau calls the ethics of the matter. Bernard poses the question explicitly and answers it forthrightly: 'Does one have the right to perform experiments on animals and to vivisect them? For my part, I think that one does, wholly and absolutely.'[11] It appears, then, that Bernard, unlike Moreau, has troubled about the rights and wrongs of experimenting on live animals and that he has considered the moral question with which I began. It *appears* that way, but in reality, as closer examination reveals, he has not. Later I shall discuss the argument he makes to support his position regarding the ethics of the matter. But it is not necessary to examine his reasoning as such. It is enough to know the frame of mind or point of view. I shall argue that to look at animals from this point of view is to cease to see them *as* animals; and if animals are not seen as animals then the moral question with which I began disappears.

Before I embark on this argument I should explain why it is worth paying attention to Bernard and Moreau. After all, both figures are larger than life. Moreau is an anti-hero in the fictional tradition of Frankenstein: a human being more monstrous than the monsters he creates. Bernard, who is widely acclaimed as a founder of modern experimental physiology, was an innovator and pioneer. Neither man is typical of today's research scientists, most of whom are humble men and women performing routine experiments, and many of whom would call Bernard and Moreau callous.

At the very least, most people in science today would find their language overblown. But it is precisely this latter quality that is useful. Bernard and Moreau might be guilty of hyperbole but their words have the merit of presenting, writ large, the perspective of the pure research scientist *per se*. Furthermore, in privileging this perspective, they express an attitude that people, both inside and outside science, often have without always knowing it or admitting it. Bernard's case is, I believe, especially relevant because what applies to him applies also to many others who tend to take his position on the ethics of the matter; that is to say, they *answer* the moral question with which I began without ever truly *asking* it. They do not take the question to heart. And they do not take it to heart because they approach it in the wrong mind – in the sort of mind expressed by Bernard in the passage quoted above.

I turn now to an examination of this passage. Notice, to begin with, to whom Bernard refers. 'The physiologist', he says, 'is not a layman.'[12] It is natural to suppose that he is speaking about himself. No doubt he is; but he writes in the third person and the subject of the statement is 'the physiologist', not Claude Bernard *per se*. (I shall use the word 'physiologist' as an umbrella term for scientists whose research could be in any one of a broad range of biological disciplines. I realize this is a somewhat archaic use of the word but it is convenient to use it in the same way that Bernard and Wells use it.) The statement Bernard makes is general and not specifically about himself. Notice, however, that he speaks of *the physiologist* and not of *physiologists*; and when I say that his statement is general, I do not mean that he is making a *generalization*. That is to say, he is not making an empirical claim about how actual physiologists do in fact, or do in general, think or feel. What he gives us is a *type*: he is describing what the physiologist is like *in principle*. He is saying, in other words, that this is what it means to be a physiologist; as if someone who did not feel or think along the lines that he describes would not be the real thing. He is giving us, in effect, a definition.

Bernard defines the physiologist as 'a scientist', a man who is 'gripped and absorbed by the scientific idea that he pursues'. Note how Bernard characterizes a scientist. A scientist is someone whose mind is on a certain kind of object and in a certain state. The object is an idea; specifically a *scientific* idea. The state is that of being 'gripped and absorbed' by this idea. Now, 'gripped and absorbed' might seem to be strong words to describe the state of mind of a scientist, which we tend to think of as detached and dispassionate. But Bernard's scientist *is* detached, as the rest of his description vividly asserts: 'he no longer hears the cries of animals, he no longer sees the blood that flows . . .'. The point is that detachment is relative; that is to say, it is relative to the object of interest. Bernard's scientist is detached from the suffering of animals precisely because he or she is 'gripped and absorbed' by a 'scientific idea': these are two sides of one coin. There is, and there can be, no such thing as a mind that is *absolutely* detached – unless it is a mind that takes an interest in absolutely nothing. And the word that describes someone who takes an interest in nothing is 'apathetic', not 'scientific'.

However, there is a question about the *degree* of interest one takes in something; and it might be thought that Bernard's scientist takes an inordinate interest in research. Perhaps the words 'gripped and absorbed' conjure up the stock figure of the mad scientist for whom science is an all-consuming obsession. But that would be to miss the point of Bernard's description. You could say that Bernard gives us a highly romanticized version of the pure research scientist. Alternatively, you could say, as I shall say, that what he gives us is a highly rhetorical account of what it means to take a purely scientific interest in a piece of research. On this reading, the words 'gripped and absorbed' serve to emphasize that the point of view that Bernard describes is pure (purely scientific). What he is saying in this passage amounts to this: that the physiologist, looking at animals in the laboratory from a purely scientific point of view, is interested only in data – data that bear upon 'the problem he wants to solve'.

Moreau, hell-bent on performing his diabolical experiments in his secret island hideaway, comes closer to the stock figure of the mad scientist. I dare say he *is* crazy and that Wells meant to depict him this way. However, I am interested only in the logic of what Moreau says when he explains himself to Prendick, not in his character as such. And the logic of what he says is the same as that of Bernard. Like Bernard's physiologist, he is detached, in the sense that he experiences no feelings of sympathy for the animals on which he experiments. But he is certainly not without feeling of *some* kind, for he speaks of his 'intellectual passion' and of 'the strange colourless delight' of his 'intellectual desires'. Once again, as with Bernard, we are looking at two sides of one coin. That is to say, Moreau's feeling for his subject ('the study of the plasticity of living forms') is one side of the coin of which his lack of feeling for the animals on which he experiments is the other. It might not be clear how delight can be 'colourless', or passion and desire 'intellectual'; but the point is that it is *delight*, *passion*, and *desire* of which he speaks. The adjectives ('colourless', 'intellectual') are cerebral and point to the scientific nature of the object of his interest: the 'problem' concerning 'the extreme limit of plasticity in a living shape'. The substantives ('delight', 'passion', 'desire') express the fact that the interest he takes in this problem is total; and, being total, he is only interested in whatever sheds light on his problem. By Bernard's definition, he is a physiologist to the core. In short, both men, Moreau and Bernard, give us a graphic picture of someone who single-mindedly looks at animals from the angle of one particular interest: physiology.

Seen from this angle, what does the physiologist perceive? In Bernard's words, 'only organisms that conceal from him the problems he wants to solve'. Lurking in this metaphor of concealment is a Baconian view of science in which the researcher seeks to extract 'the secrets still locked in Nature's bosom'.[13] This puts the whole of what Bernard says about the physiologist in a certain light; and in order to understand him fully it is necessary to place his words within the larger context of the rhetoric associated with the rise of modern (experimental) science from the six-teenth century on.[14] However, this is not necessary for the present purpose. Rather, what I wish to draw attention to is the word 'organism', the word Bernard uses to refer to that which 'conceals' the scientific problem from the physiologist.

Is the organism an animal? Of course it is. Then why does Bernard not refer to it as such? The answer is that the physiologist, according to Bernard, 'sees only his idea', and consequently is aware of the animal only in terms of that idea; and at the heart of physiology is the idea of the organism. And *is* not the animal an organism? Certainly it is. But it is also an animal. The physiologist, you might say, is not interested in the animal as such. That is what it means to say that the physiologist 'no longer hears the cries of animals' nor 'sees the blood that flows'. Bernard does not mean that people who study physiology suffer from impaired hearing or need their eyes tested. It is not that they do not hear the cries of pain, it is that they do not hear them *as* cries of pain. It is a matter of what they do or do not tune out. By the same token, it is not that they are unaware of the blood but that they are aware of it only as, say, a bodily fluid composed of certain chemical constituents and performing certain organic functions – and not as an injury or loss suffered by the animal as such. Moreau puts it this way: 'The thing before you', he says, 'is no longer an animal, a fellow-creature, but a problem.' When he says 'before you' he means before *him*, Dr Moreau, the physiologist. And when he says that the animal 'is no longer an animal' he does not mean that by some alchemy or miracle it ceases to be what it is. He is saying that *to the physiologist* the animal is not an animal. It is not, that is to say, 'a fellow-creature'.

It is not a *fellow*-creature because there is no such creature – no such animal, you could say, – as a physiologist. None was created on the sixth day. This is not to say that there are no physiologists in the world. It is only to say that all of them are human beings.

This brings me to the crux of the matter. I began with the following question: May we ever perform experiments on animals that cause them harm or suffering, or kill them, or otherwise prevent them from living their lives? I said that by 'we' I mean human beings in general and research scientists in particular. Now, the words *general* and *particular* are important here: they imply that research scientists are included in the same 'we' as everyone else. Singling them out does not make them a breed apart; does not exclude them from the category of human being. The sole reason for singling them out is that they are the ones amongst us who perform experiments on live animals. In performing these experiments, they are concerned with questions that are scientific in nature, questions that arise for them as scientists. But the question of whether it is right or wrong to perform these experiments at all is a *moral* question and it arises for them in the same way that it arises for everyone else: as human beings, not as scientists. This is not to say that the moral question about using live animals in laboratory research is never complicated by considerations that are technical and scientific. It is to say, on the contrary, that even when such considerations apply, the questions to which they give rise are not exclusively, or not necessarily, technical and scientific. There is always logical space for a moral question. That is because experts are never *merely* experts: they are, in the first place, human beings. Calling a question moral is to call attention to this fact: to the fact that we are human beings first, whatever the particular angle of our professional interest.

You could say that this is something about themselves that both Moreau and Bernard forget. (That is to say, they forget *themselves*.) But Moreau, in a way, understands the logic of his position better than Bernard does. He recognizes that, speaking purely as a physiologist, he is not concerned with the ethics of the matter. Or, to put it another way, the question of whether or not Prendick is right in calling his work 'an abomination' is not a question within physiology: it is not a physiological question. Moreau understands this. What is disturbing about him is the fact that the question does not concern him at all: does not concern him, that is, as a human being. So that when he says, 'The thing before you is no longer an animal', it is as if *he* were no longer a *man*. (This is what makes him, as I put it earlier, more monstrous than the monsters he creates.) Bernard, however, as we noted earlier, does concern himself with the ethics of the matter; or at least he purports to. He certainly takes a moral position, claiming that he has the right, 'wholly and absolutely', to perform experiments on animals.

But, as we shall see by examining his argument, the position he takes is really nothing more than the refusal (or inability) to relinquish the point of view of the physiologist: to see animals as anything other than organisms. His point of view is the same as Moreau's, except that unlike Moreau he confuses physiology and ethics.

Bernard's argument depends on the contrast he draws between the physiologist and the layman.[15] 'The physiologist', he says, 'is not a layman, he is a scientist.' This means, on his account, that the physiologist is someone whose thoughts and perceptions are governed by a special idea; that is to say, a *scientific* idea. Then what is a layman? Bernard writes as if a similar sort of account can be given of what it means to be a layman, except that the special idea that governs the thoughts and perceptions of the layman is not scientific: it is lay:

> I understand perfectly . . . that laymen, who are moved by ideas totally different from those that animate the physiologist, judge vivisection completely differently. It could not be otherwise. We have said in some part of this introduction that in science it is the idea that gives facts their value and their significance. It is the same in morals, it is the same everywhere.[16]

So, there are laymen and there are physiologists. The layman is moved by one set of ideas, the physiologist by another. Both judge the rights and wrongs of vivisection accordingly and come to incompatible conclusions. And that's that: there is nothing more to be said; nothing more that *can* be said, according to Bernard, since the moral disagreement between physiologist and layman is simply a function of the different ideas that go with the two different points of view. Hence he declares, 'I shall not try . . . to justify physiologists against the reproach of cruelty made by people who are strangers to science; the difference in ideas explains everything.'[17] This might sound plausible at first but the reasoning is doubly fallacious. In the first place, the concepts of physiologist and layman are not symmetrical. Being a layman is not, logically speaking, on a par with being a physiologist. A physiologist is someone who specializes in a particular field or discipline, namely, physiology. But there is no field or discipline that corresponds to being lay; no point of view either. The concept is purely negative; or, rather, it is purely relative to some profession or other. The layman of whom Bernard speaks is simply someone – anyone – who is *not* a physiologist. Non-physiologists do not compose a group; they do not belong to the same clubs, go to the same places, share the same tastes and come to the same conclusions. They do not all agree about the rights and wrongs of vivisection. Nor, for that matter, do all physiologists. This brings me to the second fallacy in his reasoning. For even if all physiologists were unanimous on this score, their opinion would not flow from the principles of physiology; only *moral* principles can lead to moral conclusions.

What about the moral conclusion for which Bernard argues, namely, that he has a right, 'wholly and absolutely', to perform experiments on animals? Where does this come from? Well, on his account, given the contrast that he draws between physiologist and layman, and given that he is the one and not the other, it follows that this moral conclusion is supposed to spring from the premises of his discipline. This is asking for the logically impossible; it is what I meant when I said that Bernard confuses physiology and ethics. It is also what I was alluding to when I said that he never truly considers the ethics of the matter. Here is how he concludes the portion of the *Introduction* with which I have been dealing:

> After what has preceded, we consider all discussion of vivisection futile or absurd. It is impossible for men who judge the facts with such different ideas ever to agree; and as it is impossible to satisfy everybody, the scientist should be concerned only with the opinion of scientists who understand him, and should extract rules of conduct only from his own conscience.[18]

Given 'what has preceded' (that is to say, given his argument so far), when Bernard refers to 'the opinion of scientists' he can only mean their opinion *as* scientists. This makes the use of the word 'conscience' positively weird, since conscience is a moral category, not a scientific one. What he is doing, in reality, is substituting the dictates of his discipline for the dictates of conscience. And when he asserts his absolute right to perform experiments on animals, his argument boils down to this: there is nothing in physiology to oppose the practice. This is not exactly a knockdown moral argument. In short, what Bernard does is to take an imperative of his research (or what he sees as an imperative) and turn it into an absolute right – without giving any *moral* argument whatsoever.

Once we have got the dust of Bernard's confusion out of our eyes, we can see clearly that his real position regarding the moral question with which I began is bound to be essentially the same as Moreau's, since it is inherent in the frame of mind or point of view that they share. That is to say, the question does not concern them. It does not concern them as physiologists who are looking at animals and thinking about them purely in terms derived from their science. But as human beings it *does* concern them; which is to say, it *should* concern them; it should concern *us*. This means restoring the very frame of mind or point of view that the physiologist, *qua* physiologist, suspends. It means turning Moreau and Bernard on their heads. If, in Moreau's words, 'The thing before you is no longer an animal, a fellow-creature', then it must once again become one in our eyes. If, in Bernard's words, the physiologist 'no longer hears the cries of animals' and 'no longer sees the blood that flows', then we must hear those cries once more, hearing them as cries of pain, of anguish and distress; must see that blood again, seeing it as a loss sustained, an injury inflicted. And, hearing and seeing such things, we must be appalled. Normal human sensibility must be resumed; otherwise a person is not in a position even to think about right and wrong.

I do not mean to beg the question with which I began. There might be good reasons, even compelling ones, for sanctioning experiments on animals in the interests of certain kinds of scientific research. But weighty reasons have a habit of dulling the senses. Before, during, and after the weighing of reasons, we must keep our human reactions intact – and wince at the thought of what we might be justifying. Without our ordinary human reactions, all our arguing is jaded. And if we are jaded, then the moral question about the use of animals in scientific research, however copiously discussed, is not truly on the agenda.

18

Tyrants, Stewards – or Just Kings?

Huw Spanner

'How much more valuable' says Jesus in Matthew 12.12, 'is a man than a sheep!'[1] For many Christians, the remark precludes debate. Of course there is no comparison between a human being and an animal! Many of us say without thinking that we are 'infinitely precious' to God. The sentiment is well meant; but the logical implication, whether we acknowledge it or not, is that if all other creatures on earth are of finite worth, in the end they amount to nothing – when measured against infinity, all finite values tend to zero. This unconscious arithmetic may not lead us to a conscious belief that other species are worthless, but it surely disinclines many people to stand up for them. We may allow that God likes animals – loves them, even – and cares for them; and yet, weighed in the balance against us, they do not even trouble the scales. Indeed, some Christians seem to quote Psalm 8.6 – 'You made [Man] ruler over the works of your hands; you put everything under his feet' – with a certain grim satisfaction. There is in our thinking more than a hint of human supremacism.

But the question is worth asking: How much more valuable, according to the Bible, *is* a human being than a sheep? If our supremacism in large measure derives from Hellenistic thought which has profoundly influenced the church's teaching for centuries, evangelicals have a crucial contribution to make to this debate, since we strive to build our theology solidly on the testimony of scripture. Our problem, of course, is that as we search the Bible for guidance on this issue we tend to read our own prejudices into it and imagine that we find them confirmed there with the authority of divine inspiration.[2] Thus we need to admit, and make allowance for, our bias in favour of our own kind, because it will direct us towards those statements that seem to favour us and away from those that seem to favour other species. Unfortunately, whereas our natural tendency to read our own sexist or racist assumptions into scripture can be corrected by others of the opposite sex or a different race, there are no equivalent voices to correct us when our bias in favour of our own species misleads us. And our bias is real: consider how loaded the very words 'animal', 'beast', and 'brute' are!

We lose our way, perhaps, in the opening chapters. 'For Genesis,' writes one commentator, 'the creation of man is the goal of creation.'[3] But whether 'the goal' means the object or the *terminus ad quem*, this is surely wrong: it is implicit in Genesis 1.31 that the purpose of creation is to bring pleasure to God,[4] and explicit in 2.2 that the process concludes with the Sabbath.[5] The distinction is important. If (in both senses) the end of creation is God's enjoyment of it, then the value of other creatures is determined by God's pleasure in them; on the other hand, if everything else is merely the prelude and the means to the arrival of humankind, we may be encouraged to think that everything exists for us and we are 'the measure of all things'.

I do not wish to deny the pre-eminence of humankind in God's affections or purposes, but to draw attention to some of the ways in which scripture qualifies it, which we tend to ignore. In fact, Genesis 1 and 2 observe a delicate balance in stating but not overstating the unique importance of our kind. We are crucial to the plot but we are not the whole story. So, for example, though humans are created last, we share the sixth day with every other animal that lives on dry land. The division of days makes more distinction between birds and insects than between insects and us. Again, though the writer visualizes God breathing into the nostrils only of the man (and not even the woman), on several occasions all animals are characterized as having 'the breath of life' (Gen. 1.30, 6.17, 7.22). God blesses humankind, but blesses too 'every living and moving thing with which the water teems' – including not only 'the great creatures' but also, presumably, the small fry they feed on (Gen. 1.20 ff.).[6] In common with 'all the beasts of the field and all the birds of the air', the first man is made by hand, out of the soil (though only he is made *out of the dust* of the soil, Gen. 2.7 – a distinction which does not obviously mark him out as superior!). The Hebrew word for soil here is *adamah*, which is echoed by the word for man, *adam*; and the fact that the man was made from soil is underlined in God's curse in Genesis 3.17, 19, and 23. Subsequently, though the first woman is given a name, Eve, which looks forward to her role as 'the mother of all the living', the first man is only ever known by the name which recalls his common origin with the other animals.[7]

Again, we are very familiar with the ways in which Genesis 1 gives peculiar prominence to the creation of humankind, but we tend to ignore the remarkable hiatus which follows it. At the end of the first, third, fourth, and fifth days, God pronounced the handiwork 'good', and likewise after making everything except humankind on the sixth day. Then, contrary to our expectation, God did not express any satisfaction with us as such but instead 'saw *all that he had made* that it was really very good' (Gen. 1.31).[8]

God is like a chef who kisses his fingers in delight as he unveils each successive course, and then, as he lifts the lid off his *pièce de résistance*, says: 'You know, the whole meal is superb.' We may infer that it is the last item that inspires this remark, that its supreme quality confirms, and even improves, the quality of the whole; but the whole is what matters, and it is only in its context and by implication that we know how good the final part is. Changing the metaphor, humankind may be the jewel in the crown, but it is the crown which is praised, not the jewel which enhances it. We may say that God loves creation, and especially human beings;[9] but we cannot impose on scripture the weaker formulation, 'God loves us. Of course, he also values the rest of his works.'

The currency among many evangelicals of the Hellenistic belief that other species exist for us (and are vastly inferior to us) is remarkable given all that scripture says to the contrary. Consider the book of Job: in chapters 38 to 41, God speaks with a glorious pride in creation and overwhelms Job with a vision of mysteries and intimacies unknown to him. We cannot be surprised when naturalists tell us that the most wonderful creatures on earth live far removed from human eyes.[10] The Creator's praise of Behemoth ('first among the works of God') and Leviathan ('nothing on earth is his equal') rolls out like thunder. Job takes the point: 'I spoke of things I did not understand, things too wonderful for me to know . . . Therefore I despise myself' (Job 42.3b, 6a). He is not affirmed, but humbled. Yet we, too often, do not take the point. We presume to explain away such passages as poetic hyperbole and are quick to distinguish human beings from 'mere animals'. Our frequent response to the reductionism of scientists such as Richard Dawkins, who argues that all living things are no more than 'survival machines' for their genes, is not to reassert the glory of animals in the eyes of God but to distance ourselves from them. In fact, the more science degrades animals – both in theory and in such practices as cloning and genetic engineering – the more some Christians try to deny our common nature. Ironically, the same response is often made to the 'anti-reductionism' of modern Pagans and others who seek to re-establish the ancient – and biblical[11] – idea that the physical world is not merely material. Their pleas that we should recognize the integrity and worth of all living creatures seem to be almost wilfully misheard as a call to worship them. On all sides we seem to be trying to defend our status as humans at the expense of other creatures.

It is often said that when the first man named all the birds and beasts (Gen. 2.18 ff.) he became the first scientist. If anything, he was the first poet. The act of naming the animals recognizes precisely what 'value-free' science does not: their inner meaning and intrinsic worth. There is a depth of significance in this which defies the word 'only' that so often we apply to animals. 'And whatever *adam* called each living creature, that was its name.' Even as we are reminded again that the man is made of soil, the writer seems to imply that, uniquely, he has the authority in some sense to define absolutely what his fellow creatures amount to. God has brought them to him to see, almost literally, what he will make of them. In some sense, *adam*'s subjective opinion becomes objective fact. If this is indeed a meaning of the text, it places a remarkable weight on our response to other species. When God sees the children of *adam* describing the great blue whales as 'floating meatballs' and hunting them to effectual extinction, it is hard not to believe that it is a cause of intense disappointment to their Creator, even grief.[12]

This capacity of ours to judge – to discern, to appraise, and to decide – I attribute to the 'image of God' in which we are made. This is perhaps the most resonant phrase in the account of creation, and to some extent it has prompted and validated some of the misreadings of the text. Five times in Genesis (1.26f., 5.1, 9.6) human beings are explicitly and uniquely said to resemble God. Clearly, this confers upon us an extraordinary distinction. But what exactly does it mean? Barth complains that 'expositors have . . . pursued all kinds of arbitrarily invested interpretations'.[13] At some time or another, almost everything we have thought (or would like to think) peculiar to our kind has been identified as part of the divine image, as proof that we are 'not just animals'. At the same time, the assumption that no other creature carries that image has encouraged us to suppose that everything that is characteristic of God must be foreign to other species. If any property can be said to be Godlike, the logic runs, we may possess it but no one else can.

These two lines of thought have combined to produce a very long list to our credit, which has been extended by other prejudices from less Christian sources. For example, we often seem more disposed to believe Descartes' pronouncement that the reason why animals do not speak as we do is not that they lack the organs but that they have no thoughts[14] than to accept the contrary assumption of Numbers 22.28 ff.[15] The idea that human beings are essentially other than and superior to other species has so pervaded our culture that such fancies often persist in the face of both reason and evidence. Some would be impossible to prove. How do we know, for example, that no other species is rational?[16] How could we know, until we had deciphered not only their vocalizations but their mental processes, that no other species uses language?[17] How could we substantiate the common claim that only we have a sense of humour? Montaigne's unanswerable point – 'by the same reason they may think us to be beasts as we think them'[18] – could be applied to another question that goes closer to the bone: How could we establish that no other species has a moral sense? What evidence do whales have that *we* know the difference between right and wrong?[19]

Some fond illusions, perhaps, have gone. For example, the boast that only humans use tools has had to be revised, again and again. Careful and sympathetic observation of the 'higher' mammals suggests that they are much closer to us than we care to admit. So, for example, the zoologist Cynthia Moss writes: 'Elephants are . . . intelligent, complicated, intense, tender, powerful, and funny . . . watching [them] is like reading an engrossing, convoluted novel . . .'[20] Jacques Cousteau speaks of whales as 'sociable, affectionate, devoted, gentle, captivating, high-spirited creatures'.[21] Sue Savage-Rumbaugh reports:

> It is possible, if one looks beyond the slightly differently shaped face, to read the emotions of apes as easily and as accurately as one reads the emotions and feelings of other human beings. There are few feelings that apes do not share with us, except perhaps self-hatred. They certainly experience and express exuberance, joy, guilt, remorse, disdain, disbelief, awe, sadness, wonder, tenderness, loyalty, anger, distrust and love . . . Only those who live and interact with apes as closely as they do with members of their own species will be able to understand the immense depth of the behavioral similarities between ape and man.[22]

Jane Goodall, who has spent a lifetime studying chimpanzees in the wild, crosses a further boundary: 'Like us . . . they . . . are capable of true altruism.'[23]

Here we come close to the heart of human supremacism, the belief that we alone are 'spiritual beings'. But what are we saying here? If we accept that other species can relate to humans (and given that Genesis 1 and 2 imply that our interaction with them is part of the original design of creation it would be perverse if this appearance of relationship was no more than an illusion), how can we deny that they can, and must, enjoy a relationship with their Creator? We read in scripture that they look to God, and that God makes covenants with them.[24] If a dog can return her 'owner's' affection, why should she not also love God who made her? One theologian recently declared: 'No group of chimpanzees will ever sit around the table arguing about the doctrine of the Trinity or the relative merits of

Calvinism or Arminianism!'[25] Thank God for that! But is it impossible to detect in the placid demeanour of a gorilla a humble, thankful heart? C. S. Lewis once speculated about life on other planets: 'There might be creatures genuinely spiritual, whose powers of manufacture and abstract thought were so humble that we should mistake them for mere animals.'[26] And what if earth's 'mere animals' were just such?

Perhaps the English language misleads us here: the very word 'animal' is almost the opposite to 'spiritual' – which is why many Christians strongly reject the idea that human beings are animals, because they assume that this means we do not have spirits, or souls. But of course the soul – the distinct 'immortal' part which inhabits our bodies much as our bodies inhabit our clothes – is a Greek concept which is quite foreign to the Bible.[27] In Hebrew, the words for 'animal', 'breath', and 'spirit' are often related (as, indeed, in Latin: our word 'animal' is derived from a family of words, of which *anima* means 'breath' or 'spirit' and *animus* means 'mind'). The Hebrew word translated 'creature' in Genesis 1 and 2 is *nephesh*, whose root means 'breathe' – and which is frequently (and tendentiously) translated 'soul' in human contexts throughout the Old Testament. The 'breath' of life is *ruach*, which elsewhere is rendered 'spirit' (or even 'Spirit'). Likewise, the standard Greek word for 'animal' is *zoon*, which is related to *zoe*, 'life' (as in Jesus' declaration in John 14.6, *eimi he zoe*: 'I am Life'). In other words, whereas English suggests a distinction between the animal kingdom and the world of the spirit, these ancient languages tend to imply a continuum.

But if the question 'Do other species have souls?' is not a biblical one, the question, 'Where do their spirits go when they die?' is (Eccles. 3.21). We are given no categorical answer – and why should we be? Perhaps the Bible addresses in detail only the issue of human status and salvation because only humans read it. When Peter asks Jesus what lies in store for John, he is told: 'What is that to you? You must follow me' (John 21.22). Nevertheless, there are indications that the world to come will be populated by more than the rational human souls of Hellenistic-Christian imagination. The *cherubim* of the Old Testament are portrayed as elemental wind-creatures, part human, part beast. In Revelation 4 and 5, the four 'animals' (the Greek word is *zoa*) who are closest to the throne of God have the appearance respectively of a lion, an ox, a man, and an eagle. Isaiah's vision sees the wolf, the leopard, the lion, the bear, and the cobra living in harmony with the lamb, the goat, the yearling, and the cow, 'and a little child will lead them' (11.6–9).[28] Finally, Paul hints that 'the glory that will be revealed to us' will somehow, through the agency of redeemed human beings, involve the liberation of the whole creation to share in 'the glorious freedom of the children of God' (Rom. 8.18–25).

Yet if there is no compelling evidence that reason, or conscience, or a 'soul' sets us apart, does the phrase 'the image of God' serve no purpose except to make us feel, in a vague way, supremely important? To my mind, its meaning is provided by the great commission which immediately follows it in Genesis 1.26ff.: we were created to subdue the earth and to rule over all other species. The *imago Dei* consists in our 'dominion'. According to D. J. A. Clines, 'the image is to be understood not so much ontologically as existentially: it comes to expression not in the nature of man so much as in his activity and function.'[29] Ian Hart expresses this function as 'exercising dominion over the natural world'. 'In the last twenty years or so [this] has become the interpretation supported by the overwhelming majority of Old Testament scholars.'[30]

This understanding turns our supremacism upside-down, for if we resemble God in that we have dominion, we must be called to be 'imitators of God' (Eph. 5.1) in the way we exercise it. Indeed, far from giving us a free hand on the earth, the *imago Dei* constrains us. We must be kings, not tyrants – if we become the latter we deny, and even destroy, that image in us. How, then, does God exercise dominion? Psalm 145 tells us that God is gracious, compassionate, good, faithful, loving, generous, and protective, not to humankind only but to 'all he has made'. God's characteristic act is to bless, and it is God's constant care that ensures that the cattle, the lions, and even the birds are fed and watered (Ps. 104; Matt. 6.26).

Perhaps because the duty of 'dominion' has been twisted into a right of domination, many green Christians today are promoting instead the idea that we are stewards of the earth. Although there is no obvious scriptural warrant for it, it is easy to see why this is attractive. Stewards, after all, are entrusted with what does not belong to them, and are accountable for its well-being to a higher authority. Their obligation is to their master, to be faithful and prudent. The problem is that this model does not really challenge the prevailing ethos of our science, which is reductive, and of our technology, which is exploitative. It no more than qualifies the modern idea that the world and its non-human inhabitants are a resource for our use: yes, they are a resource but they belong to God; yes, we can use them, but we must use them with care. Nor does it challenge our supremacism: we think of a steward as other than and superior to the property he or she manages.[31] A king, on the other hand, does not manage things: he rules over living beings. He too must answer to God, but he also has obligations to his subjects. Furthermore, he is essentially of the same kind as them, though as 'the Lord's anointed' he has privileges as well as responsibilities.[32] The Bible has no time for the fiction of royal blood: the greatest kings of Israel were chosen from among the common people – created, one might almost say, from the dust.[33] God introduces Saul simply as 'a man from the land of Benjamin' (I Sam. 9.16). David, the exemplar of kingship, was only a shepherd boy, and the youngest of eight brothers. Nor does the true king try to exalt himself by debasing his subjects, as the tyrant Rehoboam did (II Chron. 10), but he rejoices in their nobility, for their greatness only makes him greater. Think of the catalogue of David's 'mighty men' (II Sam. 23.8–39). Their prowess does not detract from his – on the contrary, the higher they are praised, the higher he is exalted, because he is still their lord. Perhaps most importantly, the king is essentially a servant to his subjects. Ezekiel 34 sets out most movingly what God expects of those who have dominion, expressed in terms of a shepherd's unstinting care for his sheep. The most glorious king of Israel, Solomon, daunted by his duty to 'this great people', pleases God by asking 'for discernment in administering justice' rather than for long life or wealth or security (I Kings 3.5–14).[34] The wisdom God gives him is at once exercised on behalf of the least of those people, in his famous judgment of the dispute between two prostitutes over a baby.[35]

This idea of servant-kingship is fully realized in Jesus, the Good Shepherd, whom the New Testament identifies as the actual image of God.[36] He himself tells his disciples: 'The kings of the Gentiles lord it over them . . . but you are not to be like that. Instead, the greatest among you should be like the youngest, and the one who rules like the one who serves . . . I am among you as one who serves' (Luke 22.25ff.). Our own understanding of kingship is more likely to be informed by ideas put about in Shakespeare's day, that a king is essentially different from his people, set above and apart from them not just by his status but by his very nature. So Richard II finds his own mere humanity a puzzle:

> I live with bread like you, feel want,
> Taste grief, need friends: subjected thus,
> How can you say to me I am a king?
> (*Richard II*, III.ii)

But this 'subjection' is precisely what the true king of kings embraced. He demonstrated his kingship over us not by asserting that he was different from us but by becoming like us: not by oppressing us or putting us down but by serving us and raising us up – and it was precisely because he identified with his subjects that he was given the highest honour (Phil. 2.6–11). The Person by whom and for whom all creatures were made, by whose word of power they are sustained and in whom they hold together – and to whom they will all one day sing praises – established for all time the principle that lordship entails solidarity and sacrifice.[37]

If we have dominion over God's other creatures, then we are called to live in peace with them, as good shepherds and humble servants. We cannot say that we are made in the image of God and then use that as our pretext to abuse, neglect, or even belittle other species, when God does none of those things. As kings, we have the power of life and death over them, and the right to exercise it in accordance with the principles of justice and mercy; but we have the parallel duty, not only to God but to them, to love them and protect them – looking forward to the day when they and we shall live in harmony in 'the glorious freedom of the children of God'. The patterns the Bible offers us include the first man, who gave names to all the beasts and birds, and whose own name recalls his common origin with them; the exemplar of kingship, David, who took the relationship that a man has with the animals in his care as a model for God's love and provision for us; and Jesus himself, who taught that the good shepherd not only knows his sheep by name but ultimately is willing to lay down his life for them. There is no basis here for arrogant human supremacism.

19

Compassion or Justice?
What is our Minimum Ethical
Obligation to Animals?

Paul Brett

In the middle of Essex there is a fine eighteenth-century house set in parkland. To its left is an animal cemetery, in which stones dating back to the beginning of the century are inscribed with names such as Katy, Pinny, Holly, Bob, Lassie, Mary, Psyche, Sonny, and Massa. What is the significance of this practice? What is there in the relationship between humans and animals that suggests a decent burial with a carved headstone is appropriate? Is the fact that many of the names are human names significant? In the working partnership on the estate, are animals in effect an extension of the family? Some of the names express a spiritual aspect of the creature (Psyche) or the relationship between master and servant (Massa). There seems to be a degree of uncertainty here. Animals are one of us – but not quite! Or is the practice just an exercise in whimsy, little more than sentiment enabled by an excess of riches?

The dilemma of our minimum ethical obligation to animals is encapsulated in this plot of mid-Essex ground. The names all seem to be those of dogs – or possibly cats – and there appear to be no cows, sheep, or horses among them. Is there in our minds a sort of hierarchy of respect, promoting those animals *with* which we live and work above those *on* which we work? If, in the end, this is all no more than an expression of sentiment, why should that be less worthy of our examination? We are creatures of passion as well as intellect, with affective as well as cognitive powers.

Dominion

Today there is growing recognition within the Christian churches that the ancient tradition that animals lack rationality and feel no pain, and are there for human use, is no longer acceptable. We acknowledge that human beings are not over against nature, but are part of it. The 'dominion' given to us in Genesis 1 can no longer be understood in terms of exploitation, but in terms of stewardship, nurture, and conservation. On the level of expediency, we damage ourselves if we do not conserve the environment on which we are dependent. The Christian churches, however, do not base their attitudes simply on utilitarian considerations. Running through the scriptures is a strong theme of humankind and nature as all of a piece, all part of God's creation, all dependent upon one another, and all within the scope of God's loving concern.

But if this is the current interpretation of what the Christian tradition says about our ethical obligation to animals, how does actual practice match up to it? Do farmers or participants in field sports, biology teachers or laboratory researchers and technicians, those who use animals in entertainment or own them as domestic pets act with this sort of tenderness and sensitivity in their everyday dealings with animals? And if they do not, what might the churches have to say about it?

Much disturbing literature has been produced by animal welfare organizations to suggest that all is not well. Farm animals are kept in unacceptably crowded conditions, wild animals are pursued more for sport than in order to control their numbers, small animals are cut open so that children can learn about anatomy, mice and rabbits are used to test new drugs and cosmetics, and many domestic pets are cruelly treated or abandoned. In the next sections I examine the literature produced by a range of organizations, both official and voluntary, concerned with the treatment of animals within the United Kingdom. This reveals a variety of approaches, some practical, some more idealistic. There appears to be a growing dissatisfaction with a concern merely for the welfare of animals, and increasing support for the attribution of rights to them.

Official agencies

Since the early 1970s, a number of organizations have produced Codes of Conduct to regulate their public activities. The very existence of these Codes indicates, on the one hand, that problems have been identified which need attention and, on the other, that some minimum form of ethical obligation has at least been recognized.

The Farm Animal Welfare Council (FAWC) is an independent body appointed by the government which advises agriculture ministers about all aspects of animal production and welfare. In a recent leaflet, *Welfare and Some of the Issues Involved*, the Council declared: 'No enlightened society would seriously contest the view that man has an inescapable responsibility to ensure the well-being of those animals over which he exercises complete control.' The FAWC is concerned 'to identify systems which go beyond the range of acceptability', while accepting that 'in the vast majority of cases the farmers are the best guardians of the welfare of their stock'. It tries to keep an open mind on questions about the treatment of animals at the point of slaughter – whether the heart should be kept beating to pump blood out of a carcass; whether animals suffer more from being placed in an enclosed stunning box than they do from observing the slaughter of their fellows – and encourages more scientific investigation of these matters.

The Ministry of Agriculture, Fisheries, and Food (MAFF) has produced separate Codes of Recommendations and Codes of Practice for the welfare of livestock.[1] These originated in the Brambell Report of 1965, and all Codes of Recommendations – except those concerning sheep, goats, and farmed deer – contain a Preface discussing the 'basic needs' of animals and provisions to meet them. The needs listed are as follows:

* comfort and shelter;
* readily accessible fresh water and a diet to maintain the animals in full health and vigour;
* freedom of movement;
* the company of other animals, particularly of like kind;
* the opportunity to exercise most natural patterns of behaviour;
* light during the hours of daylight, and lighting readily available to enable the animals to be inspected at any time;
* flooring which neither harms the animals nor causes undue strain;
* the prevention, or rapid diagnosis and treatment, of vice, injury, parasitic infestation, and disease;
* the avoidance of unnecessary mutilation;
* emergency arrangements to cover outbreaks of fire, the breakdown of essential mechanical services, and the disruption of supplies.

In a *Report on Priorities in Animal Welfare Research and Development*, the FAWC identified 'five freedoms': freedom from malnutrition; thermal and physical discomfort; injury and disease; fear and stress; and severe restriction on behaviour.[2] It states: 'Public opinion and scientific evidence both point to clear deficiencies in many conventional husbandry systems, especially in regard to comfort and behaviour.' The Report goes on to attack common practices such as 'castration, tail docking, disbudding/ dehorning, debeaking and ear tagging/punching'. It acknowledges that transportation of animals exposes them to a number of stress factors, which include 'handling, mixing, noise, vibration, thermal discomfort, denial of food and water and exposure to pathogens'. It considers the stunning of animals prior to slaughter, and entertains the possibility of 'radical alternatives . . . to reduce or circumvent as many as possible of the insults to animals during the last day(s) of life'. The FAWC places its faith in more research and development and the acquisition of new knowledge, and is well aware that economic considerations also have to be taken seriously – farming is a business – although it looks to the government to judge where the right balance between welfare and efficiency actually lies.

These Codes lay considerable emphasis on procedures which minimize suffering and distress. One even advises that male animals should be carried at the front of an aircraft and females at the rear, 'so that the air flow prevents the female odours causing unnecessary sexual stimulation to the males'.[3] Failure to observe the provisions of the various Codes can render a person liable to prosecution under the law.

Animal welfare organizations

What do the secular animal welfare organizations say about the treatment of animals? Freed from the constraints of the market place and the legislative chamber, have they a more uncompromising attitude to our minimum ethical obligation to animals? I select a few British examples.

The Royal Society for the Prevention of Cruelty to Animals (RSPCA), founded in 1824, is the largest of the animal welfare charities. Its 'Declaration of Animal Rights' appeared at the front of its booklet *Policies on Animal Welfare* (1977, revised 1984):

> Inasmuch as there is ample evidence that many animal species are capable of feeling, we condemn totally the infliction of suffering upon our fellow creatures and the curtailment of their behavioural and other needs save where this is necessary for their own individual benefit.
>
> We do not accept that a difference in species alone (any more than a difference in race) can justify wanton exploitation or oppression in the name of science or sport, or for use as food, for commercial profit or for any other human gain.
>
> We believe in the evolutionary and moral kinship of all animals and

declare our belief that all sentient creatures have rights to life, liberty and natural enjoyment.

We therefore call for the protection of these rights.

The booklet goes on to offer detailed policy statements on a number of matters. Its main concern is to prevent distress and suffering, and it strongly opposes battery cage systems for hens, the rearing of veal calves in crates (now banned in Britain), and intensive pig farming. It also opposes unnecessary mutilation and the slaughter of any food animal without prior stunning. It is against all experiments or procedures which cause pain, suffering, or distress, as well as experiments that involve unnecessary repetitions, are for trivial ends, or involve techniques for which satisfactory humane alternatives have already been developed. It opposes the use of animals in the testing of inessential substances such as cosmetics. It argues, overall, for the reduction, refinement, and replacement (the '3Rs') of existing techniques and applauds the setting up of local ethical committees with both lay and animal welfare representation.

The booklet also opposes in principle the taking or killing of wild animals, or the infliction of any suffering upon them, and urges more protection for them under the law. The Society deplores changes made in the environment which disturb the balance of nature, such as the removal of hedgerows, the destruction of wetland, stubble burning, and the pollution of land, air, or water by chemical substances and waste products.

The Society has also set itself against the use of animals in any form of entertainment which is likely to cause them distress or suffering. It opposes the hunting of animals with dogs, angling practices which cause pain to fish, and shooting for sport – it urges 'those shooters who see fit to pursue their sports' to adopt a simple Code of Practice (p. 20). In schools, it opposes the keeping of animals in classrooms, and the practice of dissection, believing that this 'can readily lead to a desensitisation and a lessening of respect for life itself' (p. 23).

However, the RSPCA has been equivocal about its ethical basis. Another leaflet, *Animal–Human Relationships: An Ethical Overview* (1988), when discussing the contrast between a 'welfare' view based in compassion with a 'rights' view based in justice, declares: 'The Society does not align itself with any particular ethical viewpoint' (p. 1).

A similar approach can be found in the literature of Compassion in World Farming (CIWF, founded 1967), which campaigns for the abolition of factory farming and for a new status of 'sentient beings' within the treaties governing European trade.[4] CIWF has spoken of 'our kinship with all life' and the need for 'a new initiative asserting that animals – even those destined for the table – have certain rights'.

Other animal welfare organizations include The Humane Research Trust, which promotes medical and scientific research that will reduce and eventually replace the use of animals, while the Vegetarian Society bases a part of its appeal on the natural disgust people feel when they are confronted with pictures of abattoirs and some intensive farming practices.

Christian animal groups

One of the oldest Christian animal groups is Quaker Concern for Animal Welfare, founded in 1891 as the Friends' Anti-Vivisection Society. In one of its booklets it opposed the infliction of suffering, physical or mental, upon animals, as well as 'taking advantage of the helplessness and defence-lessness of fellow-beings much smaller and weaker than ourselves'.[5] 'A truly noble soul', the author declares, 'would surely scorn to stoop to such baseness.' Vivisection involves injustice because it 'makes innocent animals the scapegoats of humanity's wrong-doing'. The cure of disease caused by our own failure to put right 'overcrowding in slums, bad sanitation, undrained swamps, foul air, wrong diet, malnutrition due to excessive poverty, and so on' cannot provide a moral justification for research inflicting harm on animals. The term 'sub-human kinsfolk' is used, and vivisection is said to be 'a crime against both animals and humans, and indeed against the creator, desecrating all that is noblest in human character and idealism'. In a more recent publication, the basis of the offence is said to be the treatment of animals as property to be bought and sold, and the system of mass production 'where the individual animal ceases to count'.[6] A redirection of minds, energies, and resources is called for, into health procedures 'which would seem to our deepest insights to be in line with loving, creative processes'. The weak should not be exploited by the strong, 'regardless of their capacity to experience pain, pleasure, frustration, fulfilment, distress or contentment at their own level'.

Roman Catholics, on the other hand, have traditionally held to the position developed by Aquinas out of Aristotle, that animals have no rights because they have no rationality. They are created for human use and benefit and we have no direct duties towards them. Cruelty to animals is only sinful inasmuch as it degrades the perpetrator. A different voice, however, has sounded from the pages of *The Ark*, the journal of the Catholic

Study Centre for Animal Welfare. Here, as early as 1952, Father Basil
Wrighton summarized the case for attributing rights to animals:

> To sum up: what 'rights' have I tried to vindicate for the animals? Only
> such as would save them from cruel abuses. What human rights would I
> curtail? Only the assumed right, on the score of rationality, to behave like
> brutes – or rather, demons. What novel principles have I introduced?
> Only such as decent people already act on without reflection. I insist only
> that natural affinity and God's justice entitle these fellow-creatures to be
> treated by us as more than 'things' if less than 'persons'; to be spared
> from pain and terror as far as rests with us; not to be killed without some
> sort of necessity; and, when they must be killed, to receive as swift and
> painless a death as our 'anxious care' can devise. Without obliterating the
> distinction between man and beast, or forgetting the superior rights of
> rational nature, I suggest that sentient nature in proportion to its God-
> given capacity for perception, feeling and desire, of itself constitutes
> some sort of 'right'; or claim to be treated as an end in itself, in due pro-
> portion to other and superior ends, but not merely as a means to them;
> and that violation of this 'right' is an injustice and therefore cruel and
> sinful.[7]

A similar point was made in the *Bulletin* of the Anglican Society for the
Welfare of Animals, which was founded after the Church Assembly Report
Man in his Living Environment was published in 1970: 'Surely we must
stand up loud and clear and declare the intrinsic worth of every creature,
[and] our responsibility towards each animal . . .'.[8] The purposes of the
Society include the promotion of prayer, study, and action on behalf of
animals.

Other Christian sources

The Report *Animals and Ethics*, published in 1980, contains a short but
significant contribution to the debate about the treatment of animals.[9]
Arguing for a greater exercise of responsibility in face of the pressure of
advancing technology, the Report sets out a series of guidelines derived
from the basic behavioural needs of animals. These include:

- freedom to perform natural physical movements;
- association with other animals, where appropriate, of their own kind;
- facilities for comfort activities, e.g. rest, sleep, and body care;

- provision of food and water to maintain full health;
- ability to perform daily routines of natural activities;
- opportunity for the activities of exploration and play, especially for young animals;
- satisfaction of minimal spatial and territorial requirements, including a visual field and 'personal' space.

The Report also includes a longer list of recommendations concerning the use of animals in research. Its basic principles are declared to be: 'Partnership between different orders of creation living side by side in the one world; also that of man as a steward, a trustee with special responsibility vested in him'. Its moral concern is for the reduction of 'avoidable suffering'.

A much more powerful case, going far beyond this welfare approach, has been put forward by Andrew Linzey in *Christianity and the Rights of Animals*,[10] which claims what are called 'theos-rights' (God-rights) for animals. They are spirit-filled, living creatures, and God has the right 'to have his creatures treated with respect'. Linzey continues: 'Animals have a God-given right to be animals. The natural life of a spirit-filled creature is a gift from God. When we take over the life of an animal to the extent of distorting its natural life for no other purpose than our own gain, we fall into sin.' From this flows a plan of 'progressive disengagement from exploitation' of animals. Ways of liberation are described – from wanton injury, from institutionalized suffering, from oppressive control, from primary products and from by-products of slaughter.

This practical concern is also illustrated in a Report to the World Council of Churches, as part of its 'Justice, Peace and the Integrity of Creation' programme.[11] The Report encourages members of the Christian community to act according to such guidelines as the following:

- Avoid cosmetics and household products that have been cruelly tested on animals. Instead buy cruelty-free items.
- Avoid clothing and other aspects of fashion that have a history of cruelty to animals, products of the fur industry in particular. Instead, purchase clothes that are 'cruelty-free'.
- Avoid meat and animal products that have been produced on factory farms. Instead purchase meat and animal products from sources where the animals have been treated with respect, or abstain from these products altogether.

• Avoid patronizing forms of entertainment that treat animals as mere means to human ends. Instead, seek benign forms of entertainment, ones that nurture a sense of the wonder of God's creation and reawaken that duty of conviviality which we can discharge by living respectfully in community with all life, the animals included.

Compassion and justice

How are we to assess all this material? What are the grounds on which our ethical obligation to animals may be built? There seem to be many imperatives at work.

A fundamental human revulsion at the suffering endured by animals in some intensive farming methods, in the field, or in the laboratory finds regular expression in the literature. But emotion is an uncertain basis for ethics. There is scope for too great a reaction, out of balance with other concerns. How could it be right, for example, to be revolted by the suffering of a laboratory mouse if we are not also opposed to the suffering of the poor or the human victims of violence? Can we be convinced and active animal welfarists without also being pacifists, and without being active politically in favour of a more equitable distribution of wealth in human society? At the same time, there is an essential rightness about emotion as the basis for concern about the treatment of animals. We do not feel emotion about the stone a child idly kicks in the gutter. It is 'inanimate'. But animate creatures have an affinity with each other that makes fellow-feeling an appropriate response. We feel about them because, in some sense, we are one with them. This line of argument, so natural and so widespread, contests the ancient tradition that there is discontinuity between humans and animals, since animals have no reason. We now understand more clearly that feelings and reason both belong to being human and alive.

It is also hard to accept that part of the tradition which proposes a hierarchy of creatures. We cannot today escape obligations to animals on the grounds that they are lower in the scale than us any more than we can deploy this argument to support the subordination of women, the practice of slavery, or racial discrimination. To speak of 'sub-human' or 'lower' creatures, or to describe certain human actions as 'noble' or 'base', is to betray a dependence on this way of thinking. We need a moral language which does not carry these Aristotelian overtones. It is true, of course, that animals prey on each other, the stronger on the weaker – the lion hunts the zebra, the pike eats the minnow – but this is not a *moral* consideration. Questions about human obligation are in a different category altogether. It is the possibility, and the inescapable challenge, of acting morally that is our especial characteristic as humankind.

Are we then to think of 'responsibilities' towards animals and the natural environment? If we are to some extent dependent on the rest of creation for our own survival, and if we sense some fellow-feeling with it, particularly with the animate part of it, is the call for responsibility merely a form of enlightened self-interest? Of course, self-interest is not synonymous with selfishness, and without some degree of self-regard we can hardly stay alive, let alone respond to any demands made upon us by others. However, responsibility is a weak concept. At its weakest, it can assume ownership – I am responsible for keeping my garden tidy – or paternalism – I am responsible for the behaviour of my children. If I neglect all this, the worst criticism that can be made of me is that I have been 'irresponsible'. In a stronger sense, however, to be responsible is to answer for our behaviour, to give account, to be reliable in the performance of some contractual obligation. It is a moral quality because it depends on free choice. Christians talk of being responsible to God for all we do in this life. The word itself contains the assumption that we must 'respond' to claims that come to us from outside, and not withdraw into the personal and the spiritual, narrowly conceived. But the idea of responsibility is basically anthropocentric, concerned with conscience and our own integrity. It fails to give full place to the equal claim from the rest of creation to exist in its own right alongside human beings. Therefore in the end it is an inadequate basis on which to build a theory of moral obligation to those with whom we share the world.

Is 'stewardship' any better? It is increasingly common to interpret the idea of dominion in Genesis (Gen. 1.28, 2.15) in terms of stewardship, and to link it with the commission from God to till the Garden of Eden and care for it. As such the term has a richer meaning than responsibility. We cannot be stewards, we cannot nurture, protect, conserve, enable things to grow, without due attention to the inherent nature of the objects of our concern. The word has overtones of mutual respect; it is less anthropocentric. But it suffers from the same problems. Stewardship can also be simple self-interest – if we do not alter the content of certain foodstuffs we give to animals, or reduce the hormones we inject into them, we will end up poisoning ourselves. The concern to prevent the extinction of certain species in case something irreplaceable is lost to our environment, whose value we cannot now see but may one day come to appreciate, can be equally self-serving. It still presupposes that the world of nature is there, outside us, separate from us, for us to manage and manipulate.

But if emotion, used according to some imagined hierarchy, responsibility, and stewardship are all, in the end, unsatisfactory bases on which to build a theory of moral obligation, where else can we look? Might 'compassion' be the word to characterize a more sensitive and thoroughgoing Christian approach?

In some interpretations, compassion is also a weak word, signifying little more than pity or mercy in the popular use of these unfashionable terms. It stoops only to relieve an animal of excessive pain, putting it 'out of its misery' when caught in a trap. But understood at a deeper level it can be more useful. To have compassion is to recognize a continuity of existence with the other. It is to suffer, to feel with – not just for – other creatures. It is to recognize with the heart and with the head that human and animal are made of the same stuff and that moral obligations arise from this. It is to recognize that using a fellow creature who is an animal for selfish purposes is no more morally acceptable than using a fellow creature who is an unborn baby or a marriage partner. That we are all involved, willy nilly, in such 'using' of each other, often with disastrous consequences, does not mean that it has to be so, or that it is good or right for it to be so. To have compassion is to go out of our way to share what we have with those who, though different, are yet of our kind – as the Good Samaritan did (Luke 10.25–37). Compassion leads not just to benevolence, fellow-feeling, but to acts that are both reasoned and practically effective. It involves an 'imaginative dwelling on the condition of the other . . . an active regard for his good'.[12]

But there is a point beyond compassion to which the argument seems irresistibly to lead. To recognize the otherness of animals, and their place alongside human beings, is to recognize that they belong here as of right, no less than we do. It is to begin to see our relationship with animals as a question of justice. It is only with the attribution of rights to animals that a secure basis can be found on which to work out our detailed ethical obligations, although the nature of these rights needs careful consideration.

It might be said that it is hard to see how a category based on justice can easily be applied to animals or to nature, when they cannot answer back or come with us to a court of law to plead their case. We have already seen that rights language can be used merely as a term to support a case being advanced on other grounds. But to attribute a right to a creature is to recognize its existence whether human beings find it convenient or not. It is to build on the sense that animals have a claim on us, and a claim that needs to be stated and protected in case it is overlooked. To attribute rights is also to imply duties or obligations; it demands a proper response from us.

For Christians these rights have their origin both in natural law and in the divine will expressed in creation.

Something of this can be found in the Codes of Conduct already mentioned. We are not encouraged to give animals freedom and space to go about their natural activities just because it appeals to us aesthetically or emotionally. We are to give them these things because it is, in some sense, their right to have them. But this cannot remain in the realm of encouragement. The right treatment of animals is not just a matter of recommendation or of voluntary compliance. Without some means of enforcing these provisions they are hardly rights at all. The law needs to be strengthened and developed to give substance to the claims of justice.

And so the conclusion seems inexorably to emerge that our minimum ethical obligation to animals is a question of justice. It is to recognize that we share this world with them, that we each have a place and a right to be here and to fulfil whatever purposes God in providence has determined for us all. We are to enshrine this fundamental insight in the law of the land, and ensure that our practice on the farm, in the wild, in the school, the research establishment, the circus ring, and the home matches up to it.

There can be little doubt that this work needs to be more fully recognized and more adequately performed. In the end, to call a companion animal by the name 'Psyche', as the mid-Essex landowner did, and to give that animal a decent burial seems little more than its due.

20

Is the Consistent Ethic of Life Consistent without a Concern for Animals?

John Berkman

The notion of a 'consistent ethic of life' was popularized in the United States in the mid-1980s through the lectures and writings of the late Archbishop of Chicago, Joseph, Cardinal Bernardin. In ten addresses delivered between 1983 and 1986, Bernardin sought to draw a 'linkage' between a large set of moral problems – for example, abortion, capital punishment, euthanasia, poverty, genetic engineering, and war – and concluded that the fundamental principle which linked these issues was that of reverence towards life.[1] Bernardin's 'consistent ethic' has been widely adopted as a key for understanding contemporary Catholic social thought, and has found resonance in the *Catechism of the Catholic Church* and in John Paul II's encyclical *Evangelium Vitae*. Although the 'consistent ethic of life' has been applied to a wide variety of issues, it has not, to my knowledge, been applied to the question of the relationship between humans and other animals.

An ethos for a new context: Bernardin's consistent ethic of life

According to Bernardin, the consistent ethic of life is fundamentally an ethos and an attitude towards a wide range of moral and social problems as they present themselves in the United States of America. Bernardin subtitled his first essay 'An American-Catholic Dialogue', because of his concern that American Catholics tend to accept uncritically one of the two mainstream political 'options' offered to them. That is, in standard American political discourse, if you are on the 'left' you are anti-capital punishment but pro-choice, while if you are on the 'right' you are anti-abortion but pro-capital punishment. Bernardin's consistent ethic of life was meant to signal that American Catholics should reject both of these options, which are a part of the *status quo*. He recognized that American Catholics were being consumed by a political logic antithetical to that of Catholicism. He was noting what the British philosopher Anthony Kenny observed at the same time: 'It is a pathological feature of the intellectual climate of our time that so few people are consistent in their attitude to the killing of the innocent.'[2] Bernardin's hope was that the 'consistent ethic' would help American Catholics become more conversant with authentic Catholic theological and moral discourse, so that they could better live out the gospel of Jesus Christ in their society.

Bernardin's attempt to articulate a broad and explicitly Catholic social vision was not new. In terms of the history of Christian social thought, his efforts can be located most immediately in the context of the Papal social encyclicals. These letters, beginning with Leo XIII's *Rerum Novarum* in 1891, have sought to provide a distinctively Catholic perspective on some of the pressing social questions of their day. However, one would be mistaken to conclude that, in calling for a consistent ethic of life, Bernardin was merely restating and reaffirming the tradition. Bernardin challenged American Catholics to do what Christians must do anew in each generation, namely, to articulate their theological convictions and embody them in contemporary witness to their society. In calling Catholics to do this in the political context that is the USA in the late twentieth century, Bernardin saw new implications.

For instance, in a 1983 lecture, Bernardin noted a shift in the 'pastoral practice' of the church with regard to the death penalty. While the church had continued to acknowledge in principle the right of the state to resort to capital punishment, Paul VI and John Paul II both argued against the exercise of that right. Why? Because 'more humane methods of defending the state exist and should be used'.[3] Bernardin then went on to say that it was important to understand the theological rationale for this shift, and argued that it should be seen as one element in promoting a consistent ethic of life. What was fundamental to this shift in Catholic perception regarding the death penalty was 'a more acute perception of the multiple ways in which life is threatened today'.[4] Bernardin was increasingly coming to see that the justifications that had previously sanctioned the employment of the death penalty were either no longer relevant (the defence of society) or no longer defensible (retribution/vengeance) in light of the Christian commitment to defend the dignity and sanctity of life. Furthermore, in the context of a society which was increasingly threatening life, Bernardin believed it was incumbent upon Christians to defend all the more vigorously the sanctity of life.[5]

The scope of John Paul II's gospel of life

Bernardin's advancing of a consistent ethic of life was an important and prophetic calling to a particularly American audience. Since that time we have seen the call to respect life become an increasingly important theme both in the teachings of Pope John Paul II and in the church more generally. John Paul II has provided a richer and deeper theological basis for this call, and has broadened the discussion to include questions regarding non-human life. His many addresses on these themes culminated with the issue in 1995 of the encyclical *Evangelium Vitae* (The Gospel of Life).

Like Bernardin, the Pope is acutely aware of his cultural context and historical moment. Thus, at the beginning of *Evangelium Vitae* he looks back to *Rerum Novarum*, an encyclical written to promote the dignity of workers at a time when they particularly needed defending against those who would oppress them. The Pope notes that *Evangelium Vitae* is written in a similar spirit for a new social and cultural context, at a time when 'another class of persons is being oppressed in the fundamental right to life'. Who in particular needs defending in our day? Those, the Pope says, who have no voice, 'a great multitude of weak and defenceless human beings, unborn children in particular, whose fundamental right to life is being trampled upon'.[6]

What can be said about a culture that tramples on the lives of its weakest and most defenceless members? John Paul II calls it a 'culture of death'. In contrast to a culture that is devoted to death, the Pope proclaims the good news of life and calls Christians to preach, celebrate, and serve the gospel of life in everything they do.[7] The light of this gospel of life must be shone not only in Christian communities – which are especially called to renewal[8] – but also to the wider society for the benefit of everyone.[9] Like Bernardin, the Pope calls for Christians to be consistent and unrelenting in their promotion of the gospel of life, whether the issue be war, abortion, capital punishment, poverty, euthanasia, or the arms race.

Furthermore, the Pope goes on to affirm the goodness of non-human life. Since it is God who has given life to all creatures, 'life, especially human life, belongs only to God'.[10] On this perspective, all creatures are created to celebrate this God who gives life, in a manner fitting to the form of life they have been apportioned by God.[11] While it is not the central theme of *Evangelium Vitae*, the great goodness of non-human life is affirmed repeatedly.[12] For example, the Pope notes that part of the gospel of life is the 'ecological question', any adequate answer to which 'respects the great good of life, of every life'.[13] In addition, *Evangelium Vitae* notes that the

growing attention paid to ecological questions is for Christians a great sign
of hope, for it is one of the contemporary movements which is 'rais[ing]
social awareness in defence of life'.[14]

To understand adequately the Pope's defence of life in *Evangelium Vitae*
one must understand the ways in which it is informed by Christian
doctrines of creation, nature, the Fall, the Trinity, and eschatology. For
instance, his overall defence of life is dependent upon his account of God's
plan for creation. For what lies at the heart of the culture of death is a
failure to comprehend God's creation. 'It is clear that the loss of contact
with God's wise design is the deepest root of modern man's confusion
. . .'[15] Human alienation from the 'truth of creation', as John Paul puts it,
arises from two errors. On the one hand, there is the error of seeing creation
as 'mere matter' to be manipulated. On the other hand, there is the error of
romanticizing or 'divinizing' nature so that it cannot be interfered with at
all.[16]

The first error – *the instrumentalization of nature* – occurs when nature
is given only instrumental value, when it no longer has its God-given
integrity and dignity: 'Nature itself, from being "mater" (mother), is now
reduced to being matter, and is subjected to every kind of manipulation.'[17]
Often, this view goes further and 'rejects the very idea that there is a
truth of creation which must be acknowledged, or a plan of God for life
which must be respected'.[18] In contrast to these views, John Paul argues
repeatedly that humans must observe moral laws in regard to other
creatures in particular and to nature more generally. Although the Pope
does not elaborate extensively on the causes of this loss of the 'truth in
creation',[19] he does indicate two key factors. One is 'a certain technical and
scientific way of thinking, prevalent in present-day culture'.[20] A second
aspect of the problem is associated with a particular view of humans and
human rights, where rights are assigned only to those who enjoy full or
incipient autonomy. What begins the downward spiral is the 'affirmation
that the human person, unlike animals and things, cannot be subjected to
domination by others'.[21] It is certainly a good thing to affirm that humans
are not to be dominated. However, the corresponding, tacit affirmation
that all other creatures may be dominated seizes on a view which links
the autonomy of persons to certain capacities of communication and/or
rationality. As John Paul II notes, on 'these presuppositions there is no
place in the world for anyone who, like the unborn or the dying, is a weak
element in the social structure'.[22] The Pope concludes that such a view,
which he sees as an element in the culture of death, 'betrays a completely
individualistic concept of freedom, which ends up by becoming the free-

dom of "the strong" against the weak who have no choice but to submit'.[23]

The second error – *the divinization of nature* – is typical of theologies which idealize old-growth forests or other untouched nature. Such theologies usually wind up affirming the 'naturalness' of predation and parasitism in nature.[24] For if 'untouched' or 'pristine' nature is what we consider to be the ideal, then we would seem to have to affirm the continuous cycles of predation, death, and decay as necessary and good. If one sees the 'creation' in Genesis and the 'nature' of the present as synonymous, it is almost impossible to avoid the conclusion that the law of 'the survival of the fittest' applies to all aspects of the natural world – which I take to be incompatible with the gospel of life. For the Darwinians are right that nature is 'at war' – so to speak – with itself. Some animals eat other animals, and we human animals will eat all the other animals if we consider it necessary (or even if we simply prefer) to do so. Unless we can provide an account of why this is inherently tragic, we end up affirming the world of original violence rather than that of ontological peace.[25] Thus the importance of the Fall in the Christian metanarrative. For when one speaks of 'nature' as it presently exists, one is speaking of what St Paul refers to as 'creation in bondage'.[26]

The state of 'creation' prior to the Fall is that of 'original justice'.[27] In this paradisal condition, humans live in friendship with God and in harmony with the other living creatures. A sign of harmony in the state of original justice is that both humans and animals are vegetarians. God gives them seed-bearing fruits and plants to eat. Considering that we are informed of the 'vegetarian' state of Eden immediately after God gives humans 'dominion' over the other animals, it would seem clear that whatever else it means for humans to have dominion over the other animals, it does not – at least in the state of original justice – include eating them.[28]

So, what does 'dominion' mean? The *Catechism* and *Evangelium Vitae* provide general principles: it is not absolute but ministerial, and to be exercised with wisdom and love.[29] Too often, accounts of human dominion are reduced to efforts to differentiate humans from animals, usually drawing on the argument that only humans are made in the image of God. I have discussed this subject elsewhere,[30] and it is also taken up at some length in *Evangelium Vitae*.[31]

With the Fall, original justice and original peace vanish. Because of the sin of humans, not only will humans themselves suffer, so too will the rest of creation. Humans are no longer at peace with God, with each other, with the other animals, or with the environment. The alienation between God and humans is exemplified by their expulsion from the garden (Gen. 3.23);

the alienation between men and women is exemplified by Eve's subjugation (Gen. 3.16); the alienation between parents and children is exemplified in the pain of bringing forth children (Gen. 3.16); the alienation between humans is exemplified by the murder of Abel (Gen. 4.8); the alienation between humans and their environment is exemplified by the fact that humans must now till the earth (Gen. 3.17–19); and the alienation between humans and animals is exemplified by the fact that humans now wear them (Gen. 3.21) and eat them (Gen. 9.3).[32] It is important to note that these forms of post-lapsarian alienation are not given as *prescriptions* for a post-lapsarian world (that is, it is not the case that this is the way a fallen world *ought* to be), but are rather *descriptions* of a post-lapsarian world (that is, this is the way things *are* in a fallen world).[33] As such, all these forms of alienation are evils of the Fall, that is, privations of good relations among humans, between humans and God, and between humans and the rest of God's creation.

If the theological account provided by John Paul II were to end with the doctrines of creation and Fall, the reality of a tragic and predatory existence would be the fate to which we and the other animals have been abandoned. But this is not the last word, and this is why Christian theology must insist that the doctrine of creation is never self-sufficient for theological reflection but must be understood as deriving from the Christian doctrine of the Trinity, with particular emphasis upon a strong eschatology.

Concerning the importance of the Christian doctrine of the Trinity, it is essential to recognize that Christians do not worship a Deist God, one who acts merely as 'first cause' to set the world in motion, nor any notion of God as Creator which is conceptually self-sufficient. In worshipping God as Trinity, Christians proclaim that one must first understand the truth of Christ and the truth of the Holy Spirit to understand the 'truth of creation'.[34] As the *Catechism of the Catholic Church* puts it, 'We must know Christ as the source of grace in order to know Adam as the source of sin.'[35] The Spirit-Paraclete, sent by the risen Christ, came to 'convict the world concerning sin', by revealing him who is its Redeemer.[36] Thus Christians cannot adequately understand what it means for us to be creatures apart from the context of Trinitarian beliefs. This is because 'The first creation finds its meaning and its summit in the new creation in Christ, the splendor of which surpasses that of the first creation.'[37]

This brings us to the importance of Christian eschatology. For in the same way that the world of 'original justice' is not our present world of 'nature', the kingdom of God for which Christians aim and to which the pilgrim church travels is not the same as our present world. When St Paul gives his vision of a redeemed creation, it is one which overcomes all the forms of alienation brought about by the Fall.[38] Thus the *Catechism* notes that the pilgrim church of God 'takes her place among the creatures which groan and travail yet and await the revelation of the sons of God'.[39] Thus, this 'truth of creation' – that the *fundamental* purpose of the lives of animals is not to serve the needs and desires of humans but to manifest God's glory – is affirmed eschatologically, because humans share a common destiny of fellowship with God with other living creatures.[40]

This longing for the kingdom of God is also envisioned by a number of the prophets, including Isaiah, who portrays an eschatological state akin to that of original justice in which 'the lion shall eat hay like the ox, and the baby shall play by the cobra's den' (11.7, 8). This is the kingdom of God of which those who live in Christ have tasted the 'first fruits'.[41] For Christians live in a world where the kingdom has both come (a 'realized' eschatology) and yet is not consummated (the 'not yet' eschatology). When Christians pray the Lord's Prayer, they pray for the further realization of God's kingdom in this world.

The *Catechism* urges Christians to 'realize' the kingdom in all that they do. While Christians 'must be careful to distinguish earthly progress clearly from the kingdom of Christ, such progress is of vital concern to the kingdom of God, insofar as it can contribute to the better ordering of human society'.[42] In *Evangelium Vitae*, John Paul II calls for a 'general mobilization of consciences' towards the goal of a 'united ethical effort to activate a great campaign in support of life'.[43] This goal is sustained eschatologically, in the confidence that comes from the resilient faith and hope which knows 'that the Gospel of Life, like the Kingdom of God itself, is growing and producing abundant fruit'.[44]

Acting prophetically in defence of life

Having analysed the 'consistent ethic of life' and *Evangelium Vitae*, we may summarize three shared guideposts for action: first, we live in a new context, which calls Catholics to respond in new ways to the gospel; second, Catholics are called to be unconditionally pro-life, understood and sustained in the faith that all life comes from God and is good, and the hope that all life is destined for fellowship with God; and third, Catholics are called to proclaim this evangelical and prophetic message in new and more vigorous ways.

I will now discuss the first of these guideposts, the new context, in relation to the United States of America. Over the last generation,

American society has shown an increased attraction to a culture of death, an increasing eagerness to kill. For instance, despite appeals to the contrary during the Gulf War, it is clear that the political leadership in the USA has become increasingly incapable of recognizing, much less fighting, a just war. We have witnessed the legalization of what is practically abortion on demand. Most American states have revived the death penalty, are making defence appeals increasingly difficult, and seem allergic to the concept of 'clemency'. The gap between rich and poor has grown over the last twenty years in this, the richest country in the world, and the hungry and home-less are as likely to meet contempt as to be given food and shelter. Legalized euthanasia or doctor-assisted suicide is just over the horizon. Finally, in the post-Cold-War 'new world order', the West continues to spend obscenely immoral billions on weapons, and, most egregiously of all, has promoted the new arms race in Central and South America. In the political sphere, whereas a generation ago one could count on most Democrats and Republicans being 'pro-life' on at least four of the above six issues, today so-called 'moderate' Republicans and 'conservative' Democrats (in other words, the mainstream in American political life) are much more likely to embrace a culture of death on five or all of these issues than they are to espouse a culture of life on even two or three of them.

Faced with a society in a headlong rush towards a culture of death, John Paul II and Cardinal Bernardin have sounded the call for all Christians to speak and act in stronger and more prophetic ways for a consistent gospel of life. In answer to any demand upon us to cause the death of the innocent, the gospel of life 'requires the exercise of conscientious objection'.[45]

We may note three relatively uncelebrated examples of the church's prophetic pro-life stance: on war; on capital punishment; and on the treat-ment of animals. First, there is the fact that in 1991 a quasi-official Vatican newspaper could conclude that the possibility of a just war is all but eclipsed, that 'modern war is always immoral'.[46] Similarly, John Paul II's recent declaration that situations justifying the death penalty are 'practi-cally non-existent' – which he announced in *Evangelium Vitae* and which has been incorporated into the 1997 edition of the *Catechism* – is another sign that it is perhaps more crucial now than it ever has been since the time of the early church for Christians to address their culture with a prophetic voice that is unconditionally pro-life. To focus more precisely on this recent evolution in church teaching on capital punishment, we must com-pare the language of the 1994 and the 1997 editions of the *Catechism*. The 1994 edition acknowledged the right of the state to inflict capital punish-ment in cases of 'extreme gravity', whereas the 1997 edition maintains that 'today [cases where capital punishment are allowed] are very rare, if not practically non-existent'. In terms of the rationale for capital punishment, the 1994 edition kept open the possibility that it might be a penalty 'commensurate' with some crimes, whereas in the 1997 edition no such commensuration is acknowledged, and capital punishment is allowed only when 'this is the only practicable way to defend the lives of human beings effectively against the aggressor'. It goes on to note that in most nations such situations would practically never occur.[47]

What has changed? John Paul II thinks it is even more necessary now to witness to the dignity and sacredness of life by refusing to execute those who 'deserve' it, because the notion that anybody – including murderers – deserves to die is inconsistent with the gospel of life. This move is a rejection of retribution in favour of mercy, a witness to Jesus' peaceableness in the midst of violence. As Bernardin puts it, 'To take any human life, even that of someone who is not innocent, is awesome and tragic.'[48] Similarly, in the words of John Paul II, 'Not even a murderer loses his personal dignity.'[49]

There are also concrete signs that the church's magisterium is quietly but increasingly challenging many of our culturally conditioned practices with regard to other animals, and bringing the gospel of life to bear on specific issues. For example, in February 1997, in the context of the Vatican call for a ban on human cloning, Reuters news service included the following item:

> Monsignor Elio Sgreccia, director of the institute of bioethics at the Catholic University in Rome, also argued today that animal experimentation was valid only under very precise circumstances. 'It is justified only when there are serious and important reasons for the benefit of humanity or also for the benefit of the animals themselves,' Sgreccia told Vatican Radio.[50]

It has become increasingly evident in our culture that, for the most part, the killing of animals is superfluous and gratuitous: as such, it is part of a culture of death. The bottom line is this: in the Western cultural context to which Cardinal Bernardin and Pope John Paul II are addressing their concerns, humans – with rare exception – have absolutely no need to eat animals to survive and flourish. Thus, there is no reason to perpetuate the evil of the slaughter of countless animals for our daily sustenance. Rather, if Christians are to be faithful to the call to be witnesses to a consistent gospel of life, and if we are to speak prophetically as Christians to our culture, we will not want to cause needless suffering and death to animals.[51]

As with the example given by John Paul II concerning the evil of capital punishment, we should seek to witness to the dignity of life in everything we do, even in those areas of our lives where it has not been our custom. As at some times in the past – and in some places at present – capital punishment was (or is) a necessary evil to safeguard the lives of humans, in a comparable way, in much of past history, and in some places in the world today, eating animals remains a necessary evil. As one can argue that it is not wrong to kill an unrestrainable aggressor to preserve life, so one can also argue that it is not morally wrong to kill an animal if that is necessary to preserve human life. These are two of the tragic elements of what it means to live in a fallen world.

While some will argue that the gospel of life only applies to humans, this is simply not true. While the main focus of *Evangelium Vitae* is of course directed to human life, the intrinsic value of animals is recognized, as is their place in the kingdom of God. Some will no doubt argue that I am calling for a 'broadening' of the consistent ethic of life which will make them uncomfortable. Yet it has been Cardinal Bernardin and John Paul II who have been calling for such a broadening. Some no doubt will argue that it is inappropriate to draw any connection between the goodness and dignity of the lives of animals and humans on Death Row. But my argument requires no commensuration or comparison of their respective dignities, only an acknowledgment that the goodness of both kinds of lives are due respect and protection.[52] As the *Catechism* puts it, 'It is contrary to human dignity to cause animals to suffer or die needlessly.'[53]

Conclusion

While I see signs of hope for the future – for example, in the vegetarianism willingly espoused by a great number of young people today – I do not expect great success until two serious problems, one practical and one theological, are overcome. The practical problem is the intractability of the eating habits of our culture. Perhaps we may begin by making people realize that certain practices – eating and wearing animals – that they take for granted as good and natural are neither 'good' nor 'natural' in a theological perspective. The theological problem has to do with a failure of imagination, in particular of an eschatological imagination. In *Crossing the Threshold of Hope*, John Paul II notes that the eschatological vision of the peaceable kingdom of God and the redemption of all creation which has been emphasized in this chapter and in *Evangelium Vitae* 'was only faintly present in traditional preaching'.[54] Furthermore, prior to the Vatican II

Council, what was emphasized was an 'individual eschatology', rather than an 'eschatology of the church and of the world'.[55] What is needed now?

> The truth which the gospel teaches about God requires a certain change in focus with regard to eschatology. First of all, eschatology is not what will take place in the future, something happening only after earthly life is finished. Eschatology has already begun with the coming of Christ. The ultimate eschatological event was His redemptive Death and His Resurrection. This is the beginning of 'a new heaven and a new earth' (cf. Rev. 21.1).[56]

The Pope is calling for Catholics to have a more realized eschatology, a greater sense that no matter how small or symbolic our steps may be, they contribute to the gospel of life, which 'is growing and producing abundant fruit'.[57] At this time when St Thérèse of Lisieux is promoted to the status of a doctor of the church, Catholics have much to learn from her 'little way'.

Striving to live peaceably, not only with other humans who are voiceless and helpless, vulnerable and dying, but also with the other animals, and not killing them needlessly and gratuitously, may be foolishness in the eyes of the world. However, in eschatological perspective, it is surely part of the witness and 'inescapable responsibility of choosing to be unconditionally pro-life'.[58]

Notes on Contributors

Paul Badham is Professor of Theology and Religious Studies and Director of the Master of Arts course in Death and Immortality at the University of Wales, Lampeter, where he has been teaching since 1973. His publications include *Christian Beliefs about Life after Death* (1978), *Immortality or Extinction?* (1984), *Death and Immortality in the Religions of the World* (1987), *Ethics on the Frontiers of Human Existence* (1992), and *Facing Death* (1996). Beliefs about life after death have been his main research interest throughout his academic career.

Richard Bauckham was formerly Reader in the History of Christian Thought at the University of Manchester and is now Professor of New Testament Studies at St Mary's College at the University of St Andrews. His publications include *The Bible in Politics* (1989), *Jude and the Relatives of Jesus in the Early Church* (1990), *The Theology of the Book of Revelation* (1993), and *The Theology of Jürgen Moltmann* (1995); he has also edited several collections of essays and has published over 100 articles in books and major theological journals.

John Berkman is a member of the department of theology at The Catholic University of America. His publications include 'How Important is the Doctrine of Double Effect? Contextualizing the Controversy', *Christian Bioethics* 3/2 (1997); (with Frederick Bauerschmidt) 'Absolutely Fabulous and Civil: Milbank's Post-Critical Augustinianism', *Theology and Philosophy* 9 (1995); 'Truth and Martyrdom: The Structure of Discipleship in *Veritatis Splendor*', *New Blackfriars* (Nov. 1994); 'Medicine, Animals, and Theology', *St Mark's Review (Australia)* 150 (Winter 1992); (with Stanley Hauerwas) 'A Trinitarian Theology of the Chief End of All Flesh', *Theology Today* XLIX/2 (July 1992).

Paul Brett was ordained into the Anglican ministry in 1965 and, after working in industrial mission, for the General Synod and as Director of

Social Responsibility in the Diocese of Chelmsford, has been Rector of Shenfield, Essex, since 1994. He is a Fellow of the Centre for the Study of Theology at Essex University and an executive committee member of the Christian Ethical Investment Group. He has contributed articles on 'Automation', 'Computers' and 'Robots' to *A New Dictionary of Christian Ethics* (1986), and his other publications include *Rethinking Christian Attitudes to Sex* (1991) and *Love Your Neighbour: The Bible and Christian Ethics Today* (1992).

Gillian Clark is a classicist. She has taught at the universities of Oxford, Leicester, Glasgow, St Andrews, and Manchester, as well as Liverpool, where she is now Senior Lecturer in Classics. She is especially interested in the social and intellectual context of patristics, and is joint General Editor of two series, *Translated Texts for Historians* and *Oxford Early Christian Studies*. Her publications include *Women in Late Antiquity* (1993) and *Augustine: Confessions 1–4* (1995) and she is currently working on an annotated translation of Porphyry, *On Abstinence from Animate Food*.

Stephen R. L. Clark is Professor of Philosophy and Dean of the Arts Faculty at the University of Liverpool. He was a Fellow of All Souls 1968–75, Lecturer in Moral Philosophy at Glasgow University 1974–83, Gifford Lecturer 1982, Stanton Lecturer 1986–89, and Wilde Lecturer 1990. He is editor of the *Journal of Applied Philosophy*, and the author of a number of books which include *The Moral Status of Animals* (1977, 1983), *The Nature of the Beast* (1982), *How to Think about the Earth* (1993), and *Animals and their Moral Standing* (1997). His chief interests are political philosophy, animals, metaphysics, and the philosophy of religion, especially in connection with Neoplatonism.

John B. Cobb, Jr studied at the University of Chicago and has taught at Young Harris College, Emory University, and the School of Theology at Claremont, California, where he is Professor Emeritus and co-director of the Center for Process Studies. His recent books include (with Charles Birch) *The Liberation of Life* (1982), (with Herman Daly) *For the Common Good* (1989), *Matters of Life and Death* (1991), *Can Christ Become Good News Again?* (1991), *Sustainability* (1992), and *Sustaining the Common Good* (1994).

James Gaffney holds degrees in biology, psychology, and African studies as well as a doctorate in theology. He was previously Supple Professor of

Religion at Iowa State University and is currently Professor of Ethics at Loyola University in New Orleans. He is the author or editor of ten books and has also contributed to many collections and journals. He is presently preparing a volume of annotated readings in the history of Christian ethics and is engaged in research on the ethical debates that accompanied the Spanish conquests in America.

Thomas E. Hosinski is a Roman Catholic priest and a member of the Congregation of Holy Cross. He is currently Associate Professor and Chair of Theology at the University of Portland, Oregon, where he has served since 1978. He is the author of *Stubborn Fact and Creative Advance: An Introduction to the Metaphysics of Alfred North Whitehead* (1993) as well as several articles in scholarly books and journals. His research is in philosophical and systematic theology, with a special interest in the doctrines of God and creation, the relation between science and religion, and process theology.

Walter Houston is a minister of the United Reformed Church and Tutor in Biblical Studies at Northern College (United Reformed and Congregational), Manchester. He also teaches at Sheffield and Manchester Universities, and was formerly Director of Old Testament Studies at Westminster College, Cambridge. He is the author of *Purity and Monotheism: Clean and Unclean Animals in Biblical Law* (1993), and is at present working on problems of ethics and ideology in the Hebrew Bible.

Scott Ickert was Lutheran Fellow in church history and theology at Mansfield College, Oxford from 1990 to 1995 and was also a member of staff at Ripon College, Cuddesdon. He is presently pastor of the Resurrection Lutheran Church in Arlington, Virginia. He has published a number of articles on theology and ecclesiology, and contributed to the third edition of the *Oxford Dictionary of the Christian Church*.

Brian Klug is Associate Professor and Chair of the Department of Philosophy at Saint Xavier University, Chicago. He is currently an Adviser for the Food Animals Concerns Trust and a Consulting Editor of *Patterns of Prejudice*. He has published numerous articles on the subject of animals, including two in *Judaism and Animal Rights* ed. R. Kalechofsky (1992), and has designed and taught a variety of courses on animals, including Animals and Ethics, Images of Nature, and Wolves and People.

Andrew Linzey holds the world's first post in theology and animal welfare – the IFAW Senior Research Fellowship at Mansfield College, Oxford. He was Special Professor at the University of Nottingham 1992–96, and is currently Special Professor at Saint Xavier University, Chicago, and Honorary Professor at the University of Birmingham. He has written or edited 19 books, including major works on theology and animals: *Animal Rights* (1976), *Christianity and the Rights of Animals* (1987), (with Tom Regan) *Animals and Christianity: A Book of Readings* (1989), *Animal Theology* (1994), and (with Dan Cohn-Sherbok) *After Noah: Animals and the Liberation of Theology* (1997). He is co-editor of the *Dictionary of Ethics, Theology and Society* (1996).

Michael Lloyd wrote his D.Phil. thesis on 'The Cosmic Fall and the Free Will Defence' (1996). He was Chaplain and Director of Studies in Theology at Christ's College, Cambridge, 1990–94; he was then Chaplain at Fitzwilliam College, Cambridge, and is now Honorary Curate at St James the Less in Pimlico. His publications include the entry on 'The Fall' in the *Dictionary of Ethics, Theology and Society*, and an article on 'The Humanity of Fallenness' for a forthcoming volume to mark the 1998 Lambeth Conference. He is currently working to turn his D.Phil. thesis into the first of three volumes on the problem of evil.

Jay B. McDaniel received his Ph.D. in the philosophy of religion and theology from Claremont Graduate School in California, where he studied under John B. Cobb, Jr. He is Professor of Religion and Director of the Steel Center for the Study of Religion and Philosophy at Hendrix College, Conway, Arkansas. His books on ecotheology, *Of God and Pelicans* (1989), *Earth, Sky, Gods and Mortals* (1990), and *With Roots and Wings* (1995), emphasize the intrinsic value of individual animals both domestic and wild. He has also written on Buddhist-Christian dialogue and the relation of Christianity to other world religions.

John Muddiman is G. B. Caird Fellow in New Testament Studies at Mansfield College, and Lecturer in the Faculty of Theology at the University of Oxford. He was until recently Co-Director of the Oxford Centre for the Environment, Ethics and Society. His publications include *The Bible: Fountain and Well of Truth* (1983) and *The Epistle to the Ephesians: A Commentary* (1996), and he has contributed to *The World's Religions* ed. S. Sutherland, L. Houlden, P. Clarke and F. Hardy (1988), *The Companion Encyclopedia of Theology* ed. J. L. Houlden (1995), and the

Dictionary of Ethics, Theology and Society ed. P. B. Clarke and A. Linzey (1996).

J. W. Rogerson is an Emeritus Canon of Sheffield Cathedral. From 1964 to 1979 he taught in the Department of Theology, Durham University, and from 1979 to 1994 he was Professor and Head of the Department of Biblical Studies at Sheffield University. He retired in 1996 and is Professor Emeritus. His many books include *Myth in Old Testament Interpretation* (1974), *Anthropology and the Old Testament* (1978), (with P. R. Davies) *The Old Testament World* (1989), *Genesis 1–11* (1991), and *The Bible and Criticism in Victorian Britain: Profiles of F. D. Maurice and W. Robertson Smith* (1995). He is currently writing a Theology of the Old Testament and is researching social, ethical, aesthetic, and economic aspects of the Old Testament.

Huw Spanner was Managing Editor of the evangelical current-affairs magazine *Third Way* from 1993 to 1997 and remains a consulting editor. He has recently edited Roy McCloughry's *Belief in Politics: People, Policies and Personal Faith* (1996).

Eldred Willey was formerly assistant editor of *The Tablet* and is now a freelance editor and writer on religious affairs. His publications include (with Petroc Willey) 'The Earth is a Gift', *New Blackfriars* (1991). Among his research interests are ecumenism, Christian East-West relations, and the work of G. K. Chesterton.

Petroc Willey did research on environmental ethics as a doctoral student at Liverpool University, and from 1985 to 1992 was tutor in Catholic ethics at Plater College, Oxford. He is currently editor of *The Sower: A Journal for Religious Educators in School and Parish*, and Dean of Higher Education, Maryvale Institute, Birmingham. His publications include (with Katherine Willey) *Become What You Are: The Call and Gift of Marriage* (1992). Among his research interests are the theology and ethics of love and marriage, catechetics, and moral and religious education.

Dorothy Yamamoto is a mediaevalist. She has taught at Westminster College, Oxford, and at Oxford Brookes University, where she wrote her doctoral thesis on the boundary between humans and animals in mediaeval culture. She has published a number of articles in scholarly journals, including *Neuphilologische Mitteilungen* and *The Chaucer Review*, and has recently finished writing a book based on her thesis.

Notes

Introduction: Is Christianity Irredeemably Speciesist?

1. Daphne Hampson, *Theology and Feminism*, Blackwell 1990.
2. Daphne Hampson, *After Christianity*, SCM Press 1996, p. 6. See also Iain Torrance, 'Is Christianity Irredeemably Sexist?' in *Who Needs Feminism? Men Respond to Sexism in the Church* ed. Richard Holloway, SPCK 1991, and Hampson's comments, *After Christianity*, pp. 287–88.
3. Editorial, *Daily Telegraph*, 10 January 1995, my emphasis. See also my response, 'A Christian Shield for Animals', *The Spectator*, 6 April 1996, pp. 18–19.
4. Andrew Linzey and Paul Waldau, 'Speciesism' in *Dictionary of Ethics, Theology and Society* ed. Paul Barry Clarke and Andrew Linzey, Routledge 1996, p. 788; my emphasis.
5. For a discussion of this material see Andrew Linzey and Dan Cohn-Sherbok (eds), *After Noah: Animals and the Liberation of Theology*, Cassell 1997, ch. 4: 'Christ and the stories of Christlike compassion'.
6. I am often accused of focussing only on the negative aspects of the tradition in relation to animals. *After Noah* is an attempt to outline the resources within Judaism and Christianity for a positive view of animals, and ch. 6 shows how 'Animals can liberate Jewish and Christian theology' by rejecting the contemporary deification of humans in theology and ethics. See also my thumbnail sketch of the positive tradition in 'Animals', *Oxford Companion to Christian Thought* ed. Adrian Hastings, forthcoming Oxford University Press.
7. Aristotle, *The Politics*, trs. T. A. Sinclair, rev. T. J. Saunders, Penguin Books 1985, p. 79.
8. Augustine, *City of God*, 1.20; cited and discussed by Gillian Clark in ch. 6, below.
9. Aquinas, *Summa contra Gentiles*, trs. English Dominican Fathers, Benzger Brothers 1928, Third Book, Part II, ch. cxii; also cited and discussed in Andrew Linzey, *Christianity and the Rights of Animals*, SPCK/Crossroad 1987, pp. 22f.

10. See e.g. P. Palazzini (ed.), *Dictionary of Moral Theology*, comp. F. Roberti, trs. H. Y. Yannone, Burns & Oates 1962, pp. 73f.

11. John Canon McCarthy, *Problems in Theology*, vol. ii: *The Commandments*, Browne & Nolan 1960, pp. 156–57. Far from falling out of use, the view that the virtue of 'temperance' is sufficient for understanding our obligations to animals was maintained by a leading Dominican at a conference on animals in Oxford in 1996.

12. William Cowper, 'Winter Walk at Noon', extract in *Song of Creation* ed. Andrew Linzey and Tom Regan, Marshall Pickering 1989, p. 48. Cowper's poem is an impressive essay on the theology of the Fall and restoration of the animal creation.

13. For some recent 'animal blind' discussions of creation liturgy, see Celia Deane-Drummond, *A Handbook in Theology and Ecology*, SCM Press 1996; Deiter T. Hessell, *Theology for Earth Community: A Field Guide*, Orbis Books 1996; and Ralph N. McMichael, Jr (ed.), *Creation and Liturgy*, The Pastoral Press 1993. I hope to remedy this deficiency in my *Animal Rites: Liturgies for Animal Care*, forthcoming SCM Press.

14. John Puddefoot, 'Perhaps God really is an alien', *Church Times*, 29 August 1997, p. 8.

15. Andrew Linzey, *Animal Theology*, SCM Press/University of Illinois Press 1994, p. viii.

16. Ibid., p. 47.

17. Karl Barth, *Church Dogmatics*, III/1, *The Doctrine of Creation* ed. G. W. Bromiley and T. F. Torrance, T. & T. Clark 1960, pp. 16, 18; my emphases.

18. For two outstanding discussions on the patristic and biblical evidence see Allan D. Galloway, *The Cosmic Christ*, Nisbet & Co. 1951, and Robert Murray, *The Cosmic Covenant: Biblical Themes of Justice, Peace and the Integrity of Creation*, Sheed & Ward 1992.

19. I develop this point elsewhere: see *After Noah*, ch. 6, and my 'The Theological Basis of Animal Rights', *The Christian Century* 108/28, 9 October 1991, pp. 906–10.

20. Andrew Linzey and Paul Waldau, 'The Dog's Mess: Theology as if Animals Mattered', *AARSBL Abstracts*, 1994 Annual Meeting, Chicago, para. A179.

21. See Albert Schweitzer, *Civilization and Ethics*, trs. C. T. Campion, A. & C. Black 1967, and discussion in Barth, *Church Dogmatics*, III/4, p. 349; also discussed in Linzey, *Animal Theology*, p. 7.

22. Alasdair MacIntyre, *After Virtue*, 2nd edn, Duckworth 1985, pp. 221–22, 223.

23. David Jenkins, *God, Miracle and the Church of England*, SCM Press 1987,

p. 100; I am grateful to Jenkins for his insightful discussion of MacIntyre. On the need for a new *pneuma*-based paradigm, see my 'On Theology' in *Theology, the University and the Modern World* ed. P. A. B. Clarke and Andrew Linzey, Lester Crook Academic Press 1988, pp. 29–66.

24. There have been some other theological pioneers – notably Gary Comstock, John B. Cobb, Jr, Jay B. McDaniel, Stephen R. L. Clark, and John Berkman – but not many. There are only two other anthologies on theology and animals: Charles Pinches and Jay B. McDaniel (eds), *Good News for Animals? Christian Approaches to Animal Well-Being*, Orbis Books 1993, and Andrew Linzey and Tom Regan (eds), *Animals and Christianity: A Book of Readings*, SPCK/Crossroad 1989.

1 What was the Meaning of Animal Sacrifice?

1. Paul Radin, *Primitive Man as Philosopher*, Dover 1959. See especially ch. xix.

2. For an account of the rise of the views that follow, see my *Old Testament Criticism in the Nineteenth Century: England and Germany*, SPCK 1984.

3. A classical account of this, as well as of the consensus just described, is given by W. Robertson Smith, *The Old Testament in the Jewish Church*, Edinburgh 1881 (revd edn 1892).

4. W. Robertson Smith, *Lectures on the Religion of the Semites. First Series: The Fundamental Institutions*, 3rd edn, A. & C. Black 1927; H. Hubert and M. Mauss, 'Essai sur la nature et la fonction du sacrifice', *L'Année sociologique* ii, 1899, pp. 89ff.

5. G. B. Gray, *Sacrifice in the Old Testament: Its Theory and Practice*, Clarendon Press 1925.

6. See my *Anthropology and the Old Testament*, Blackwell 1978; reissued JSOT Press 1984, pp. 24–26.

7. E. R. Leach, *Culture and Communication: The Logic by which Symbols are Connected*, Cambridge University Press 1976; D. Davies, 'An Interpretation of Sacrifice in Leviticus', *Zeitschrift für die alttestamentliche Wissenschaft* 89, 1977, pp. 388–98, reprinted in B. Lang (ed.), *Anthropological Approaches to the Old Testament*, SPCK 1985, pp. 151–62.

8. The view that transgressions by individual Israelites of various ranks as well as the people as a whole defile the sanctuary, which must be cleansed by animal sacrifice and blood sprinkling, is clearly expressed in Lev. 4–6. See my 'Sacrifice in the Old Testament: Problems of Method and Approach', *Sacrifice* ed. M. F. C. Bourdillon and M. Fortes, Academic Press 1980, pp. 45–60, esp. pp. 49 and 54.

9. On 'lepers' see G. R. Driver, 'Leprosy', *Hastings Dictionary of the Bible* ed.

F. C. Grant and H. H. Rowley, T. & T. Clark 1963. By 'leprosy' is meant a curable skin disorder.

10. R. Girard, *La Violence et le sacré*, Paris: Grasset 1972; trs. by P. Gregory, *Violence and the Sacred*, Baltimore: Johns Hopkins University Press 1978. An extensive bibliography on Girard and responses to him is given by N. Lohfink in N. Lohfink (ed.), *Gewalt und Gewaltlosigkeit im Alten Testament* (Quaestiones disputae 96), Freiburg: Herder Verlag 1983, pp. 245–47.

11. See J. W. Rogerson, *Genesis 1–11* (Old Testament Guides), Sheffield Academic Press 1991.

12. N. Lohfink, 'Die Schichten des Pentateuch und der Krieg', *Gewalt und Gewaltlosigkeit*, pp. 51–110. P^g denotes the historical narrative of the Priestly source.

13. For information on the relationship with domestic animals in the Talmudic period, see S. Krauss, *Talmudische Archäologie* 2, reissued Hildesheim: Georg Olms 1966, pp. 111–17. Krauss details various ways in which these animals were helped when giving birth or when sick, 'aus Barmherzigkeit gegen das Tier' (p. 114). He also draws attention to the problem of castration of oxen, which was held to be forbidden to Jews, although a castrated animal was worth more than an intact one (p. 116). Whatever may have been the practice in the biblical period, it would certainly have been contrary to the law to offer a castrated animal in sacrifice (Lev. 1.3).

14. See A. Bialik, 'baqar', in *Encyclopaedia Biblica* (Hebrew), Jerusalem: Bialik Institute 1954, pp. 312–16.

15. D. Hopkins, *The Highlands of Canaan: Agricultural Life in the Early Iron Age* (Social World of Biblical Antiquity Series 3), Almond Press 1985, pp. 245–50.

16. For milch cows, see I Sam. 6.7–14.

17. On the extent of territory and its enlargement in the second and first centuries BCE, see M. Avi-Yonah, 'Historical Geography of Palestine', *The Jewish People in the First Century: Historical Geography, Political History, Social, Cultural and Religious Life and Institutions* ed. S. Safrai and M. Stern, vol. 1, Assen: Van Gorcum 1974, pp. 78–95. For the concentration on vines and olives, see H. Kippenberg, *Religion und Klassenbildung in antiken Judäa*, 2nd edn, Göttingen: Vandenhoeck & Ruprecht 1982, p. 47. See also the observation of I. Finkelstein: 'cereal growing was a wrong economic strategy in these hilly parts of the highlands', in 'The Great Transformation: The "Conquest" of the Highlands Frontiers and the Rise of the Territorial States', *The Archaeology of Society in the Holy Land* ed. T. E. Levy, Leicester University Press 1995, pp. 349–65 (p. 353). In the early centuries CE there was considerable poverty in Palestine, which

would hardly have provided an economic base for temple sacrifices. On this poverty, see Krauss, *Talmudische Archäologie*, vol. 2, p. 116, and, generally, D. Sperber, *Roman Palestine 200–400: The Land, Crisis and Change in Agrarian Society as Reflected in Rabbinic Sources* (Bar-Ilan Studies in Near Eastern Languages and Culture), Ramat-Gan: Bar-Ilan University 1978.

18. See also Rogerson, 'Sacrifice in the Old Testament', p. 58 (n. 8 above).

2 *What was the Meaning of Classifying Animals as Clean or Unclean?*

1. My own translation, but based on the Revised English Bible (REB).
2. REB.
3. Daniel L. Smith, *The Religion of the Landless: The Social Context of the Babylonian Exile*, Bloomington, Ind.: Meyer-Stone Books 1989, esp. pp. 145–49.
4. Walter Houston, *Purity and Monotheism: Clean and Unclean Animals in Biblical Law* (JSOT Supplement Series 140), JSOT Press 1993.
5. *Purity and Danger: An Analysis of Concepts of Pollution and Taboo*, Routledge 1966; *Natural Symbols: Explorations in Cosmology*, New York: Barrie & Rockliff 1970 (2nd edn Penguin Books 1973); 'Deciphering a Meal' and 'Self-Evidence', *Implicit Meanings: Essays in Anthropology*, Routledge 1975, pp. 249–75, 276–318.
6. Houston, *Purity and Monotheism*, pp. 65–66, 118, and elsewhere.
7. Letter of Aristeas, 146; Mishnah, *Hullin* 3.6; discussion in Babylonian Talmud, *Hullin* 61a–65a.
8. Houston, *Purity and Monotheism*, table on pp. 178–80, summarizing many specialist studies, discussion on pp. 129–45, 148–50.
9. Cf. Edwin B. Firmage, 'The Biblical Dietary Laws and the Concept of Holiness', *Studies in the Pentateuch* ed. J. A. Emerton (VT Sup. 41), Leiden: Brill 1990, pp. 177–208.
10. Houston, *Purity and Monotheism*, pp. 149 f.
11. Ibid., pp. 161–68.
12. Ibid., pp. 150–61.
13. Ibid., pp. 168–72.
14. Liora Kolska Horwitz, 'Faunal Remains from the Early Iron Age Site of Mount Ebal', *Tel Aviv* 13–14, 1986–87, pp. 173–89.
15. Houston, *Purity and Monotheism*, pp. 180–217.
16. *On Abstinence*, 2.25.
17. Houston, *Purity and Monotheism*, pp. 204 f.
18. Johnson M. Kimuhu, 'The Kikuyu Bible Rendering of Hebrew Words that Function to Mark Off an Untouchable Zone or Objects or Impose

Restrictions in Relation to Sancta', M.Th. thesis, University of Glasgow 1995.

19. Cf. Edmund Leach, 'Anthropological Aspects of Language: Animal Categories and Verbal Abuse', *New Directions in the Study of Language* ed. H. Lenneberg, Cambridge, Mass.: MIT Press 1964, pp. 23–64 (reprinted in *Reader in Comparative Religion: An Anthropological Approach* ed. W. A. Lessa and E. Z. Vogt, 4th edn, New York: Harper & Row 1965, pp. 153–66).

20. Ibid., p. 31.

21. Houston, *Purity and Monotheism*, pp. 251 f. See also below.

22. Ibid., pp. 255–56.

3 A New Testament Doctrine of Creation?

1. See R. Hays, *Echoes of Scripture in the Letters of Paul*, New Haven: Yale University Press 1989; R. Riesner, *Jesus als Lehrer*, Tübingen: Mohr 1981.

2. See C. Westermann, *Creation*, SPCK 1974; B. Anderson (ed.), *Creation in the Old Testament*, SPCK 1984.

3. See H. Jonas, *Gnosis und spätantike Geist*, Göttingen: Vandenhoeck & Ruprecht 1954.

4. See J. R. Levison, *The Portrait of Adam in Early Judaism*, Sheffield Academic Press 1988; *Journal for the Study of the Pseudepigrapha*, Supplement Series 1; R. Scroggs, *The Last Adam*, Blackwell 1966; J. Jervell, *Imago Dei*, Göttingen: Vandenhoeck & Ruprecht 1960; E. Brandenburger, *Adam und Christus*, Neukirchen: Neukirchener Verlag 1962.

5. Genesis Rabba 12.6. See W. D. Davies, *Paul and Rabbinic Judaism*, 4th edn, Philadelphia: Fortress Press 1980.

6. On this see e.g. E. P. Sanders, *Paul and Palestinian Judaism*, SCM Press/Fortress Press 1977, pp. 419 ff. The Apocalypse of Baruch (II Baruch), though comparable, is less severe in its treatment of Adam.

7. See the discussion of Rom. 5.12 in J. D. G. Dunn, *Commentary on Romans 1–8*, Waco: Word 1988.

8. See further J. Muddiman, 'Adam, the Type of the One to Come', *Theology* lxxxvii, 1984, pp. 101–10.

9. See E. Käsemann, *Commentary on Romans*, SCM Press 1980; cf. also R. Murray, *The Cosmic Covenant*, Sheed & Ward 1992, pp. 129–32, and F. Bridger, 'Ecology and Eschatology', *Tyndale Bulletin* 41, 1990, pp. 297–300.

10. See W. Wink, *Naming the Powers*, Philadelphia: Fortress Press 1984; G. Twelftree, *Christ Triumphant*, IVP 1985.

11. See B. S. Childs, *Myth and Reality in the Old Testament*, SCM Press 1960.

12. Cf. R. H. Lightfoot, *The Gospel Message of Mark*, Oxford University Press 1950, and *St John's Gospel: A Commentary*, Oxford University Press 1956.

13. Some exegetes take the phrase less positively and see 'wild beasts' as symbolic of the desert as inhospitable or even as haunted by demons; cf. W. Schulze, 'Der Heilige und die wilden Tiere: zur Exegese von Mc. 1.13b', *ZNW* 46, 1955, pp. 280–83.

14. See further Murray, *Cosmic Covenant*, pp. 127 ff.

15. See J. Bogart, *Orthodox and Heretical Perfectionism*, Missoula: Scholars Press 1977.

16. See esp. J. L. Martyn, *History and Theology in the Fourth Gospel*, New York: Harper & Row 1968; revd edn 1979.

17. See R. E. Brown, *The Gospel According to John*, Anchor Bible, vol. 1, New York: Doubleday 1966.

18. See C. K. Barrett, *The Gospel of John and Judaism*, SPCK 1975.

4 Jesus and Animals I: What did he Teach?

1. On this verse, see esp. R. Murray, *The Cosmic Covenant*, Heythrop Monographs 7, Sheed & Ward 1992, p. 113.

2. The general scholarly opinion is that this, like the other Testaments of the Twelve Patriarchs, is an originally Jewish work, which has received some Christian editing. But the argument of H. W. Hollander and M. de Jonge, *The Testaments of the Twelve Patriarchs: A Commentary*, SVTP 8, Leiden: Brill 1985, pp. 82–85, that the Testaments as we have them are a Christian work, whose Jewish sources cannot be reconstructed, should also be noted.

3. See ibid., pp. 254–55.

4. The point is not quite clear, because of the difference between the two recensions of the work: see the translations of 58.4–6 in MSS J and A in F. I. Andersen, '2 (Slavonic Apocalypse of) Enoch', *The Old Testament Pseudepigrapha*, vol. 1, ed. J. H. Charlesworth, Darton, Longman & Todd 1983, pp. 184–85.

5. This may also be the sin to which Pseudo-Phocylides 139 refers. P. W. Van der Horst translates: 'Take not for yourself a mortal beast's ration of food.' But the Greek is very obscure: see P. W. Van der Horst, *The Sentences of Pseudo-Phocylides*, Leiden: Brill 1978, p. 206. Cf. also b. Gitt. 62a; Ber. 40a.

6. For this interpretation, see Andersen, '2 (Slavonic Apocalypse of) Enoch', pp. 184–85 n. a. For Jewish condemnation of bestiality, see Ex. 22.18; Lev. 18.23; 20.15–16; Deut. 27.21; Philo, Spec. Leg. 3.43–50; Sib. Or. 5.393; T. Levi 17.11; Pseudo-Phocylides 188; m. Sanh. 7.4; m. Ker. 1.1; m. 'Abod. Zar. 2.1; b. Yeb. 59b.

7. Cf. Targums Pseudo-Jonathan and Neofiti to Gen. 22.10, where Isaac asks Abraham to bind him well for precisely this reason. I owe this point to Professor Philip Alexander.

8. See e.g. b. Ber. 33b; b. B. M. 31a–32b, 87b; b. Shabb. 128b; Lev. R. 27.11; Deut. R. 6.1.

9. For a recent discussion, see Murray, *Cosmic Covenant*, pp. 114–19.

10. P. W. van der Horst's discussion (*Sentences*, 172–3) seems to overlook the fact that the law is not here interpreted as a matter of kindness to the bird, as it is in other Jewish sources.

11. E. J. Schochet, *Animal Life in Jewish Tradition*, New York: Ktav 1984, p. 151.

12. This otherwise unknown law is also found in a lost work of Philo (*Hypothetica*), quoted in Eusebius, *Praep. Evang.* 8.7.

13. Translation from H. St J. Thackeray, *Josephus*, vol. 1, Loeb Classical Library, Heinemann 1926, p. 379.

14. Philo adopted the Stoic view that animals are distinguished from humans by their lack of reason. For Philo's views of animals and his relationship on this point to Hellenistic philosophy, see A. Terian, *Philonis Alexandrini De Animalibus: The Armenian Text with an Introduction, Translation and Commentary*, Chico, Calif.: Scholars Press 1981.

15. See n. 8 above.

16. For the probably early date of this particular tradition, see M. McNamara, *The New Testament and the Palestinian Targum to the Pentateuch*, AnBib 27, Rome: Pontifical Biblical Institute 1966, pp. 136–37. It was later criticized and censured by rabbis who objected to the giving of reasons for commandments of the Torah, because this reduced the ordinances of God to mere acts of mercy: m. Ber. 5.3; b. Ber. 33b; y. Ber. 5.3.9c; y. Meg. 4.9.75c. See E. E. Urbach, *The Sages: Their Concepts and Beliefs*, Jerusalem: Magnes Press 1975, pp. 382–85, 452; Schochet, *Animal Life*, pp. 179–83; E. Segal, 'Justice, Mercy and a Bird's Nest', *Journal of Jewish Studies* 42, 1991, pp. 176–95.

17. Biblical quotations in this chapter are from the NRSV, unless otherwise stated.

18. The best manuscript evidence is divided between *huios* (child) and *onos* (donkey, as in Luke 13.15). The textual question is discussed by I. H. Marshall, *The Gospel of Luke*, NIGTC, Paternoster Press 1978, pp. 579–80; J. A. Fitzmyer, *The Gospel According to Luke (X–XXIV)*, AB 28A, New York: Doubleday 1985, pp. 1041–42. Both accept *huios*, as the harder reading.

19. Matt. 12.11 and Luke 14.5 are probably variant forms of the same saying, though probably not derived by Matthew and Luke from the same source.

Of course, Jesus could well have made the same point in the context of two debates about his practice of healing on the sabbath.

20. For differences in interpretation of the sabbath law in New Testament times, see E. P. Sanders, *Jewish Law from Jesus to the Mishnah*, SCM Press 1990, pp. 6–23.

21. Translation from G. Vermes, *The Dead Sea Scrolls in English*, 3rd edn, Penguin 1987, p. 95.

22. My translation from the German translation of the Coptic in J. Boehmer, *Neutestamentliche Parallelen und Verwandte aus altchristlicher Literatur*, Stuttgart: Greiner & Pfeiffer 1903, pp. 26–27. There are also English translations in B. Pick, *Paralipomena: Remains of Gospels and Sayings of Christ*, Chicago: Open Court 1908, pp. 58–59, and Roderick Dunkerley, *Beyond the Gospels*, Penguin 1957, pp. 143–44; also cited and discussed in *After Noah: Animals and the Liberation of Theology* ed. Andrew Linzey and Dan Cohn-Sherbok, Cassell 1997, pp. 65–66.

23. Boehmer gives its source merely as 'Coptic Bible'.

24. For this interpretation of these texts, see b. B. M. 31a–32b; b. Sanh. 128b.

25. There is a remarkable parallel in the saying attributed to the second-century Rabbi Gamliel III: 'Whosoever has compassion upon his fellow-creatures, upon him will God have compassion' (b. Shabb. 77b; y. Ber. 9.3.13c; quoted in Schochet, *Animal Life*, p. 164). See also the story of Rabbi Judah ha-Nasi, of which this is the moral: ibid.

26. See also Pss. 104.10–11, 14, 21, 27–8, 145.15–16; Job 38.39–41. M. F. Olsthoorn, *The Jewish Background and the Synoptic Setting of Mt 6.25–33 and Lk 12.22–31*, Studium Biblicum Franciscanum Analecta 10, Jerusalem: Franciscan Printing House 1975, p. 36, calls this 'one of the most common beliefs of listeners . . . familiar with the Jewish tradition'.

27. V. C. Holmgren, *Bird Walk Through the Bible*, 2nd edn, New York: Dover 1988, p. 146.

28. Ravens were also generally disliked: I Enoch 90.8–19; Jub. 12.18–21; b. Sanh. 108b; t. Shabb. 6.6; Barn. 10.4 (where their idleness is precisely the point). Cf. Olsthoorn, *Jewish Background*, p. 35.

29. Translation from R. B. Wright, 'Psalms of Solomon', *The Old Testament Pseudepigrapha*, vol. 2, ed. J. H. Charlesworth, Darton, Longman & Todd 1985, p. 657.

30. The point is therefore rather different from that in m. Qidd. 4.14 (quoted below), where R. Simeon ben Eleazar observes that animals and birds do not have to work to gain a living, whereas humans do. His point is that humans would be sustained without effort, had they not forfeited this right through sin (cf. Gen. 3.17–19).

31. A. Deissmann, *Light from the Ancient East*, 4th edn, Hodder & Stoughton

1927, pp. 273–74; O. Bauernfeind in *Theological Dictionary of the New Testament* ed. G. Kittel and G. Friedrich, trs. G. W. Bromiley, vol. 7, Grand Rapids: Eerdmans 1971, pp. 730 n. 10, 732 n. 19. Marshall, *Luke*, p. 514, appears to be mistaken when he says that sparrows were not in fact eaten for food and that *strouthion* here must mean any small bird eaten for food.

32. Cf. Deut. R. 6.2, which calls it the least weighty of the commandments, whereas Ex. 20.12, for which the same reward is specified, is the weightiest.

33. The Romans reckoned an *assarion* (Latin *as*) as one sixteenth of a denarius, the rabbis as one twenty-fourth of a denarius: see H. L. Strack and P. Billerbeck, *Kommentar zum Neuen Testament aus Talmud und Midrasch*, vol. 1, Munich: Beck 1922, p. 291.

34. e.g. W. D. Davies and D. C. Allison, *A Critical and Exegetical Commentary on the Gospel according to Saint Matthew*, vol. 2, T. & T. Clark 1991, p. 208.

35. See the comments on Amos 3.5 in W. R. Harper, *A Critical and Exegetical Commentary on Amos and Hosea*, ICC, T. & T. Clark 1905, pp. 70–71; J. L. Mays, *Amos*, OTL, SCM Press 1969, p. 61.

36. Translation from H. Freedman, *Midrash Rabbah: Genesis*, vol. 2, Soncino Press 1939, p. 730. The story also appears in y. Sheb. 9.22.38d; Eccles. R. 10.8; Midr. Ps. 17.13.

37. For a modern discussion of this issue in relation to animal suffering, which takes Jesus' saying as its starting-point, see J. B. McDaniel, *Of God and Pelicans: A Theology of Reverence for Life*, Louisville, Ky.: Westminster/John Knox Press 1989, ch. 1.

38. Cf. also Mekilta to Ex. 12.1, quoted in Olsthoorn, *Jewish Background*, p. 37.

39. Translation from H. Danby, *The Mishnah*, Clarendon Press 1933, p. 329.

40. Translation from H. Freedman, *The Babylonian Talmud: Kiddushin*, Soncino Press 1936, p. 425. See also y. Qidd. 4.11.66d.

41. Quoted in G. Friedlander, *The Jewish Sources of the Sermon on the Mount*, Routledge 1911, p. 194.

42. Translation from J. Rabbinowitz, *Midrash Rabbah: Deuteronomy*, Soncino Press 1939, p. 124.

43. This point is neglected in the following *non sequitur*: 'Men and women are worth more than the birds or the grass of the field. The real value of beasts and trees lies in how far they enrich human life, for nourishment, protection or beauty' (E. Marshall, 'Jesus and the Environment: How Green is Christianity?', *Modern Churchman* 33, 1992, p. 4).

44. e.g. Aristotle, *Polit.* 1.8; Cicero, *De natura deorum* 2. See my article, 'Attitudes to the Non-Human Creation in the History of Christian Thought',

Stewarding Creation: Christian Perspectives on the Non-Human Creation (forthcoming).

45. See Terian, *Philonis Alexandrini De animalibus*, 51; C. J. Glacken, *Traces on the Rhodian Shore: Nature and Culture in Western Thought from Ancient Times to the End of the Eighteenth Century*, Berkeley and Los Angeles: University of California Press 1967, pp. 57, 61. For a rabbinic example, see b. Shabb. 77b.

46. See Bauckham, 'Attitudes to the Non-Human Creation'.

47. As Maimonides argued: Schochet, *Animal Life*, pp. 204–6.

48. *De moribus Manichaeorum* 17.54. Augustine is followed by Marshall, 'Jesus and the Environment', p. 4, who takes the story to show that Jesus put humans 'in a class apart from other living creatures'.

49. See Terian, *Philonis Alexandrini De animalibus*, 52.

50. e.g. Thomas Aquinas, *Summa theologiae*, 2.65.3.

51. G. H. Twelftree, *Christ Triumphant: Exorcism Then and Now*, Hodder & Stoughton 1985, p. 66.

52. Cf. ibid. 77–82.

5 Jesus and Animals II: What did he Practise?

1. See R. Bauckham, 'Jesus' Demonstration in the Temple', *Law and Religion* ed. B. Lindars, James Clarke 1988, pp. 72–89.

2. Note also Luke 17.14 (cf. Lev. 14.1–32).

3. For a general account of sacrifices in the time of Jesus, see E. P. Sanders, *Judaism: Practice and Belief: 63 BCE–66 CE*, SCM Press/TPI 1992, ch. 7.

4. In context, Stephen's quotation of Amos 5.25–7 (Acts 7.42–3) means that Israel in the wilderness failed to offer the sacrifices to God which they should have offered, but offered sacrifices to idols instead.

5. According to Acts 21.26, even Paul participated in sacrifices in the temple.

6. The passages in the Pseudo-Clementine literature which treat the laws in the Pentateuch prescribing sacrifices and other aspects of the temple cult as later additions to the law of Moses, not belonging to the law originally given by God (*Clem. hom.* 2.44, 3.52), are probably of Ebionite origin.

7. See G. Howard, 'The Gospel of the Ebionites' in W. Haase, *Aufstieg und Niedergang der romischen Welt*, vol. 2/25/5, Berlin and New York: de Gruyter 1988, pp. 4034–53.

8. See E. J. Schochet, *Animal Life in Jewish Tradition*, New York: Ktav 1984, pp. 15–17.

9. On Jewish and Christian vegetarianism in New Testament times, see R. T. Beckwith, 'The Vegetarianism of the Therapeutae, and the Motives for Vegetarianism in Early Jewish and Christian Circles', *Revue de Qumran* 13,

1988, pp. 407–10 (but he overlooks some evidence: Dan. 10.2; IV Ezra 9.23–6, 12.51; T. Reub. 1.9–10; T. Jud. 15.4; Eusebius, *Hist. eccl.* 2.23.5). He divides his evidence into five categories of vegetarianism, but it can all be included in my two categories, with the exception of his fourth category. This is a single reference in Philo (*Providentia*, fragment 2, 69–70), which commends vegetarianism on the grounds that eating meat reduces humans 'to the savagery of wild beasts'. On the more general question of vegetarianism in the ancient world, see D. E. Aune in *Plutarch's Theological Writings and Early Christian Literature* ed. H. D. Betz, Studia ad Corpus Hellenisticum Novi Testamenti 3, Leiden: Brill 1975, pp. 305–8.

10. It is not very clear whether, in Jewish and early Christian eschatology, people in the messianic age are expected to be vegetarian, though it is clear that they will drink wine (I Enoch 10.19; Mark 14.25). But if wild animals are to be once again vegetarian (Isa. 11.6–9; Sib. Or. 3.788–95; cf. Gen. 1.30), it would seem that humans must also be, and the abundance of food which is to be provided without human effort (II Bar. 29.5; I Enoch 10.19; Papias, ap. Irenaeus, *Adv. haer.* 5.33.5–6) is to be vegetarian. On the other hand, Leviathan and Behemoth are to be slaughtered to provide food (IV Ezra 6.52; II Bar. 29.4).

11. For an argument for vegetarianism which takes account of the fact that Jesus was not a vegetarian, see A. Linzey, 'The Bible and Killing for Food', *Using the Bible Today* ed. D. Cohn-Sherbok, Bellew Publishing 1991.

12. For a much fuller discussion of this text and a defence of the interpretation adopted here, against other interpretations, see R. Bauckham, 'Jesus and the Wild Animals (Mark 1:13): A Christological Image for an Ecological Age', *Jesus of Nazareth: Lord and Christ: Essays on the Historical Jesus and New Testament Christology*, Festschrift for I. Howard Marshall ed. J. B. Green and M. Turner, Grand Rapids: Eerdmans 1994, pp. 3–21.

13. J. Pedersen, *Israel: Its Life and Culture*, trs. A. Moller, Oxford University Press 1926, pp. 454–60; G. H. Williams, *Wilderness and Paradise in Christian Thought*, New York: Harper 1962, pp. 12–13.

14. Cf. J. Cohen, *'Be Fertile and Increase, Fill the Earth and Master It': The Ancient and Medieval Career of a Biblical Text*, Ithaca: Cornell University Press 1989, pp. 87, 100–1, 103, where additional references are given. See also T. Napht. 8.4, 6; T. Iss. 7.7; T. Benj. 3.4–5; 5.2.

15. On this passage, see R. Murray, *The Cosmic Covenant*, Heythrop Monographs 7, Sheed & Ward 1992, pp. 103–10.

16. For this (not exhaustive) list of animals to be found in such areas of Palestine, I am indebted to H. B. Tristram, *The Natural History of the*

Bible, SPCK 1875; F. S. Bodenheimer, *Animal Life in Palestine*, Jerusalem: L. Mayer 1935; G. Cansdale, *Animals of Bible Lands*, Paternoster 1970. Some Old Testament passages are informative as to the animals generally associated with the desert: Deut. 8.15; Job 24.5, 39.6–8; Isa. 13.21–22, 32.14, 34.11–15; Jer. 2.24, 5.6, 10.22; Zeph. 2.14–15; Mal. 1.8.

6 The Fathers and Animals: The Rule of Reason?

1. Translations are my own. References to patristic works are followed, for those who want to consult the original, by volume and page number in one of the following series: CCL (*Corpus Christianorum, series Latina*), CSEL (*Corpus Scriptorum Ecclesiasticorum Latinorum*), PG (*Patrologia Graeca*), PL (*Patrologia Latina*).

2. R. Renehan, 'The Greek Anthropocentric View of Man', *Harvard Studies in Classical Philology* 85, 1981, pp. 239–59; R. R. K. Sorabji, *Animal Minds and Human Morals*, Duckworth 1993, p. 90; Origen, *Contra Celsum* 4.74–99 (trs. H. Chadwick, Oxford University Press 1953, pp. 242–63).

3. *83 Questions* 13 (*CCL* 44A: 20).

4. Porphyry, *On Abstinence* 3.3–5; Sorabji, *Animal Minds*, pp. 80–86.

5. *On Free Choice (De libero arbitrio)* 1.53 (*CSEL* 74: 16).

6. Ibid., 54–8 (*CSEL* 74: 17–18).

7. Ibid., 59–61 (*CSEL* 74: 18–19).

8. Ibid., 61–65 (*CSEL* 74: 18–19); see further Sorabji, *Animal Minds*, pp. 89–93, and M. Baltes, *Animal: I, Allgemein*, entry in *Augustinus-Lexicon* vol. 1 ed. C. Mayer, Basle: Schwabe 1994, cols. 358–60.

9. *On Free Choice* 2.38–41 (*CSEL* 74: 47–8).

10. *Confessions* 7.17.23 (*CCL* 27: 107); my emphasis.

11. R. French, *Ancient Natural History*, Routledge 1994; A. Wallace-Hadrill, *The Greek Patristic View of Nature*, Manchester University Press 1968.

12. *On the Six Days of Creation (Hexaemeron)* 5.18.58 (*CSEL* 32.1: 184).

13. Plutarch, *Moralia* 987b–991d.

14. *On Providence* 5.553c–554a (*PG* 83: 632–33).

15. *Six Days* 6.5.31–6 (*CSEL* 32.1: 224–28).

16. *Literal Commentary on Genesis (De Genesi ad litteram)* 3.20 (*CSEL* 28.1: 86).

17. *Expositions of the Psalms (Enarrationes in psalmos)* 146.18 (*CCL* 40: 2136).

18. Ibid., 103, sermon 3.22 (*CCL* 40: 1517–18).

19. Ibid., 145.13–14 (*CCL* 40: 2114–15).

20. *Literal Commentary on Genesis* 3.16 (*CSEL* 28.1: 81–82).

21. Ibid.

22. *City of God (De civitate dei)* 19.14–15 (*CCL* 48: 681–82). See further R. A.

Markus, *Saeculum: History and Society in the Theology of St Augustine*, 2nd edn, Cambridge University Press 1988, pp. 197–210.

23. *Confessions* 8.6.14–15 (*CCL* 27: 122); *Life of Antony* 7 (*PG* 26: 853).

24. *Life of Augustine* 22 (*PL* 32: 33–66); G. Lawless, *Augustine of Hippo and his Monastic Rule*, Oxford University Press 1987, pp. 84–85.

25. *Confessions* 10.31.46 (*CCL* 27: 179–80).

26. S. Lieu, *Manichaeism in the Later Roman Empire and Medieval China*, Manchester University Press 1985.

27. *City of God* 1.20 (*CCL* 47: 22); Sorabji, *Animal Minds*, pp. 195–98.

28. *On the Magnitude of the Soul (De quantitate animi)* 14.24 (*PL* 32: 1049); on elephants, see J. M. C. Toynbee, *Animals in Roman Life and Art*, Thames & Hudson 1973, pp. 22–23, 48–49.

29. *City of God* 8.17 (*CCL* 47: 234).

30. *On the Magnitude of the Soul* 28.54 (*PL* 32: 1066).

31. *Literal Commentary on Genesis* 3.8 (*CSEL* 28.1: 71). For 'fish stories', see Toynbee, *Animals*, pp. 210–11.

32. G. O'Daly, *Augustine's Theory of Mind*, Duckworth 1987.

33. A. Smith, 'Porphyrian Studies since 1913', *Aufstieg und Niedergang der romischen Welt* II.36.2 ed. H. Temporini, Berlin: de Gruyter 1987, pp. 768–71.

34. G. Clark, *Porphyry, 'On Abstinence from Animate Food'* (forthcoming); D. Dombrowski, 'Porphyry and Vegetarianism: A Contemporary Philosophical Approach', *Aufstieg und Niedergang der romischen Welt* ed. Temporini, pp. 774–91; Sorabji, *Animal Minds*, pp. 180–94.

35. A. Elliott, *Roads to Paradise: Reading the Lives of the Early Saints*, Hanover, NH: University Press of New England 1987.

36. *Confessions* 10.35.57 (*CCL* 27: 186).

37. On ecological concern in antiquity, J. D. Hughes, *Pan's Travail: Environmental Problems of the Ancient Greeks and Romans*, Baltimore: Johns Hopkins University Press 1994, pp. 91–111; cf. O. Rackham, 'Ecology and Pseudo-Ecology', *Human Landscapes in Classical Antiquity* (Leicester-Nottingham Studies in Ancient Society, 6) ed. G. Shipley and J. Salmon, Routledge 1996, pp. 16–43.

38. Sorabji, *Animal Minds*, pp. 184–88; G. Clark, 'Cosmic Sympathies: Nature as Microcosm and as Message from God', *Human Landscapes in Classical Antiquity* ed. Shipley and Salmon, pp. 310–29.

39. Toynbee, *Animals*, pp. 16–23; S. Brown, 'Death as Decoration: Scenes from the Arena in Roman Domestic Mosaics', *Pornography and Representation in Greece and Rome* ed. A. Richlin, Oxford University Press 1992, pp. 180–211.

40. *Confessions* 6.7.11–8.13 (*CCL* 27: 80–83).

7 Aquinas and Animals: Patrolling the Boundary?

1. St Thomas Aquinas, *Summa theologiae*, Part 1, Q. 64.1; reprinted in *Political Theory and Animal Rights* ed. P. A. B. Clarke and Andrew Linzey, Pluto Press 1990, p. 103.
2. St Thomas Aquinas, *Summa contra Gentiles*: ibid., p. 9.
3. The Bestiary, the main body of which is a descriptive catalogue of animals with moral and spiritual lessons attached, had its origins in the Greek *Physiologus*, written some time between the second and the fourth centuries, probably in Alexandria. It was an enormously popular text in mediaeval England: over 40 copies survive, many of them richly illustrated. For the development of the Bestiary, see Florence McCulloch, *Medieval Latin and French Bestiaries*, Chapel Hill, NC: University of North Carolina Press 1962. T. H. White's *The Book of Beasts* (THW below), Jonathan Cape 1954, is an amusing, although rather idiosyncratic, popular version; a more scholarly translation (with colour pictures) is Richard Barber, *Bestiary* (RB below), The Folio Society 1992.
4. Ostrich: THW p. 121, RB p. 137; mouse: THW p. 91, RB p. 109.
5. THW pp. 204–6.
6. THW p. 131, RB p. 145.
7. THW pp. 142–43, RB p. 160.
8. David Attenborough, *The Trials of Life*, Collins/BBC Books 1990, p. 10.
9. RB p. 138 (THW pp. 122–23).
10. *The General Prologue*, ll. 165–207: *The Riverside Chaucer* ed. Larry D. Benson, 3rd edn, Oxford University Press 1987, p. 26.
11. *The Complete Works of John Gower* ed. G. C. Macaulay, 4 vols, Oxford University Press 1899–1902, vol. iv: *The Latin Works*, 4.281–90. The translation is by Eric W. Stockton, *The Major Latin Works of John Gower*, Seattle: University of Washington Press 1962, pp. 171–72.
12. Ludwig Wittgenstein, *Philosophical Investigations*, trs. G. E. M. Anscombe, Blackwell 1953, IIxi (p. 223).
13. St Thomas Aquinas, *Summa contra Gentiles* in *Political Theory* ed. Clarke and Linzey, p. 12.
14. See John Block Friedman, *The Monstrous Races in Medieval Art and Thought*, Cambridge, Mass.: Harvard University Press 1981.
15. Augustine, *City of God*, trs. Henry Bettenson, introd. John O'Meara, Penguin Books 1984, Bk XVI, ch. 8 (p. 662).
16. *Mandeville's Travels* ed. M. C. Seymour, Oxford University Press 1967, p. 33. The original version of the story is in Jerome's *Vita S. Pauli primi eremitate*, in J.-P. Migne, *Patrologia Latina*, vol. 23, col. 23.
17. See Vern L. Bullough, 'Medieval Medical and Scientific Views of Women', *Viator*, 4 (1973), p. 497 and n. 57.

18. *Summa theologiae*, Part 1, Q. 92.2: Rome: Editiones Paulinae 1962, pp. 445–46. The translation is by Bullough, 'Medieval Medical and Scientific Views', p. 487.

19. See Anna Abulafia, 'Bodies in the Jewish-Christian Debate' in *Framing Medieval Bodies* ed. Sarah Kay and Miri Rubin, Manchester: Manchester University Press 1994, pp. 123–37. As Abulafia writes: 'doctrinal differences between Christianity and Judaism encouraged twelfth-century Christian polemicists to transpose the generally accepted polarities of mind/body, spirit/flesh and man/beast on to the existing opposition between Christians and Jews' (ibid., p. 129).

20. See Richard Bernheimer, *Wild Men in the Middle Ages: A Study in Art, Sentiment and Demonology*, Cambridge, Mass.: Harvard University Press 1952.

21. Examples are Orfeo ('Sir Orfeo', *Middle English Romances* ed. A. C. Gibbs, York Medieval Texts, Edward Arnold 1966), Owein ('The Lady of the Fountain', *The Mabinogion*, trs. Gwyn Jones and Thomas Jones, revd edn, Everyman's Library, Dent 1989), and Yvain ('Yvain', Chrétien de Troyes, *Arthurian Romances*, trs. D. D. R. Owen, Everyman's Library, Dent 1987).

22. *The Complete Works of John Gower* ed. G. C. Macaulay, 4 vols, Oxford University Press 1899–1902, vol. ii: *The English Works*, Bk 1, ll. 2785–3042. For the story of Nebuchadnezzar in mediaeval times, see Penelope Doob, *Nebuchadnezzar's Children: Conventions of Madness in Middle English Literature*, New Haven: Yale University Press 1974.

23. See e.g. Maximilian Novak, 'The Wild Man Comes to Tea', *The Wild Man Within: An Image in Western Thought from the Renaissance to Romanticism* ed. Edward Dudley and Maximilian E. Novak, Pittsburgh: University of Pittsburgh Press 1972, pp. 183–221; Harlan Lane, *The Wild Boy of Aveyron*, Allen & Unwin 1979; Lucien Malson, *Wolf Children*, NLB 1972; Roger Shattuck, *The Forbidden Experiment: The Story of the Wild Boy of Aveyron*, Secker & Warburg 1980.

24. S. Zuckerman, 'Apes R Not Us', *New York Review of Books*, 30 May 1991, pp. 43–49. A compendium of the latest thinking on the status of the great apes (a category which encompasses humans) is Paola Cavalieri and Peter Singer (eds), *The Great Ape Project: Equality Beyond Humanity*, Fourth Estate 1993.

25. For a trenchant criticism of the attempt to find a simple final distinction, see Mary Midgley, *Beast and Man*, Methuen 1980, pp. 203–7; reprinted in *Political Theory* ed. Clarke and Linzey, pp. 46–48.

8 *Luther and Animals: Subject to Adam's Fall?*

1. *Luther's Works*, American Edition, St Louis and Philadelphia 1958–86, 1.66 (*D. Martin Luthers Werke: Kritische Gesamtausgabe*, 61 vols, Weimar: Hermann Böhlaus Nachfolger 1883–1983, 42.49, 21–22). (Henceforth *LW*, *WA*.)

2. *LW* 2.141 (*WA* 42.361, 20–21).

3. *LW* 1.66 (*WA* 42.49, 18–20). See also Luther on Gen. 2.19: 'God brought all the animals to Adam; and when he had assigned to each of them its name, he found none that was like himself. Here again we are reminded of the superior knowledge and wisdom of Adam, who was created in innocence and righteousness . . . From this enlightenment there also followed, of course, the rule over all the animals, something which is also pointed out here, since they were named in accordance with Adam's will.' Cf. *LW* 1.183 (*WA* 42.137, 20–21) where Luther contrasts irrational nature (animals) with intelligent nature (humankind). Also *LW* 2.135 (*WA* 42.357, 13–14), on Gen. 9.3, where Luther deals with the question why, if after the Flood the animals are to fear human beings, humans are terrified by animals such as wolves, lions, bears, boars, and tigers. 'Why . . . are they [human beings] filled with fear when they [these animals] are stronger? My answer is that they know that the human being is endowed with reason, which has the advantage over all the animals.'

4. Augustine, *De civ. dei* 12.23; *De Trin.* 14.4; *In Joannis evan. tract.* tract 3.4.

5. Cf. *LW* 51.10 (*WA* 4.593, 4–9). And yet, though irrational, animals are often examples of compassion and faith. In one of Luther's first sermons (1510 or 1512) he castigates human beings who show no compassion for their fellows. Even wild beasts and irrational animals observe this law, he says. When animals 'see one of their own kind in trouble, they quite naturally grieve with it and are sad, and if they can, they help it'. Only the human being, who is rational, does not help his neighbour or have pity on him. When Luther's dog Tölpel was at the table looking for a bit of food from his master, Luther commented: 'Oh, if I could only pray the way this dog watches the meat! All his thoughts are concentrated on the piece of meat. Otherwise he has no thought, wish, or hope' (*LW* 54.37–8; *D. Martin Luthers Werke: Kritische Gesamtausgabe, Tischreden* (henceforth *TR*), 6 vols, Weimar: Hermann Böhlaus Nachfolger 1912–21, 274).

6. *LW* 1.67 (*WA* 42.50, 13–15). Cf. Augustine, *Serm.* 88.6; *Ep.* 92.3.

7. *Sent.* II, Dist. 16, 683–85; cf. *LW* 1.68 (*WA* 42.51, 22–25): 'In the remaining creatures God is recognized as by His footprints; but in the human being, especially in Adam, He is recognized, because in him there is such wisdom, justice, and knowledge of all things that he may rightly be called

a world in miniature. He had understanding of heaven, earth, and the entire creation.'

8. *LW* 1.73 (*WA* 42.55, 34–36). Cf. *LW* 1.81 (*WA* 42.61, 30–32): 'man was created not for this physical life only, *like the other animals*, but for eternal life, just as God . . . is eternal' (emphasis added). See also 91 (*WA* 42.69, 11–14): 'Moses is intent on having it clearly understood [in Gen. 2.8] that man is a far nobler and better creature than the others. The brute animals have the earth on which they may feed; for man the Lord Himself provides a more excellent dwelling place.' Cf. *LW* 22.30 (*WA* 46.561, 39–562, 3); also *LW* 2.58 (*WA* 42.303, 1–4): the beasts of creation did not fall by sinning. 'No, they were created merely for this physical life. Therefore they do not hear the Word, and the Word does not concern itself with them; they are altogether without the Law of the First and the Second Table. Hence these words [Gen. 6.11, 'Now the earth was corrupt in God's sight, and the earth was filled with violence'] must be applied only to man.'

9. *LW* 2.58–59 (*WA* 42.303, 16–18).

10. *WA, TR* 1150. See Roland Bainton, 'Luther on Birds, Dogs, and Babies', *Luther Today* (Martin Luther Lectures), vol. 1, Decorah, Iowa: Luther College Press 1957, pp. 8–9.

11. *LW* 1.73 (*WA* 42.56, 5–7).

12. *LW* 1.66 (cf. *WA* 42.49, 29–38). See also *LW* 1.141 (*WA* 42.106, 12–15) on Gen. 3.1: as a result of the Fall 'we have lost a most beautifully enlightened reason and a will in agreement with the Word and will of God. We have also lost the glory of our bodies . . . and the unique prerogative of the human race over all the other animals.'

13. *LW* 1.67 (*WA* 42.50, 18–19).

14. Cf. *LW* 2.74 (*WA* 42.315, 1–6).

15. *LW* 1.67 (*WA* 42.50, 30–35).

16. *LW* 2.58 (*WA* 42.303, 6–8).

17. *LW* 2.132 (*WA* 42.355, 7–9).

18. *LW* 2.132 (*WA* 42.355, 11–13).

19. *LW* 2.139 (*WA* 42.359, 41–360, 1). Luther continues: 'wanton and irreverent killing or slaughter is forbidden. For it is a matter of good order not to kill animals without a purpose and not to consume their raw flesh' (*WA* 42.360, 3–5).

20. *LW* 2.132–3 (*WA* 42.355, 18–20).

21. *LW* 2.133 (*WA* 42.355, 33–35).

22. *LW* 2.133–4 (cf. *WA* 42.355, 37–356, 10).

23. *LW* 2.134 (*WA* 42.356, 11–17).

24. *LW* 2.134 (*WA* 42.356, 18–24).

25. *LW* 2.135 (*WA* 42.357, 23–26).
26. *LW* 28.189 (cf. *WA* 36.659, 22–36).
27. *LW* 28.190 (cf. *WA* 36.661, 21–24).
28. Augustine, *De Trin.* 14.4.
29. Cf. *LW* 1.104 (*WA* 42.79, 22–23).
30. *LW* 46.237–8 (*WA* 30/2.555, 20–34).
31. *LW* 46.251–2 (*WA* 30/2.578, 22–24).

9 Can Catholic Morality Make Room for Animals?

1. Joseph Rickaby, *Moral Philosophy*, vol. ii, Longman 1901, pp. 248 ff.
2. For a serious discussion, see *Human Sentience Before Birth*, A Report by the Commission of Inquiry into Fetal Sentience, CARE Trust, October 1996.
3. John Henry Newman, 'The Crucifixion' (1842), *Parochial and Plain Sermons*, 8 vols, Rivingtons 1868, vol. vii, pp. 136–37.
4. Peter Kropotkin, *Mutual Aid: A Factor in Evolution*, foreword by H. L. Beales, Pelican Books 1939, esp. pp. 21–73; extracts in *Political Theory and Animal Rights* ed. P. A. B. Clarke and Andrew Linzey, Pluto Press 1990, pp. 88–90.
5. Thomas More, *Utopia*, trs. and ed. Robert M. Adams, New York: Norton 1975, p. 59.
6. Ibid., p. 58.
7. Ibid., p. 81.
8. Ibid.
9. See e.g. Matt Cartmill, *A View to a Death in the Morning: Hunting and Nature through History*, Cambridge, Mass.: Harvard University Press 1991, who argues that 'The hunting hypothesis originated as a myth, concocted out of antique preconceptions and wishful thinking' (p. 224).
10. Cited and discussed in Matt Cartmill, 'Four Legs Good, Two Legs Bad', *Natural History* 11, 1983, p. 69.
11. William Golding, *The Inheritors*, Faber 1995.
12. Cited and discussed in Cartmill, 'Four Legs Good', p. 69.

10 Is Nature God's Will?

A shorter version of this chapter has been published in *Argument* 1, 1990, pp. 9–16. Further work on the topic is to be found in *How to Think about the Earth*, Mowbray 1993, being the Scott Holland Lectures for 1992, and in 'Global Religions', *Philosophy and the Natural Environment* ed. R. Attfield and A. Belsey, Cambridge University Press 1994, pp. 113–29.

1. A. Toynbee and D. Ikeda, *Choose Life*, Oxford University Press 1976, p. 324.
2. J. Lovelock, *The Ages of Gaia*, Oxford University Press 1989.
3. R. Dawkins, *The Selfish Gene*, Oxford University Press 1976; E. O. Wilson, *Sociobiology: A New Synthesis*, Cambridge, Mass.: Harvard University Press 1975.
4. R. A. Pois, *National Socialism and the Religion of Nature*, New York: St Martin's Press 1986, p. 58; see also Anna Bramwell, *Ecology in the Twentieth Century*, New Haven: Yale University Press 1989; C. Spretnak and F. Capra, *Green Politics*, Paladin 1985, p. 127.
5. Wrongly, since we need exactly that distinction if we are to hate the sin and love the sinner: without it, sinners are only aggregated sins.
6. 'What attitude should the advancing sector of humanity adopt towards static and decidedly unprogressive ethnic groups?' (Teilhard de Chardin, writing in 1937, cited by R. Speaight, *Teilhard de Chardin: A Biography*, Collins 1967, p. 234; see also H. de Lubac, *The Religion of Teilhard de Chardin*, Collins 1967).
7. On which see John Hick, *Evil and the God of Love*, Macmillan 1996; revd edn Collins/Fontana 1968. Hick does acknowledge 'the permanent significance and value of the natural order' (p. 295, Fontana edn), but subordinates that value to ours.
8. Hans Jonas, *The Imperative of Responsibility*, trs. H. Jonas and D. Herr, Chicago: University of Chicago Press 1984, p. 77.
9. Plotinus, *Enneads* 2.9.16, 26 ff.: trs. A. H. Armstrong, Loeb Classical Library, Heinemann 1979, vol. 2, p. 289; see also my 'Objective Values, Final Causes', *Electronic Journal of Analytical Philosophy*, 3, 1995, pp. 117 ff.
10. L. H. Bailey, *The Holy Earth*, New York: Macmillan 1923, pp. 16, 21.
11. P. Kropotkin, *Mutual Aid*, Pelican 1939.
12. A 'really selfish' – or selfishly philoprogenitive – gene would not permit others to propagate and would insist on reproducing itself exactly: successful genes, by contrast, reproduce themselves inexactly, and in co-operation with any available others. 'Selfish genes', it is worth adding, are not – as too many 1980s ideologues imagined – the same as 'genes for selfishness'.
13. Alfred Tennyson, *In Memoriam*, canto 131, stanza 37: *Poems* ed. T. H. Warren, Oxford University Press 1912, p. 448.
14. Ibid., canto 56, stanza 1: p. 393.
15. I. H. Angus, *George Grant's Platonic Rejoinder to Heidegger*, Lewiston and Queenston: Edwin Mellen Press 1987, p. 36.
16. C. S. Lewis, *The Abolition of Man*, 2nd edn, Bless 1946.

17. Ernst Krieck, 1936: cited in Pois, *National Socialism*, p. 117.
18. L. Pearsall Smith, *All Trivia*, Constable 1933, p. 81: 'The Wrong Word'.
19. It is hard, as Haldane commented, 'to worship one's own moral convictions, as Mr Bertrand Russell does, while believing that they are an unimportant byproduct of a universe which, as a whole, is indifferent to them': J. B. S. Haldane, *Possible Worlds and Other Essays*, Chatto & Windus 1927, p. 235.
20. 'Down, down, down with the defeated! Victory is the only ultimate fact!' as the devil-worshipping intellectual remarks in G. K. Chesterton's *The Ball and the Cross*, Darwen Finlayson 1963, p. 81.
21. *The Collected Poems of G. K. Chesterton*, 3rd edn, Methuen 1933, p. 268.
22. See 'How Chesterton Read History', *Inquiry* 39, 1996, pp. 343–58.
23. J. L. Mackie, *Ethics: Inventing the Difference between Right and Wrong*, Penguin Books 1976, p. 10. Alan Donagan rightly commented that such rules had no moral force at all (*The Theory of Morality*, Chicago: University of Chicago Press 1977, pp. 91f.).
24. Lev. 26.34.
25. Tennyson, *In Memoriam*, canto 55, stanza 2: p. 392.
26. I have explored this doctrine further in *God's World and the Great Awakening*, Clarendon Press 1991, pp. 131ff.
27. H. Richard Niebuhr, *Radical Monotheism and Western Culture*, New York: Harper & Brothers 1960, p. 126.
28. W. Wink, *Naming the Powers*, Philadelphia: Fortress Press 1984, p. 115.

11 How does God's Providential Care Extend to Animals?

1. William Paley, *Natural Theology: Selections* ed. Frederick Ferre, The Library of Liberal Arts, Indianapolis: Bobbs-Merrill 1963, p. 54.
2. Charles Darwin, letter to J. D. Hooker, 13 July 1856, *More Letters of Charles Darwin* ed. Francis Darwin and A. C. Seward, 2 vols, John Murray 1903, vol. i, p. 94.
3. I am drawing this summary from Stephen Jay Gould, *Wonderful Life: The Burgess Shale and the Nature of History*, W. W. Norton 1989, pp. 58–60.
4. Ibid., pp. 299–308.
5. Ibid., pp. 277–323.
6. See e.g. John Polkinghorne, *Science and Providence: God's Interaction with the World*, Boston, Mass.: Shambhala Publications 1989, which summarizes much of the evidence for this view.
7. See e.g. Langdon Gilkey, *Message and Existence*, New York: Seabury 1980, chs 4 and 5; Langdon Gilkey, *Reaping the Whirlwind: A Christian Interpretation of History*, New York: Seabury 1976, ch. 12; John B. Cobb, Jr and

David Ray Griffin, *Process Theology*, Philadelphia: Westminster Press 1976; Marjorie Hewitt Suchocki, *God-Christ-Church: A Practical Guide to Process Theology*, New York: Crossroad 1982; Jürgen Moltmann, *God in Creation: A New Theology of Creation and the Spirit of God*, trs. Margaret Kohl, SCM Press/Harper & Row 1985; Ian Barbour, *Religion in an Age of Science*, The Gifford Lectures 1989–91, vol. 1, SCM Press/Harper & Row 1990, esp. ch. 9; Arthur Peacocke, *God and the New Biology*, San Francisco: Harper & Row 1986; Polkinghorne, *Science and Providence*; Sallie McFague, *Models of God: Theology for an Ecological, Nuclear Age*, Philadelphia: SCM Press/Fortress Press 1987.

8. This expresses the major difference between the 'process' theologians, who generally treat freedom as inherent in actuality because of the operation of creativity in every actual thing, and those theologians who treat freedom as a gift to creation because of God's free self-limitation.

9. See Alfred North Whitehead, *Process and Reality: An Essay in Cosmology*, corrected edn, ed. David Ray Griffin and Donald W. Sherburne, New York: The Free Press 1978; and Thomas E. Hosinski, *Stubborn Fact and Creative Advance: An Introduction to the Metaphysics of Alfred North Whitehead*, Lanham, Md.: Rowman & Littlefield 1993, chs 7 and 8.

10. Alfred North Whitehead, *Religion in the Making*, New York: Macmillan 1926, p. 156. See also Hosinski, *Stubborn Fact*, ch. 7.

11. Jeffrey G. Sobosan has articulated the implications of Christian faith for the care of animals in his *Bless the Beasts: A Spirituality of Animal Care*, New York: Crossroad 1991.

12. See Whitehead, *Process and Reality*, Part V, ch. 2, and Hosinski, *Stubborn Fact*, chs 8 and 9.

12 Are Animals Fallen?

1. Quentin Smith, 'An Atheological Argument from Evil Natural Laws', *International Journal for Philosophy of Religion*, 29/3, June 1991, pp. 159–74.

2. Ibid., p. 173.

3. See e.g. Charles Raven, *The Creator Spirit*, Martin Hopkinson and Co. 1927, p. 120, and Dom Illtyd Trethowan, *An Essay in Christian Philosophy*, Longmans, Green & Co. 1954, pp. 41, 92.

4. See e.g. Peter Geach, *Providence and Evil*, Cambridge University Press 1977, pp. 77–79.

5. *Love Almighty and Ills Unlimited*, Collins 1962; Fontana 1966, p. 53.

6. Ibid.

7. It is of course true that God seeks ultimately to be 'all in all' (I Cor. 15.28),

but precisely in such a way as to preserve and even enhance the true self-being of that 'all'.

8. This is more true of those positions which see human freedom as the 'greater good'.

9. *Encountering Evil* ed. Stephen T. Davis, Atlanta: John Knox Press 1981, p. 47 (my italics).

10. Ibid., pp. 67–68.

11. 'An Atheological Argument', p. 169.

12. *Evil and the God of Love*, Macmillan 1966, 2nd revd edn 1985, p. 258.

13. I say 'the good that it would do *us*' because those for whom the greater good is human freedom believe that animal suffering is justified not by any good that it might do *them*, but by the good it ultimately does to humanity. Of course, the problem is even more intense for those who see the greater good as being some aesthetic quality; they have to see animal and human suffering as being justified by the aesthetic quality of the whole, which can presumably be appreciated fully only by One whose perspective is total.

14. *Love Almighty*, Fontana edn, p. 12.

15. T. F. Torrance, *Divine and Contingent Order*, Oxford University Press 1981, p. 134.

16. Ibid., p. 139.

17. N. P. Williams pointed out that to see nature as fallen is to increase 'the scope, the amplitude, and the magnificence of redemption' (*The Ideas of the Fall and of Original Sin*, Longmans, Green & Co. 1927, p. 524).

18. An example of this latter position is Andrew Elphinstone, whose *Freedom, Suffering and Love* (SCM Press 1976) likens the evolutionary process, with its in-built pain and aggression, to the essential but expendable role of scaffolding in the making of a building (p. 65).

19. C. W. Formby, *The Unveiling of the Fall*, Williams & Norgate 1923, pp. 38–39. It would not amount to self-contradiction if it could be shown, logically or metaphysically, that predation and pain were the only way to produce creatures capable of freedom and love. It would still, however, be vulnerable to Smith's point that 'No omnibenevolent creator would use animals as a mere means to the end of human welfare, treating them as if they had no value or rights by themselves and could be tortured with complacency on a mass scale for the sake of "spiritual benefits" to the human species'. Furthermore, any metaphysical construct in which the creation of beings capable of freedom and love was only possible via predation and pain would be likely so to limit the power of God as to reduce eschatology to wishful thinking.

20. Elphinstone, *Freedom, Suffering and Love*, p. 39.

21. *Divine and Contingent Order*, p. 139.
22. We shall address the eschatological roots of this suggestion below.
23. Pt. ll, Bk V, ch. 4.
24. I would argue that the instrumental accounts of natural evil provide a dangerous divine precedent for human wrongdoing in the name of good.
25. From my article on 'The Fall' in *Dictionary of Ethics, Theology and Society* ed. Paul Barry Clarke and Andrew Linzey, Routledge 1996, p. 370.
26. *Principalities and Powers*, Clarendon Press 1956, p. 59.
27. Gen. 1.28. Interestingly, the word suggests that, even before the human Fall, there was something within creation which needed to be subdued.
28. See Isa. 11 and 65.25, on which passages John Eaton comments, 'great prophets, looking deep into the nature of love, still knew that an age would come again when the creatures would not harm each other, but live together in trust under a king who mirrored God's goodness and power' (*The Circle of Creation*, SCM Press 1995, p. 4).
29. *The Ideas of the Fall*, pp. 522–23.
30. Ibid., p. 519.
31. Ibid., p. 513.
32. Ibid.
33. Ibid., p. 524.
34. Ibid., p. 495.
35. Ibid., p. 510.
36. Ibid., p. 520, though I am not sure how it can be termed 'modern': the relatedness of humanity with the rest of the cosmos seems to have been recognized as much by ancient Hebrew theology as it is by modern Western ecology.
37. I use the word 'reality' rather than 'creation' because process thought rejects the notion of creation *ex nihilo*. In Whitehead's famous statement, 'It is as true to say that God creates the world, as that the world creates God.'
38. David Ray Griffin, 'Creation out of Chaos and the Problem of Evil', *Encountering Evil* ed. Davis, pp. 111–12.
39. 'Occasion' is a technical process term for the basic unit of space-time.
40. See Charles Hartshorne, *Omnipotence and Other Theological Mistakes*, Albany, NY: State University of New York Press 1984.
41. See, however, Marjorie Hewitt Suchocki's attempt to formulate a process eschatology in *The End of Evil*, Albany, NY: State University of New York Press 1988.
42. See e.g. Paul Fiddes in his *The Creative Suffering of God*, Clarendon Press 1990.
43. William Temple wrote that 'whenever you trace any event or observed fact

to the action of intelligent purpose you have explained it' (*Christian Faith and Life*, SCM Press 1931, p. 13). To trace the dividedness of nature back to the action of a personal World-Soul or to the actions of personal spiritual beings is thus (on these terms) to have explained it. But it is not clear that to trace it back to the agency of sub-personal levels of reality is to have explained it at all. This would not matter perhaps within a full-blown process metaphysic in which God is not omnipotent and could not therefore be held to account for the ways in which those sub-personal levels malfunction. But in those positions which seek to combine a process theodicy with a more traditional Christian metaphysic, there could be no such defence, and God's would seem to be the only intelligent purpose which could be blamed.

44. It could, of course, be argued that, whilst such sub-personal freedom is not in itself a good great enough to justify the ills that it allows, nevertheless full human freedom and moral responsibility is at the end of (and dependent upon) the chain of increasing creaturely freedom, and that that human freedom and responsibility *is* a good great enough to justify the suffering involved. To say that, however, would turn this position into an instrumental answer to the problem of natural evil, and make it subject to all the criticisms we levelled against instrumental answers in the second section of this chapter.

45. *The Problem of Pain*, Geoffrey Bless 1940.

46. *Christian Theology and Natural Science*, Longmans, Green & Co. 1956.

47. *An Essay in Christian Philosophy*, Longmans, Green & Co. 1954.

48. *Theo-Drama*, vol. iii, *Dramatis Personae*, San Francisco: Ignatius Press 1992, IV, pp. 466–501; and vol. iv, *The Action*, San Francisco: Ignatius Press 1994, D, pp. 137–201.

49. *God, Freedom and Evil*, New York: Harper & Row 1974.

50. 'Free Will and Evil', *Encountering Evil* ed. Davis.

51. Mascall, *Christian Theology*, p. 36.

52. Thus C. S. Lewis wonders 'whether man, at his first coming into the world, had not already a redemptive function to perform. . . . It may have been one of man's functions to restore peace to the animal world, and if he had not joined the enemy he might have succeeded in doing so to an extent now hardly imaginable' (*The Problem of Pain*, p. 124).

53. Clearly, to argue this exegetical case is beyond the scope of a work of this length. See my D.Phil. dissertation, 'The Cosmic Fall and the Free Will Defence', Oxford 1996.

13 Can Animal Suffering be Reconciled with Belief in an All-Loving God?

1. Gary Snyder, *The Practice of the Wild*, Berkeley, Calif.: North Point Press 1990, p. 102.
2. Ibid., p. 110.
3. Ibid.
4. Quoted in *Liberating Life: Contemporary Approaches to Ecological Theology* ed. Charles Birch, William Eakin and Jay McDaniel, Maryknoll, NY: Orbis Books 1990, frontispiece.
5. To say that process theology is influenced by the Bible is not to say that all process theologians appeal to the Bible as an authority. Some, I among them, are interested in biblical perspectives as a distinct source of insight, itself nourished by the inspiration of God as influential in the history of Israel up to, and including, Jesus. Others are shaped by biblical perspectives, as was Whitehead, without appealing to it as a distinct source of intellectual insight.
6. John Wesley, 'The General Deliverance', *Sermons on Several Occasions*; included in *Animals and Christianity: A Book of Readings* ed. Andrew Linzey and Tom Regan, New York: Crossroad 1988, p. 102.

14 All Things in Christ?

1. Calvin, *Institutes of the Christian Religion*, bk 1, sect. 1, trs. Ford Lewis Battles, The Library of the Christian Classics, vol. 20, SCM Press/ Westminster Press 1960, p. 35.
2. See e.g. the recent work of Brian Horne, which corrects earlier views: 'It is true that when the Early Church spoke of the process of divinization which was begun in the incarnation of the Word of God . . . it often spoke from the categories of the Greek philosophical tradition with its basic assumption of a dichotomy between body and soul. The Fathers, therefore, frequently saw divinization as the soul's achievement of its desire for, and longing to share in, a spiritual immaterial existence out of reach of the hampering clay of the body. But there is much more to the concept than can be contained in the terms of Greek philosophy, and we need not use the categories of body and soul at all. The supernatural destiny of man does not stand as a contradiction of man's natural existence . . . What is involved here is the transformation of matter itself, an eschatological concept which sees the whole creation caught up in the promise of God to man' (*A World to Gain: Incarnation and the Hope of Renewal*, Darton, Longman & Todd 1983, p. 19).
3. 'Nothing can be more express. Away with vulgar prejudices, and let the plain word of God take place. They shall be delivered from the bondage of

corruption; into glorious liberty . . . they shall enjoy happiness suited to their state, without alloy, without interruption, and without end' (John Wesley, 'The General Deliverance', *Sermons on Several Occasions*, biographical note by John Beecham, Wesleyan Conference Office 1874, vol. ii, LXV, pp. 128–29: included in *Animals and Christianity: A Book of Readings* ed Andrew Linzey and Tom Regan, New York: Crossroad 1988, p. 102).

15 Do Animals have Immortal Souls?

1. St Thomas Aquinas, *Summa theologiae*, vol. 11, trs. Timothy Suttor, Eyre & Spottiswoode for Blackfriars 1970, p. 15 (1a. 75, 3). (The words I cite form the Counter-Thesis (*Sed contra*) of the issue under discussion, but it is clear from the Reply (*Responsio*) that follows that it is the view of the soul which Aquinas himself supports and therefore that Gennadius' comment does indeed represent Aquinas' own view.)
2. Cited from Michael Coughlan, *The Vatican, the Law and the Human Embryo*, Macmillan 1990, p. 23.
3. Aquinas, *Summa theologiae*, vol. 11, p. 17 (1a. 75, 3).
4. John Habgood, *Religion and Science*, Mills & Boon 1964, p. 59.
5. Theodosius Dobzhansky, *The Biology of Ultimate Concern*, Fontana 1971, p. 19.
6. J. C. Eccles, *Facing Reality*, New York: Springer-Verlag 1970, p. 173.
7. Descartes, *Discourse on Method*, trs. F. E. Sutcliffe, Penguin 1968, pp. 162–63.
8. Ibid., p. 58.
9. Charles Raven, 'The Continuing Vision: A Personal Retrospect', *Biology and Personality* ed. I. T. Ramsey, Blackwell 1965, p. 12.
10. Descartes, *Discourse on Method*, p. 54.
11. P. and L. Badham, *Immortality or Extinction?*, Macmillan 1982; reissued SPCK 1984, p. 40.
12. Antony Flew, *A Dictionary of Philosophy*, Pan 1979, p. 236.
13. Coughlan, *The Vatican*, p. 83.
14. Cardinal Mercier, *A Manual of Modern Scholastic Philosophy*, vol. 1, p. 318, cited in Coughlan, *The Vatican*, p. 84.
15. D. Hume, *On Religion* ed. R. Wollheim, Fount 1963, p. 264.
16. W. H. Thorpe, 'Reductionism in Biology', *Studies in the Philosophy of Biology* ed. F. J. Ayala and T. Dobzhansky, University of California 1974, p. 129.
17. Descartes, *Discourse on Method*, p. 75 (actual quotation is from a different translation cited in M. Midgley, *Beast and Man*, Methuen 1979, p. 211).

18. J. Neuner and J. Dupuis, *The Christian Faith in the Doctrinal Documents of the Catholic Church*, Collins 1983, p. 691.
19. Cited from 'early in *The German Ideology*' by Karl Marx in Midgley, *Beast and Man*, p. 207.
20. John Hick, *Biology and the Soul*, Cambridge University Press 1972, p. 2.
21. *The Letters of John Keats* ed. M. B. Forman, Oxford University Press 1952, pp. 334–35 (letter of April 1819), cited in John Hick, *Evil and the God of Love*, Macmillan 1966, p. 295.
22. Richard Swinburne, *The Evolution of the Soul*, Clarendon Press 1986, p. 1.
23. Ibid., p. 10.
24. Ibid., p. 2.
25. Keith Ward, *The Battle for the Soul*, Hodder 1985, pp. 149–50.
26. For philosophical defence of my use of this argument see my 'A Case for Mind Body Dualism', *The Modern Churchman* 34/3, 1992, pp. 19–25. For discussion of the data see ch. 5 of my *Immortality or Extinction?*
27. Jacques Monod, *Chance and Necessity*, Collins 1971, p. 30.
28. For development of this argument see my 'God, the Soul and the Future Life', *Death and Afterlife* ed. S. Davis, Macmillan 1989.

16 Will Animals be Redeemed?

1. *Lumen gentium* 48; *Gaudium et spes* 39.
2. E. Schurer, *The History of the Jewish People in the Age of Christ* ed. G. Vermes, F. Millar, and M. Black, T. & T. Clark 1979, vol. ii, pp. 537ff.
3. See E. P. Sanders, *Judaism: Practice and Belief 63BCE–66CE*, SCM Press 1992, pp. 279–303.
4. See A. Harnack, *A History of Dogma*, trs. N. Buchanan, Dover 1961, pp. 295f.
5. *Against Heresies*: 5.32.2; 5.33.3 f.; 5.35.
6. T. Roszak, *Person/Planet*, Gollancz 1979, p. 54.
7. See M. Eliade, *The Forge and the Crucible*, Rider 1962.
8. Rainer Maria Rilke, *Duino Elegies*, trs. Stephen Cohn, Carcanet Press 1989. Used by permission.
9. P. W. Watts, *Nicolaus Cusanus: A Fifteenth Century Vision of Man*, E. J. Brill 1982, pp. 101ff.
10. Cf. Augustine, *Expositions on the Book of Psalms*, 148.
11. Cf. K. Ward, *Rational Theology and the Creativity of God*, Blackwell 1982, pp. 197ff.
12. J. Hick, *Evil and the God of Love*, Macmillan 1966; revd edn Collins/Fontana 1968, pp. 351ff.
13. Cf. R. Nozick, *Anarchy, State and Utopia*, Blackwell 1974, pp. 34f.

14. K. Rahner, *Foundations of Christian Faith*, Crossroad 1978, p. 444.
15. In a beautiful passage the scriptures speak of burying Israel's sins at the bottom of the sea (see Isa. 43.25).
16. G. Berkeley, *Works* ed. A. A. Luce and T. E. Jessop, 9 vols, Nelson & Sons 1948–56, vol. ii, pp. 254f.
17. O. O'Donovan, *Begotten or Made?*, Oxford University Press 1984, p. 50.
18. *Pace* O'Donovan, animal tales such as *Born Free* and *Ring of Bright Water* remain popular, which suggests that many people perceive animals as having life-stories sufficiently analogous to our own to be of interest.
19. D. Hume, *A Treatise of Human Nature* ed. L. A. Selby-Bigge, Oxford University Press 1951, I, IV, sects. 5, 6.
20. G. G. Gallop, Jr., 'Self-Recognition in Primates: A Comparative Approach to the Bidirectional Approach to Consciousness', *Am. Psychol.* 32, 1977, pp. 329–38. For a full discussion of recent experiments concerned with animal self-awareness see D. R. Griffin, *The Question of Animal Awareness*, revd edn, New York: Rockefeller University Press 1981, pp. 30–33, 87–98.
21. Cf. B. B. Dragle, *Being Forgotten: An Invitation to Return*, Hamilton 1996.
22. Gerard Manley Hopkins, 'Carrion Comfort' in, e.g., *Gerard Manley Hopkins* ed. Catherine Phillips, The Oxford Authors, Oxford University Press 1986, p. 168.
23. G. B. Caird, *St Luke*, Penguin Books 1963, p. 121.
24. See also H. Waddell, *Beasts and Saints*, Constable 1934.

17 Can we See a Moral Question about Animals?

1. H. D. Thoreau, 'Autumnal Tints', *The Selected Works of Thoreau* ed. W. Harding, Boston, Mass.: Houghton Mifflin 1975, p. 709. The essay was first published in the *Atlantic Monthly*, October 1862. Here is the phrase in context: 'A man sees only what concerns him. A botanist absorbed in the study of grasses does not distinguish the grandest pasture oaks. He, as it were, tramples down oaks unwittingly in his walk, or at most only sees their shadows. I have found that it required a different intention of the eye, in the same locality, to see different plants, even when they were closely allied, as *Juncaceae* and *Gramineae*: when I was looking for the former, I did not see the latter in the midst of them. How much more, then, it requires different intentions of the eye and of the mind to attend to different departments of knowledge! How differently the poet and the naturalist look at objects!'
2. H. G. Wells, *The Island of Doctor Moreau*, Everyman 1993, p. 32.
3. Ibid., pp. 33, 32.

4. Ibid., p. 48.

5. Ibid., p. 69.

6. Ibid., p. 73.

7. Ibid.

8. Ibid., p. 27 *re* Prendick.

9. Wells' article 'The Way the World is Going', justifying animal experimentation, was published in the *Sunday Express*, 24 July 1927. George Bernard Shaw's reply, 'These Scoundrels', was published in the same newspaper, 27 August 1927. See E. Westacott, *A Century of Vivisection and Anti-Vivisection*, C. W. Daniel 1949, p. 589.

10. Claude Bernard, *Introduction à l'étude de la médecine expérimentale*, Paris: Cres et Cie 1926, vol. ii, p. 41. Translations from the French are mine, although I consulted the translation by Henry Copley Greene, New York: Macmillan 1927. I owe knowledge of this passage to J. Vyvyan, *In Pity and In Anger: A Study of the Use of Animals in Science*, Michael Joseph 1969, p. 44; reissued Marblehead: Micah Publications 1988.

11. Bernard, *Introduction*, p. 38.

12. 'Le physiologiste n'est pas un homme du monde.' Greene translates 'un homme du monde' as 'a man of fashion' (p. 103). Vyvyan translates the phrase as 'an ordinary man' (p. 44). I have chosen 'layman' as closest to what I think Bernard is saying in the larger context of his discussion in this portion of the book. I am grateful to Dr Kathleen Alaimo for her advice on this point. See also n. 15.

13. Francis Bacon, 'Thoughts and Conclusions on the Interpretation of Nature', *The Philosophy of Francis Bacon* ed. and trs. B. Farrington, Chicago: University of Chicago Press 1966, p. 96. The original essay, in Latin, was written in 1607.

14. A recent work in this general area is William Eamon, *Science and the Secrets of Nature*, Princeton: Princeton University Press 1994. I have discussed Bacon's rhetoric, and its relevance to animal experimentation, in 'Lab Animals, Francis Bacon and the Culture of Science', *Listening* 18/1, Winter 1983, reprinted in *Judaism and Animal Rights: Classical and Contemporary Responses* ed. R. Kalechofsky, Marblehead: Micah Publications 1992.

15. See n. 12. If 'un homme du monde' were not translated as 'layman', some adjustment would have to be made in the discussion that follows. It would not, however, affect the main thrust of my criticism of Bernard's reasoning. The male gender – 'layman' rather than 'layperson' – reflects the French 'homme'.

16. Bernard, *Introduction*, p. 40. I have followed Bernard in the use of commas in the first sentence. The punctuation is important: the commas mean that

the relative pronoun 'who' ('qui') refers to the *whole* class of 'laymen' ('les gens du monde'), not to a subclass. In other words, Bernard is saying that *all* laymen, not just *some*, are moved by ideas totally different from those that animate the physiologist, and therefore judge vivisection differently.

17. Ibid., p. 41. The passage that begins 'The physiologist is not a layman' follows immediately in the text.

18. Ibid., pp. 41–42.

18 Tyrants, Stewards – or Just Kings?

1. All biblical quotations are from the NIV unless otherwise stated.

2. So, for example, those who think that women are the weaker sex find in Genesis 2 that the first woman was created to be the man's 'helper'. Others might notice that the first man couldn't manage without help. Likewise, it is sometimes cited as evidence of the absolute inferiority of animals that when God brought all the beasts and birds to the man 'no suitable helper was found'. What impresses me is that the writer even entertains the idea that it might have proved otherwise. The story may be *faux naïf* – of course the man is not going to mate with an elephant – but there is no trace of irony in it.

3. Gordon J. Wenham, *Word Biblical Commentary*, vol. 1: *Genesis 1–15*, Word Books 1987, p. 9.

4. Borne out by Col. 1.16 (and arguably Prov. 8.31).

5. For a full discussion of this latter point, see Jürgen Moltmann, *God in Creation: An Ecological Doctrine of Creation*, SCM Press/Harper 1985, pp. 5ff.

6. God also commands them, as well as us, to 'be fruitful and increase in number'.

7. Note that, according to Gen. 5.2, the name *adam* is given by God to the whole human race.

8. My italics. The translation is from Wenham, *Genesis 1–15*.

9. Prov. 8.39f. might be the proof text here – and note that though, once again, our kind is singled out, the parallelism of Hebrew poetry at the same time aligns us with the whole of creation.

10. Thus, the great nineteenth-century naturalist Alfred Russel Wallace wrote of the birds of paradise he saw in New Guinea: 'I thought of the long ages of the past, during which the successive generations of these things of beauty had run their course, year by year being born and living and dying amid these dark and gloomy woods with no intelligent eye to gaze upon their loveliness, to all appearances such a wanton waste of beauty. It seems sad that . . . such exquisite creatures should live out their lives and

exhibit their charms only in these wild, inhospitable regions. This consideration must surely tell us that all living things were *not* made for man. Many of them have no relation to him' (*The Malay Archipelago*, 2 vols, Macmillan 1869, quoted by David Attenborough in 'The Natural World Special: Attenborough in Paradise', broadcast 8 April 1996, BBC2).

11. See e.g. Josh. 24.27; Ps. 19.1–4; Isa. 55.12; Rom. 8.22.

12. Ben Elton would seem closer to the spirit of the Bible when he observes in his comic novel *Stark*: 'Everything pales in comparison to a creation of this awesome magnitude. What is the Taj Mahal or the Golden Gate Bridge to a living force with arteries so huge a child could crawl along them? Yet they [are] being wiped off the face of the earth to make soap.'

13. Karl Barth, *Church Dogmatics*, III/1, T. & T. Clark 1964, p. 195. Of attempts to locate the *imago Dei* in various mental and spiritual faculties, Wenham observes: 'It is impossible to demonstrate any of these suggestions. In every case there is the suspicion that the commentator may be reading his own values into the text as to what is most significant about man' (*Genesis 1–15*, p. 30).

14. See 'Discourse V', *René Descartes: A Discourse on Method*, trs. John Veitch, Everyman edn, Dent 1912, Part V, pp. 43–46. Montaigne's point still stands: 'The defect that hinders communication betwixt them and us, why may it not be on our part as well as theirs? 'Tis yet to determine where the fault lies that we understand not one another; for we understand them no more than they do us' (*Essais*, trs. Charles Cotton, 1693).

15. To my mind, the writer is clear that two preternatural events occur in this incident, which he indicates with the formula 'The Lord opened . . .'. God first enables the ass to speak, and, second, enables Balaam to see what she sees. That the ass has something to say seems to be taken for granted. Of course, one can dismiss the story as a fable; but even fables have their own integrity. It is interesting, too, that the angel tells Balaam so pointedly, 'I would certainly have killed you . . . but I would have spared her.' These last five words, like the curious verse which concludes the book of Jonah, undermine our assumption that the lives only of human beings matter in themselves.

16. There are references in scripture to the fact that (some?) animals have no understanding or reason, e.g. Ps. 32.9, II Peter 2.12. I take it, however, that these are using a popular perception to make a different point. (On the same basis, I do not believe that Prov. 6.6 ff. actually means that the ant is as sensible as the writer implies.)

17. Karl-Erik Fichtelius and Sverre Sjölander write: 'The intricate combination of phenomena necessary for a complex language like ours could very well exist in other animals, for example dolphins . . . But it may employ a

logic that is entirely foreign to us, and treat information in a way that seems to us backwards' (*Man's Place: Intelligence in Whales, Dolphins and Humans*, Gollancz 1973). Certainly, dolphins have demonstrated a much greater capacity to imitate and apparently understand human speech than we have to either imitate or understand theirs.

18. *Essais.* Douglas Adams sardonically observes in *The Hitch Hiker's Guide to the Galaxy* (Heinemann 1986): 'Man had always assumed that he was more intelligent than dolphins because he had achieved so much – the wheel, New York, wars and so on – whilst all the dolphins had ever done was muck about in the water having a good time. But conversely, the dolphins had always believed that they were far more intelligent than man – for precisely the same reasons.'

19. As Carl Sagan noted: 'They have behaved benignly and in many cases affectionately toward us. We have systematically slaughtered them' (*The Cosmic Connection*, New York: Doubleday 1973).

20. *Elephant Memories: Thirteen Years in the Life of an Elephant Family*, Elm Tree Books 1988.

21. J. Cousteau and Y. Paccalet, *Whales*, trs. I. M. Paris, New York: Harry N. Abrams 1988.

22. E. S. Savage-Rumbaugh, *Ape Language: From Conditioned Response to Symbol*, New York: Columbia University Press 1986, p. 25.

23. Cited in *Third Way*, May 1994, p. 11. Frans de Waal cites many examples of apparent altruism in other species in *Good Natured: The Origin of Right and Wrong in Humans and Other Animals*, Cambridge, Mass.: Harvard University Press 1996.

24. See Ps. 104.21, 27, and many other references, and Gen. 9.8–17, Hos. 2.18.

25. Wayne Grudem, *Systematic Theology*, IVP 1993, p. 446.

26. C. S. Lewis, 'Religion and Rocketry' in *'Fern-Seed and Elephants' and Other Essays on Christianity* ed. Walter Hooper, Fount edn 1975, p. 88.

27. Thus in Gen. 2.7 the first man is created as a body into which life is breathed, not (as Plato would have had it) as a soul which is then embodied. The importance of this – and the contrast with Plato's doctrine of the soul – cannot be overemphasized. It is his body (which is unique) which makes *adam* human; the breath of God (which he shares with every other animal) gives him life. Note too that when *adam* first sees the woman he welcomes her not as a kindred spirit but as 'bone of my bones and flesh of my flesh' (2.23).

28. Even if we spiritualize this vision – and it is interesting to ask ourselves why we should want to – it is notable that the biblical paradise is a place where human beings live in harmony with their traditional rivals and enemies. Today we are more likely to visualize paradise as a place from

which every wolf and cobra – and every wasp and spider – has been exterminated.

29. Quoted in I. Hart, 'Genesis 1.1–2.3 as a Prologue to the Book of Genesis', *Tyndale Bulletin*, 46/2, November 1995, p. 317.

30. Ibid.

31. Perhaps because many leading green Christians are scientists, their statements are often distanced and dispassionate. They speak in terms of vast, impersonal abstractions, of 'creation' or 'the environment' (a word which Christians should reject, since it defines the earth entirely in relation to us). Animals seem to be seen as adjuncts to the earth, no more than a vital component in its self-regulating mechanism – essential to the ecosystem, valuable biodiversity.

    Thus *An Evangelical Declaration on the Care of Creation* (published 1994 by the Evangelical Environmental Network) seems to envisage 'the creation' as something other than us, 'in which we are embedded, and through which . . . we are sustained'. It goes on to issue the vague and strangely bloodless call: 'We urge individual Christians and churches to be centers of creation's care and renewal, both delighting in creation as God's gift, and enjoying it as God's provision, in ways which sustain and heal the damaged fabric of the creation which God has entrusted to us.' What a chasm there is between this kind of language and the passionate and particular words of scripture! Even Paul, the most metropolitan of biblical writers, personifies creation in Rom. 8 as a woman in labour, and feels her struggle between agony and hope. Evangelicals especially seem to be unsettled by too much enthusiasm for trees and whales (though we are comfortable enough quoting the opening words of Ps. 19). I suspect that this is because we are afraid of conceding too much to the New Age movement – yet it strikes me that every book of the Bible I have quoted here was written at a time when paganism was a much greater threat to the purity of the faith than it is now.

32. One such privilege is illustrated in I Sam. 26.7–11 and II Sam. 1.1–16. There is an obvious parallel here with Gen. 9.5f.

33. See also Deut. 17.14–20.

34. Long life, wealth, and security could well stand as the three primary motivations for humankind's abuse of other species.

35. It is striking that the wisdom of the king demands empathy: his judgment shows that he has understood both the love of the real mother and the bitterness of the one who has been bereaved. One might compare Prov. 12.10a: 'A righteous man cares for the needs of [AV: 'regardeth the life of'] his animal', which implies understanding gained through sympathetic observation.

36. II Cor. 4.4; Col. 1.15; Heb. 1.3. See also II Cor. 3.18.
37. Col. 1.16 f.; Heb. 1.2 f.; Rev. 5.13 f.

19 Compassion or Justice? What is our Minimum Ethical Obligation to Animals?

1. There are separate Codes of Recommendations for the welfare of livestock cattle, pigs, domestic fowls, turkeys, sheep, ducks, rabbits, farmed deer, and goats. There are Codes of Practice for the 'Guidance of Operators of Horse, Pony and Donkey Markets, Sales and Fairs'; for the 'Care and Feeding of Farm Animals in Government Approved Export Lairages'; on the 'Care of Farm Animals and Horses during their Transport on Roll On/Roll Off Ferries'; for the 'Transport by Air of Cattle, Sheep, Pigs, Goats and Horses'; and for the 'Slaughter of Farmed Deer'.
2. FAWC, *Report on Priorities in Animal Welfare Research and Development*, March 1988, pp. 6–8.
3. FAWC, 'Transport by Air' (n. 1, above), p. 6.
4. *Aims and Ambitions*. A European protocol (Amsterdam 1997) accepted that animals should be classed as 'sentient beings'.
5. Frieda Le Pla, *Vivisection: Right or Wrong?*, 1954. Quotations are from pp. 1, 2, 9.
6. *Regarding Animals*, 1985; 2nd edn 1989. Quotations are from pp. 4, 6, 8, 10.
7. Basil Wrighton, 'Justice and the Animals', reprinted in *Reason, Religion and the Animals*, Catholic Study Circle for Animal Welfare 1987.
8. The Anglican Society for the Welfare of Animals, *Bulletin* 34, Autumn 1989, p. 17.
9. *Animals and Ethics: The Report of a Working Party Convened by Edward Carpenter*, 1980, p. 38; subsequent quotations from pp. 3, 10.
10. Andrew Linzey, *Christianity and the Rights of Animals*, SPCK 1987. Quotations are from pp. 74, 104, 112.
11. Report to World Council of Churches, *The Liberation of Life*, reprinted in Charles Birch, William Eakin, Jay B. McDaniel (eds), *Liberating Life: Contemporary Approaches to Ecological Theology*, Maryknoll, NY: Orbis Books 1990 (see Appendix).
12. James Childress, 'Compassion', *A New Dictionary of Christian Ethics*, SCM Press 1986, p. 109.

20 *Is the Consistent Ethic of Life Consistent without a Concern for Animals?*

Thanks to James Fodor, David Cunningham, Bill Cavanaugh, and Brian Doyle for comments on an earlier draft of this chapter.

1. These essays, along with eight analytical essays by a variety of scholars, are gathered in Joseph, Cardinal Bernardin, *Consistent Ethic of Life*, Kansas City: Sheed & Ward 1988. Henceforth *CEL*.
2. Anthony Kenny, *A Path from Rome*, Sidgwick & Jackson 1985, p. 207. Kenny continues: 'When I am with people who share my opposition to nuclear deterrence, I commonly find I am alone in disapproving of abortion: if I want to find company which opposes abortion it is easiest to do so among those who are hawks on the arms race. This is true not only of secular society but of the Catholic Church: the strengthening of the opposition among bishops to nuclear war has gone hand in hand with a weakening among priests and nuns of their abhorrence of abortion.'
3. *CEL*, p. 6.
4. *CEL*, p. 6.
5. *CEL*, p. 6.
6. Pope John Paul II, *Evangelium Vitae*, Encyclical Letter, 25 March 1995, §5. Henceforth *EV*.
7. *EV*, §79.
8. *EV*, §§95–100.
9. *EV*, §101.
10. *EV*, §9.
11. 'We must celebrate Eternal Life, from which every other life proceeds. From this, in proportion to its capacities, every being which in any way participates in life, receives life' (*EV*, §84).
12. *EV*, §42. To avoid misunderstanding, it is important to emphasize at this juncture that the primary aim of *Evangelium Vitae* is a vigorous defence of human life in particular, especially the lives of those who are without voices. This is an extremely important message, which urgently needs to be heard. For this reason I am a little ambivalent in drawing on *Evangelium Vitae* at length without that as my primary focus, for fear of giving a false impression regarding its message. Having said that, if this chapter is properly and generously understood, I believe that no reader will conclude that the kind of concern I am advocating for non-human animals takes away from our concern for our fellow humans, but will rather conclude that in relating to animals in the light of our hope of the kingdom of God, our hearts will be 'dilated' so that we will have more, not less, compassion for our fellow humans.
13. *EV*, §42.

14. *EV*, §27.
15. *EV*, §22.
16. *EV*, §22. *Evangelium Vitae* distinguishes the life given to humans from that given to other living creatures in §§34–35.
17. *EV*, §22.
18. *EV*, §22.
19. In his 1989 address 'The Ecological Crisis: A Common Responsibility', John Paul II uses the term 'the integrity of creation' (§7).
20. *EV*, §22. On this, see also Mary Midgley, *Science as Salvation: A Modern Myth and its Meaning*, Routledge 1992.
21. *EV*, §19.
22. *EV*, §19.
23. *EV*, §19. This issue is very closely tied to the Pope's critiques of erroneous views of human freedom. On this, see John Berkman, 'Truth and Martyrdom: The Structure of Discipleship in *Veritatis Splendor*', *New Blackfriars*, November 1994, pp. 534–37.
24. Thus it is that one very influential recent book in Christian ecological ethics refuses to see the natural world as fallen, and thus advocates that humans become 'altruistic predators' as opposed to 'profligate predators'.
25. John Milbank notes that to the extent that liberalism has abandoned the Christian metanarrative of ontological peace for one of original violence, it serves as one of the great heresies of modernity (*Theology and Social Theory*, Blackwell 1990).
26. See also *The Catechism of the Catholic Church*, §1046. Henceforth *CCC*.
27. *CCC*, §376.
28. If this is true, then Gen. 9.2–4, often seen as a hermeneutical key for the notion of 'dominion', is in fact describing a relationship between humans and animals very different from what Gen. 1.26, 28 means by dominion.
29. *EV*, §§52, 34, 42.
30. See John Berkman and Stanley Hauerwas, 'The Chief End of All Flesh', *Theology Today* XLIX/2, July 1992, pp. 199–200, 204–6; also published as 'A Trinitarian Theology of the "Chief End" of "All Flesh"', *Good News for Animals?* ed. Jay McDaniel and Charles Pinches, New York: Orbis 1992, reprinted in Stanley Hauerwas, *In Good Company*, South Bend, Ill.: UNDP 1996.
31. *EV*, §§34–5.
32. In terms of the sources for Gen. 1–11, whereas the second creation story and the Fall in ch. 3 form one unit (written by J), one may helpfully understand Gen. 9 as the 'Fall' narrative for the first creation story (both by P).
33. *Evangelium Vitae* provides a similar description in §9: 'Murderous violence profoundly changes man's environment. From being the "garden of Eden"

(Gen. 2.15), a place of plenty, of harmonious interpersonal relationships and of friendship with God, the earth becomes "the land of Nod" (Gen. 4.16), a place of scarcity, loneliness and separation from God.'

34. The importance of locating the 'truth of creation' in the context of salvation history and Trinitarian belief may be better understood in the following: the conviction that the God who has discovered us in Jesus of Nazareth, the God who intends for us to share the kingdom of God, is a saving God from the beginning. In other words, 'creation' is part of a narrative of fulfilment for Christians; from the Christian conviction that God redeems all of creation Christians learn that God, having created all things, wills that all things enjoy their status as God's creatures.

35. *CCC* §388 says that the ultimate meaning of the story of the Fall can only be understood in the light of the death and resurrection of Jesus Christ. See also *CCC* §§349.

36. *CCC*, §388.

37. *CCC*, §349.

38. See Rom. 8.19–23.

39. *CCC*, §671.

40. *CCC*, §1046 and *EV*, §§38, 80.

41. *CCC*, §655.

42. *CCC*, §1049.

43. *EV*, §95.

44. *EV*, §100.

45. *EV*, §89.

46. *La Civiltà Cattolica*, 'Modern War and the Christian Conscience' cited in David Decosse (ed.), *But was it Just?*, New York: Doubleday 1992, p. 120.

47. *EV*, §§2266, 2267 (1997 revisions). See *Origins*, 25 September 1997.

48. Joseph, Cardinal Bernardin, 'The Death Penalty in our Time', *CEL*, p. 64.

49. *EV*, §9.

50. Reuters, Vatican City, 26 February 1997.

51. *EV*, §100.

52. On the other hand, some may argue that animals, who have done ill to no one, deserve even less to be killed than those convicted of murder and/or other traditionally capital crimes. But neither is this view a consistent gospel of life.

53. *CCC*, §2418.

54. Pope John Paul II, *Crossing the Threshold of Hope*, Knopf 1994, p. 182.

55. Ibid., p. 181.

56. Ibid., pp. 184–85.

57. *EV*, §100.

58. *EV*, §28.

Index

UNIVERSITY OF ILLINOIS PRESS
1325 SOUTH OAK STREET
CHAMPAIGN, ILLINOIS 61820-6903
WWW.PRESS.UILLINOIS.EDU